LLEWELLYN'S
2·0

ASTROL

POCKET PLANNER

Daily Ephemeris & Aspectarian
2024-2026

Cover design by Shannon McKuhen
Edited by Hanna Grimson

A special thanks to Beth Koch Rosato for astrological proofreading.

Astrological calculations compiled and programmed by Rique Pottenger, based on
the earlier work of Neil F. Michelsen. Reuse is prohibited.

Published by
LLEWELLYN WORLDWIDE LTD.
2143 Wooddale Drive
Woodbury, MN 55125-2989
www.llewellyn.com

Printed in China
Typography property of Llewellyn Worldwide Ltd.

Table of Contents

Mercury Retrograde 2025

	DATE	ET	PT			DATE	ET	PT
Mercury Retrograde	3/14		11:46 pm	—	Mercury Direct	4/7	**7:08 am**	4:08 am
Mercury Retrograde	3/15	**2:46 am**		—	Mercury Direct	4/7	**7:08 am**	4:08 am
Mercury Retrograde	7/17		9:45 pm	—	Mercury Direct	8/11	**3:30 am**	12:30 am
Mercury Retrograde	7/18	**12:45 am**		—	Mercury Direct	8/11	**3:30 am**	12:30 am
Mercury Retrograde	11/9	**2:02 pm**	11:02 am	—	Mercury Direct	11/29	**12:38 pm**	9:38 am

Moon Void-of-Course 2025

Times are listed in Eastern time in this table only. All other information in the *Pocket Planner* is listed in both Eastern time and Pacific time. Note: All times are corrected for Daylight Saving Time.

Last Aspect		Moon Enters New Sign		Last Aspect		Moon Enters New Sign		Last Aspect		Moon Enters New Sign	
Date	Time	Date	Sign Time	Date	Time	Date	Sign Time	Date	Time	Date	Sign Time
JANUARY				**FEBRUARY**				**MARCH**			
1	1:02 am	1	≈ 5:50 am	1	5:06 pm	1	♈ 8:10 pm	1	3:05 am	1	♈ 4:52 am
2	11:13 pm	3	♓ 10:21 am	3	5:19 am	3	♉ 10:33 pm	2	8:52 am	3	♉ 5:37 am
5	9:30 am	5	♈ 2:01 pm	5	10:29 pm	5	♊ 1:44 am	5	5:53 am	5	♊ 7:29 am
7	4:16 pm	7	♉ 5:11 pm	8	2:52 am	8	⊛ 6:04 am	7	9:57 am	7	⊛ 11:29 am
9	5:50 pm	9	♊ 8:07 pm	10	8:49 am	10	♌ 12:01 pm	9	5:32 pm	9	♌ 6:59 pm
11	7:03 pm	11	⊛ 11:24 pm	12	2:12 pm	12	♍ 8:07 pm	11	4:16 pm	12	♍ 3:56 am
13	11:46 pm	14	♌ 4:12 am	15	3:36 am	15	♎ 6:45 am	14	1:47 pm	14	♎ 2:59 pm
15	11:10 pm	16	♍ 11:46 am	17	6:24 pm	17	♏ 7:19 pm	16	5:53 am	17	♏ 3:30 am
18	9:01 pm	18	♎ 10:33 am	20	5:06 am	20	♐ 7:55 am	19	3:28 pm	19	♐ 4:17 pm
20	11:34 pm	21	♏ 11:20 am	22	2:38 pm	22	♑ 6:09 pm	22	2:53 am	22	♑ 3:29 am
23	7:03 pm	23	♐ 11:29 pm	25	10:28 pm	25	≈ 12:40 am	24	11:01 am	24	≈ 11:25 am
26	4:40 am	26	♑ 8:43 am	26	5:04 pm	27	♓ 3:46 am	26	6:15 am	26	♓ 3:31 pm
28	10:48 am	28	≈ 2:31 pm					28	4:30 pm	28	♈ 4:36 pm
30	6:29 am	30	♓ 5:52 pm					30	5:18 am	30	♉ 4:16 pm

Moon Void-of-Course 2025 (cont.)

APRIL

Last Aspect Date	Time	Moon Enters New Sign Date	Sign	Time
1	1:43 pm	1	♊	4:26 pm
3	2:26 pm	3	♋	6:50 pm
5	6:54 pm	6	♌	12:34 am
8	12:08 am	8	♍	9:40 am
10	3:49 pm	10	♎	9:12 pm
13	6:01 am	13	♏	9:54 am
15	10:24 pm	15	♐	10:37 pm
17	7:38 am	18	♑	10:12 am
20	1:21 pm	20	♒	7:22 pm
22	5:55 pm	23	♓	1:07 am
24	10:57 pm	25	♈	3:24 am
26	12:18 pm	27	♉	3:17 am
29	1:18 am	29	♊	2:34 am
30	11:49 pm	5/1	♋	3:23 am

MAY

Last Aspect Date	Time	Moon Enters New Sign Date	Sign	Time
4/30	11:49 pm	1	♋	3:23 am
3	4:02 am	3	♌	7:29 am
5	9:03 am	5	♍	3:40 pm
8	12:11 am	8	♎	3:06 am
10	2:17 am	10	♏	3:58 pm
13	2:37 am	13	♐	4:35 am
15	2:29 pm	15	♑	3:58 pm
18	12:27 am	18	♒	1:29 am
20	7:59 am	20	♓	8:28 am
22	12:06 pm	22	♈	12:26 pm
24	7:44 am	24	♉	1:38 pm
26	9:52 am	26	♊	1:21 pm
28	9:01 am	28	♋	1:33 pm
30	12:50 pm	30	♌	4:17 pm

JUNE

Last Aspect Date	Time	Moon Enters New Sign Date	Sign	Time
1	7:38 pm	1	♍	11:00 pm
4	7:11 am	4	♎	9:38 am
6	9:04 pm	6	♏	10:23 pm
8	8:06 am	9	♐	10:56 am
11	3:58 pm	11	♑	9:55 pm
14	4:52 am	14	♒	7:00 am
16	1:31 pm	16	♓	2:09 pm
18	5:34 pm	18	♈	7:08 pm
20	9:49 pm	20	♉	9:53 pm
22	9:50 pm	22	♊	10:57 pm
23	4:26 am	24	♋	11:44 pm
27	1:16 am	27	♌	2:05 am
29	7:03 am	29	♍	7:44 am

JULY

Last Aspect Date	Time	Moon Enters New Sign Date	Sign	Time
1	4:47 pm	1	♎	5:16 pm
2	3:30 pm	4	♏	5:33 am
6	6:04 pm	6	♐	6:06 pm
7	5:29 pm	9	♑	4:55 am
10	4:37 pm	11	♒	1:21 pm
12	3:45 pm	13	♓	7:45 pm
15	1:10 pm	16	♈	12:32 am
17	8:38 pm	18	♉	3:59 am
20	2:43 am	20	♊	6:22 am
21	3:52 pm	22	♋	8:26 am
23	8:42 pm	24	♌	11:28 am
26	7:02 am	26	♍	4:55 pm
28	8:57 pm	29	♎	1:43 am
29	11:59 pm	31	♏	1:25 pm

AUGUST

Last Aspect Date	Time	Moon Enters New Sign Date	Sign	Time
2	9:07 pm	3	♐	2:00 am
5	11:29 am	5	♑	1:04 pm
6	1:40 pm	7	♒	9:18 pm
9	3:55 am	10	♓	2:50 am
11	2:55 am	12	♈	6:33 am
13	6:54 pm	14	♉	9:22 am
16	1:12 am	16	♊	12:01 pm
18	7:53 am	18	♋	3:05 pm
20	8:27 am	20	♌	7:17 pm
21	2:13 pm	23	♍	1:24 am
25	9:53 am	25	♎	10:08 am
26	10:06 pm	27	♏	9:28 pm
29	8:47 pm	30	♐	10:04 am

SEPTEMBER

Last Aspect Date	Time	Moon Enters New Sign Date	Sign	Time
1	9:39 pm	1	♑	9:45 pm
4	6:08 am	4	♒	6:32 am
5	4:51 pm	6	♓	11:54 am
8	1:44 pm	8	♈	2:37 pm
10	2:54 am	10	♉	4:03 pm
12	4:14 pm	12	♊	5:38 pm
14	6:46 pm	14	♋	8:30 pm
16	11:14 pm	17	♌	1:20 am
19	8:21 am	19	♍	8:23 am
21	3:54 pm	21	♎	5:41 pm
23	12:02 pm	24	♏	5:00 am
26	1:44 pm	26	♐	5:37 pm
29	1:44 am	29	♑	5:55 am

OCTOBER

Last Aspect Date	Time	Moon Enters New Sign Date	Sign	Time
1	11:33 am	1	♒	3:52 pm
3	2:15 pm	3	♓	10:07 pm
5	8:30 pm	6	♈	12:48 am
7	2:24 pm	8	♉	1:12 am
9	8:31 pm	10	♊	1:12 am
11	10:56 pm	12	♋	2:37 am
14	1:05 am	14	♌	6:47 am
16	1:06 am	16	♍	2:06 pm
18	5:10 pm	19	♎	12:01 am
21	8:25 am	21	♏	11:42 am
24	12:14 am	24	♐	12:19 am
26	12:42 pm	26	♑	12:53 pm
28	11:38 pm	28	♒	11:55 pm
31	2:15 am	31	♓	7:46 am

NOVEMBER

Last Aspect Date	Time	Moon Enters New Sign Date	Sign	Time
2	10:15 am	2	♈	10:39 am
4	6:21 am	4	♉	11:16 am
6	9:51 am	6	♊	10:20 am
8	9:32 am	8	♋	10:06 am
10	12:23 pm	10	♌	12:34 pm
12	6:29 pm	12	♍	6:52 pm
15	4:08 am	15	♎	4:44 am
17	6:51 am	17	♏	4:44 pm
20	4:24 am	20	♐	5:26 am
22	4:48 pm	22	♑	5:53 pm
25	4:10 am	25	♒	5:16 am
27	12:53 pm	27	♓	2:24 pm
29	7:05 pm	29	♈	8:07 pm

DECEMBER

Last Aspect Date	Time	Moon Enters New Sign Date	Sign	Time
1	1:14 pm	1	♉	10:13 pm
3	8:50 pm	3	♊	9:48 pm
5	7:55 pm	5	♋	8:54 pm
7	8:45 pm	7	♌	9:48 pm
9	11:56 pm	10	♍	2:20 am
12	9:51 am	12	♎	11:04 am
14	10:36 pm	14	♏	10:51 pm
17	10:24 am	17	♐	11:38 am
19	10:41 pm	19	♑	11:53 pm
22	9:44 am	22	♒	10:52 am
24	4:42 pm	24	♓	8:09 pm
27	2:03 am	27	♈	3:02 am
28	9:13 pm	29	♉	6:57 am
31	7:25 am	31	♊	8:13 am

How to Use the *Pocket Planner*

by Leslie Nielsen

This handy guide contains information that can be most valuable to you as you plan your daily activities. As you read through the first few pages, you can start to get a feel for how well organized this guide is.

Read the Symbol Key on the next page, which is rather like astrological shorthand. The characteristics of the planets can give you direction in planning your strategies. Much like traffic signs that signal "go," "stop," or even "caution," you can determine for yourself the most propitious time to get things done.

You'll find tables that show the dates when Mercury is retrograde (Rx) or direct (D). Because Mercury deals with the exchange of information, a retrograde Mercury makes miscommunication more noticeable.

There's also a section dedicated to the times when the Moon is void-of-course (V/C). These are generally poor times to conduct business because activities begun during these times usually end badly or fail to get started. If you make an appointment during a void-of-course, you might save yourself a lot of aggravation by confirming the time and date later. The Moon is only void-of-course for 7 percent of the time when business is usually conducted during a normal workday (that is, 8:00 am to 5:00 pm). Sometimes, by waiting a matter of minutes or a few hours until the Moon has left the void-of-course phase, you have a much better chance to make action move more smoothly. Moon voids can also be used successfully to do routine activities or inner work, such as dream therapy or personal contemplation.

You'll find Moon phases, as well as each of the Moon's entries into a new sign. Times are expressed in Eastern time (in bold type) and Pacific time (in regular type). The New Moon time is generally best for beginning new activities, as the Moon is increasing in light and can offer the element of growth to our endeavors. When the Moon is Full, its illumination is greatest and we can see the results of our efforts. When it moves from the Full stage back to the New stage, it can best be used to reflect on our projects. If necessary, we can make corrections at the New Moon.

The section of "Planetary Stations" on page 7 will give you the times when the planets are changing signs or direction, thereby affording us opportunities for new starts.

The ephemeris in the back of your *Pocket Planner* can be very helpful to you. As you start to work with the ephemeris, you may notice that not all planets seem to be comfortable in every sign. Think of the planets as actors and the signs as the costumes they wear. Sometimes, costumes just itch. If you find this to be so for a certain time period, you may choose to delay your plans for a time or be more creative with the energies at hand.

As you turn to the daily pages, you'll find information about the Moon's sign, phase, and the time it changes phase. You'll find icons indicating the best days to plant and fish. Also, you will find times and dates when the planets and asteroids change signs and go either retrograde or direct, major holidays, a three-month calendar, and room to record your appointments.

This guide is a powerful tool. Make the most of it!

Symbol Key

Planets:	☉ Sun	⚳ Ceres	♄ Saturn
	☽ Moon	⚴ Pallas	⚷ Chiron
	☿ Mercury	⚵ Juno	♅ Uranus
	♀ Venus	⚶ Vesta	♆ Neptune
	♂ Mars	♃ Jupiter	♇ Pluto
Signs:	♈ Aries	♌ Leo	♐ Sagittarius
	♉ Taurus	♍ Virgo	♑ Capricorn
	♊ Gemini	♎ Libra	♒ Aquarius
	♋ Cancer	♏ Scorpio	♓ Pisces
Aspects:	☌ Conjunction (0°)	⚺ Semisextile (30°)	✶ Sextile (60°)
	□ Square (90°)	△ Trine (120°)	
	⚻ Quincunx (150°)	☍ Opposition (180°)	
Motion:	℞ Retrograde	D Direct	
Best Days for Planting: 🌿		Best Days for Fishing: 🐟	

Planetary Stations for 2025

	JAN	FEB	MAR	APR	MAY	JUN	JUL	AUG	SEP	OCT	NOV	DEC
☿			3/15–4/7				7/18–8/11				11/9–11/29	
♀			3/1–4/12									
♂	12/6/24–2/23											
♃	10/9/24–2/4											
♄							7/13–11/27					11/11–3/10/26
♅	9/1/24–1/30								9/6–2/3/26			
♆							7/4–12/10					
♇					5/4–10/13							
⚷								7/30–1/2/26				
⚳						6/9–10/4						
⚴								8/11–11/21				
⚵			3/19–7/11									
⚶			3/21–6/14									

The Year 2025

January
S	M	T	W	T	F	S
			1	2	3	4
5	6	7	8	9	10	11
12	13	14	15	16	17	18
19	20	21	22	23	24	25
26	27	28	29	30	31	

February
S	M	T	W	T	F	S
						1
2	3	4	5	6	7	8
9	10	11	12	13	14	15
16	17	18	19	20	21	22
23	24	25	26	27	28	

March
S	M	T	W	T	F	S
						1
2	3	4	5	6	7	8
9	10	11	12	13	14	15
16	17	18	19	20	21	22
23	24	25	26	27	28	29
30	31					

April
S	M	T	W	T	F	S
		1	2	3	4	5
6	7	8	9	10	11	12
13	14	15	16	17	18	19
20	21	22	23	24	25	26
27	28	29	30			

May
S	M	T	W	T	F	S
				1	2	3
4	5	6	7	8	9	10
11	12	13	14	15	16	17
18	19	20	21	22	23	24
25	26	27	28	29	30	31

June
S	M	T	W	T	F	S
1	2	3	4	5	6	7
8	9	10	11	12	13	14
15	16	17	18	19	20	21
22	23	24	25	26	27	28
29	30					

July
S	M	T	W	T	F	S
		1	2	3	4	5
6	7	8	9	10	11	12
13	14	15	16	17	18	19
20	21	22	23	24	25	26
27	28	29	30	31		

August
S	M	T	W	T	F	S
					1	2
3	4	5	6	7	8	9
10	11	12	13	14	15	16
17	18	19	20	21	22	23
24	25	26	27	28	29	30
31						

September
S	M	T	W	T	F	S
	1	2	3	4	5	6
7	8	9	10	11	12	13
14	15	16	17	18	19	20
21	22	23	24	25	26	27
28	29	30				

October
S	M	T	W	T	F	S
			1	2	3	4
5	6	7	8	9	10	11
12	13	14	15	16	17	18
19	20	21	22	23	24	25
26	27	28	29	30	31	

November
S	M	T	W	T	F	S
						1
2	3	4	5	6	7	8
9	10	11	12	13	14	15
16	17	18	19	20	21	22
23	24	25	26	27	28	29
30						

December
S	M	T	W	T	F	S
	1	2	3	4	5	6
7	8	9	10	11	12	13
14	15	16	17	18	19	20
21	22	23	24	25	26	27
28	29	30	31			

The Year 2026

January

S	M	T	W	T	F	S
				1	2	3
4	5	6	7	8	9	10
11	12	13	14	15	16	17
18	19	20	21	22	23	24
25	26	27	28	29	30	31

February

S	M	T	W	T	F	S
1	2	3	4	5	6	7
8	9	10	11	12	13	14
15	16	17	18	19	20	21
22	23	24	25	26	27	28

March

S	M	T	W	T	F	S
1	2	3	4	5	6	7
8	9	10	11	12	13	14
15	16	17	18	19	20	21
22	23	24	25	26	27	28
29	30	31				

April

S	M	T	W	T	F	S
			1	2	3	4
5	6	7	8	9	10	11
12	13	14	15	16	17	18
19	20	21	22	23	24	25
26	27	28	29	30		

May

S	M	T	W	T	F	S
					1	2
3	4	5	6	7	8	9
10	11	12	13	14	15	16
17	18	19	20	21	22	23
24	25	26	27	28	29	30
31						

June

S	M	T	W	T	F	S
	1	2	3	4	5	6
7	8	9	10	11	12	13
14	15	16	17	18	19	20
21	22	23	24	25	26	27
28	29	30				

July

S	M	T	W	T	F	S
			1	2	3	4
5	6	7	8	9	10	11
12	13	14	15	16	17	18
19	20	21	22	23	24	25
26	27	28	29	30	31	

August

S	M	T	W	T	F	S
						1
2	3	4	5	6	7	8
9	10	11	12	13	14	15
16	17	18	19	20	21	22
23	24	25	26	27	28	29
30	31					

September

S	M	T	W	T	F	S
		1	2	3	4	5
6	7	8	9	10	11	12
13	14	15	16	17	18	19
20	21	22	23	24	25	26
27	28	29	30			

October

S	M	T	W	T	F	S
				1	2	3
4	5	6	7	8	9	10
11	12	13	14	15	16	17
18	19	20	21	22	23	24
25	26	27	28	29	30	31

November

S	M	T	W	T	F	S
1	2	3	4	5	6	7
8	9	10	11	12	13	14
15	16	17	18	19	20	21
22	23	24	25	26	27	28
29	30					

December

S	M	T	W	T	F	S
		1	2	3	4	5
6	7	8	9	10	11	12
13	14	15	16	17	18	19
20	21	22	23	24	25	26
27	28	29	30	31		

30 Monday
4th ♈
New Moon   **5:27 pm**   2:27 pm

31 Tuesday
1st ♈
☽ v/c   10:02 pm

New Year's Eve

1 Wednesday
1st ♈
☽ v/c   **1:02 am**
☽ enters ≈   **5:50 am**   2:50 am

Kwanzaa ends • New Year's Day

2 Thursday
1st ≈
♅ enters ♏   **6:15 pm**   3:15 pm
♀ enters ♓   **10:24 pm**   7:24 pm
☽ v/c   **11:13 pm**   8:13 pm

Hanukkah ends

3 Friday
1st ≈
☽ enters ♓ **10:21 am** 7:21 am

4 Saturday
1st ♓

5 Sunday
1st ♓
☽ v/c   **9:30 am** 6:30 am
☽ enters ♈ **2:01 pm** 11:01 am

December 2024						
S	M	T	W	T	F	S
1	2	3	4	5	6	7
8	9	10	11	12	13	14
15	16	17	18	19	20	21
22	23	24	25	26	27	28
29	30	31				

January 2025						
S	M	T	W	T	F	S
			1	2	3	4
5	6	7	8	9	10	11
12	13	14	15	16	17	18
19	20	21	22	23	24	25
26	27	28	29	30	31	

February 2025						
S	M	T	W	T	F	S
						1
2	3	4	5	6	7	8
9	10	11	12	13	14	15
16	17	18	19	20	21	22
23	24	25	26	27	28	

6 Monday

1st ♈
♂ enters ♋ **5:44 am** 2:44 am
2nd Quarter **6:56 pm** 3:56 pm

7 Tuesday

2nd ♈
☽ v/c **4:16 pm** 1:16 pm
☽ enters ♉ **5:11 pm** 2:11 pm

8 Wednesday

2nd ♉
☿ enters ♑ **5:30 am** 2:30 am

9 Thursday

2nd ♉
☽ v/c **5:50 pm** 2:50 pm
☽ enters ♊ **8:07 pm** 5:07 pm

Eastern time in bold type
Pacific time in medium type

10 Friday
2nd ♊

11 Saturday
2nd ♊
☽ v/c **7:03 pm** 4:03 pm
☽ enters ♋ **11:24 pm** 8:24 pm

12 Sunday
2nd ♋

December 2024								January 2025								February 2025					
S	M	T	W	T	F	S		S	M	T	W	T	F	S		S	M	T	W	T	F	S
1	2	3	4	5	6	7					1	2	3	4								1
8	9	10	11	12	13	14		5	6	7	8	9	10	11		2	3	4	5	6	7	8
15	16	17	18	19	20	21		12	13	14	15	16	17	18		9	10	11	12	13	14	15
22	23	24	25	26	27	28		19	20	21	22	23	24	25		16	17	18	19	20	21	22
29	30	31						26	27	28	29	30	31			23	24	25	26	27	28	

13 Monday

2nd ♋
Full Moon **5:27 pm** 2:27 pm
☽ v/c **11:46 pm** 8:46 pm

14 Tuesday

3rd ♋
☽ enters ♌ **4:12 am** 1:12 am

15 Wednesday

3rd ♌
☽ v/c **11:10 pm** 8:10 pm

16 Thursday

3rd ♌
☽ enters ♍ **11:46 am** 8:46 am

Eastern time in bold type
Pacific time in medium type

17 Friday
3rd ♍

18 Saturday
3rd ♍
☽ v/c **9:01 pm** 6:01 pm
☽ enters ♎ **10:33 pm** 7:33 pm

19 Sunday
3rd ♎
☉ enters ≈ **3:00 pm** 12:00 pm

Sun enters Aquarius

December 2024								January 2025								February 2025					
S	M	T	W	T	F	S		S	M	T	W	T	F	S		S	M	T	W	T	F	S
1	2	3	4	5	6	7					1	2	3	4								1
8	9	10	11	12	13	14		5	6	7	8	9	10	11		2	3	4	5	6	7	8
15	16	17	18	19	20	21		12	13	14	15	16	17	18		9	10	11	12	13	14	15
22	23	24	25	26	27	28		19	20	21	22	23	24	25		16	17	18	19	20	21	22
29	30	31						26	27	28	29	30	31			23	24	25	26	27	28

20 Monday
3rd ♎︎
☽ v/c   **11:34 pm**   8:34 pm

Martin Luther King Jr. Day • Inauguration Day

21 Tuesday

3rd ♎︎
☽ enters ♏︎ **11:20 am**   8:20 am
4th Quarter   **3:31 pm** 12:31 pm

22 Wednesday

4th ♏︎

23 Thursday

4th ♏︎
☽ v/c   **7:03 pm**   4:03 pm
☽ enters ♐︎ **11:29 pm**   8:29 pm

Eastern time in bold type
Pacific time in medium type

24 Friday
4th ♐

25 Saturday
4th ♐

26 Sunday
4th ♐
☽ v/c   **4:40 am** 1:40 am
☽ enters ♑   **8:43 am** 5:43 am

December 2024						
S	M	T	W	T	F	S
1	2	3	4	5	6	7
8	9	10	11	12	13	14
15	16	17	18	19	20	21
22	23	24	25	26	27	28
29	30	31				

January 2025						
S	M	T	W	T	F	S
			1	2	3	4
5	6	7	8	9	10	11
12	13	14	15	16	17	18
19	20	21	22	23	24	25
26	27	28	29	30	31	

February 2025						
S	M	T	W	T	F	S
						1
2	3	4	5	6	7	8
9	10	11	12	13	14	15
16	17	18	19	20	21	22
23	24	25	26	27	28	

27 Monday

4th ♑
☿ enters ♒   **9:53 pm** 6:53 pm

28 Tuesday

4th ♑
☽ v/c   **10:48 am** 7:48 am
☽ enters ♒   **2:31 pm** 11:31 am

29 Wednesday

4th ♒
New Moon   **7:36 am** 4:36 am

Lunar New Year (Snake)

30 Thursday

1st ♒
☽ v/c   **6:29 am** 3:29 am
♅ D   **11:22 am** 8:22 am
☽ enters ♓   **5:52 pm** 2:52 pm

31 Friday
1st ♓

1 Saturday
1st ♓
☽ v/c	**5:06 pm**	2:06 pm
☽ enters ♈	**8:10 pm**	5:10 pm

2 Sunday
1st ♈

Imbolc • Groundhog Day

January 2025						
S	M	T	W	T	F	S
			1	2	3	4
5	6	7	8	9	10	11
12	13	14	15	16	17	18
19	20	21	22	23	24	25
26	27	28	29	30	31	

February 2025						
S	M	T	W	T	F	S
						1
2	3	4	5	6	7	8
9	10	11	12	13	14	15
16	17	18	19	20	21	22
23	24	25	26	27	28	

March 2025						
S	M	T	W	T	F	S
						1
2	3	4	5	6	7	8
9	10	11	12	13	14	15
16	17	18	19	20	21	22
23	24	25	26	27	28	29
30	31					

3 Monday

1st ♈
☽ v/c	**5:19 am**	2:19 am
☽ enters ♉	**10:33 pm**	7:33 pm
♀ enters ♈		11:57 pm

4 Tuesday

1st ♉
♀ enters ♈	**2:57 am**	
♃ D	**4:40 am**	1:40 am

5 Wednesday

1st ♉
2nd Quarter	**3:02 am**	12:02 am
☽ v/c	**10:29 pm**	7:29 pm
☽ enters ♊		10:44 pm

6 Thursday

2nd ♉
☽ enters ♊	**1:44 am**

Eastern time in bold type
Pacific time in medium type

7 Friday
2nd ♊
☽ v/c   11:52 pm

8 Saturday
2nd ♊
☽ v/c   **2:52 am**
☽ enters ♋ **6:04 am** 3:04 am

9 Sunday
2nd ♋

January 2025						
S	M	T	W	T	F	S
			1	2	3	4
5	6	7	8	9	10	11
12	13	14	15	16	17	18
19	20	21	22	23	24	25
26	27	28	29	30	31	

February 2025						
S	M	T	W	T	F	S
						1
2	3	4	5	6	7	8
9	10	11	12	13	14	15
16	17	18	19	20	21	22
23	24	25	26	27	28	

March 2025						
S	M	T	W	T	F	S
						1
2	3	4	5	6	7	8
9	10	11	12	13	14	15
16	17	18	19	20	21	22
23	24	25	26	27	28	29
30	31					

Eastern time in bold type
Pacific time in medium type

10 Monday

2nd ♋

| ☽ v/c | **8:49 am** | 5:49 am |
| ☽ enters ♌ | **12:01 pm** | 9:01 am |

11 Tuesday

2nd ♌

12 Wednesday

2nd ♌

Full Moon	**8:53 am**	5:53 am
☽ v/c	**2:12 pm**	11:12 am
☽ enters ♍	**8:07 pm**	5:07 pm

13 Thursday

3rd ♍

Eastern time in bold type
Pacific time in medium type

14 Friday
3rd ♍
☿ enters ♓   **7:06 am**   4:06 am

Valentine's Day

15 Saturday
3rd ♍
☽ v/c   **3:36 am** 12:36 am
☽ enters ♎   **6:45 am** 3:45 am

16 Sunday
3rd ♎
♀ enters ♒   **2:26 pm** 11:26 am

January 2025						
S	M	T	W	T	F	S
			1	2	3	4
5	6	7	8	9	10	11
12	13	14	15	16	17	18
19	20	21	22	23	24	25
26	27	28	29	30	31	

February 2025						
S	M	T	W	T	F	S
						1
2	3	4	5	6	7	8
9	10	11	12	13	14	15
16	17	18	19	20	21	22
23	24	25	26	27	28	

March 2025						
S	M	T	W	T	F	S
						1
2	3	4	5	6	7	8
9	10	11	12	13	14	15
16	17	18	19	20	21	22
23	24	25	26	27	28	29
30	31					

Eastern time in bold type
Pacific time in medium type

17 Monday

3rd ♎
☽ v/c **6:24 pm** 3:24 pm
☽ enters ♏ **7:19 pm** 4:19 pm

Presidents' Day

18 Tuesday

3rd ♏
☉ enters ♓ **5:07 am** 2:07 am

Sun enters Pisces

19 Wednesday

3rd ♏
⚡ enters ♐ **10:30 pm** 7:30 pm

20 Thursday

3rd ♏
☽ v/c **5:06 am** 2:06 am
☽ enters ♐ **7:55 am** 4:55 am
4th Quarter **12:33 pm** 9:33 am

Eastern time in bold type
Pacific time in medium type

21 Friday
4th ♐

22 Saturday
4th ♐
| ☽ v/c | **3:38 pm** | 12:38 pm |
| ☽ enters ♑ | **6:09 pm** | 3:09 pm |

23 Sunday
4th ♑
| ♀ enters ♓ | **5:55 pm** | 2:55 pm |
| ♂ D | **9:00 pm** | 6:00 pm |

January 2025								February 2025								March 2025						
S	M	T	W	T	F	S		S	M	T	W	T	F	S		S	M	T	W	T	F	S
			1	2	3	4								1								1
5	6	7	8	9	10	11		2	3	4	5	6	7	8		2	3	4	5	6	7	8
12	13	14	15	16	17	18		9	10	11	12	13	14	15		9	10	11	12	13	14	15
19	20	21	22	23	24	25		16	17	18	19	20	21	22		16	17	18	19	20	21	22
26	27	28	29	30	31			23	24	25	26	27	28			23	24	25	26	27	28	29
																30	31					

24 Monday

4th ♈
☽ v/c   **10:28 pm**   7:28 pm
☽ enters ♒   9:40 pm

25 Tuesday

4th ♈
☽ enters ♒ **12:40 am**

26 Wednesday

4th ♒
☽ v/c   **5:04 pm**   2:04 pm

27 Thursday

4th ♒
☽ enters ♓   **3:46 am** 12:46 am
New Moon   **7:45 pm**   4:45 pm

Eastern time in bold type
Pacific time in medium type

28 Friday
1st ♓

Ramadan begins at sundown

1 Saturday
1st ♓
☽ v/c   **3:05 am** 12:05 am
☽ enters ♈   **4:52 am** 1:52 am
♀ ℞   **7:36 pm** 4:36 pm

2 Sunday
1st ♈
☽ v/c   **8:52 am** 5:52 am

February 2025						
S	M	T	W	T	F	S
						1
2	3	4	5	6	7	8
9	10	11	12	13	14	15
16	17	18	19	20	21	22
23	24	25	26	27	28	

March 2025						
S	M	T	W	T	F	S
						1
2	3	4	5	6	7	8
9	10	11	12	13	14	15
16	17	18	19	20	21	22
23	24	25	26	27	28	29
30	31					

April 2025						
S	M	T	W	T	F	S
		1	2	3	4	5
6	7	8	9	10	11	12
13	14	15	16	17	18	19
20	21	22	23	24	25	26
27	28	29	30			

Eastern time in bold type
Pacific time in medium type

3 Monday
1st ♈
☿ enters ♈   **4:04 am**   1:04 am
☽ enters ♉   **5:37 am**   2:37 am

4 Tuesday
1st ♉

Mardi Gras (Fat Tuesday)

5 Wednesday
1st ♉
☽ v/c   **5:53 am**   2:53 am
☽ enters ♊   **7:29 am**   4:29 am

Ash Wednesday

6 Thursday
1st ♊
2nd Quarter **11:32 am**   8:32 am

7 Friday

2nd ♊

☽ v/c	**9:57 am**	6:57 am
☽ enters ♋	**11:29 am**	8:29 am

8 Saturday

2nd ♋

9 Sunday

2nd ♋

☽ v/c	**5:32 pm**	2:32 pm
☽ enters ♌	**6:59 pm**	3:59 pm

Daylight Saving Time begins at 2 am

February 2025						
S	M	T	W	T	F	S
						1
2	3	4	5	6	7	8
9	10	11	12	13	14	15
16	17	18	19	20	21	22
23	24	25	26	27	28	

March 2025						
S	M	T	W	T	F	S
						1
2	3	4	5	6	7	8
9	10	11	12	13	14	15
16	17	18	19	20	21	22
23	24	25	26	27	28	29
30	31					

April 2025						
S	M	T	W	T	F	S
		1	2	3	4	5
6	7	8	9	10	11	12
13	14	15	16	17	18	19
20	21	22	23	24	25	26
27	28	29	30			

Eastern time in bold type
Pacific time in medium type

10 Monday
2nd ♌

11 Tuesday
2nd ♌
☽ v/c   **4:16 pm** 1:16 pm

12 Wednesday
2nd ♌
☽ enters ♍ **3:56 am** 12:56 am

13 Thursday

2nd ♍
Full Moon   11:55 pm

Purim begins at sundown

Eastern time in bold type
Pacific time in medium type

14 Friday

2nd ♍

Full Moon	**2:55 am**	
☽ v/c	**1:47 pm**	10:47 am
☽ enters ♎	**2:59 pm**	11:59 am
☿ ℞		11:46 pm

Lunar Eclipse 23° ♍ 57' • Mercury retrograde until 4/7 (PDT)

15 Saturday

3rd ♎

☿ ℞	**2:46 am**

Mercury retrograde until 4/7 (EDT)

16 Sunday

3rd ♎

☽ v/c	**5:53 am**	2:53 am

February 2025						
S	M	T	W	T	F	S
						1
2	3	4	5	6	7	8
9	10	11	12	13	14	15
16	17	18	19	20	21	22
23	24	25	26	27	28	

March 2025						
S	M	T	W	T	F	S
						1
2	3	4	5	6	7	8
9	10	11	12	13	14	15
16	17	18	19	20	21	22
23	24	25	26	27	28	29
30	31					

April 2025						
S	M	T	W	T	F	S
		1	2	3	4	5
6	7	8	9	10	11	12
13	14	15	16	17	18	19
20	21	22	23	24	25	26
27	28	29	30			

Eastern time in bold type
Pacific time in medium type

17 Monday
3rd ♎︎
☽ enters ♏︎ **3:30 am** 12:30 am

St. Patrick's Day

18 Tuesday
3rd ♏︎

19 Wednesday
3rd ♏︎
✷ ℞   **2:00 pm** 11:00 am
☽ v/c   **3:28 pm** 12:28 pm
☽ enters ♐︎ **4:17 pm** 1:17 pm

20 Thursday
3rd ♐︎
☉ enters ♈︎ **5:01 am** 2:01 am

International Astrology Day
Sun enters Aries • Ostara • Spring Equinox • 5:01 am EDT/2:01 am PDT

21 Friday
3rd ♐
♅ R̥   **6:10 am**   3:10 am
☽ v/c   11:53 pm

22 Saturday

3rd ♐
☽ v/c   **2:53 am**
☽ enters ♑   **3:29 am** 12:29 am
4th Quarter   **7:29 am**   4:29 am

23 Sunday

4th ♑

February 2025						
S	M	T	W	T	F	S
						1
2	3	4	5	6	7	8
9	10	11	12	13	14	15
16	17	18	19	20	21	22
23	24	25	26	27	28	

March 2025						
S	M	T	W	T	F	S
						1
2	3	4	5	6	7	8
9	10	11	12	13	14	15
16	17	18	19	20	21	22
23	24	25	26	27	28	29
30	31					

April 2025						
S	M	T	W	T	F	S
		1	2	3	4	5
6	7	8	9	10	11	12
13	14	15	16	17	18	19
20	21	22	23	24	25	26
27	28	29	30			

24 Monday
4th ♑
☽ v/c **11:01 am** 8:01 am
☽ enters ♒ **11:25 am** 8:25 am

25 Tuesday
4th ♒

26 Wednesday
4th ♒
☽ v/c **6:15 am** 3:15 am
☽ enters ♓ **3:31 pm** 12:31 pm

27 Thursday
4th ♓
♀ enters ♓ **4:41 am** 1:41 am

Eastern time in bold type
Pacific time in medium type

28 Friday
4th ♓
| ☽ v/c | **4:30 pm** | 1:30 pm |
| ☽ enters ♈ | **4:36 pm** | 1:36 pm |

29 Saturday
4th ♈
| New Moon | **6:58 am** | 3:58 am |
| ☿ enters ♓ | **10:18 pm** | 7:18 pm |

Solar Eclipse 9° ♈ 00'

30 Sunday
1st ♈
☽ v/c	**5:18 am**	2:18 am
♆ enters ♈	**8:00 am**	5:00 am
☽ enters ♉	**4:16 pm**	1:16 pm

Eid al-Fitr begins at sundown (Ramadan ends)

February 2025								March 2025								April 2025					
S	M	T	W	T	F	S		S	M	T	W	T	F	S		S	M	T	W	T	F	S
						1								1				1	2	3	4	5
2	3	4	5	6	7	8		2	3	4	5	6	7	8		6	7	8	9	10	11	12
9	10	11	12	13	14	15		9	10	11	12	13	14	15		13	14	15	16	17	18	19
16	17	18	19	20	21	22		16	17	18	19	20	21	22		20	21	22	23	24	25	26
23	24	25	26	27	28			23	24	25	26	27	28	29		27	28	29	30			
								30	31													

31 Monday
1st ♉

1 Tuesday
1st ♉
☽ v/c   **1:43 pm** 10:43 am
☽ enters ♊ **4:26 pm** 1:26 pm

April Fools' Day (All Fools' Day—Pagan)

2 Wednesday
1st ♊

3 Thursday
1st ♊
☽ v/c   **2:26 pm** 11:26 am
☽ enters ♋ **6:50 pm** 3:50 pm

Eastern time in bold type
Pacific time in medium type

4 Friday
1st ♋
2nd Quarter **10:15 pm** 7:15 pm

5 Saturday
2nd ♋
☽ v/c   **6:54 pm** 3:54 pm
☽ enters ♌   9:34 pm

6 Sunday
2nd ♋
☽ enters ♌ **12:34 am**

March 2025						
S	M	T	W	T	F	S
						1
2	3	4	5	6	7	8
9	10	11	12	13	14	15
16	17	18	19	20	21	22
23	24	25	26	27	28	29
30	31					

April 2025						
S	M	T	W	T	F	S
		1	2	3	4	5
6	7	8	9	10	11	12
13	14	15	16	17	18	19
20	21	22	23	24	25	26
27	28	29	30			

May 2025						
S	M	T	W	T	F	S
				1	2	3
4	5	6	7	8	9	10
11	12	13	14	15	16	17
18	19	20	21	22	23	24
25	26	27	28	29	30	31

Eastern time in bold type
Pacific time in medium type

7 Monday

2nd ♌
☿ D   **7:08 am**   4:08 am
☽ v/c   9:08 pm

8 Tuesday

2nd ♌
☽ v/c   **12:08 am**
☽ enters ♍   **9:40 am**   6:40 am

9 Wednesday

2nd ♍

10 Thursday

2nd ♍
☽ v/c   **3:49 pm**   12:49 pm
☽ enters ♎   **9:12 pm**   6:12 pm

11 Friday
2nd ♎

12 Saturday
2nd ♎
Full Moon **8:22 pm** 5:22 pm
♀ D **9:02 pm** 6:02 pm

Passover begins at sundown

13 Sunday
3rd ♎
☽ v/c **6:01 am** 3:01 am
☽ enters ♏ **9:54 am** 6:54 am

Palm Sunday

March 2025						
S	M	T	W	T	F	S
						1
2	3	4	5	6	7	8
9	10	11	12	13	14	15
16	17	18	19	20	21	22
23	24	25	26	27	28	29
30	31					

April 2025						
S	M	T	W	T	F	S
		1	2	3	4	5
6	7	8	9	10	11	12
13	14	15	16	17	18	19
20	21	22	23	24	25	26
27	28	29	30			

May 2025						
S	M	T	W	T	F	S
				1	2	3
4	5	6	7	8	9	10
11	12	13	14	15	16	17
18	19	20	21	22	23	24
25	26	27	28	29	30	31

14 Monday
3rd ♏

♅ enters ♏   11:30 pm

15 Tuesday
3rd ♏

♅ enters ♏   **2:30 am**
☽ v/c   **10:24 pm**   7:24 pm
☽ enters ♐ **10:37 pm**   7:37 pm
☿ enters ♈   11:25 pm

16 Wednesday
3rd ♐
☿ enters ♈   **2:25 am**

17 Thursday
3rd ♐
♂ enters ♌   9:21 pm

Eastern time in bold type
Pacific time in medium type

18 Friday

3rd ♐
♂ enters ♌ **12:21 am**
☽ v/c   **7:38 am** 4:38 am
☽ enters ♑ **10:12 am** 7:12 am

Good Friday • Orthodox Good Friday

19 Saturday

3rd ♑
☉ enters ♉ **3:56 pm** 12:56 pm

Sun enters Taurus

20 Sunday

3rd ♑
☽ v/c   **1:21 pm** 10:21 am
☽ enters ♒ **7:22 pm** 4:22 pm
4th Quarter **9:36 pm** 6:36 pm

Easter • Orthodox Easter • Passover ends

March 2025						
S	M	T	W	T	F	S
						1
2	3	4	5	6	7	8
9	10	11	12	13	14	15
16	17	18	19	20	21	22
23	24	25	26	27	28	29
30	31					

April 2025						
S	M	T	W	T	F	S
		1	2	3	4	5
6	7	8	9	10	11	12
13	14	15	16	17	18	19
20	21	22	23	24	25	26
27	28	29	30			

May 2025						
S	M	T	W	T	F	S
				1	2	3
4	5	6	7	8	9	10
11	12	13	14	15	16	17
18	19	20	21	22	23	24
25	26	27	28	29	30	31

21 Monday
4th ≈

22 Tuesday
4th ≈
☽ v/c   **5:55 pm**   2:55 pm
☽ enters ♓   10:07 pm

Earth Day

23 Wednesday
4th ≈
☽ enters ♓   **1:07 am**

24 Thursday
4th ♓
☽ v/c   **10:57 pm**   7:57 pm

Eastern time in bold type
Pacific time in medium type

25 Friday

4th ♓

☽ enters ♈   **3:24 am** 12:24 am

26 Saturday

4th ♈

☽ v/c   **12:18 pm** 9:18 am

27 Sunday

4th ♈

☽ enters ♉   **3:17 am** 12:17 am

New Moon   **3:31 pm** 12:31 pm

		March 2025				
S	M	T	W	T	F	S
						1
2	3	4	5	6	7	8
9	10	11	12	13	14	15
16	17	18	19	20	21	22
23	24	25	26	27	28	29
30	31					

		April 2025				
S	M	T	W	T	F	S
		1	2	3	4	5
6	7	8	9	10	11	12
13	14	15	16	17	18	19
20	21	22	23	24	25	26
27	28	29	30			

		May 2025				
S	M	T	W	T	F	S
				1	2	3
4	5	6	7	8	9	10
11	12	13	14	15	16	17
18	19	20	21	22	23	24
25	26	27	28	29	30	31

Llewellyn's 2025 Pocket Planner and Ephemeris

28 Monday

1st ♉
☽ v/c   10:18 pm
☽ enters ♊   11:34 pm

29 Tuesday
1st ♉
☽ v/c   **1:18 am**
☽ enters ♊ **2:34 am**

30 Wednesday
1st ♊
♀ enters ♈ **1:16 pm** 10:16 am
☽ v/c   **11:49 pm** 8:49 pm

1 Thursday

1st ♊
☽ enters ♋ **3:23 am** 12:23 am

Beltane

Eastern time in bold type
Pacific time in medium type

2 Friday
1st ♋

3 Saturday
1st ♋
| ☽ v/c | **4:02 am** | 1:02 am |
| ☽ enters ♌ | **7:29 am** | 4:29 am |

4 Sunday
1st ♌
| 2nd Quarter | **9:52 am** | 6:52 am |
| ♀ ℞ | **11:27 am** | 8:27 am |

April 2025						
S	M	T	W	T	F	S
		1	2	3	4	5
6	7	8	9	10	11	12
13	14	15	16	17	18	19
20	21	22	23	24	25	26
27	28	29	30			

May 2025						
S	M	T	W	T	F	S
				1	2	3
4	5	6	7	8	9	10
11	12	13	14	15	16	17
18	19	20	21	22	23	24
25	26	27	28	29	30	31

June 2025						
S	M	T	W	T	F	S
1	2	3	4	5	6	7
8	9	10	11	12	13	14
15	16	17	18	19	20	21
22	23	24	25	26	27	28
29	30					

Eastern time in bold type
Pacific time in medium type

5 Monday

2nd ♌
☽ v/c   **9:03 am** 6:03 am
☽ enters ♍ **3:40 pm** 12:40 pm

Cinco de Mayo

6 Tuesday

2nd ♍

7 Wednesday

2nd ♍
☽ v/c   9:11 pm

8 Thursday

2nd ♍
☽ v/c   **12:11 am**
☽ enters ♎ **3:06 am** 12:06 am

Eastern time in bold type
Pacific time in medium type

9 Friday
2nd ♎
☽ v/c   11:17 pm

10 Saturday
2nd ♎
☽ v/c   **2:17 am**
☿ enters ♉   **8:15 am**   5:15 am
☽ enters ♏   **3:58 pm** 12:58 pm

11 Sunday
2nd ♏

Mother's Day

April 2025						
S	M	T	W	T	F	S
		1	2	3	4	5
6	7	8	9	10	11	12
13	14	15	16	17	18	19
20	21	22	23	24	25	26
27	28	29	30			

May 2025						
S	M	T	W	T	F	S
				1	2	3
4	5	6	7	8	9	10
11	12	13	14	15	16	17
18	19	20	21	22	23	24
25	26	27	28	29	30	31

June 2025						
S	M	T	W	T	F	S
1	2	3	4	5	6	7
8	9	10	11	12	13	14
15	16	17	18	19	20	21
22	23	24	25	26	27	28
29	30					

12 Monday

2nd ♏
Full Moon **12:56 pm** 9:56 am
☽ v/c 11:37 pm

13 Tuesday
3rd ♏
☽ v/c **2:37 am**
☽ enters ♐ **4:35 am** 1:35 am

14 Wednesday
3rd ♐

15 Thursday
3rd ♐
☽ v/c **2:29 pm** 11:29 am
☽ enters ♑ **3:58 pm** 12:58 pm

16 Friday
3rd ♑
♀ enters ♈ **2:23 pm** 11:23 am

17 Saturday
3rd ♑
☽ v/c   9:27 pm
☽ enters ♒   10:29 pm

18 Sunday
3rd ♑
☽ v/c   **12:27 am**
☽ enters ♒   **1:29 am**

April 2025						
S	M	T	W	T	F	S
		1	2	3	4	5
6	7	8	9	10	11	12
13	14	15	16	17	18	19
20	21	22	23	24	25	26
27	28	29	30			

May 2025						
S	M	T	W	T	F	S
				1	2	3
4	5	6	7	8	9	10
11	12	13	14	15	16	17
18	19	20	21	22	23	24
25	26	27	28	29	30	31

June 2025						
S	M	T	W	T	F	S
1	2	3	4	5	6	7
8	9	10	11	12	13	14
15	16	17	18	19	20	21
22	23	24	25	26	27	28
29	30					

19 Monday
3rd ≈

20 Tuesday

3rd ≈
☽ v/c	**7:59 am**	4:59 am
4th Quarter	**7:59 am**	4:59 am
☽ enters ♓	**8:28 am**	5:28 am
☉ enters ♊	**2:55 pm**	11:55 am

Sun enters Gemini

21 Wednesday

4th ♓

22 Thursday

4th ♓
| ☽ v/c | **12:06 pm** | 9:06 am |
| ☽ enters ♈ | **12:26 pm** | 9:26 am |

23 Friday
4th ♈

24 Saturday
4th ♈
☽ v/c	**7:44 am**	4:44 am
☽ enters ♉	**1:38 pm**	10:38 am
♄ enters ♈	**11:35 pm**	8:35 pm

25 Sunday
4th ♉

| ☿ enters ♊ | **8:59 pm** | 5:59 pm |

April 2025						
S	M	T	W	T	F	S
		1	2	3	4	5
6	7	8	9	10	11	12
13	14	15	16	17	18	19
20	21	22	23	24	25	26
27	28	29	30			

May 2025						
S	M	T	W	T	F	S
				1	2	3
4	5	6	7	8	9	10
11	12	13	14	15	16	17
18	19	20	21	22	23	24
25	26	27	28	29	30	31

June 2025						
S	M	T	W	T	F	S
1	2	3	4	5	6	7
8	9	10	11	12	13	14
15	16	17	18	19	20	21
22	23	24	25	26	27	28
29	30					

26 Monday
4th ♉
☽ v/c   **9:52 am** 6:52 am
☽ enters ♊ **1:21 pm** 10:21 am
New Moon **11:02 pm** 8:02 pm

Memorial Day

27 Tuesday
1st ♊

28 Wednesday
1st ♊
☽ v/c   **9:01 am** 6:01 am
☽ enters ♋ **1:33 pm** 10:33 am

29 Thursday
1st ♋

30 Friday

1st ♋
D v/c   **12:50 pm**   9:50 am
D enters ♌   **4:17 pm**   1:17 pm

31 Saturday

1st ♌

1 Sunday

1st ♌
D v/c   **7:38 pm**   4:38 pm
D enters ♍ **11:00 pm**   8:00 pm

Shavuot begins at sundown

May 2025						
S	M	T	W	T	F	S
				1	2	3
4	5	6	7	8	9	10
11	12	13	14	15	16	17
18	19	20	21	22	23	24
25	26	27	28	29	30	31

June 2025						
S	M	T	W	T	F	S
1	2	3	4	5	6	7
8	9	10	11	12	13	14
15	16	17	18	19	20	21
22	23	24	25	26	27	28
29	30					

July 2025						
S	M	T	W	T	F	S
		1	2	3	4	5
6	7	8	9	10	11	12
13	14	15	16	17	18	19
20	21	22	23	24	25	26
27	28	29	30	31		

Eastern time in bold type
Pacific time in medium type

2 Monday

1st ℳ
2nd Quarter **11:41 pm**   8:41 pm

3 Tuesday

2nd ℳ

4 Wednesday
2nd ℳ
☽ v/c   **7:11 am**   4:11 am
☽ enters ♎   **9:38 am**   6:38 am

5 Thursday
2nd ♎
♀ enters ♉   9:43 pm

Eastern time in bold type
Pacific time in medium type

6 Friday
2nd ♎
♀ enters ♉ **12:43 am**
☽ v/c **9:04 pm** 6:04 pm
☽ enters ♏ **10:23 pm** 7:23 pm

7 Saturday
2nd ♏

8 Sunday
2nd ♏
☿ enters ♋ **6:58 pm** 3:58 pm

May 2025						
S	M	T	W	T	F	S
				1	2	3
4	5	6	7	8	9	10
11	12	13	14	15	16	17
18	19	20	21	22	23	24
25	26	27	28	29	30	31

June 2025						
S	M	T	W	T	F	S
1	2	3	4	5	6	7
8	9	10	11	12	13	14
15	16	17	18	19	20	21
22	23	24	25	26	27	28
29	30					

July 2025						
S	M	T	W	T	F	S
		1	2	3	4	5
6	7	8	9	10	11	12
13	14	15	16	17	18	19
20	21	22	23	24	25	26
27	28	29	30	31		

9 Monday

2nd ♏

☿ ℞	**5:40 am**	2:40 am
☽ v/c	**8:06 am**	5:06 am
☽ enters ♐	**10:56 am**	7:56 am
♃ enters ♋	**5:02 pm**	2:02 pm

10 Tuesday

2nd ♐

11 Wednesday

2nd ♐

Full Moon	**3:44 am**	12:44 am
☽ v/c	**3:58 pm**	12:58 pm
☽ enters ♑	**9:55 pm**	6:55 pm

12 Thursday

3rd ♑

Eastern time in bold type
Pacific time in medium type

13 Friday
3rd ♑

14 Saturday
3rd ♑

☽ v/c	**4:52 am**	1:52 am
☽ enters ♒	**7:00 am**	4:00 am
� D	**2:00 pm**	11:00 am

Flag Day

15 Sunday
3rd ♒

Father's Day

May 2025								June 2025								July 2025						
S	M	T	W	T	F	S		S	M	T	W	T	F	S		S	M	T	W	T	F	S
				1	2	3		1	2	3	4	5	6	7				1	2	3	4	5
4	5	6	7	8	9	10		8	9	10	11	12	13	14		6	7	8	9	10	11	12
11	12	13	14	15	16	17		15	16	17	18	19	20	21		13	14	15	16	17	18	19
18	19	20	21	22	23	24		22	23	24	25	26	27	28		20	21	22	23	24	25	26
25	26	27	28	29	30	31		29	30							27	28	29	30	31		

16 Monday
3rd ≈
☽ v/c   **1:31 pm** 10:31 am
☽ enters ♓   **2:09 pm** 11:09 am

17 Tuesday
3rd ♓
♂ enters ♍ **4:35 am** 1:35 am

18 Wednesday
3rd ♓
4th Quarter **3:19 pm** 12:19 pm
☽ v/c   **5:34 pm** 2:34 pm
☽ enters ♈ **7:08 pm** 4:08 pm

19 Thursday
4th ♈

Juneteenth

20 Friday
4th ♈
☽ v/c   **9:49 pm** 6:49 pm
☽ enters ♉ **9:53 pm** 6:53 pm
☉ enters ♋ **10:42 pm** 7:42 pm

Sun enters Cancer • Litha • Summer Solstice • 10:42 pm EDT/7:42 pm PDT

21 Saturday
4th ♉

22 Sunday
4th ♉
☽ v/c   **9:50 pm** 6:50 pm
☽ enters ♊ **10:57 pm** 7:57 pm

		May 2025				
S	M	T	W	T	F	S
				1	2	3
4	5	6	7	8	9	10
11	12	13	14	15	16	17
18	19	20	21	22	23	24
25	26	27	28	29	30	31

		June 2025				
S	M	T	W	T	F	S
1	2	3	4	5	6	7
8	9	10	11	12	13	14
15	16	17	18	19	20	21
22	23	24	25	26	27	28
29	30					

		July 2025				
S	M	T	W	T	F	S
		1	2	3	4	5
6	7	8	9	10	11	12
13	14	15	16	17	18	19
20	21	22	23	24	25	26
27	28	29	30	31		

Eastern time in bold type
Pacific time in medium type

23 Monday
4th ♊
☽ v/c   **4:26 am**   1:26 am

24 Tuesday
4th ♊
☽ enters ♋   **11:44 pm**   8:44 pm

25 Wednesday
4th ♋
New Moon   **6:32 am**   3:32 am

26 Thursday
1st ♋
☿ enters ♌   **3:09 pm**   12:09 pm
☽ v/c   10:16 pm
☽ enters ♌   11:05 pm

Islamic New Year begins at sundown

27 Friday

1st ♋
☽ v/c   **1:16 am**
☽ enters ♌ **2:05 am**

28 Saturday

1st ♌

29 Sunday

1st ♌
☽ v/c   **7:03 am** 4:03 am
☽ enters ♍ **7:44 am** 4:44 am

		May 2025				
S	M	T	W	T	F	S
				1	2	3
4	5	6	7	8	9	10
11	12	13	14	15	16	17
18	19	20	21	22	23	24
25	26	27	28	29	30	31

		June 2025				
S	M	T	W	T	F	S
1	2	3	4	5	6	7
8	9	10	11	12	13	14
15	16	17	18	19	20	21
22	23	24	25	26	27	28
29	30					

		July 2025				
S	M	T	W	T	F	S
		1	2	3	4	5
6	7	8	9	10	11	12
13	14	15	16	17	18	19
20	21	22	23	24	25	26
27	28	29	30	31		

30 Monday
1st ♍

1 Tuesday
1st ♍
☽ v/c   **4:47 pm**   1:47 pm
☽ enters ♎   **5:16 pm**   2:16 pm

2 Wednesday
1st ♎
☽ v/c   **3:30 pm**   12:30 pm
2nd Quarter   **3:30 pm**   12:30 pm

3 Thursday
2nd ♎

4 Friday

2nd ♎︎
)) enters ♏︎ **5:33 am** 2:33 am
♀ enters ♊︎ **11:31 am** 8:31 am
♆ R̥ **5:34 pm** 2:34 pm

Independence Day

5 Saturday

2nd ♏︎

6 Sunday

2nd ♏︎
)) v/c **6:04 pm** 3:04 pm
)) enters ♐︎ **6:06 pm** 3:06 pm

June 2025						
S	M	T	W	T	F	S
1	2	3	4	5	6	7
8	9	10	11	12	13	14
15	16	17	18	19	20	21
22	23	24	25	26	27	28
29	30					

July 2025						
S	M	T	W	T	F	S
		1	2	3	4	5
6	7	8	9	10	11	12
13	14	15	16	17	18	19
20	21	22	23	24	25	26
27	28	29	30	31		

August 2025						
S	M	T	W	T	F	S
					1	2
3	4	5	6	7	8	9
10	11	12	13	14	15	16
17	18	19	20	21	22	23
24	25	26	27	28	29	30
31						

7 Monday
2nd ♐
♅ enters ♊   **3:45 am** 12:45 am
☽ v/c   **5:29 pm** 2:29 pm

8 Tuesday
2nd ♐

9 Wednesday
2nd ♐
☽ enters ♑   **4:55 am** 1:55 am

10 Thursday
2nd ♑
☽ v/c   **4:37 pm** 1:37 pm
Full Moon   **4:37 pm** 1:37 pm
❄ D   9:01 pm

11 Friday
3rd ♈

| ☀ D | **12:01 am** | |
| ☽ enters ≈ | **1:21 pm** | 10:21 am |

12 Saturday
3rd ≈

| ☽ v/c | **3:45 pm** | 12:45 pm |
| ♄ ℞ | | 9:07 pm |

13 Sunday
3rd ≈

| ♄ ℞ | **12:07 am** | |
| ☽ enters ♓ | **7:45 pm** | 4:45 pm |

June 2025								July 2025								August 2025					
S	M	T	W	T	F	S		S	M	T	W	T	F	S		S	M	T	W	T	F	S
1	2	3	4	5	6	7				1	2	3	4	5							1	2
8	9	10	11	12	13	14		6	7	8	9	10	11	12		3	4	5	6	7	8	9
15	16	17	18	19	20	21		13	14	15	16	17	18	19		10	11	12	13	14	15	16
22	23	24	25	26	27	28		20	21	22	23	24	25	26		17	18	19	20	21	22	23
29	30							27	28	29	30	31				24	25	26	27	28	29	30
																31					

Eastern time in bold type
Pacific time in medium type

14 Monday
3rd ♓

15 Tuesday
3rd ♓
☽ v/c   **1:10 pm** 10:10 am
☽ enters ♈   9:32 pm

16 Wednesday
3rd ♓
☽ enters ♈ **12:32 am**

17 Thursday
3rd ♈
☽ v/c   **8:38 pm** 5:38 pm
4th Quarter   **8:38 pm** 5:38 pm
☿ ℞   9:45 pm

Mercury retrograde until 8/11 (PDT)

Eastern time in bold type
Pacific time in medium type

18 Friday

4th ♈︎
☿ ℞   **12:45 am**
☽ enters ♉︎ **3:59 am** 12:59 am

Mercury retrograde until 8/11 (EDT)

19 Saturday

4th ♉︎
☽ v/c   11:43 pm

20 Sunday

4th ♉︎
☽ v/c   **2:43 am**
☽ enters ♊︎ **6:22 am** 3:22 am

June 2025						
S	M	T	W	T	F	S
1	2	3	4	5	6	7
8	9	10	11	12	13	14
15	16	17	18	19	20	21
22	23	24	25	26	27	28
29	30					

July 2025						
S	M	T	W	T	F	S
		1	2	3	4	5
6	7	8	9	10	11	12
13	14	15	16	17	18	19
20	21	22	23	24	25	26
27	28	29	30	31		

August 2025						
S	M	T	W	T	F	S
					1	2
3	4	5	6	7	8	9
10	11	12	13	14	15	16
17	18	19	20	21	22	23
24	25	26	27	28	29	30
31						

21 Monday
4th ♊
☽ v/c   **3:52 pm** 12:52 pm

22 Tuesday
4th ♊
☽ enters ♋   **8:26 am** 5:26 am
☉ enters ♌   **9:29 am** 6:29 am

Sun enters Leo

23 Wednesday
4th ♋
☽ v/c   **8:42 pm** 5:42 pm

24 Thursday
4th ♋
☽ enters ♌ **11:28 am** 8:28 am
New Moon   **3:11 pm** 12:11 pm

25 Friday
1st ♌

26 Saturday
1st ♌
☽ v/c   **7:02 am**   4:02 am
☽ enters ♍   **4:55 pm**   1:55 pm

27 Sunday
1st ♍

June 2025						
S	M	T	W	T	F	S
1	2	3	4	5	6	7
8	9	10	11	12	13	14
15	16	17	18	19	20	21
22	23	24	25	26	27	28
29	30					

July 2025						
S	M	T	W	T	F	S
		1	2	3	4	5
6	7	8	9	10	11	12
13	14	15	16	17	18	19
20	21	22	23	24	25	26
27	28	29	30	31		

August 2025						
S	M	T	W	T	F	S
					1	2
3	4	5	6	7	8	9
10	11	12	13	14	15	16
17	18	19	20	21	22	23
24	25	26	27	28	29	30
31						

Eastern time in bold type
Pacific time in medium type

28 Monday

1st ♍
☽ v/c   **8:57 pm** 5:57 pm
☽ enters ♎   10:43 pm

29 Tuesday

1st ♍
☽ enters ♎ **1:43 am**
☽ v/c   **11:59 pm** 8:59 pm

30 Wednesday

1st ♎
☿ ℞   **10:42 am** 7:42 am
♀ enters ♋ **11:57 pm** 8:57 pm

31 Thursday

1st ♎
☽ enters ♏ **1:25 pm** 10:25 am

1 Friday

1st ♏
2nd Quarter **8:41 am** 5:41 am

Lammas

2 Saturday

2nd ♏
☽ v/c   **9:07 pm** 6:07 pm
☽ enters ♐   11:00 pm

3 Sunday

2nd ♏
☽ enters ♐ **2:00 am**

		July 2025							August 2025							September 2025			
S	M	T	W	T	F	S	S	M	T	W	T	F	S	S	M	T	W	T	F	S
		1	2	3	4	5						1	2		1	2	3	4	5	6
6	7	8	9	10	11	12	3	4	5	6	7	8	9	7	8	9	10	11	12	13
13	14	15	16	17	18	19	10	11	12	13	14	15	16	14	15	16	17	18	19	20
20	21	22	23	24	25	26	17	18	19	20	21	22	23	21	22	23	24	25	26	27
27	28	29	30	31			24	25	26	27	28	29	30	28	29	30				
							31													

4 Monday
2nd ♐

5 Tuesday
2nd ♐
☽ v/c   **11:29 am** 8:29 am
☽ enters ♑ **1:04 pm** 10:04 am

6 Wednesday
2nd ♑
☽ v/c   **1:40 pm** 10:40 am
♂ enters ♎ **7:23 pm** 4:23 pm

7 Thursday
2nd ♑
☽ enters ≈ **9:18 pm** 6:18 pm

8 Friday

2nd ≈

9 Saturday

2nd ≈

☽ v/c	**3:55 am**	12:55 am
Full Moon	**3:55 am**	12:55 am
☽ enters ♓		11:50 pm

10 Sunday

3rd ≈

| ☽ enters ♓ | **2:50 am** | |
| ☽ v/c | | 11:55 pm |

July 2025								August 2025								September 2025						
S	M	T	W	T	F	S		S	M	T	W	T	F	S		S	M	T	W	T	F	S
		1	2	3	4	5							1	2			1	2	3	4	5	6
6	7	8	9	10	11	12		3	4	5	6	7	8	9		7	8	9	10	11	12	13
13	14	15	16	17	18	19		10	11	12	13	14	15	16		14	15	16	17	18	19	20
20	21	22	23	24	25	26		17	18	19	20	21	22	23		21	22	23	24	25	26	27
27	28	29	30	31				24	25	26	27	28	29	30		28	29	30				
								31														

11 Monday

3rd ♓
☽ v/c	**2:55 am**	
☿ D	**3:30 am**	12:30 am
♀ ℞	**5:36 pm**	2:36 pm

12 Tuesday

3rd ♓
| ☽ enters ♈ | **6:33 am** | 3:33 am |

13 Wednesday

3rd ♈
| ☽ v/c | **6:54 pm** | 3:54 pm |

14 Thursday

3rd ♈
| ☽ enters ♉ | **9:22 am** | 6:22 am |

15 Friday

3rd ♉

| ☽ v/c | 10:12 pm |
| 4th Quarter | 10:12 pm |

16 Saturday

3rd ♉

☽ v/c	**1:12 am**	
4th Quarter	**1:12 am**	
☽ enters ♊	**12:01 pm**	9:01 am

17 Sunday

4th ♊

July 2025						
S	M	T	W	T	F	S
		1	2	3	4	5
6	7	8	9	10	11	12
13	14	15	16	17	18	19
20	21	22	23	24	25	26
27	28	29	30	31		

August 2025						
S	M	T	W	T	F	S
					1	2
3	4	5	6	7	8	9
10	11	12	13	14	15	16
17	18	19	20	21	22	23
24	25	26	27	28	29	30
31						

September 2025						
S	M	T	W	T	F	S
	1	2	3	4	5	6
7	8	9	10	11	12	13
14	15	16	17	18	19	20
21	22	23	24	25	26	27
28	29	30				

Eastern time in bold type
Pacific time in medium type

18 Monday

4th ♊
☽ v/c   **7:53 am**   4:53 am
☽ enters ♋   **3:05 pm**   12:05 pm

19 Tuesday

4th ♋

20 Wednesday

4th ♋
☽ v/c   **8:27 am**   5:27 am
☽ enters ♌   **7:17 pm**   4:17 pm

21 Thursday

4th ♌
☽ v/c   **2:13 pm**   11:13 am

22 Friday
4th ♌
☉ enters ♍ **4:34 pm** 1:34 pm
☽ enters ♍ 10:24 pm
New Moon 11:07 pm

Sun enters Virgo

23 Saturday
4th ♌
☽ enters ♍ **1:24 am**
New Moon **2:07 am**

24 Sunday
1st ♍

July 2025
S M T W T F S
1 2 3 4 5
6 7 8 9 10 11 12
13 14 15 16 17 18 19
20 21 22 23 24 25 26
27 28 29 30 31

August 2025
S M T W T F S
1 2
3 4 5 6 7 8 9
10 11 12 13 14 15 16
17 18 19 20 21 22 23
24 25 26 27 28 29 30
31

September 2025
S M T W T F S
1 2 3 4 5 6
7 8 9 10 11 12 13
14 15 16 17 18 19 20
21 22 23 24 25 26 27
28 29 30

Eastern time in bold type
Pacific time in medium type

25 Monday
1st ♍
☽ v/c	**9:53 am**	6:53 am
☽ enters ♎	**10:08 am**	7:08 am
♀ enters ♌	**12:27 pm**	9:27 am

26 Tuesday
1st ♎
☽ v/c	**10:06 pm**	7:06 pm

27 Wednesday
1st ♎
☽ enters ♏	**9:27 pm**	6:27 pm

28 Thursday
1st ♏

29 Friday
1st ♏︎
☽ v/c   **8:47 pm**   5:47 pm

30 Saturday
1st ♏︎
☽ enters ♐︎ **10:04 am** 7:04 am
2nd Quarter   11:25 pm

31 Sunday
1st ♐︎
2nd Quarter **2:25 am**

July 2025						
S	M	T	W	T	F	S
		1	2	3	4	5
6	7	8	9	10	11	12
13	14	15	16	17	18	19
20	21	22	23	24	25	26
27	28	29	30	31		

August 2025						
S	M	T	W	T	F	S
					1	2
3	4	5	6	7	8	9
10	11	12	13	14	15	16
17	18	19	20	21	22	23
24	25	26	27	28	29	30
31						

September 2025						
S	M	T	W	T	F	S
	1	2	3	4	5	6
7	8	9	10	11	12	13
14	15	16	17	18	19	20
21	22	23	24	25	26	27
28	29	30				

1 Monday

2nd ✗

♄ enters ♓	**4:07 am**	1:07 am
) v/c	**9:39 pm**	6:39 pm
) enters ♑	**9:45 pm**	6:45 pm

Labor Day

---

2 Tuesday

2nd ♑

| ☿ enters ♍ | **9:23 am** | 6:23 am |

---

3 Wednesday

2nd ♑

---

4 Thursday

2nd ♑

|) v/c | **6:08 am** | 3:08 am |
|) enters ≈ | **6:32 am** | 3:32 am |

Eastern time in bold type
Pacific time in medium type

5 Friday

2nd ≈
☽ v/c   **4:51 pm** 1:51 pm
♅ ℞   9:51 pm

6 Saturday

2nd ≈
♅ ℞   **12:51 am**
☽ enters ♓   **11:54 am** 8:54 am

7 Sunday

2nd ♓
Full Moon   **2:09 pm** 11:09 am

Lunar Eclipse 15° ♓ 23'

August 2025						
S	M	T	W	T	F	S
					1	2
3	4	5	6	7	8	9
10	11	12	13	14	15	16
17	18	19	20	21	22	23
24	25	26	27	28	29	30
31						

September 2025						
S	M	T	W	T	F	S
	1	2	3	4	5	6
7	8	9	10	11	12	13
14	15	16	17	18	19	20
21	22	23	24	25	26	27
28	29	30				

October 2025						
S	M	T	W	T	F	S
			1	2	3	4
5	6	7	8	9	10	11
12	13	14	15	16	17	18
19	20	21	22	23	24	25
26	27	28	29	30	31	

8 Monday
3rd ♓
☽ v/c   **1:44 pm** 10:44 am
☽ enters ♈ **2:37 pm** 11:37 am

9 Tuesday
3rd ♈
☽ v/c   11:54 pm

10 Wednesday
3rd ♈
☽ v/c   **2:54 am**
☽ enters ♉ **4:03 pm** 1:03 pm

11 Thursday
3rd ♉

Eastern time in bold type
Pacific time in medium type

12 Friday

3rd ♉

☽ v/c	**4:14 pm**	1:14 pm
☽ enters ♊	**5:38 pm**	2:38 pm

13 Saturday

3rd ♊

♇ enters ♐	**11:10 pm**	8:10 pm

14 Sunday

3rd ♊

4th Quarter	**6:33 am**	3:33 am
☽ v/c	**6:46 pm**	3:46 pm
☽ enters ♋	**8:30 pm**	5:30 pm

August 2025						
S	M	T	W	T	F	S
					1	2
3	4	5	6	7	8	9
10	11	12	13	14	15	16
17	18	19	20	21	22	23
24	25	26	27	28	29	30
31						

September 2025						
S	M	T	W	T	F	S
	1	2	3	4	5	6
7	8	9	10	11	12	13
14	15	16	17	18	19	20
21	22	23	24	25	26	27
28	29	30				

October 2025						
S	M	T	W	T	F	S
			1	2	3	4
5	6	7	8	9	10	11
12	13	14	15	16	17	18
19	20	21	22	23	24	25
26	27	28	29	30	31	

Eastern time in bold type
Pacific time in medium type

15 Monday
4th ♋

16 Tuesday
4th ♋
☽ v/c   **11:14 pm** 8:14 pm
☽ enters ♌   10:20 pm

17 Wednesday
4th ♋
☽ enters ♌ **1:20 am**

18 Thursday
4th ♌
☿ enters ♎ **6:06 am** 3:06 am

19 Friday

4th ♌

☽ v/c	**8:21 am**	5:21 am
☽ enters ♍	**8:23 am**	5:23 am
♀ enters ♍	**8:39 am**	5:39 am

20 Saturday

4th ♍

21 Sunday

4th ♍

☽ v/c	**3:54 pm**	12:54 pm
New Moon	**3:54 pm**	12:54 pm
☽ enters ♎	**5:41 pm**	2:41 pm

Solar Eclipse 29° ♍ 05' • UN International Day of Peace

August 2025						
S	M	T	W	T	F	S
					1	2
3	4	5	6	7	8	9
10	11	12	13	14	15	16
17	18	19	20	21	22	23
24	25	26	27	28	29	30
31						

September 2025						
S	M	T	W	T	F	S
	1	2	3	4	5	6
7	8	9	10	11	12	13
14	15	16	17	18	19	20
21	22	23	24	25	26	27
28	29	30				

October 2025						
S	M	T	W	T	F	S
			1	2	3	4
5	6	7	8	9	10	11
12	13	14	15	16	17	18
19	20	21	22	23	24	25
26	27	28	29	30	31	

Eastern time in bold type
Pacific time in medium type

22 Monday

1st ♎︎
♂ enters ♏︎ **3:54 am** 12:54 am
☉ enters ♎︎ **2:19 pm** 11:19 am

Rosh Hashanah begins at sundown
Sun enters Libra • Mabon • Fall Equinox • 2:19 pm EDT/ 11:19 am PDT

23 Tuesday

1st ♎︎
☽ v/c   **12:02 pm** 9:02 am

24 Wednesday

1st ♎︎
☽ enters ♏︎ **5:00 am** 2:00 am

25 Thursday

1st ♏︎

Eastern time in bold type
Pacific time in medium type

26 Friday
1st ♏
☽ v/c   **1:44 pm** 10:44 am
☽ enters ♐   **5:37 pm** 2:37 pm

27 Saturday
1st ♐

28 Sunday
1st ♐
☽ v/c   10:44 pm

August 2025						
S	M	T	W	T	F	S
					1	2
3	4	5	6	7	8	9
10	11	12	13	14	15	16
17	18	19	20	21	22	23
24	25	26	27	28	29	30
31						

September 2025						
S	M	T	W	T	F	S
	1	2	3	4	5	6
7	8	9	10	11	12	13
14	15	16	17	18	19	20
21	22	23	24	25	26	27
28	29	30				

October 2025						
S	M	T	W	T	F	S
			1	2	3	4
5	6	7	8	9	10	11
12	13	14	15	16	17	18
19	20	21	22	23	24	25
26	27	28	29	30	31	

Eastern time in bold type
Pacific time in medium type

29 Monday

1st ♐
☽ v/c	**1:44 am**	
☽ enters ♑	**5:55 am**	2:55 am
2nd Quarter	**7:54 pm**	4:54 pm

30 Tuesday

2nd ♑

1 Wednesday

2nd ♑
⚹ enters ♐	**3:55 am**	12:55 am
☽ v/c	**11:33 am**	8:33 am
☽ enters ≈	**3:52 pm**	12:52 pm

Yom Kippur begins at sundown

2 Thursday

2nd ≈

Eastern time in bold type
Pacific time in medium type

3 Friday
2nd ≈
☽ v/c	**2:15 pm**	11:15 am
☽ enters ♓	**10:07 pm**	7:07 pm

4 Saturday
2nd ♓

☿ D	**3:17 am**	12:17 am

5 Sunday
2nd ♓

☽ v/c	**8:30 pm**	5:30 pm
☽ enters ♈		9:48 pm

September 2025							October 2025							November 2025						
S	M	T	W	T	F	S	S	M	T	W	T	F	S	S	M	T	W	T	F	S
	1	2	3	4	5	6				1	2	3	4							1
7	8	9	10	11	12	13	5	6	7	8	9	10	11	2	3	4	5	6	7	8
14	15	16	17	18	19	20	12	13	14	15	16	17	18	9	10	11	12	13	14	15
21	22	23	24	25	26	27	19	20	21	22	23	24	25	16	17	18	19	20	21	22
28	29	30					26	27	28	29	30	31		23	24	25	26	27	28	29
														30						

6 Monday

2nd ♓
☽ enters ♈ **12:48 am**
☿ enters ♏ **12:41 pm** 9:41 am
Full Moon **11:48 pm** 8:48 pm

Sukkot begins at sundown

7 Tuesday

3rd ♈
☽ v/c **2:24 pm** 11:24 am
☽ enters ♉ 10:12 pm

8 Wednesday

3rd ♈
☽ enters ♉ **1:12 am**

9 Thursday

3rd ♉
☽ v/c **8:31 pm** 5:31 pm
☽ enters ♊ 10:12 pm

10 Friday
3rd ☿
☽ enters ♊ **1:12 am**

11 Saturday
3rd ♊
☽ v/c **10:56 pm** 7:56 pm
☽ enters ♋ 11:37 pm

12 Sunday
3rd ♊
☽ enters ♋ **2:37 am**

September 2025						
S	M	T	W	T	F	S
	1	2	3	4	5	6
7	8	9	10	11	12	13
14	15	16	17	18	19	20
21	22	23	24	25	26	27
28	29	30				

October 2025						
S	M	T	W	T	F	S
			1	2	3	4
5	6	7	8	9	10	11
12	13	14	15	16	17	18
19	20	21	22	23	24	25
26	27	28	29	30	31	

November 2025						
S	M	T	W	T	F	S
						1
2	3	4	5	6	7	8
9	10	11	12	13	14	15
16	17	18	19	20	21	22
23	24	25	26	27	28	29
30						

Eastern time in bold type
Pacific time in medium type

13 Monday

3rd ♋
4th Quarter **2:13 pm** 11:13 am
♀ enters ♎ **5:19 pm** 2:19 pm
☿ D **10:54 pm** 7:54 pm
☽ v/c 10:05 pm

Sukkot ends • Indigenous Peoples' Day

14 Tuesday

4th ♋
☽ v/c **1:05 am**
☽ enters ♌ **6:47 am** 3:47 am

15 Wednesday

4th ♌
☽ v/c 10:06 pm

16 Thursday

4th ♌
☽ v/c **1:06 am**
☽ enters ♍ **2:06 pm** 11:06 am

17 Friday
4th ♍

18 Saturday
4th ♍

☽ v/c	**5:10 pm**	2:10 pm
☽ enters ♎		9:01 pm

19 Sunday
4th ♍

☽ enters ♎ **12:01 am**

September 2025							October 2025							November 2025						
S	M	T	W	T	F	S	S	M	T	W	T	F	S	S	M	T	W	T	F	S
	1	2	3	4	5	6				1	2	3	4							1
7	8	9	10	11	12	13	5	6	7	8	9	10	11	2	3	4	5	6	7	8
14	15	16	17	18	19	20	12	13	14	15	16	17	18	9	10	11	12	13	14	15
21	22	23	24	25	26	27	19	20	21	22	23	24	25	16	17	18	19	20	21	22
28	29	30					26	27	28	29	30	31		23	24	25	26	27	28	29
														30						

20 Monday
4th ♎

21 Tuesday
4th ♎
☽ v/c   **8:25 am**   5:25 am
New Moon   **8:25 am**   5:25 am
☽ enters ♏ **11:42 am** 8:42 am

22 Wednesday
1st ♏
♆ enters ♓ **5:48 am**   2:48 am
☉ enters ♏ **11:51 pm**   8:51 pm

Sun enters Scorpio

23 Thursday
1st ♏
☽ v/c   9:14 pm
☽ enters ♐   9:19 pm

24 Friday

1st ♏
| ☽ v/c | **12:14 am** | |
| ☽ enters ♐ | **12:19 am** | |

25 Saturday

1st ♐

26 Sunday

1st ♐
| ☽ v/c | **12:42 pm** | 9:42 am |
| ☽ enters ♑ | **12:53 pm** | 9:53 am |

September 2025	October 2025	November 2025
S M T W T F S	S M T W T F S	S M T W T F S
1 2 3 4 5 6	1 2 3 4	1
7 8 9 10 11 12 13	5 6 7 8 9 10 11	2 3 4 5 6 7 8
14 15 16 17 18 19 20	12 13 14 15 16 17 18	9 10 11 12 13 14 15
21 22 23 24 25 26 27	19 20 21 22 23 24 25	16 17 18 19 20 21 22
28 29 30	26 27 28 29 30 31	23 24 25 26 27 28 29
		30

Eastern time in bold type
Pacific time in medium type

27 Monday
1st ♈︎

28 Tuesday
1st ♑︎
☽ v/c   **11:38 pm**   8:38 pm
☽ enters ♒︎ **11:55 pm**   8:55 pm

29 Wednesday

1st ♒︎
☿ enters ♐︎   **7:02 am**   4:02 am
2nd Quarter **12:21 pm**   9:21 am

30 Thursday

2nd ♒︎
☽ v/c   11:15 pm

31 Friday

2nd ≈

D v/c   **2:15 am**
D enters ♓   **7:46 am**   4:46 am

Halloween • Samhain

1 Saturday

2nd ♓

All Saints' Day

2 Sunday

2nd ♓
D v/c   **10:15 am**   7:15 am
D enters ♈   **10:39 am**   7:39 am

Daylight Saving Time ends at 2 am

October 2025						
S	M	T	W	T	F	S
			1	2	3	4
5	6	7	8	9	10	11
12	13	14	15	16	17	18
19	20	21	22	23	24	25
26	27	28	29	30	31	

November 2025						
S	M	T	W	T	F	S
						1
2	3	4	5	6	7	8
9	10	11	12	13	14	15
16	17	18	19	20	21	22
23	24	25	26	27	28	29
30						

December 2025						
S	M	T	W	T	F	S
	1	2	3	4	5	6
7	8	9	10	11	12	13
14	15	16	17	18	19	20
21	22	23	24	25	26	27
28	29	30	31			

3 Monday
2nd ♈

4 Tuesday
2nd ♈
☽ v/c	**6:21 am**	3:21 am
♂ enters ♐	**8:01 am**	5:01 am
☽ enters ♉	**11:16 am**	8:16 am

Election Day (general)

5 Wednesday
2nd ♉
| Full Moon | **8:19 am** | 5:19 am |

6 Thursday
3rd ♉
☽ v/c	**9:51 am**	6:51 am
☽ enters ♊	**10:20 am**	7:20 am
♀ enters ♏	**5:39 pm**	2:39 pm

Eastern time in bold type
Pacific time in medium type

7 Friday
3rd ♊
♅ enters ♉   **9:22 pm**   6:22 pm

8 Saturday
3rd ♊
☽ v/c   **9:32 am**   6:32 am
☽ enters ♋   **10:06 am** 7:06 am

9 Sunday
3rd ♋
☿ ℞   **2:02 pm**   11:02 am

Mercury retrograde until 11/29

October 2025							November 2025							December 2025					
S	M	T	W	T	F	S	S	M	T	W	T	F	S	S	M	T	W	T	F	S
			1	2	3	4							1		1	2	3	4	5	6
5	6	7	8	9	10	11	2	3	4	5	6	7	8	7	8	9	10	11	12	13
12	13	14	15	16	17	18	9	10	11	12	13	14	15	14	15	16	17	18	19	20
19	20	21	22	23	24	25	16	17	18	19	20	21	22	21	22	23	24	25	26	27
26	27	28	29	30	31		23	24	25	26	27	28	29	28	29	30	31			
							30													

10 Monday

3rd ♋
| ☽ v/c | **12:23 pm** | 9:23 am |
| ☽ enters ♌ | **12:34 pm** | 9:34 am |

11 Tuesday

3rd ♌
| ♃ Rx | **11:41 am** | 8:41 am |
| 4th Quarter | | 9:28 pm |

Veterans Day

12 Wednesday

3rd ♌
4th Quarter	**12:28 am**	
☽ v/c	**6:29 pm**	3:29 pm
☽ enters ♍	**6:52 pm**	3:52 pm

13 Thursday

4th ♍

Eastern time in bold type
Pacific time in medium type

14 Friday
4th ♍

15 Saturday
4th ♍

☽ v/c	**4:08 am**	1:08 am
☽ enters ♎	**4:44 am**	1:44 am
⯞ enters ♑	**5:25 am**	2:25 am

16 Sunday
4th ♎

October 2025						
S	M	T	W	T	F	S
			1	2	3	4
5	6	7	8	9	10	11
12	13	14	15	16	17	18
19	20	21	22	23	24	25
26	27	28	29	30	31	

November 2025						
S	M	T	W	T	F	S
						1
2	3	4	5	6	7	8
9	10	11	12	13	14	15
16	17	18	19	20	21	22
23	24	25	26	27	28	29
30						

December 2025						
S	M	T	W	T	F	S
	1	2	3	4	5	6
7	8	9	10	11	12	13
14	15	16	17	18	19	20
21	22	23	24	25	26	27
28	29	30	31			

17 Monday

4th ♎︎
☽ v/c   **6:51 am**   3:51 am
☽ enters ♏︎   **4:44 pm**   1:44 pm

18 Tuesday

4th ♏︎
☿ enters ♏︎   **10:20 pm**   7:20 pm

19 Wednesday

4th ♏︎
New Moon   10:47 pm

20 Thursday

4th ♏︎
New Moon   **1:47 am**
☽ v/c   **4:24 am**   1:24 am
☽ enters ♐︎   **5:26 am**   2:26 am

21 Friday

1st ♐
☿ D   **6:57 pm**   3:57 pm
☉ enters ♐   **8:36 pm**   5:36 pm

Sun enters Sagittarius

22 Saturday

1st ♐
☽ v/c   **4:48 pm**   1:48 pm
☽ enters ♑   **5:53 pm**   2:53 pm

23 Sunday

1st ♑

October 2025						
S	M	T	W	T	F	S
			1	2	3	4
5	6	7	8	9	10	11
12	13	14	15	16	17	18
19	20	21	22	23	24	25
26	27	28	29	30	31	

November 2025						
S	M	T	W	T	F	S
						1
2	3	4	5	6	7	8
9	10	11	12	13	14	15
16	17	18	19	20	21	22
23	24	25	26	27	28	29
30						

December 2025						
S	M	T	W	T	F	S
	1	2	3	4	5	6
7	8	9	10	11	12	13
14	15	16	17	18	19	20
21	22	23	24	25	26	27
28	29	30	31			

Eastern time in bold type
Pacific time in medium type

24 Monday
1st VS

25 Tuesday
1st VS
☽ v/c   **4:10 am**   1:10 am
☽ enters ≈   **5:16 am**   2:16 am

26 Wednesday
1st ≈

27 Thursday
1st ≈
☽ v/c   **12:53 pm**   9:53 am
☽ enters ♓   **2:24 pm**   11:24 am
♄ D   **10:52 pm**   7:52 pm
2nd Quarter   10:59 pm

Thanksgiving Day

Eastern time in bold type
Pacific time in medium type

28 Friday
1st ♓
2nd Quarter **1:59 am**

29 Saturday
2nd ♓
☿ D **12:38 pm** 9:38 am
☽ v/c **7:05 pm** 4:05 pm
☽ enters ♈ **8:07 pm** 5:07 pm

30 Sunday
2nd ♈
♀ enters ♐ **3:14 pm** 12:14 pm

October 2025						
S	M	T	W	T	F	S
			1	2	3	4
5	6	7	8	9	10	11
12	13	14	15	16	17	18
19	20	21	22	23	24	25
26	27	28	29	30	31	

November 2025						
S	M	T	W	T	F	S
						1
2	3	4	5	6	7	8
9	10	11	12	13	14	15
16	17	18	19	20	21	22
23	24	25	26	27	28	29
30						

December 2025						
S	M	T	W	T	F	S
	1	2	3	4	5	6
7	8	9	10	11	12	13
14	15	16	17	18	19	20
21	22	23	24	25	26	27
28	29	30	31			

Eastern time in bold type
Pacific time in medium type

1 Monday
2nd ♈
D v/c   **1:14 pm** 10:14 am
D enters ♉ **10:13 pm** 7:13 pm

2 Tuesday
2nd ♉

3 Wednesday
2nd ♉
D v/c   **8:50 pm** 5:50 pm
D enters ♊ **9:48 pm** 6:48 pm

4 Thursday
2nd ♊
Full Moon   **6:14 pm** 3:14 pm

5 Friday

3rd ♊

☽ v/c	**7:55 pm**	4:55 pm
☽ enters ♋	**8:54 pm**	5:54 pm

6 Saturday

3rd ♋

7 Sunday

3rd ♋

☽ v/c	**8:45 pm**	5:45 pm
☽ enters ♌	**9:48 pm**	6:48 pm

November 2025						
S	M	T	W	T	F	S
						1
2	3	4	5	6	7	8
9	10	11	12	13	14	15
16	17	18	19	20	21	22
23	24	25	26	27	28	29
30						

December 2025						
S	M	T	W	T	F	S
	1	2	3	4	5	6
7	8	9	10	11	12	13
14	15	16	17	18	19	20
21	22	23	24	25	26	27
28	29	30	31			

January 2026						
S	M	T	W	T	F	S
				1	2	3
4	5	6	7	8	9	10
11	12	13	14	15	16	17
18	19	20	21	22	23	24
25	26	27	28	29	30	31

8 Monday
3rd ♌

9 Tuesday
3rd ♌
☽ v/c   **11:56 pm**   8:56 pm
☽ enters ♍   11:20 pm

10 Wednesday
3rd ♌
☽ enters ♍   **2:20 am**
♆ D   **7:21 am**   4:21 am

11 Thursday

3rd ♍
4th Quarter **3:52 pm**   12:52 pm
☿ enters ♐   **5:40 pm**   2:40 pm

Eastern time in bold type
Pacific time in medium type

12 Friday
4th ♍
| ☽ v/c | **9:51 am** | 6:51 am |
| ☽ enters ♎ | **11:04 am** | 8:04 am |

13 Saturday
4th ♎

14 Sunday
4th ♎
☽ v/c	**10:36 pm**	7:36 pm
☽ enters ♏	**10:51 pm**	7:51 pm
♂ enters ♑		11:34 pm

Hanukkah begins at sundown

November 2025						
S	M	T	W	T	F	S
						1
2	3	4	5	6	7	8
9	10	11	12	13	14	15
16	17	18	19	20	21	22
23	24	25	26	27	28	29
30						

December 2025						
S	M	T	W	T	F	S
	1	2	3	4	5	6
7	8	9	10	11	12	13
14	15	16	17	18	19	20
21	22	23	24	25	26	27
28	29	30	31			

January 2026						
S	M	T	W	T	F	S
				1	2	3
4	5	6	7	8	9	10
11	12	13	14	15	16	17
18	19	20	21	22	23	24
25	26	27	28	29	30	31

Eastern time in bold type
Pacific time in medium type

15 Monday
4th ♏
♂ enters ♑ **2:34 am**

16 Tuesday
4th ♏

17 Wednesday
4th ♏
☽ v/c **10:24 am** 7:24 am
☽ enters ♐ **11:38 am** 8:38 am

18 Thursday
4th ♐

19 Friday
4th ♐

New Moon	**8:43 pm**	5:43 pm
☽ v/c	**10:41 pm**	7:41 pm
☽ enters ♑	**11:53 pm**	8:53 pm

20 Saturday
1st ♑

21 Sunday
1st ♑
☉ enters ♑ **10:03 am**　7:03 am

Sun enters Capricorn • Yule • Winter Solstice • 10:03 am EST/7:03 am PST

November 2025						
S	M	T	W	T	F	S
						1
2	3	4	5	6	7	8
9	10	11	12	13	14	15
16	17	18	19	20	21	22
23	24	25	26	27	28	29
30						

December 2025						
S	M	T	W	T	F	S
	1	2	3	4	5	6
7	8	9	10	11	12	13
14	15	16	17	18	19	20
21	22	23	24	25	26	27
28	29	30	31			

January 2026						
S	M	T	W	T	F	S
				1	2	3
4	5	6	7	8	9	10
11	12	13	14	15	16	17
18	19	20	21	22	23	24
25	26	27	28	29	30	31

22 Monday
1st ♑
☽ v/c **9:44 am** 6:44 am
☽ enters ♒ **10:52 am** 7:52 am

Hanukkah ends

23 Tuesday
1st ♒

24 Wednesday
1st ♒
♀ enters ♑ **11:26 am** 8:26 am
☽ v/c **4:42 pm** 1:42 pm
☽ enters ♓ **8:09 pm** 5:09 pm

Christmas Eve

25 Thursday
1st ♓

Christmas Day

Eastern time in bold type
Pacific time in medium type

26 Friday

1st ♓
☽ v/c   11:03 pm

Kwanzaa begins

27 Saturday

1st ♓
☽ v/c   **2:03 am**
☽ enters ♈   **3:02 am** 12:02 am
2nd Quarter **2:10 pm** 11:10 am

28 Sunday

2nd ♈
☽ v/c   **9:13 pm** 6:13 pm

November 2025						
S	M	T	W	T	F	S
						1
2	3	4	5	6	7	8
9	10	11	12	13	14	15
16	17	18	19	20	21	22
23	24	25	26	27	28	29
30						

December 2025						
S	M	T	W	T	F	S
	1	2	3	4	5	6
7	8	9	10	11	12	13
14	15	16	17	18	19	20
21	22	23	24	25	26	27
28	29	30	31			

January 2026						
S	M	T	W	T	F	S
					1	2	3
4	5	6	7	8	9	10
11	12	13	14	15	16	17
18	19	20	21	22	23	24
25	26	27	28	29	30	31

Eastern time in bold type
Pacific time in medium type

29 Monday

2nd ♈

☽ enters ♉ **6:57 am** 3:57 am
⁂ enters ♑ **9:35 am** 6:35 am

30 Tuesday

2nd ♉

31 Wednesday

2nd ♉

☽ v/c **7:25 am** 4:25 am
☽ enters ♊ **8:13 am** 5:13 am

New Year's Eve

1 Thursday

2nd ♊

☿ enters ♑ **4:11 pm** 1:11 pm

Kwanzaa ends • New Year's Day

Eastern time in bold type
Pacific time in medium type

2 Friday

2nd ♊

☽ v/c	**7:24 am**	4:24 am
☽ enters ♋	**8:09 am**	5:09 am
☿ D	**9:38 am**	6:38 am

3 Saturday

2nd ♋

| Full Moon | **5:03 am** | 2:03 am |

4 Sunday

3rd ♋

| ☽ v/c | **7:59 am** | 4:59 am |
| ☽ enters ♌ | **8:44 am** | 5:44 am |

December 2025							January 2026							February 2026						
S	M	T	W	T	F	S	S	M	T	W	T	F	S	S	M	T	W	T	F	S
	1	2	3	4	5	6					1	2	3	1	2	3	4	5	6	7
7	8	9	10	11	12	13	4	5	6	7	8	9	10	8	9	10	11	12	13	14
14	15	16	17	18	19	20	11	12	13	14	15	16	17	15	16	17	18	19	20	21
21	22	23	24	25	26	27	18	19	20	21	22	23	24	22	23	24	25	26	27	28
28	29	30	31				25	26	27	28	29	30	31							

Eastern time in bold type
Pacific time in medium type

JANUARY 2024

☽ Last Aspect day	ET / hr:mn / PT	asp	☽ Ingress sign day	ET / hr:mn / PT
2	**6:36 pm** 3:36 pm	△♇	♎ 2	**7:47 pm** 4:47 pm
5	**6:41 am** 3:41 am	□♇	♏ 5	**7:39 am** 4:39 am
7	**3:22 pm** 12:22 pm	⚹♇	♐ 7	**4:08 pm** 1:08 pm
9	**1:24 pm** 10:24 am	☌☿	♑ 9	**8:33 pm** 5:33 pm
11	**9:33 pm** 6:33 pm	☌♇	♒ 11	**10:01 pm** 7:01 pm
13	**4:59 am** 1:59 am	□♅	♓ 13	**10:29 pm** 7:29 pm
15	**11:33 pm** 8:33 pm	⚹♇	♈ 15	**11:49 pm** 8:49 pm
18	**3:03 am** 12:03 am	□♇	♉ 18	**3:12 am** 12:12 am
20	**8:57 am** 5:57 am	△☉	♊ 20	**8:58 am** 5:58 am
22	**3:40 pm** 12:40 pm	☍♀	♋ 22	**4:51 pm** 1:51 pm

☽ Last Aspect day	ET / hr:mn / PT	asp	☽ Ingress sign day	ET / hr:mn / PT
24	**5:58 pm** 2:58 pm	△♆	♌ 24	11:37 pm
24	**5:58 pm** 2:58 pm	△♆	♌ 25	**2:37 am**
26	**4:19 pm** 1:19 pm	□♅	♍ 27	**2:11 pm** 11:11 am
29	**6:20 pm** 3:20 pm	☍♆	♎ 30	**3:04 am** 12:04 am

☽ Phases & Eclipses phase	day	ET / hr:mn / PT
4th Quarter	3	**10:30 pm** 7:30 pm
New Moon	11	**6:57 am** 3:57 am
2nd Quarter	17	**10:53 pm** 7:53 pm
Full Moon	25	**12:54 pm** 9:54 am

Planet Ingress	day	ET / hr:mn / PT
♂ ♑	4	**9:58 am** 6:58 am
☿ ♑	13	**9:49 pm** 6:49 pm
☉ ♒	20	**9:07 am** 6:07 am
♇ ♒	20	**7:50 pm** 4:50 pm
♀ ♑	23	**3:50 am** 12:50 am

Planetary Motion	day	ET / hr:mn / PT
☿ D	1	**10:08 pm** 7:08 pm
⚵ R	12	**11:55 pm** 8:55 pm
♅ D	26	11:35 pm
♅ D	27	**2:35 am**

1 MONDAY
☽ △ ☉ **3:59 am** 12:59 am
♀ □ ♄ **8:26 am** 5:26 am
☽ △ ♅ **10:09 pm** 7:09 pm

2 TUESDAY
☽ □ ☿ **3:54 am** 12:54 am
☽ ☍ ♆ **9:50 am** 6:50 am
☽ □ ♂ **5:13 pm** 2:13 pm
☽ △ ♇ **6:36 pm** 3:36 pm
☽ ⚻ ♄ 11:47 pm

3 WEDNESDAY
☽ ⚻ ♄ **2:47 am**
♀ ⚻ ♃ **5:55 am** 2:55 am
☽ ⚻ ♃ **7:07 am** 4:07 am
☽ ⚹ ♀ **7:15 am** 4:15 am
♂ ⚺ ♇ **4:09 pm** 1:09 pm
☽ □ ☉ **10:30 pm** 7:30 pm

4 THURSDAY
☽ ⚻ ♅ **10:37 am** 7:37 am
☽ ⚹ ☿ **5:25 pm** 2:25 pm
☽ ⚻ ♆ **10:08 pm** 7:08 pm

5 FRIDAY
☽ □ ♇ **6:41 am** 3:41 am
☽ ⚹ ♂ **9:03 am** 6:03 am
☽ △ ♄ **2:49 pm** 11:49 am
☽ ☍ ♃ **6:35 pm** 3:35 pm
☽ ⚺ ♀ 10:03 pm

6 SATURDAY
☽ ⚺ ♀ **1:03 am**
☽ ⚹ ☉ **2:12 pm** 11:12 am
☽ ☍ ♅ **8:24 pm** 5:24 pm

7 SUNDAY
☽ ⚺ ☿ **5:15 am** 2:15 am
☽ △ ♆ **7:21 am** 4:21 am
☽ ⚹ ♇ **3:22 pm** 12:22 pm
☽ ⚺ ♂ **8:47 pm** 5:47 pm
☽ □ ♄ **11:11 pm** 8:11 pm
☽ ⚻ ♃ 11:23 pm

8 MONDAY
☽ ⚻ ♃ **2:23 am**
☽ ☌ ♀ **1:44 pm** 10:44 am
☿ □ ♆ **8:24 pm** 5:24 pm
☽ ⚺ ☉ 9:48 pm
☽ ⚻ ♅ 11:10 pm

9 TUESDAY
☽ ⚺ ☉ **12:48 am**
☽ ⚻ ♅ **2:10 am**
☽ □ ♆ **12:27 pm** 9:27 am
☽ ☌ ☿ **1:24 pm** 10:24 am
☉ △ ♅ **7:07 pm** 4:07 pm
☽ ⚺ ♇ **7:57 pm** 4:57 pm
♂ ⚹ ♄ **9:40 pm** 6:40 pm

10 WEDNESDAY
☽ ⚹ ♄ **3:29 am** 12:29 am
☽ ☌ ♂ **3:45 am** 12:45 am
☽ △ ♃ **6:14 am** 3:14 am
☽ ⚺ ♀ **9:27 pm** 6:27 pm

11 THURSDAY
☽ △ ♅ **4:26 am** 1:26 am
☽ ☌ ☉ **6:57 am** 3:57 am
☽ ⚹ ♆ **2:20 pm** 11:20 am
☽ ⚺ ☿ **6:27 pm** 3:27 pm
☽ ☌ ♇ **9:33 pm** 6:33 pm

12 FRIDAY
☽ ⚺ ♄ **5:01 am** 2:01 am
♂ △ ♃ **5:42 am** 2:42 am
☽ □ ♃ **7:29 am** 4:29 am
☽ ⚺ ♂ **7:34 am** 4:34 am
☽ ⚹ ♀ 11:32 pm

13 SATURDAY
☽ ⚹ ♀ **2:32 am**
☽ □ ♅ **4:59 am** 1:59 am
☽ ⚺ ☉ **11:05 am** 8:05 am
☽ ⚺ ♆ **2:53 pm** 11:53 am
☿ ⚺ ♇ **4:39 pm** 1:39 pm
☽ ⚺ ♇ **10:07 pm** 7:07 pm
☽ ⚹ ☿ **10:32 pm** 7:32 pm

14 SUNDAY
☽ ☌ ♄ **5:50 am** 2:50 am
♀ ⚻ ♅ **8:03 am** 5:03 am
☽ ⚹ ♃ **8:08 am** 5:08 am
☽ ⚹ ♂ **10:40 am** 7:40 am

15 MONDAY
☽ ⚹ ♅ **5:47 am** 2:47 am
☽ □ ♀ **7:48 am** 4:48 am
☽ ⚹ ☉ **3:47 pm** 12:47 pm
☽ ☌ ♆ **4:03 pm** 1:03 pm
☉ ⚹ ♆ **7:38 pm** 4:38 pm
☽ ⚹ ♇ **11:33 pm** 8:33 pm

16 TUESDAY
☽ □ ☿ **4:05 am** 1:05 am
☽ ⚺ ♄ **7:47 am** 4:47 am
☽ ⚺ ♃ **9:59 am** 6:59 am
☽ □ ♂ **3:14 pm** 12:14 pm

17 WEDNESDAY
☽ ⚺ ♅ **8:18 am** 5:18 am
☽ △ ♀ **3:22 pm** 12:22 pm
☽ ⚺ ♆ **7:10 pm** 4:10 pm
☽ □ ☉ **10:53 pm** 7:53 pm

18 THURSDAY
☽ □ ♇ **3:03 am** 12:03 am
☿ ⚹ ♄ **3:49 am** 12:49 am
☽ ⚹ ♄ **11:57 am** 8:57 am
☽ △ ☿ **12:42 pm** 9:42 am
☽ ☌ ♃ **2:05 pm** 11:05 am
☽ △ ♂ **10:26 pm** 7:26 pm

19 FRIDAY
☿ △ ♃ **4:31 am** 1:31 am
♀ □ ♆ **10:49 am** 7:49 am
☽ ☌ ♅ **1:11 pm** 10:11 am
☽ ⚹ ♆ 9:40 pm
☽ ⚻ ♀ 11:04 pm

20 SATURDAY
☽ ⚹ ♆ **12:40 am**
☽ ⚻ ♀ **2:04 am**
☉ ☌ ♇ **8:46 am** 5:46 am
☽ △ ♇ **8:56 am** 5:56 am
☽ △ ☉ **8:57 am** 5:57 am
☽ □ ♄ **6:32 pm** 3:32 pm
☽ ⚺ ♃ **8:36 pm** 5:36 pm
☽ ⚻ ☿ 9:45 pm

21 SUNDAY
☽ ⚻ ☿ **12:45 am**
☽ ⚻ ♂ **8:23 am** 5:23 am
☽ ⚺ ♅ **8:19 pm** 5:19 pm

22 MONDAY
☽ □ ♆ **8:22 am** 5:22 am
☽ ☍ ♀ **3:40 pm** 12:40 pm
☽ ⚻ ♇ **4:58 pm** 1:58 pm
☽ ⚻ ☉ **9:43 pm** 6:43 pm

23 TUESDAY
☽ △ ♄ **3:15 am** 12:15 am
☽ ⚹ ♃ **5:13 am** 2:13 am
♀ ⚺ ♇ **5:21 am** 2:21 am
☽ ☍ ☿ **3:53 pm** 12:53 pm
☽ ☍ ♂ **8:44 pm** 5:44 pm

24 WEDNESDAY
☽ ⚹ ♅ **5:24 am** 2:24 am
☽ △ ♆ **5:58 pm** 2:58 pm
☽ ☍ ♇ 11:53 pm

25 THURSDAY
☽ ☍ ♇ **2:53 am**
☽ ⚻ ♀ **7:50 am** 4:50 am
☽ ☍ ☉ **12:54 pm** 9:54 am
☽ ⚻ ♄ **1:52 pm** 10:52 am
☽ □ ♃ **3:46 pm** 12:46 pm
☉ ⚺ ♄ 10:52 pm

26 FRIDAY
☉ ⚺ ♄ **1:52 am**
☽ ⚻ ☿ **9:56 am** 6:56 am
☽ ⚻ ♂ **11:19 am** 8:19 am
☽ □ ♅ **4:19 pm** 1:19 pm
☉ □ ♃ 11:18 pm

27 SATURDAY
☉ □ ♃ **2:18 am**
☽ ⚻ ♆ **5:25 am** 2:25 am
☿ ☌ ♂ **9:59 am** 6:59 am
☽ ⚻ ♇ **2:38 pm** 11:38 am
♀ ⚹ ♄ 10:03 pm
☽ ☍ ♄ 11:20 pm
☽ △ ♀ 11:28 pm

28 SUNDAY
♀ ⚹ ♄ **1:03 am**
☽ ☍ ♄ **2:20 am**
☽ △ ♀ **2:28 am**
☽ △ ♃ **4:10 am** 1:10 am
☽ ⚻ ☉ **6:23 am** 3:23 am
☿ △ ♅ **4:07 pm** 1:07 pm
♀ △ ♃ **8:02 pm** 5:02 pm

29 MONDAY
☽ △ ♂ **3:54 am** 12:54 am
☽ △ ♅ **4:51 am** 1:51 am
☽ △ ☿ **6:38 am** 3:38 am
☽ ☍ ♆ **6:20 pm** 3:20 pm
♂ △ ♅ **6:41 pm** 3:41 pm

30 TUESDAY
☽ △ ♇ **3:41 am** 12:41 am
☽ ⚻ ♄ **3:55 pm** 12:55 pm
☽ ⚻ ♃ **5:40 pm** 2:40 pm
☽ □ ♀ **10:34 pm** 7:34 pm
☽ △ ☉ 10:07 pm

31 WEDNESDAY
☽ △ ☉ **1:07 am**
☽ ⚻ ♅ **5:48 pm** 2:48 pm
☽ □ ♂ **9:00 pm** 6:00 pm

Eastern time in bold type
Pacific time in medium type

JANUARY 2024

DATE	SID.TIME	SUN	MOON	NODE	MERCURY	VENUS	MARS	JUPITER	SATURN	URANUS	NEPTUNE	PLUTO	CERES	PALLAS	JUNO	VESTA	CHIRON
1 M	6 40 36	10♑︎02 20	6♈︎00	21♈︎05R	22♐︎17R	2♐︎37	27♐︎19	5♉︎35	3♓︎15	19♉︎23R	25♓︎05	29♑︎21	15♐︎27	17♏︎34	21♍︎19	27♍︎00R	15♈︎28
2 T	6 44 33	11 03 29	17 49	21 00	22 11D	3 50	28 03	5 35	3 20	19 22	25 05	29 23	15 51	17 57	21 24	26 45	15 28
3 W	6 48 29	12 04 38	29 37	20 58	22 14	5 03	28 48	5 36	3 25	19 21	25 06	29 25	16 15	18 20	21 29	26 30	15 29
4 Th	6 52 26	13 05 47	11♉︎30	20 57	22 26	6 16	29 32	5 36	3 31	19 19	25 07	29 27	16 40	18 43	21 33	26 16	15 29
5 F	6 56 22	14 06 56	23 33	20 57	22 46	7 29	0♑︎17	5 37	3 36	19 18	25 08	29 29	17 04	19 05	21 37	26 02	15 29
6 Sa	7 0 19	15 08 06	5♊︎51	20 57	23 13	8 42	1 01	5 38	3 42	19 17	25 09	29 31	17 28	19 28	21 41	25 48	15 30
7 Su	7 4 16	16 09 16	18 31	20 54	23 46	9 56	1 46	5 40	3 48	19 16	25 10	29 33	17 53	19 50	21 44	25 34	15 30
8 M	7 8 12	17 10 26	1♋︎35	20 49	24 26	11 09	2 31	5 41	3 53	19 15	25 11	29 35	18 17	20 12	21 46	25 21	15 31
9 T	7 12 9	18 11 36	15 06	20 42	25 09	12 22	3 16	5 43	3 59	19 14	25 13	29 37	18 41	20 34	21 48	25 08	15 31
10 W	7 16 5	19 12 46	29 05	20 31	25 59	13 36	4 01	5 45	4 05	19 13	25 14	29 39	19 05	20 56	21 50	24 56	15 32
11 Th	7 20 2	20 13 57	13♌︎27	20 19	26 52	14 49	4 46	5 47	4 11	19 12	25 15	29 40	19 29	21 18	21 51	24 43	15 32
12 F	7 23 58	21 15 07	28 08	20 07	27 49	16 03	5 31	5 50	4 17	19 12	25 16	29 42	19 53	21 40	21 52	24 31	15 33
13 Sa	7 27 55	22 16 16	12♍︎59	19 55	28 49	17 16	6 16	5 52	4 23	19 11	25 17	29 44	20 17	22 02	21 52R	24 20	15 34
14 Su	7 31 51	23 17 25	27 51	19 46	29 52	18 30	7 01	5 55	4 29	19 10	25 19	29 46	20 41	22 23	21 52	24 08	15 35
15 M	7 35 48	24 18 33	12♎︎36	19 39	0♑︎58	19 43	7 46	5 58	4 35	19 09	25 20	29 48	21 04	22 45	21 51	23 58	15 36
16 T	7 39 45	25 19 41	27 07	19 36	2 06	20 57	8 31	6 01	4 41	19 09	25 21	29 50	21 28	23 06	21 50	23 47	15 37
17 W	7 43 41	26 20 48	11♏︎22	19 34D	3 17	22 10	9 16	6 04	4 48	19 08	25 23	29 52	21 52	23 27	21 49	23 37	15 38
18 Th	7 47 38	27 21 54	25 18	19 34R	4 29	23 24	10 01	6 08	4 54	19 08	25 24	29 54	22 15	23 48	21 47	23 27	15 39
19 F	7 51 34	28 23 00	8♐︎57	19 34	5 43	24 38	10 46	6 12	5 00	19 07	25 25	29 56	22 39	24 08	21 45	23 18	15 40
20 Sa	7 55 31	29 24 04	22 20	19 32	6 59	25 51	11 32	6 15	5 07	19 07	25 27	29 58	23 02	24 29	21 42	23 09	15 42
21 Su	7 59 27	0♒︎25 08	5♑︎28	19 28	8 16	27 05	12 17	6 20	5 13	19 06	25 28	0♒︎00	23 26	24 50	21 38	23 01	15 43
22 M	8 3 24	1 26 11	18 24	19 21	9 35	28 19	13 02	6 24	5 19	19 06	25 30	0 02	23 49	25 10	21 35	22 53	15 44
23 T	8 7 20	2 27 13	1♒︎08	19 10	10 55	29 33	13 48	6 28	5 26	19 06	25 33	0 04	24 12	25 30	21 31	22 45	15 45
24 W	8 11 17	3 28 14	13 42	18 58	12 16	0♑︎47	14 33	6 33	5 33	19 06	25 34	0 06	24 35	25 50	21 26	22 38	15 47
25 Th	8 15 14	4 29 14	26 06	18 44	13 38	2 01	15 18	6 38	5 39	19 05	25 36	0 08	24 58	26 10	21 20	22 31	15 48
26 F	8 19 10	5 30 14	8♓︎21	18 31	15 01	3 14	16 04	6 43	5 46	19 05D	25 38	0 10	25 21	26 30	21 15	22 25	15 50
27 Sa	8 23 7	6 31 13	20 26	18 18	16 25	4 28	16 49	6 48	5 52	19 05	25 39	0 12	25 44	26 49	21 09	22 19	15 52
28 Su	8 27 3	7 32 10	2♈︎18	18 07	17 50	5 42	17 35	6 54	5 59	19 05	25 41	0 14	26 07	27 08	21 03	22 14	15 53
29 M	8 31 0	8 33 08	14 15	17 59	19 16	6 56	18 20	6 59	6 06	19 05	25 43	0 16	26 29	27 28	20 56	22 09	15 55
30 T	8 34 56	9 34 04	26 02	17 54	20 43	8 10	19 06	7 05	6 13	19 05	25 43	0 17	26 52	27 47	20 48	22 05	15 57
31 W	8 38 53	10 34 59	7♉︎50	17 52D	22 10	9 24	19 52	7 11	6 20	19 06	25 44	0 19	27 15	28 05	20 41	22 01	15 58

EPHEMERIS CALCULATED FOR 12 MIDNIGHT GREENWICH MEAN TIME. ALL OTHER DATA AND FACING ASPECTARIAN PAGE IN **EASTERN TIME (BOLD)** AND PACIFIC TIME (REGULAR).

FEBRUARY 2024

☽ Last Aspect day	ET / hr:mn	PT	asp	☽ Ingress sign	day	ET / hr:mn	PT
1	**4:03 am**	1:03 am	□☿	♏	1	**3:37 pm**	12:37 pm
3	**10:24 pm**	7:24 pm	⚹☿	♐	3		10:28 pm
3	**10:24 pm**	7:24 pm	⚹☿	♐	4	**1:28 am**	
5		9:06 pm	□♆	♑	6	**7:08 am**	4:08 am
6	**12:06 am**		□♆	♑	6	**7:08 am**	4:08 am
7		11:52 pm	☌♂	♒	8	**8:59 am**	5:59 am
8	**2:52 am**		☌♂	♒	8	**8:59 am**	5:59 am
9	**5:59 pm**	2:59 pm	☌☉	♓	10	**8:42 am**	5:42 am
12	**7:32 am**	4:32 am	⚹♂	♈	12	**8:26 am**	5:26 am
14	**5:21 am**	2:21 am	□♀	♉	14	**10:02 am**	7:02 am
16	**10:01 am**	7:01 am	□☉	♊	16	**2:39 pm**	11:39 am
18	**10:21 pm**	7:21 pm	△☉	♋	18	**10:25 pm**	7:25 pm
20		10:38 pm	△♆	♌	21	**8:40 am**	5:40 am
21	**1:38 am**		△♆	♌	21	**8:40 am**	5:40 am
22	**11:18 pm**	8:18 pm	□♅	♍	23	**8:38 pm**	5:38 pm
25		11:35 pm	☍♆	♎	26	**9:29 am**	6:29 am
26	**2:35 am**		☍♆	♎	26	**9:29 am**	6:29 am
27	**1:22 pm**	10:22 am	△♀	♏	28	**10:09 pm**	7:09 pm

☽ Phases & Eclipses phase	day	ET / hr:mn	PT
4th Quarter	2	**6:18 pm**	3:18 pm
New Moon	9	**5:59 pm**	2:59 pm
2nd Quarter	16	**10:01 am**	7:01 am
Full Moon	24	**7:30 am**	4:30 am

Planet Ingress		day	ET / hr:mn	PT
☿	♒	4		9:10 pm
☿	♒	5	**12:10 am**	
♀	♐	6	**3:09 am**	12:09 am
⚳	♑	7	**6:11 am**	3:11 am
♂	♒	12		10:05 pm
♂	♒	13	**1:05 am**	
♀	♒	16	**11:05 am**	8:05 am
☉	♓	18	**11:13 pm**	8:13 pm
☿	♓	22		11:29 pm
☿	♓	23	**2:29 am**	

Planetary Motion		day	ET / hr:mn	PT
⚶	D	8	**4:41 am**	1:41 am

1 THURSDAY
☽ □ ☿ **4:03 am** 1:03 am
☽ ⚻ ♆ **7:13 am** 4:13 am
☽ □ ♇ **4:23 pm** 1:23 pm

2 FRIDAY
☽ △ ♄ **4:39 am** 1:39 am
☿ ⚹ ♆ **5:55 am** 2:55 am
☽ ☍ ♃ **6:17 am** 3:17 am
☽ ⚹ ♀ **5:09 pm** 2:09 pm
☽ □ ☉ **6:18 pm** 3:18 pm

3 SATURDAY
☽ ☍ ♅ **4:55 am** 1:55 am
☽ ⚹ ♂ **11:42 am** 8:42 am
☽ △ ♆ **5:42 pm** 2:42 pm
☽ ⚹ ☿ **10:24 pm** 7:24 pm
☽ ⚹ ♇ 11:19 pm

4 SUNDAY
☽ ⚹ ♇ **2:19 am**
☽ □ ♄ **2:10 pm** 11:10 am
☽ ⚻ ♃ **3:39 pm** 12:39 pm

5 MONDAY
☉ ⚺ ♀ **4:03 am** 1:03 am
☽ ⚹ ☉ **6:55 am** 3:55 am
☽ ⚺ ♀ **6:58 am** 3:58 am
☿ ☌ ♇ **7:58 am** 4:58 am
☽ ⚻ ♅ **12:11 pm** 9:11 am
☽ ⚺ ♂ **9:40 pm** 6:40 pm
☽ □ ♆ 9:06 pm

6 TUESDAY
☽ □ ♆ **12:06 am**
☽ ⚺ ♇ **8:03 am** 5:03 am
☽ ⚺ ☿ **10:59 am** 7:59 am
☽ ⚹ ♄ **7:18 pm** 4:18 pm
☽ △ ♃ **8:41 pm** 5:41 pm

7 WEDNESDAY
☽ ⚺ ☉ **2:14 pm** 11:14 am
☽ ☌ ♀ **3:12 pm** 12:12 pm
☽ △ ♅ **3:19 pm** 12:19 pm
♀ △ ♅ **4:25 pm** 1:25 pm
♂ ⚹ ♆ **7:20 pm** 4:20 pm
☽ ⚹ ♆ 11:30 pm
☽ ☌ ♂ 11:52 pm

8 THURSDAY
☽ ⚹ ♆ **2:30 am**
☽ ☌ ♂ **2:52 am**
☉ □ ♅ **5:46 am** 2:46 am
☽ ☌ ♇ **9:57 am** 6:57 am
☽ ☌ ☿ **6:25 pm** 3:25 pm
☽ ⚺ ♄ **8:51 pm** 5:51 pm
☽ □ ♃ **10:10 pm** 7:10 pm

9 FRIDAY
☽ □ ♅ **3:35 pm** 12:35 pm
☽ ☌ ☉ **5:59 pm** 2:59 pm
☿ ⚺ ♄ **6:59 pm** 3:59 pm
☽ ⚺ ♀ **7:44 pm** 4:44 pm
☽ ⚺ ♆ 11:29 pm

10 SATURDAY
☽ ⚺ ♆ **2:29 am**
☽ ⚺ ♂ **5:17 am** 2:17 am
☿ □ ♃ **8:25 am** 5:25 am
☽ ⚺ ♇ **9:45 am** 6:45 am
☽ ☌ ♄ **8:45 pm** 5:45 pm
☽ ⚹ ♃ **10:05 pm** 7:05 pm
☽ ⚺ ☿ **11:34 pm** 8:34 pm

11 SUNDAY
☽ ⚹ ♅ **3:07 pm** 12:07 pm
☽ ⚺ ☉ **8:55 pm** 5:55 pm
☽ ⚹ ♀ **11:31 pm** 8:31 pm
☽ ☌ ♆ 11:11 pm

12 MONDAY
☽ ☌ ♆ **2:11 am**
☽ ⚹ ♂ **7:32 am** 4:32 am
☽ ⚹ ♇ **9:36 am** 6:36 am
☽ ⚺ ♄ **9:11 pm** 6:11 pm
☽ ⚺ ♃ **10:36 pm** 7:36 pm

13 TUESDAY
☽ ⚹ ☿ **5:44 am** 2:44 am
♀ ⚹ ♆ **8:36 am** 5:36 am
☽ ⚺ ♅ **3:55 pm** 12:55 pm
♂ ☌ ♇ 10:06 pm
☽ ⚹ ☉ 10:40 pm

14 WEDNESDAY
♂ ☌ ♇ **1:06 am**
☽ ⚹ ☉ **1:40 am**
☽ ⚺ ♆ **3:35 am** 12:35 am
☽ □ ♀ **5:21 am** 2:21 am
☽ □ ♇ **11:22 am** 8:22 am

☽ □ ♂ **11:56 am** 8:56 am
☽ ⚹ ♄ **11:57 pm** 8:57 pm
☽ ☌ ♃ 10:31 pm

15 THURSDAY
☽ ☌ ♃ **1:31 am**
☉ ⚺ ♆ **5:28 am** 2:28 am
☽ □ ☿ **3:36 pm** 12:36 pm
☽ ☌ ♅ **7:27 pm** 4:27 pm

16 FRIDAY
☽ ⚹ ♆ **7:55 am** 4:55 am
☽ □ ☉ **10:01 am** 7:01 am
☽ △ ♀ **3:02 pm** 12:02 pm
☽ △ ♇ **4:11 pm** 1:11 pm
☽ △ ♂ **7:56 pm** 4:56 pm
☿ □ ♅ **10:53 pm** 7:53 pm

17 SATURDAY
♀ ☌ ♇ **3:48 am** 12:48 am
☽ □ ♄ **5:57 am** 2:57 am
☽ ⚺ ♃ **7:42 am** 4:42 am
☽ ⚺ ♅ 11:12 pm

18 SUNDAY
☽ ⚺ ♅ **2:12 am**
☽ △ ☿ **6:22 am** 3:22 am
☽ □ ♆ **3:28 pm** 12:28 pm
☽ △ ☉ **10:21 pm** 7:21 pm
☽ ⚻ ♇ 9:10 pm

19 MONDAY
☽ ⚻ ♇ **12:10 am**
☽ ⚻ ♀ **4:53 am** 1:53 am
☽ ⚻ ♂ **7:38 am** 4:38 am

☽ △ ♄ **3:02 pm** 12:02 pm
☽ ⚹ ♃ **5:00 pm** 2:00 pm
☉ ⚺ ♇ **9:39 pm** 6:39 pm

20 TUESDAY
☽ ⚹ ♅ **11:45 am** 8:45 am
☽ ⚻ ☿ 10:32 pm
☽ △ ♆ 10:38 pm
☿ ⚺ ♆ 11:10 pm

21 WEDNESDAY
☽ ⚻ ☿ **1:32 am**
☽ △ ♆ **1:38 am**
☿ ⚺ ♆ **2:10 am**
☽ ☍ ♇ **10:37 am** 7:37 am
☽ ⚻ ☉ **1:53 pm** 10:53 am
☽ ☍ ♀ **10:03 pm** 7:03 pm
☽ ☍ ♂ **10:13 pm** 7:13 pm
♀ ☌ ♂ 11:14 pm
☽ ⚻ ♄ 11:28 pm

22 THURSDAY
♀ ☌ ♂ **2:14 am**
☽ ⚻ ♄ **2:28 am**
☽ □ ♃ **4:39 am** 1:39 am
☽ □ ♅ **11:18 pm** 8:18 pm

23 FRIDAY
☽ ⚻ ♆ **1:36 pm** 10:36 am
☿ ⚺ ♇ **4:31 pm** 1:31 pm
♀ ⚺ ♄ **9:26 pm** 6:26 pm
☽ ⚻ ♇ **10:46 pm** 7:46 pm
☽ ☍ ☿ **11:52 pm** 8:52 pm

24 SATURDAY
☽ ☍ ☉ **7:30 am** 4:30 am
☽ ⚻ ♂ **2:39 pm** 11:39 am
☽ ☍ ♄ **3:24 pm** 12:24 pm
☽ ⚻ ♀ **5:18 pm** 2:18 pm
☽ △ ♃ **5:49 pm** 2:49 pm
♀ □ ♃ **11:01 pm** 8:01 pm

25 SUNDAY
♂ ⚺ ♄ **4:20 am** 1:20 am
☽ △ ♅ **12:04 pm** 9:04 am
☽ ☍ ♆ 11:35 pm

26 MONDAY
☽ ☍ ♆ **2:35 am**
☽ △ ♇ **11:47 am** 8:47 am
☽ ⚻ ☿ **11:54 pm** 8:54 pm
☽ ⚻ ☉ 11:06 pm

27 TUESDAY
☽ ⚻ ☉ **2:06 am**
♂ □ ♃ **3:30 am** 12:30 am
☽ ⚻ ♄ **4:59 am** 1:59 am
☽ ⚻ ♃ **7:38 am** 4:38 am
☽ △ ♂ **7:51 am** 4:51 am
☽ △ ♀ **1:22 pm** 10:22 am
☽ ⚻ ♅ 10:06 pm

28 WEDNESDAY
☽ ⚻ ♅ **1:06 am**
☉ ☌ ☿ **3:43 am** 12:43 am
☿ ☌ ♄ **10:08 am** 7:08 am
☽ ⚻ ♆ **3:32 pm** 12:32 pm
☉ ☌ ♄ **4:25 pm** 1:25 pm
☽ □ ♇ 9:33 pm

29 THURSDAY
☽ □ ♇ **12:33 am**
☿ ⚹ ♃ **4:53 am** 1:53 am
☽ △ ♄ **5:52 pm** 2:52 pm
☽ △ ☉ **7:53 pm** 4:53 pm
☽ ☍ ♃ **8:40 pm** 5:40 pm
☽ △ ☿ **11:18 pm** 8:18 pm
☽ □ ♂ 9:08 pm

Eastern time in bold type
Pacific time in medium type

FEBRUARY 2024

DATE	SID.TIME	SUN	MOON	NODE	MERCURY	VENUS	MARS	JUPITER	SATURN	URANUS	NEPTUNE	PLUTO	CERES	PALLAS	JUNO	VESTA	CHIRON
1 Th	8 42 49	11≈35 54	19≏42	17♈51	23♑39	10♑38	20♑37	7♉03	6♓26	19♉06	25♓46	0≈21	27♐37	28♏24	20♍33R	21♊57R	16♈02
2 F	8 46 46	12 36 48	1♏42	17 52R	25 08	11 33	21 23	7 23	6 33	19 06	25 48	0 23	27 59	28 42	20 24	21 54	16 04
3 Sa	8 50 43	13 37 41	13 58	17 52	26 38	13 06	22 09	7 30	6 40	19 06	25 50	0 25	28 22	29 00	20 15	21 51	16 06
4 Su	8 54 39	14 38 34	26 33	17 51	28 09	14 20	22 55	7 36	6 47	19 07	25 51	0 27	28 44	29 19	20 05	21 49	16 08
5 M	8 58 36	15 39 26	9♏32	17 48	29 40	15 34	23 41	7 43	6 54	19 07	25 53	0 29	29 06	29 36	19 56	21 47	16 10
6 T	9 2 32	16 40 17	23 00	17 43	1≈13	16 49	24 26	7 50	7 01	19 08	25 55	0 31	29 28	29 54	19 46	21 46	16 12
7 W	9 6 29	17 41 07	6♐58	17 36	2 46	18 03	25 12	7 57	7 08	19 08	25 57	0 33	29 50	0♐11	19 35	21 45	16 14
8 Th	9 10 25	18 41 56	21 24	17 27	4 19	19 17	25 58	8 04	7 15	19 09	25 59	0 35	0♑12	0 29	19 24	21 45D	16 16
9 F	9 14 22	19 42 44	6♑58	17 18	5 54	20 31	26 44	8 11	7 22	19 10	26 01	0 36	0 33	0 46	19 13	21 45	16 19
10 Sa	9 18 19	20 43 31	21 19	17 09	7 30	21 45	27 30	8 19	7 30	19 10	26 03	0 38	0 55	1 02	19 02	21 45	16 21
11 Su	9 22 15	21 44 16	6≈14	17 01	9 06	22 59	28 16	8 27	7 37	19 11	26 05	0 40	1 16	1 19	18 50	21 46	16 23
12 M	9 26 12	22 45 00	21 19	16 56	10 43	24 13	29 02	8 35	7 44	19 12	26 07	0 42	1 38	1 35	18 38	21 48	16 25
13 T	9 30 8	23 45 42	6♓31	16 54D	12 21	25 28	29 48	8 42	7 51	19 13	26 09	0 44	1 59	1 51	18 25	21 49	16 28
14 W	9 34 5	24 46 23	21 05	16 53	13 59	26 42	0≈34	8 51	7 58	19 14	26 11	0 46	2 20	2 07	18 12	21 52	16 30
15 Th	9 38 1	25 47 02	5♉15	16 54	15 39	27 56	1 21	8 59	8 05	19 15	26 13	0 47	2 41	2 23	17 59	21 54	16 33
16 F	9 41 58	26 47 40	19 01	16 55R	17 19	29 10	2 07	9 07	8 13	19 16	26 15	0 49	3 02	2 38	17 46	21 57	16 35
17 Sa	9 45 54	27 48 15	2♊24	16 55	19 00	0≈24	2 53	9 16	8 20	19 17	26 17	0 51	3 23	2 53	17 32	22 01	16 38
18 Su	9 49 51	28 48 49	15 27	16 54	20 42	1 39	3 39	9 25	8 27	19 18	26 19	0 53	3 44	3 08	17 18	22 05	16 40
19 M	9 53 48	29 49 22	28 12	16 50	22 26	2 53	4 25	9 33	8 34	19 19	26 21	0 55	4 04	3 22	17 04	22 09	16 43
20 T	9 57 44	0♓49 52	10♋44	16 45	24 09	4 07	5 11	9 42	8 42	19 20	26 23	0 56	4 25	3 37	16 50	22 14	16 46
21 W	10 1 41	1 50 21	23 03	16 37	25 54	5 21	5 58	9 51	8 49	19 21	26 25	0 58	4 45	3 51	16 36	22 19	16 48
22 Th	10 5 37	2 50 48	5♌13	16 30	27 40	6 36	6 44	10 01	8 56	19 23	26 27	1 00	5 05	4 05	16 21	22 24	16 51
23 F	10 9 34	3 51 13	17 15	16 24	29 27	7 50	7 30	10 10	9 04	19 24	26 29	1 01	5 25	4 18	16 06	22 30	16 53
24 Sa	10 13 30	4 51 36	29 12	16 20	1♓14	9 04	8 17	10 20	9 11	19 25	26 31	1 03	5 45	4 32	15 52	22 36	16 56
25 Su	10 17 27	5 51 58	11♍03	16 06	3 03	10 18	9 03	10 29	9 18	19 27	26 34	1 05	6 05	4 44	15 37	22 43	16 59
26 M	10 21 23	6 52 18	22 52	16 01	4 52	11 33	9 49	10 39	9 25	19 28	26 36	1 07	6 25	4 57	15 22	22 50	17 02
27 T	10 25 20	7 52 36	4≏41	15 59	6 43	12 47	10 36	10 49	9 33	19 30	26 38	1 08	6 44	5 09	15 07	22 57	17 05
28 W	10 29 16	8 52 53	16 31	15 58	8 34	14 01	11 22	10 59	9 40	19 31	26 40	1 10	7 04	5 22	14 51	23 05	17 08
29 Th	10 33 13	9 53 09	28 26	15 59	10 26	15 15	12 09	11 09	9 47	19 33	26 42	1 12	7 23	5 33	14 36	23 13	17 11

EPHEMERIS CALCULATED FOR 12 MIDNIGHT GREENWICH MEAN TIME. ALL OTHER DATA AND FACING ASPECTARIAN PAGE IN **EASTERN TIME (BOLD)** AND PACIFIC TIME (REGULAR).

MARCH 2024

☽ Last Aspect day	ET / hr:mn / PT		asp	☽ Ingress sign day	ET / hr:mn / PT	
1		11:47 pm	△♆	♐ 2	**8:56 am**	5:56 am
2	**2:47 am**		△♆	♐ 2	**8:56 am**	5:56 am
4	**10:41 am**	7:41 am	□♆	♑ 4	**4:15 pm**	1:15 pm
6	**2:35 pm**	11:35 am	⚹♆	♒ 6	**7:38 pm**	4:38 pm
8	**1:56 pm**	10:56 am	☌♀	♓ 8	**8:03 pm**	5:03 pm
10	**3:45 pm**	12:45 pm	☌♆	♈ 10	**8:19 pm**	5:19 pm
12	**7:08 am**	4:08 am	⚹♂	♉ 12	**8:28 pm**	5:28 pm
14	**6:29 pm**	3:29 pm	⚹♆	♊ 14	**11:16 pm**	8:16 pm
16		9:43 pm	□♆	♋ 17	**5:40 am**	2:40 am
17	**12:43 am**		□♆	♋ 17	**5:40 am**	2:40 am

☽ Last Aspect day	ET / hr:mn / PT		asp	☽ Ingress sign day	ET / hr:mn / PT	
19	**2:52 pm**	11:52 am	△☉	♌ 19	**3:33 pm**	12:33 pm
21		11:34 pm	☍♂	♍ 22	**3:42 am**	12:42 am
22	**2:34 am**		☍♂	♍ 22	**3:42 am**	12:42 am
24	**11:49 am**	8:49 am	☍♆	♎ 24	**4:37 pm**	1:37 pm
26	**7:09 pm**	4:09 pm	☍☿	♏ 27	**5:03 am**	2:03 am
29	**11:40 am**	8:40 am	△♆	♐ 29	**3:52 pm**	12:52 pm
31	**8:16 pm**	5:16 pm	□♆	♑ 31		9:05 pm
31	**8:16 pm**	5:16 pm	□♆	♑ 4/1	**12:05 am**	

☽ Phases & Eclipses phase	day	ET / hr:mn / PT	
4th Quarter	3	**10:23 am**	7:23 am
New Moon	10	**5:00 am**	1:00 am
2nd Quarter	16		9:11 pm
2nd Quarter	17	**12:11 am**	
Full Moon	25	**3:00 am**	12:00 am
●	25	5° ♎ 07'	

Planet Ingress		day	ET / hr:mn / PT	
☿	♈	9	**11:03 pm**	8:03 pm
♀	♓	11	**5:50 pm**	2:50 pm
☉	♈	19	**11:06 pm**	8:06 pm
♂	♓	22	**7:47 pm**	4:47 pm
⚶	♋	31	**7:02 am**	4:02 am

Planetary Motion		day	ET / hr:mn / PT	
⚴	℞	29	**9:17 am**	6:17 am

1 FRIDAY
☽□♂ 12:08 am
☉⚹♃ **7:15 am** 4:15 am
☿⊻♂ **7:41 am** 4:41 am
☽□♀ **8:09 am** 5:09 am
☽☍♅ **12:53 pm** 9:53 am
☽△♆ 11:47 pm

2 SATURDAY
☽△♆ **2:47 am**
☽⚹♇ **11:20 am** 8:20 am

3 SUNDAY
☽□♄ **4:12 am** 1:12 am
☽⊼♃ **7:04 am** 4:04 am
♀□♅ **8:17 am** 5:17 am
☽□☉ **10:23 am** 7:23 am
☽⚹♂ **1:11 pm** 10:11 am
☽□☿ **6:39 pm** 3:39 pm
☽⊼♅ **9:39 pm** 6:39 pm
☽⚹♀ **11:01 pm** 8:01 pm

4 MONDAY
☽□♆ **10:41 am** 7:41 am
☿⚹♅ **3:24 pm** 12:24 pm
☽⊻♇ **6:35 pm** 3:35 pm

5 TUESDAY
☽⚹♄ **10:38 am** 7:38 am
☽△♃ **1:30 pm** 10:30 am
☽⚹☉ **8:01 pm** 5:01 pm
☽⊻♂ **9:37 pm** 6:37 pm
☽△♅ 11:28 pm

6 WEDNESDAY
☽△♅ **2:28 am**
☽⚹☿ **7:54 am** 4:54 am
☽⊻♀ **8:37 am** 5:37 am
☽⚹♆ **2:35 pm** 11:35 am
☿⊻♀ **9:00 pm** 6:00 pm
☽☌♇ **9:54 pm** 6:54 pm

7 THURSDAY
☽⊻♄ **1:14 pm** 10:14 am
☽□♃ **4:08 pm** 1:08 pm
☽⊻☉ 10:12 pm
☽☌♂ 10:51 pm

8 FRIDAY
☽⊻☉ **1:12 am**
☽☌♂ **1:51 am**
☽□♅ **3:50 am** 12:50 am
☿☌♆ **10:06 am** 7:06 am
☽☌♀ **1:56 pm** 10:56 am
☽⊻♆ **3:21 pm** 12:21 pm
☽⊻☿ **4:07 pm** 1:07 pm
☽⊻♇ **10:18 pm** 7:18 pm

9 SATURDAY
♀⊻♆ **7:49 am** 4:49 am
☽☌♄ **1:23 pm** 10:23 am
☽⚹♃ **4:24 pm** 1:24 pm
♂□♅ **5:55 pm** 2:55 pm
☉⚹♅ **6:01 pm** 3:01 pm
☉⊻♂ **6:20 pm** 3:20 pm

10 SUNDAY
☽⚹♅ **4:22 am** 12:22 am
☽⊻♂ **4:52 am** 12:52 am
☽☌☉ **5:00 am** 1:00 am
☽☌♆ **3:45 pm** 12:45 pm
☿⚹♇ **6:21 pm** 3:21 pm
☽⊻♀ **6:25 pm** 3:25 pm
☽⚹♇ **10:38 pm** 7:38 pm
☽☌☿ **11:15 pm** 8:15 pm

11 MONDAY
☽⊻♄ **2:08 pm** 11:08 am
☽⊻♃ **5:24 pm** 2:24 pm

12 TUESDAY
☽⊻♅ **4:07 am** 1:07 am
☽⚹♂ **7:08 am** 4:08 am
☽⊻☉ **8:06 am** 5:06 am
☽⊻♆ **3:52 pm** 12:52 pm
☽⚹♀ **10:56 pm** 7:56 pm
☽□♇ **10:57 pm** 7:57 pm
♀⊻♇ **11:11 pm** 8:11 pm

13 WEDNESDAY
☽⊻☿ **6:43 am** 3:43 am
☽⚹♄ **3:30 pm** 12:30 pm
☽☌♃ **7:13 pm** 4:13 pm

14 THURSDAY
☽☌♅ **6:00 am** 3:00 am
☽□♂ **12:01 pm** 9:01 am
☽⚹☉ **1:57 pm** 10:57 am
☽⚹♆ **6:29 pm** 3:29 pm
☽△♇ 11:00 pm

15 FRIDAY
☽△♇ **2:00 am**
☽□♀ **6:59 am** 3:59 am
☽⚹☿ **6:11 pm** 3:11 pm
☽□♄ **8:06 pm** 5:06 pm
☽⊻♃ 9:22 pm

16 SATURDAY
☽⊻♃ **12:22 am**
☿⊻♄ **9:57 am** 6:57 am
☽⊻♅ **11:20 am** 8:20 am
☽△♂ **9:02 pm** 6:02 pm
☽□☉ 9:11 pm
☽□♆ 9:43 pm

17 SUNDAY
☽□☉ **12:11 am**
☽□♆ **12:43 am**
☉☌♆ **7:22 am** 4:22 am
☽⊼♇ **8:42 am** 5:42 am
☽△♀ **7:55 pm** 4:55 pm
☿⊻♃ 10:02 pm

18 MONDAY
☿⊻♃ **1:02 am**
☽△♄ **4:29 am** 1:29 am
☽⚹♃ **9:24 am** 6:24 am
☽□☿ **10:29 am** 7:29 am
☽⚹♅ **8:20 pm** 5:20 pm

19 TUESDAY
☽⊼♂ **10:20 am** 7:20 am
☽△♆ **10:30 am** 7:30 am
♂⊻♆ **12:57 pm** 9:57 am
☽△☉ **2:52 pm** 11:52 am
☽☍♇ **6:49 pm** 3:49 pm

20 WEDNESDAY
☽⊼♀ **1:13 pm** 10:13 am
☽⊼♄ **4:02 pm** 1:02 pm
☽□♃ **9:35 pm** 6:35 pm

21 THURSDAY
☽△☿ **5:57 am** 2:57 am
☽□♅ **8:07 am** 5:07 am
☉⚹♇ **4:03 pm** 1:03 pm
♀☌♄ **7:09 pm** 4:09 pm
☽⊼♆ **10:42 pm** 7:42 pm
☿⊻♅ 11:27 pm
☽☍♂ 11:34 pm

22 FRIDAY
☿⊻♅ **2:27 am**
☽☍♂ **2:34 am**
☽⊼♇ **7:09 am** 4:09 am
☽⊼☉ **8:30 am** 5:30 am

23 SATURDAY
☽☍♄ **5:17 am** 2:17 am
☽☍♀ **8:54 am** 5:54 am
☽△♃ **11:22 am** 8:22 am
☽△♅ **9:10 pm** 6:10 pm
☽⊼☿ 10:37 pm

24 SUNDAY
☽⊼☿ **1:37 am**
☽☍♆ **11:49 am** 8:49 am
♀⚹♃ **12:37 pm** 9:37 am
☽⊼♂ **7:47 pm** 4:47 pm
☽△♇ **8:11 pm** 5:11 pm
♂⊻♇ 10:58 pm

25 MONDAY
♂⊻♇ **1:58 am**
☽☍☉ **3:00 am** 12:00 am
☽⊼♄ **6:45 pm** 3:45 pm
☽⊼♃ 10:15 pm

26 TUESDAY
☽⊼♃ **1:15 am**
☽⊼♀ **4:47 am** 1:47 am
☽⊼♅ **10:06 am** 7:06 am
☽☍☿ **7:09 pm** 4:09 pm
☽⊼♆ 9:31 pm

27 WEDNESDAY
☽⊼♆ **12:31 am**
☽□♇ **8:37 am** 5:37 am
☽△♂ **12:18 pm** 9:18 am
☽⊼☉ **8:35 pm** 5:35 pm

28 THURSDAY
☽△♄ **7:11 am** 4:11 am
♀⚹♅ **9:58 am** 6:58 am
☽☍♃ **1:59 pm** 10:59 am
☽☍♅ **9:46 pm** 6:46 pm
☽△♀ **11:02 pm** 8:02 pm

29 FRIDAY
☽⊼☿ **9:10 am** 6:10 am
☽△♆ **11:40 am** 8:40 am
☽⚹♇ **7:23 pm** 4:23 pm
☽□♂ 11:43 pm

30 SATURDAY
☽□♂ **2:43 am**
☽△☉ **11:44 am** 8:44 am
☽□♄ **5:29 pm** 2:29 pm
☽⊼♃ 9:26 pm

31 SUNDAY
☽⊼♃ **12:26 am**
☽⊼♅ **7:06 am** 4:06 am
☽□♀ **2:06 pm** 11:06 am
☽△☿ **6:54 pm** 3:54 pm
☽□♆ **8:16 pm** 5:16 pm

Eastern time in bold type
Pacific time in medium type

MARCH 2024

DATE	SID.TIME	SUN	MOON	NODE	MERCURY	VENUS	MARS	JUPITER	SATURN	URANUS	NEPTUNE	PLUTO	CERES	PALLAS	JUNO	VESTA	CHIRON
1 F	10 37 10	10♓53 22	10♏29	16♈00	12♓19	16≈30	12≈55	11♉19	9♓55	19♉35	26♓44	1≈13	7♑42	5♐45	14♉21R	23♑21R	17♈14
2 Sa	10 41 6	11 53 35	22 45	16 02	14 13	17 44	13 42	11 29	10 02	19 36	26 47	1 15	8 01	5 56	14 06	23 30	17 17
3 Su	10 45 3	12 53 45	5♐18	16 03R	16 08	18 58	14 28	11 40	10 09	19 38	26 49	1 16	8 20	6 07	13 50	23 39	17 20
4 M	10 48 59	13 53 55	18 13	16 03	18 03	20 12	15 15	11 50	10 17	19 40	26 51	1 18	8 39	6 17	13 35	23 49	17 23
5 T	10 52 56	14 54 02	1♑33	16 02	19 59	21 27	16 01	12 01	10 24	19 42	26 53	1 19	8 57	6 27	13 20	23 58	17 26
6 W	10 56 52	15 54 09	15 21	16 00	21 55	22 41	16 48	12 11	10 31	19 44	26 56	1 21	9 16	6 37	13 05	24 09	17 29
7 Th	11 0 49	16 54 13	29 37	15 56	23 52	23 55	17 34	12 22	10 39	19 46	26 58	1 22	9 34	6 46	12 50	24 19	17 32
8 F	11 4 45	17 54 17	14≈18	15 52	25 48	25 10	18 21	12 33	10 46	19 48	27 00	1 24	9 52	6 56	12 35	24 30	17 36
9 Sa	11 8 42	18 54 18	29 20	15 48	27 45	26 24	19 07	12 44	10 53	19 50	27 02	1 25	10 10	7 04	12 20	24 41	17 39
10 Su	11 12 39	19 54 17	14♓33	15 45	29 41	27 38	19 54	12 55	11 01	19 52	27 05	1 26	10 28	7 13	12 05	24 52	17 42
11 M	11 16 35	20 54 15	29 48	15 43	1♈36	28 52	20 41	13 07	11 08	19 54	27 07	1 27	10 46	7 21	11 51	25 04	17 45
12 T	11 20 32	21 54 10	14♈54	15 42D	3 30	0♓07	21 27	13 18	11 15	19 56	27 09	1 29	11 03	7 28	11 37	25 16	17 48
13 W	11 24 28	22 54 04	29 43	15 43	5 23	1 21	22 14	13 29	11 22	19 58	27 11	1 31	11 20	7 36	11 22	25 28	17 52
14 Th	11 28 25	23 53 55	14♉09	15 44	7 13	2 35	23 00	13 41	11 30	20 01	27 14	1 32	11 37	7 42	11 08	25 40	17 55
15 F	11 32 21	24 53 44	28 08	15 45	9 02	3 49	23 47	13 52	11 37	20 03	27 16	1 33	11 54	7 49	10 55	25 53	17 58
16 Sa	11 36 18	25 53 31	11♊41	15 46	10 48	5 04	24 34	14 04	11 44	20 05	27 18	1 35	12 11	7 55	10 41	26 06	18 02
17 Su	11 40 14	26 53 16	24 49	15 47R	12 31	6 18	25 20	14 16	11 51	20 08	27 21	1 36	12 28	8 01	10 28	26 20	18 05
18 M	11 44 11	27 52 59	7♋59	15 47	14 10	7 32	26 07	14 28	11 58	20 10	27 23	1 37	12 44	8 06	10 15	26 33	18 08
19 T	11 48 8	28 52 39	20 02	15 46	15 45	8 46	26 54	14 40	12 05	20 12	27 25	1 38	13 00	8 11	10 02	26 47	18 12
20 W	11 52 4	29 52 17	2♌15	15 44	17 15	10 01	27 40	14 52	12 13	20 15	27 27	1 39	13 16	8 15	9 50	27 01	18 15
21 Th	11 56 1	0♈51 53	14 17	15 42	18 40	11 15	28 27	15 04	12 20	20 17	27 30	1 41	13 32	8 19	9 37	27 16	18 19
22 F	11 59 57	1 51 26	26 12	15 39	20 00	12 29	29 14	15 16	12 27	20 20	27 32	1 42	13 48	8 23	9 26	27 30	18 22
23 Sa	12 3 54	2 50 58	8♍02	15 37	21 14	13 43	0♓01	15 28	12 34	20 23	27 34	1 43	14 03	8 26	9 14	27 45	18 25
24 Su	12 7 50	3 50 27	19 51	15 36	22 22	14 58	0 47	15 40	12 41	20 25	27 36	1 44	14 18	8 29	9 03	28 00	18 29
25 M	12 11 47	4 49 54	1♎40	15 35	23 23	16 12	1 34	15 53	12 48	20 28	27 39	1 45	14 33	8 31	8 52	28 16	18 32
26 T	12 15 43	5 49 19	13 32	15 34D	24 17	17 26	2 20	16 05	12 55	20 30	27 41	1 46	14 48	8 33	8 41	28 31	18 36
27 W	12 19 40	6 48 42	25 28	15 34	25 04	18 40	3 07	16 18	13 02	20 33	27 43	1 47	15 03	8 34	8 31	28 47	18 39
28 Th	12 23 37	7 48 03	7♏32	15 35	25 44	19 54	3 54	16 30	13 09	20 36	27 45	1 48	15 17	8 35	8 21	29 03	18 43
29 F	12 27 33	8 47 22	19 45	15 36	26 17	21 08	4 41	16 43	13 16	20 39	27 48	1 49	15 31	8 36R	8 11	29 19	18 46
30 Sa	12 31 30	9 46 39	2♐09	15 36	26 42	22 23	5 27	16 56	13 22	20 41	27 50	1 50	15 45	8 36	8 02	29 36	18 50
31 Su	12 35 26	10 45 55	14 49	15 37	27 00	23 37	6 14	17 08	13 29	20 44	27 52	1 51	15 59	8 35	7 53	29 52	18 53

EPHEMERIS CALCULATED FOR 12 MIDNIGHT GREENWICH MEAN TIME. ALL OTHER DATA AND FACING ASPECTARIAN PAGE IN **EASTERN TIME (BOLD)** AND PACIFIC TIME (REGULAR).

APRIL 2024

☽ Last Aspect day	ET / hr:mn / PT		asp	☽ Ingress sign	day	ET / hr:mn / PT	
3/31	**8:16 pm**	5:16 pm	□♆	♑	3/31		9:05 pm
3/31	**8:16 pm**	5:16 pm	□♆	♑	1	**12:05 am**	
2		10:40 pm	⚹♆	♒	3	**5:08 am**	2:08 am
3	**1:40 am**		⚹♆	♒	3	**5:08 am**	2:08 am
4		10:40 pm	⚹☿	♓	5	**7:13 am**	4:13 am
5	**1:40 am**		⚹☿	♓	5	**7:13 am**	4:13 am
7	**4:27 am**	1:27 am	☌♆	♈	7	**7:25 am**	4:25 am
8	**10:39 pm**	7:39 pm	☌☿	♉	9	**7:23 am**	4:23 am
11	**6:04 am**	3:04 am	⚹♆	♊	11	**8:59 am**	5:59 am
13	**10:46 am**	7:46 am	□♆	♋	13	**1:45 pm**	10:45 am

☽ Last Aspect day	ET / hr:mn / PT		asp	☽ Ingress sign	day	ET / hr:mn / PT	
15	**7:22 pm**	4:22 pm	△♆	♌	15	**10:24 pm**	7:24 pm
18	**8:02 am**	5:02 am	△☉	♍	18	**10:10 am**	7:10 am
20	**8:20 pm**	5:20 pm	☍♆	♎	20	**11:08 pm**	8:08 pm
22	**7:24 pm**	4:24 pm	☍♀	♏	23	**11:20 am**	8:20 am
25	**7:17 pm**	4:17 pm	△♆	♐	25	**9:37 pm**	6:37 pm
28	**3:31 am**	12:31 am	□♆	♑	28	**5:37 am**	2:37 am
30	**11:19 am**	8:19 am	⚹♂	♒	30	**11:20 am**	8:20 am

☽ Phases & Eclipses phase	day	ET / hr:mn / PT	
4th Quarter	1	**11:15 pm**	8:15 pm
New Moon	8	**2:21 pm**	11:21 am
●	8	13° ♈ 24'	
2nd Quarter	15	**3:13 pm**	12:13 pm
Full Moon	23	**7:49 pm**	4:49 pm

Planet Ingress		day	ET / hr:mn / PT	
♀	♈	4		9:00 pm
♀	♈	5	**12:00 am**	
☉	♉	19	**10:00 am**	7:00 am
♀	♉	29	**7:31 am**	4:31 am
♂	♈	30	**11:33 am**	8:33 am

Planetary Motion		day	ET / hr:mn / PT	
☿	℞	1	**6:14 pm**	3:14 pm
⚵	D	21	**10:58 pm**	7:58 pm
☿	D	25	**8:54 am**	5:54 am

1 MONDAY
☽ ⚺ ♇ **3:29 am** 12:29 am
☽ ⚹ ♂ **1:49 pm** 10:49 am
☽ □ ☉ **11:15 pm** 8:15 pm
☽ ⚹ ♄ 9:46 pm

2 TUESDAY
☽ ⚹ ♄ **12:46 am**
☽ △ ♃ **7:44 am** 4:44 am
☽ △ ♅ **1:20 pm** 10:20 am
☿ ⚺ ♀ **4:58 pm** 1:58 pm
☉ ⚺ ♄ **10:42 pm** 7:42 pm
☽ □ ☿ 9:11 pm
☽ ⚹ ♀ 9:58 pm
☽ ⚹ ♆ 10:40 pm

3 WEDNESDAY
☽ □ ☿ **12:11 am**
☽ ⚹ ♀ **12:58 am**
☽ ⚹ ♆ **1:40 am**
☽ ☌ ♇ **8:23 am** 5:23 am
♀ ☌ ♆ **9:10 am** 6:10 am
☽ ⚺ ♂ **9:04 pm** 6:04 pm

4 THURSDAY
☽ ⚺ ♄ **4:47 am** 1:47 am
☽ ⚹ ☉ **6:45 am** 3:45 am
☽ □ ♃ **11:43 am** 8:43 am
☽ □ ♅ **4:24 pm** 1:24 pm
☽ ⚹ ☿ 10:40 pm

5 FRIDAY
☽ ⚹ ☿ **1:40 am**
☽ ⚺ ♆ **4:03 am** 1:03 am
☽ ⚺ ♀ **7:52 am** 4:52 am
☽ ⚺ ♇ **10:21 am** 7:21 am
☽ ☌ ♂ 10:08 pm

6 SATURDAY
☽ ☌ ♂ **1:08 am**
☽ ☌ ♄ **6:10 am** 3:10 am
☽ ⚺ ☉ **11:08 am** 8:08 am
☽ ⚹ ♃ **1:13 pm** 10:13 am
♀ ⚹ ♇ **1:46 pm** 10:46 am
☽ ⚹ ♅ **5:11 pm** 2:11 pm
☽ ⚺ ☿ 9:36 pm

7 SUNDAY
☽ ⚺ ☿ **12:36 am**
☽ ☌ ♆ **4:27 am** 1:27 am
☽ ⚹ ♇ **10:31 am** 7:31 am
☽ ☌ ♀ **12:22 pm** 9:22 am

8 MONDAY
☉ ⚺ ♃ **3:11 am** 12:11 am
☽ ⚺ ♂ **3:39 am** 12:39 am
☽ ⚺ ♄ **6:23 am** 3:23 am
☽ ⚺ ♃ **1:46 pm** 10:46 am
☽ ☌ ☉ **2:21 pm** 11:21 am
☽ ⚺ ♅ **5:12 pm** 2:12 pm
☽ ☌ ☿ **10:39 pm** 7:39 pm

9 TUESDAY
☽ ⚺ ♆ **4:30 am** 1:30 am
☽ □ ♇ **10:35 am** 7:35 am
☽ ⚺ ♀ **4:48 pm** 1:48 pm

10 WEDNESDAY
☽ ⚹ ♂ **6:49 am** 3:49 am
☽ ⚹ ♄ **7:16 am** 4:16 am
☉ ⚺ ♅ **12:00 pm** 9:00 am
☽ ☌ ♃ **3:19 pm** 12:19 pm
♂ ☌ ♄ **4:36 pm** 1:36 pm
☽ ☌ ♅ **6:18 pm** 3:18 pm
☽ ⚺ ☉ **6:44 pm** 3:44 pm
☽ ⚺ ☿ **9:31 pm** 6:31 pm

11 THURSDAY
☽ ⚹ ♆ **6:04 am** 3:04 am
☽ △ ♇ **12:23 pm** 9:23 am
☉ ☌ ☿ **7:03 pm** 4:03 pm
☽ ⚹ ♀ **11:47 pm** 8:47 pm

12 FRIDAY
☽ □ ♄ **10:39 am** 7:39 am
☽ □ ♂ **12:51 pm** 9:51 am
☽ ⚺ ♃ **7:43 pm** 4:43 pm
☽ ⚺ ♅ **10:13 pm** 7:13 pm
☽ ⚹ ☿ **10:43 pm** 7:43 pm
☽ ⚹ ☉ 11:35 pm

13 SATURDAY
☽ ⚹ ☉ **2:35 am**
☿ ⚺ ♅ **6:47 am** 3:47 am
☽ □ ♆ **10:46 am** 7:46 am
☽ ⚻ ♇ **5:26 pm** 2:26 pm

14 SUNDAY
☽ □ ♀ **11:24 am** 8:24 am
☿ ⚺ ♃ **3:38 pm** 12:38 pm
☽ △ ♄ **5:48 pm** 2:48 pm
☽ △ ♂ **11:17 pm** 8:17 pm

15 MONDAY
☽ □ ☿ **3:12 am** 12:12 am
☽ ⚹ ♃ **4:05 am** 1:05 am
☽ ⚹ ♅ **6:01 am** 3:01 am
☽ □ ☉ **3:13 pm** 12:13 pm
☽ △ ♆ **7:22 pm** 4:22 pm
☽ ☍ ♇ 11:23 pm

16 TUESDAY
☽ ☍ ♇ **2:23 am**
☿ ⚺ ♂ **10:46 am** 7:46 am

17 WEDNESDAY
☽ △ ♀ **4:03 am** 1:03 am
☽ ⚻ ♄ **4:42 am** 1:42 am
♀ ⚺ ♄ **10:53 am** 7:53 am
☽ △ ☿ **11:01 am** 8:01 am
☽ ⚻ ♂ **2:04 pm** 11:04 am
☽ □ ♃ **4:11 pm** 1:11 pm
☽ □ ♅ **5:20 pm** 2:20 pm
☉ ⚺ ♆ **9:31 pm** 6:31 pm

18 THURSDAY
☽ ⚻ ♆ **7:12 am** 4:12 am
☽ △ ☉ **8:02 am** 5:02 am
☽ ⚻ ♇ **2:20 pm** 11:20 am

19 FRIDAY
☿ ☌ ♀ **4:59 am** 1:59 am
♂ ⚹ ♃ **11:28 am** 8:28 am
☽ ☍ ♄ **5:53 pm** 2:53 pm
♂ ⚹ ♅ **7:56 pm** 4:56 pm
☽ ⚻ ☿ **9:10 pm** 6:10 pm
☽ ⚻ ♀ **11:47 pm** 8:47 pm

20 SATURDAY
☽ △ ♃ **6:14 am** 3:14 am
☽ △ ♅ **6:28 am** 3:28 am
☽ ☍ ♂ **7:09 am** 4:09 am
☽ ☍ ♆ **8:20 pm** 5:20 pm
♃ ☌ ♅ **10:27 pm** 7:27 pm
☽ ⚻ ☉ 11:28 pm

21 SUNDAY
☽ ⚻ ☉ **2:28 am**
☽ △ ♇ **3:20 am** 12:20 am
☉ □ ♇ **1:02 pm** 10:02 am

22 MONDAY
☽ ⚻ ♄ **7:08 am** 4:08 am
☽ ☍ ☿ **8:10 am** 5:10 am
♀ ⚺ ♅ **6:25 pm** 3:25 pm
☽ ⚻ ♅ **7:18 pm** 4:18 pm
☽ ☍ ♀ **7:24 pm** 4:24 pm
☽ ⚻ ♃ **7:58 pm** 4:58 pm
☽ ⚻ ♂ **11:51 pm** 8:51 pm
♀ ⚺ ♃ 11:04 pm

23 TUESDAY
♀ ⚺ ♃ **2:04 am**
☽ ⚻ ♆ **8:45 am** 5:45 am
☽ □ ♇ **3:27 pm** 12:27 pm
☽ ☍ ☉ **7:49 pm** 4:49 pm

24 WEDNESDAY
☿ ⚺ ♄ **5:14 am** 2:14 am
☽ ⚻ ☿ **6:41 pm** 3:41 pm
☽ △ ♄ **6:52 pm** 3:52 pm

25 THURSDAY
☽ ☍ ♅ **6:26 am** 3:26 am
☽ ☍ ♃ **7:55 am** 4:55 am
☽ ⚻ ♀ **12:42 pm** 9:42 am
☽ △ ♂ **2:25 pm** 11:25 am
☽ △ ♆ **7:17 pm** 4:17 pm
☽ ⚹ ♇ 10:36 pm

26 FRIDAY
☽ ⚹ ♇ **1:36 am**
☽ ⚻ ☉ **10:36 am** 7:36 am

27 SATURDAY
☽ △ ☿ **3:59 am** 12:59 am
☽ □ ♄ **4:21 am** 1:21 am
♀ ⚺ ♂ **8:36 am** 5:36 am
☽ ⚻ ♅ **3:18 pm** 12:18 pm
☽ ⚻ ♃ **5:30 pm** 2:30 pm
☽ □ ♂ 11:15 pm
☽ △ ♀ 11:56 pm

28 SUNDAY
☽ □ ♂ **2:15 am**
☽ △ ♀ **2:56 am**
☽ □ ♆ **3:31 am** 12:31 am
♀ ⚺ ♆ **9:13 am** 6:13 am
☽ ⚺ ♇ **9:27 am** 6:27 am
☿ ⚺ ♄ **6:49 pm** 3:49 pm
☽ △ ☉ **10:28 pm** 7:28 pm
♂ ☌ ♆ 9:31 pm

29 MONDAY
♂ ☌ ♆ **12:31 am**
☽ ⚹ ♄ **11:28 am** 8:28 am
☽ □ ☿ **11:45 am** 8:45 am
☽ △ ♅ **9:49 pm** 6:49 pm
☽ △ ♃ 9:39 pm

30 TUESDAY
☽ △ ♃ **12:39 am**
☽ ⚹ ♆ **9:25 am** 6:25 am
☽ ⚹ ♂ **11:19 am** 8:19 am
☽ □ ♀ **2:04 pm** 11:04 am
☽ ☌ ♇ **3:00 pm** 12:00 pm
♀ □ ♇ 9:30 pm

Eastern time in bold type
Pacific time in medium type

APRIL 2024

DATE	SID.TIME	SUN	MOON	NODE	MERCURY	VENUS	MARS	JUPITER	SATURN	URANUS	NEPTUNE	PLUTO	CERES	PALLAS	JUNO	VESTA	CHIRON
1 M	12 39 23	11 Υ 45 09	27 ♐ 46	15 Υ 37	27 Υ 10R	24 ♓ 51	7 ♓ 01	17 ♉ 21	13 ♓ 36	20 ♉ 47	27 ♓ 54	1 ♒ 52	16 ♑ 13	8 ♒ 34R	7 ♍ 45R	0 ♌ 09	18 Υ 57
2 T	12 43 19	12 44 21	11 ♑ 03	15 37R	27 13	26 05	7 47	17 34	13 43	20 50	27 57	1 53	16 26	8 33	7 37	0 26	19 00
3 W	12 47 16	13 43 31	24 42	15 37	27 09	27 19	8 34	17 47	13 49	20 53	27 59	1 54	16 39	8 31	7 29	0 44	19 04
4 Th	12 51 12	14 42 40	8 ♒ 45	15 37 D	26 58	28 33	9 21	18 00	13 56	20 56	28 01	1 55	16 52	8 29	7 22	1 01	19 07
5 F	12 55 9	15 41 47	23 09	15 37	26 41	29 48	10 07	18 13	14 03	20 59	28 03	1 55	17 04	8 26	7 15	1 19	19 11
6 Sa	12 59 6	16 40 52	7 ♓ 53	15 37	26 18	1 Υ 02	10 54	18 26	14 09	21 02	28 05	1 56	17 17	8 23	7 08	1 37	19 15
7 Su	13 3 2	17 39 55	22 51	15 37	25 49	2 16	11 41	18 39	14 16	21 05	28 08	1 57	17 29	8 19	7 02	1 55	19 18
8 M	13 6 59	18 38 56	7 Υ 54	15 38R	25 16	3 30	12 27	18 53	14 22	21 08	28 10	1 58	17 41	8 14	6 57	2 13	19 22
9 T	13 10 55	19 37 55	22 56	15 37	24 39	4 44	13 14	19 06	14 29	21 11	28 12	1 58	17 52	8 10	6 51	2 31	19 25
10 W	13 14 52	20 36 52	7 ♉ 46	15 36	23 58	5 58	14 01	19 19	14 35	21 14	28 14	1 59	18 04	8 04	6 46	2 50	19 29
11 Th	13 18 48	21 35 48	22 18	15 35	23 15	7 12	14 47	19 33	14 42	21 17	28 16	2 00	18 15	7 59	6 42	3 09	19 32
12 F	13 22 45	22 34 41	6 Ⅱ 27	15 36	22 31	8 26	15 34	19 46	14 48	21 20	28 18	2 00	18 25	7 52	6 38	3 28	19 36
13 Sa	13 26 41	23 33 32	20 09	15 35	21 45	9 41	16 21	19 59	14 54	21 24	28 20	2 01	18 36	7 45	6 34	3 47	19 39
14 Su	13 30 38	24 32 20	3 ♋ 25	15 34	21 00	10 55	17 07	20 13	15 01	21 27	28 23	2 01	18 46	7 38	6 31	4 06	19 43
15 M	13 34 35	25 31 07	16 16	15 34D	20 16	12 09	17 54	20 26	15 07	21 30	28 25	2 02	18 56	7 31	6 28	4 26	19 46
16 T	13 38 31	26 29 51	28 46	15 34	19 34	13 23	18 40	20 40	15 13	21 33	28 27	2 02	19 06	7 22	6 25	4 45	19 50
17 W	13 42 28	27 28 33	10 ♌ 59	15 34	18 54	14 37	19 27	20 54	15 19	21 36	28 29	2 03	19 15	7 14	6 23	5 05	19 53
18 Th	13 46 24	28 27 12	22 59	15 35	18 17	15 51	20 13	21 07	15 25	21 40	28 31	2 03	19 25	7 04	6 21	5 25	19 57
19 F	13 50 21	29 25 50	4 ♍ 51	15 36	17 44	17 05	21 00	21 21	15 31	21 43	28 33	2 04	19 33	6 55	6 20	5 45	20 01
20 Sa	13 54 17	0 ♉ 24 25	16 39	15 37	17 15	18 19	21 46	21 35	15 37	21 46	28 35	2 04	19 42	6 45	6 19	6 05	20 04
21 Su	13 58 14	1 22 58	28 27	15 39	16 50	19 33	22 33	21 48	15 43	21 49	28 37	2 04	19 50	6 34	6 18	6 26	20 08
22 M	14 2 10	2 21 29	10 ♎ 19	15 39R	16 30	20 47	23 19	22 02	15 49	21 53	28 39	2 05	19 58	6 23	6 18D	6 46	20 11
23 T	14 6 7	3 19 58	22 17	15 39	16 15	22 01	24 06	22 16	15 54	21 56	28 41	2 05	20 06	6 12	6 18	7 07	20 14
24 W	14 10 3	4 18 26	4 ♏ 24	15 38	16 05	23 15	24 52	22 30	16 00	21 59	28 43	2 05	20 13	6 00	6 19	7 27	20 18
25 Th	14 14 0	5 16 51	16 41	15 36	16 00D	24 29	25 38	22 44	16 06	22 03	28 45	2 05	20 21	5 48	6 19	7 48	20 21
26 F	14 17 57	6 15 15	29 09	15 35	15 59	25 43	26 25	22 58	16 11	22 06	28 47	2 06	20 27	5 35	6 21	8 09	20 25
27 Sa	14 21 53	7 13 36	11 ♐ 50	15 30	15 54	26 57	27 11	23 11	16 17	22 10	28 48	2 06	20 34	5 22	6 22	8 31	20 28
28 Su	14 25 50	8 11 57	24 45	15 27	16 14	28 11	27 57	23 25	16 22	22 13	28 50	2 06	20 40	5 08	6 24	8 52	20 32
29 M	14 29 46	9 10 15	7 ♑ 54	15 24	16 28	29 25	28 44	23 39	16 28	22 16	28 52	2 06	20 46	4 54	6 27	9 13	20 35
30 T	14 33 43	10 08 33	21 18	15 22	16 47	0 ♉ 38	29 30	23 53	16 33	22 20	28 54	2 06	20 51	4 40	6 29	9 35	20 39

EPHEMERIS CALCULATED FOR 12 MIDNIGHT GREENWICH MEAN TIME. ALL OTHER DATA AND FACING ASPECTARIAN PAGE IN **EASTERN TIME (BOLD)** AND PACIFIC TIME (REGULAR).

MAY 2024

☽ Last Aspect day	ET / hr:mn / PT		asp	☽ Ingress sign	day	ET / hr:mn / PT	
2	**5:28 am**	2:28 am	□ ♃	♓	2	**2:52 pm**	11:52 am
4	**3:06 pm**	12:06 pm	☌ ♆	♈	4	**4:41 pm**	1:41 pm
5		10:57 pm	☌ ☿	♉	6	**5:42 pm**	2:42 pm
6	**1:57 am**		☌ ☿	♉	6	**5:42 pm**	2:42 pm
8	**5:55 pm**	2:55 pm	⚹ ♆	♊	8	**7:20 pm**	4:20 pm
10	**9:49 pm**	6:49 pm	□ ♆	♋	10	**11:13 pm**	8:13 pm
13	**5:13 am**	2:13 am	△ ♆	♌	13	**6:36 am**	3:36 am
15	**12:41 pm**	9:41 am	□ ♃	♍	15	**5:33 pm**	2:33 pm
18	**5:09 am**	2:09 am	☍ ♆	♎	18	**6:23 am**	3:23 am
19	**11:48 am**	8:48 am	☍ ♂	♏	20	**6:34 pm**	3:34 pm
23	**3:28 am**	12:28 am	△ ♆	♐	23	**4:24 am**	1:24 am
25	**10:47 am**	7:47 am	□ ♆	♑	25	**11:36 am**	8:36 am
27	**4:02 pm**	1:02 pm	⚹ ♆	♒	27	**4:45 pm**	1:45 pm
29	**10:20 am**	7:20 am	□ ♅	♓	29	**8:33 pm**	5:33 pm
31	**10:55 pm**	7:55 pm	☌ ♆	♈	31	**11:28 pm**	8:28 pm

☽ Phases & Eclipses phase	day	ET / hr:mn / PT	
4th Quarter	1	**7:27 am**	4:27 am
New Moon	7	**11:22 pm**	8:22 pm
2nd Quarter	15	**7:48 am**	4:48 am
Full Moon	23	**9:53 am**	6:53 am
4th Quarter	30	**1:13 pm**	10:13 am

Planet Ingress		day	ET / hr:mn / PT	
☿	♉	15	**1:05 pm**	10:05 am
♀	♏	16	**1:23 pm**	10:23 am
☉	♊	20	**8:59 am**	5:59 am
♀	♊	23	**4:30 pm**	1:30 pm
♃	♊	25	**7:15 pm**	4:15 pm

Planetary Motion		day	ET / hr:mn / PT	
♇	℞	2	**1:46 pm**	10:46 am
⚳	℞	14		10:34 pm
⚳	℞	15	**1:34 am**	

1 WEDNESDAY
♀ □ ♇ **12:30 am**
☽ □ ☉ **7:27 am** 4:27 am
☽ ⚺ ♄ **4:17 pm** 1:17 pm
☽ ⚹ ☿ **5:48 pm** 2:48 pm
☽ □ ♅ 11:06 pm

2 THURSDAY
☽ □ ♅ **2:06 am**
☽ □ ♃ **5:28 am** 2:28 am
☽ ⚺ ♆ **1:08 pm** 10:08 am
☽ ⚺ ♂ **5:48 pm** 2:48 pm
☽ ⚺ ♇ **6:24 pm** 3:24 pm
☽ ⚹ ♀ **10:21 pm** 7:21 pm

3 FRIDAY
♂ ⚹ ♇ **5:06 am** 2:06 am
☽ ⚹ ☉ **1:55 pm** 10:55 am
☽ ☌ ♄ **7:05 pm** 4:05 pm
☽ ⚺ ☿ **10:18 pm** 7:18 pm

4 SATURDAY
☽ ⚹ ♅ **4:28 am** 1:28 am
☽ ⚹ ♃ **8:22 am** 5:22 am
☽ ☌ ♆ **3:06 pm** 12:06 pm
☽ ⚹ ♇ **8:08 pm** 5:08 pm
☽ ☌ ♂ **10:17 pm** 7:17 pm

5 SUNDAY
☽ ⚺ ♀ **4:32 am** 1:32 am
☽ ⚺ ☉ **6:42 pm** 3:42 pm
☽ ⚺ ♄ **8:35 pm** 5:35 pm
☽ ☌ ☿ 10:57 pm

6 MONDAY
☽ ☌ ☿ **1:57 am**
☽ ⚺ ♅ **5:46 am** 2:46 am
☽ ⚺ ♃ **10:14 am** 7:14 am
☽ ⚺ ♆ **4:14 pm** 1:14 pm
☽ □ ♇ **9:08 pm** 6:08 pm
☉ ⚹ ♄ 10:42 pm
☽ ⚺ ♂ 11:01 pm

7 TUESDAY
☉ ⚹ ♄ **1:42 am**
☽ ⚺ ♂ **2:01 am**
☽ ☌ ♀ **10:05 am** 7:05 am
☽ ⚹ ♄ **10:02 pm** 7:02 pm
☽ ☌ ☉ **11:22 pm** 8:22 pm

8 WEDNESDAY
☽ ⚺ ☿ **6:14 am** 3:14 am
☽ ☌ ♅ **7:19 am** 4:19 am
☽ ☌ ♃ **12:30 pm** 9:30 am
☽ ⚹ ♆ **5:55 pm** 2:55 pm
☽ △ ♇ **10:52 pm** 7:52 pm
☿ ⚺ ♅ 9:17 pm

9 THURSDAY
☿ ⚺ ♅ **12:17 am**
☽ ⚹ ♂ **6:47 am** 3:47 am
☽ ⚺ ♀ **5:08 pm** 2:08 pm
☽ □ ♄ 10:03 pm

10 FRIDAY
☽ □ ♄ **1:03 am**
☽ ⚺ ☉ **6:00 am** 3:00 am
☽ ⚺ ♅ **10:44 am** 7:44 am
☽ ⚹ ☿ **1:13 pm** 10:13 am
☽ ⚺ ♃ **4:54 pm** 1:54 pm
☽ □ ♆ **9:49 pm** 6:49 pm
☽ ⚻ ♇ 11:57 pm

11 SATURDAY
☽ ⚻ ♇ **2:57 am**
☽ □ ♂ **2:36 pm** 11:36 am

12 SUNDAY
☽ ⚹ ♀ **3:57 am** 12:57 am
☽ △ ♄ **7:11 am** 4:11 am
☽ ⚹ ☉ **4:34 pm** 1:34 pm
☽ ⚹ ♅ **5:29 pm** 2:29 pm
☿ ⚺ ♃ 9:00 pm
☽ ⚹ ♃ 9:52 pm
☽ □ ☿ 9:56 pm

13 MONDAY
☿ ⚺ ♃ **12:00 am**
☽ ⚹ ♃ **12:52 am**
☽ □ ☿ **12:56 am**
☽ △ ♆ **5:13 am** 2:13 am
☉ ☌ ♅ **5:14 am** 2:14 am
☽ ☍ ♇ **10:35 am** 7:35 am
♀ ⚹ ♄ **3:45 pm** 12:45 pm
☽ △ ♂ 11:49 pm

14 TUESDAY
☽ △ ♂ **2:49 am**
☽ ⚻ ♄ **5:06 pm** 2:06 pm
☽ □ ♀ **7:47 pm** 4:47 pm
☿ ⚺ ♆ **11:45 pm** 8:45 pm

15 WEDNESDAY
☽ □ ♅ **3:58 am** 12:58 am
☽ □ ☉ **7:48 am** 4:48 am
☽ □ ♃ **12:41 pm** 9:41 am
☽ ⚻ ♆ **4:12 pm** 1:12 pm
☽ △ ☿ **6:04 pm** 3:04 pm
☽ ⚻ ♇ **9:42 pm** 6:42 pm

16 THURSDAY
☽ ⚻ ♂ **6:48 pm** 3:48 pm

17 FRIDAY
☿ □ ♇ **3:44 am** 12:44 am
☽ ☍ ♄ **5:48 am** 2:48 am
☽ △ ♀ **3:15 pm** 12:15 pm
☽ △ ♅ **4:53 pm** 1:53 pm
☽ △ ☉ 10:53 pm
☽ △ ♃ 11:42 pm

18 SATURDAY
☽ △ ☉ **1:53 am**
☽ △ ♃ **2:42 am**
☽ ☍ ♆ **5:09 am** 2:09 am
♀ ☌ ♅ **7:41 am** 4:41 am
☽ △ ♇ **10:32 am** 7:32 am
☽ ⚻ ☿ **2:29 pm** 11:29 am
☉ ☌ ♃ **2:45 pm** 11:45 am

19 SUNDAY
☽ ☍ ♂ **11:48 am** 8:48 am
☉ ⚹ ♆ **6:45 pm** 3:45 pm
☽ ⚻ ♄ **6:52 pm** 3:52 pm

20 MONDAY
☽ ⚻ ♅ **5:43 am** 2:43 am
☽ ⚻ ♀ **10:41 am** 7:41 am
☽ ⚻ ♃ **4:11 pm** 1:11 pm
☽ ⚻ ♆ **5:29 pm** 2:29 pm
☽ ⚻ ☉ **7:23 pm** 4:23 pm
☽ □ ♇ **10:34 pm** 7:34 pm

21 TUESDAY
☽ ☍ ☿ **10:18 am** 7:18 am
☽ ⚻ ♂ 11:49 pm

22 WEDNESDAY
☽ ⚻ ♂ **2:49 am**
☽ △ ♄ **6:03 am** 3:03 am
☉ △ ♇ **11:14 am** 8:14 am
☽ ☍ ♅ **4:24 pm** 1:24 pm

23 THURSDAY
☽ ☍ ♀ **3:07 am** 12:07 am
☽ ☍ ♃ **3:13 am** 12:13 am
☽ △ ♆ **3:28 am** 12:28 am
♀ ☌ ♃ **4:29 am** 1:29 am
♀ ⚹ ♆ **6:50 am** 3:50 am
☽ ⚹ ♇ **8:10 am** 5:10 am
☽ ☍ ☉ **9:53 am** 6:53 am
♃ ⚹ ♆ **5:44 pm** 2:44 pm

24 FRIDAY
☽ ⚻ ☿ **3:05 am** 12:05 am
♂ ⚺ ♄ **12:23 pm** 9:23 am
☽ □ ♄ **2:29 pm** 11:29 am
☽ △ ♂ **2:36 pm** 11:36 am
☽ ⚻ ♅ 9:21 pm

25 SATURDAY
☽ ⚻ ♅ **12:21 am**
♀ △ ♇ **7:16 am** 4:16 am
☽ □ ♆ **10:47 am** 7:47 am
☽ ⚻ ♃ **11:28 am** 8:28 am
☽ ⚺ ♇ **3:10 pm** 12:10 pm
☽ ⚻ ♀ **3:58 pm** 12:58 pm
☽ ⚻ ☉ **9:06 pm** 6:06 pm

26 SUNDAY
☽ △ ☿ **4:49 pm** 1:49 pm
☽ ⚹ ♄ **8:33 pm** 5:33 pm
☽ □ ♂ **11:37 pm** 8:37 pm

27 MONDAY
☽ △ ♅ **6:05 am** 3:05 am
☽ ⚹ ♆ **4:02 pm** 1:02 pm
☽ △ ♃ **5:32 pm** 2:32 pm
☽ ☌ ♇ **8:10 pm** 5:10 pm
☿ ⚹ ♄ **11:22 pm** 8:22 pm
☽ △ ♀ 11:10 pm

28 TUESDAY
☽ △ ♀ **2:10 am**
☽ △ ☉ **5:54 am** 2:54 am
☽ ⚺ ♄ 10:00 pm

29 WEDNESDAY
☽ ⚺ ♄ **1:00 am**
☽ □ ☿ **4:36 am** 1:36 am
☽ ⚹ ♂ **6:46 am** 3:46 am
☽ □ ♅ **10:20 am** 7:20 am
☽ ⚺ ♆ **7:55 pm** 4:55 pm
☽ □ ♃ **10:12 pm** 7:12 pm
☽ ⚺ ♇ **11:51 pm** 8:51 pm

30 THURSDAY
☿ ⚺ ♂ **7:54 am** 4:54 am
☽ □ ♀ **10:43 am** 7:43 am
☽ □ ☉ **1:13 pm** 10:13 am
☿ ☌ ♅ 10:54 pm

31 FRIDAY
☿ ☌ ♅ **1:54 am**
☽ ☌ ♄ **4:24 am** 1:24 am
☽ ⚺ ♂ **12:45 pm** 9:45 am
☽ ⚹ ♅ **1:36 pm** 10:36 am
☽ ⚹ ☿ **3:19 pm** 12:19 pm
☽ ☌ ♆ **10:55 pm** 7:55 pm
☽ ⚹ ♃ 10:57 pm
☽ ⚹ ♇ 11:41 pm

Eastern time in bold type
Pacific time in medium type

MAY 2024

DATE	SID.TIME	SUN	MOON	NODE	MERCURY	VENUS	MARS	JUPITER	SATURN	URANUS	NEPTUNE	PLUTO	CERES	PALLAS	JUNO	VESTA	CHIRON
1 W	14 37 39	11♉06 48	4≈58	15♈21D	17♈11	1♉52	0♈16	24♉07	16♓43	22♉23	28♓56	2≈06	20♑56	4♈25R	6♊32	9♋57	20♈42
2 Th	14 41 36	12 05 02	18 53	15 21	17 39	3 06	1 03	24 21	16 49	22 27	28 58	2 06R	21 01	4 10	6 36	10 18	20 45
3 F	14 45 33	13 03 15	3♓00	15 22	18 11	4 20	1 49	24 35	16 54	22 30	29 01	2 06	21 06	3 55	6 39	10 40	20 49
4 Sa	14 49 29	14 01 26	17 27	15 23	18 47	5 34	2 35	24 49	16 59	22 34	29 01	2 06	21 10	3 39	6 43	11 02	20 52
5 Su	14 53 26	14 59 36	2♈02	15 24R	19 26	6 48	3 21	25 04	17 04	22 37	29 03	2 06	21 14	3 23	6 48	11 25	20 55
6 M	14 57 22	15 57 44	16 43	15 25	20 10	8 02	4 07	25 18	17 09	22 41	29 04	2 06	21 17	3 07	6 52	11 47	20 59
7 T	15 1 19	16 55 51	1♉24	15 24	20 57	9 16	4 53	25 32	17 13	22 44	29 06	2 06	21 20	2 51	6 57	12 09	21 02
8 W	15 5 15	17 53 56	16 00	15 21	21 48	10 30	5 39	25 46	17 18	22 47	29 08	2 06	21 23	2 34	7 03	12 32	21 05
9 Th	15 9 12	18 52 00	0♊23	15 17	22 42	11 44	6 25	26 00	17 23	22 51	29 09	2 06	21 26	2 17	7 08	12 54	21 08
10 F	15 13 8	19 50 02	14 29	15 12	23 39	12 57	7 11	26 14	17 27	22 54	29 11	2 06	21 28	2 00	7 14	13 17	21 12
11 Sa	15 17 5	20 48 02	28 12	15 07	24 39	14 11	7 57	26 28	17 32	22 58	29 13	2 05	21 29	1 42	7 21	13 40	21 15
12 Su	15 21 2	21 46 00	11♋30	15 01	25 42	15 25	8 43	26 42	17 36	23 01	29 14	2 05	21 31	1 25	7 27	14 03	21 18
13 M	15 24 58	22 43 57	24 25	14 57	26 48	16 39	9 29	26 57	17 41	23 05	29 16	2 05	21 32	1 07	7 34	14 26	21 21
14 T	15 28 55	23 41 52	6♌58	14 54	27 56	17 53	10 15	27 11	17 45	23 08	29 17	2 04	21 32	0 49	7 41	14 49	21 24
15 W	15 32 51	24 39 45	19 12	14 53D	29 08	19 07	11 01	27 25	17 49	23 12	29 19	2 04	21 32R	0 31	7 49	15 12	21 27
16 Th	15 36 48	25 37 37	1♍13	14 53	0♉23	20 21	11 46	27 39	17 53	23 15	29 20	2 04	21 32	0 13	7 56	15 36	21 30
17 F	15 40 44	26 35 26	13 05	14 54	1 38	21 34	12 32	27 53	17 57	23 19	29 22	2 04	21 32	29♓55	8 04	15 59	21 33
18 Sa	15 44 41	27 33 14	24 54	14 55	2 57	22 48	13 18	28 07	18 01	23 22	29 23	2 03	21 31	29 37	8 13	16 23	21 36
19 Su	15 48 37	28 31 01	6≏43	14 56R	4 19	24 02	14 03	28 21	18 05	23 26	29 24	2 03	21 30	29 19	8 21	16 46	21 39
20 M	15 52 34	29 28 45	18 39	14 57	5 43	25 16	14 49	28 36	18 09	23 29	29 26	2 02	21 28	29 00	8 30	17 10	21 42
21 T	15 56 31	0♊26 28	0♏44	14 55	7 09	26 29	15 35	28 50	18 12	23 33	29 27	2 02	21 27	28 42	8 39	17 34	21 45
22 W	16 0 27	1 24 10	13 01	14 52	8 38	27 43	16 21	29 04	18 16	23 36	29 28	2 02	21 24	28 24	8 48	17 58	21 48
23 Th	16 4 24	2 21 50	25 33	14 46	10 09	28 57	17 06	29 18	18 20	23 40	29 30	2 01	21 22	28 06	8 58	18 22	21 51
24 F	16 8 20	3 19 30	8♐21	14 39	11 42	0♊11	17 51	29 32	18 23	23 43	29 31	2 00	21 19	27 48	9 08	18 46	21 54
25 Sa	16 12 17	4 17 07	21 23	14 31	13 18	1 25	18 36	29 46	18 26	23 47	29 32	1 59	21 15	27 30	9 18	19 10	21 57
26 Su	16 16 13	5 14 44	4♑41	14 23	14 56	2 38	19 22	0♊00	18 30	23 50	29 33	1 59	21 11	27 13	9 28	19 34	22 00
27 M	16 20 10	6 12 20	18 11	14 15	16 36	3 52	20 07	0 15	18 33	23 53	29 35	1 58	21 07	26 55	9 39	19 58	22 02
28 T	16 24 6	7 09 55	1≈52	14 08	18 19	5 06	20 52	0 29	18 36	23 57	29 36	1 58	21 03	26 38	9 49	20 22	22 05
29 W	16 28 3	8 07 28	15 43	14 04	20 04	6 20	21 37	0 43	18 39	24 00	29 37	1 57	20 58	26 20	10 00	20 47	22 08
30 Th	16 32 0	9 05 01	29 41	14 02D	21 51	7 33	22 23	0 57	18 42	24 04	29 38	1 56	20 53	26 03	10 11	21 11	22 11
31 F	16 35 56	10 02 33	13♓46	14 01	23 41	8 47	23 08	1 11	18 42	24 07	29 39	1 55	20 47	25 46	10 23	21 36	22 13

EPHEMERIS CALCULATED FOR 12 MIDNIGHT GREENWICH MEAN TIME. ALL OTHER DATA AND FACING ASPECTARIAN PAGE IN **EASTERN TIME (BOLD)** AND PACIFIC TIME (REGULAR).

☽ Last Aspect day	ET / hr:mn / PT	asp	☽ Ingress sign day	ET / hr:mn / PT
2	**6:04 pm** 3:04 pm	☌♂	♉ 2	10:55 pm
2	**6:04 pm** 3:04 pm	☌♂	♉ 3	**1:55 am**
5	**4:09 am** 1:09 am	⚹♆	♊ 5	**4:36 am** 1:36 am
7	**8:16 am** 5:16 am	□♆	♋ 7	**8:41 am** 5:41 am
9	**3:05 pm** 12:05 pm	△♆	♌ 9	**3:29 pm** 12:29 pm
11	**3:16 pm** 12:16 pm	□♅	♍ 11	10:39 pm
11	**3:16 pm** 12:16 pm	□♅	♍ 12	**1:39 am**
14	**1:54 pm** 10:54 am	☍♆	♎ 14	**2:12 pm** 11:12 am
16	11:05 pm	△☿	♏ 16	11:38 pm
17	**2:05 am**	△☿	♏ 17	**2:38 am**
19	**12:19 pm** 9:19 am	△♆	♐ 19	**12:32 pm** 9:32 am
21	**6:58 pm** 3:58 pm	□♆	♑ 21	**7:08 pm** 4:08 pm
23	**11:05 pm** 8:05 pm	⚹♆	♒ 23	**11:14 pm** 8:14 pm
25	**6:30 pm** 3:30 pm	□♅	♓ 25	11:08 pm
25	**6:30 pm** 3:30 pm	□♅	♓ 26	**2:08 am**
28	**4:45 am** 1:45 am	☌♆	♈ 28	**4:52 am** 1:52 am
29	9:56 pm	□☿	♉ 30	**8:00 am** 5:00 am
30	**12:56 am**	□☿	♉ 30	**8:00 am** 5:00 am

☽ Phases & Eclipses phase	day	ET / hr:mn / PT
New Moon	6	**8:38 am** 5:38 am
2nd Quarter	13	10:18 pm
2nd Quarter	14	**1:13 am**
Full Moon	21	**9:08 pm** 6:08 pm
4th Quarter	28	**5:53 pm** 2:53 pm

Planet Ingress	day	ET / hr:mn / PT
☿ ♊	3	**3:37 am** 12:37 am
♂ ♉	8	9:35 pm
♂ ♉	9	**12:35 am**
♀ ♋	16	11:20 pm
♀ ♋	17	**2:20 am**
☿ ♋	17	**5:07 am** 2:07 am
⚵ ♌	19	**6:11 pm** 3:11 pm
☉ ♋	20	**4:51 pm** 1:51 pm

Planetary Motion	day	ET / hr:mn / PT
♄ ℞	29	**3:07 pm** 12:07 pm

1 SATURDAY
- ☽ ⚹ ♃ **1:57 am**
- ☽ ⚹ ♇ **2:41 am**
- ♂ ⚺ ♅ **6:07 am** 3:07 am
- ☽ ⚹ ♀ **6:15 pm** 3:15 pm
- ☽ ⚹ ☉ **7:35 pm** 4:35 pm

2 SUNDAY
- ☽ ⚺ ♄ **7:08 am** 4:08 am
- ☽ ⚺ ♅ **4:18 pm** 1:18 pm
- ☽ ☌ ♂ **6:04 pm** 3:04 pm
- ♃ △ ♇ **8:13 pm** 5:13 pm
- ☿ ⚹ ♆ **11:57 pm** 8:57 pm
- ☽ ⚺ ♆ 10:25 pm
- ☽ ⚺ ☿ 10:39 pm

3 MONDAY
- ☽ ⚺ ♆ **1:25 am**
- ☽ ⚺ ☿ **1:39 am**
- ☽ □ ♇ **5:05 am** 2:05 am
- ☽ ⚺ ♃ **5:14 am** 2:14 am
- ☽ ⚺ ♀ 10:27 pm
- ☽ ⚺ ☉ 10:39 pm
- ☿ △ ♇ 11:12 pm

4 TUESDAY
- ☽ ⚺ ♀ **1:27 am**
- ☽ ⚺ ☉ **1:39 am**
- ☿ △ ♇ **2:12 am**
- ☿ ☌ ♃ **6:23 am** 3:23 am
- ☽ ⚹ ♄ **9:46 am** 6:46 am
- ☉ ☌ ♀ **11:32 am** 8:32 am
- ☽ ☌ ♅ **7:04 pm** 4:04 pm
- ☽ ⚺ ♂ **11:28 pm** 8:28 pm

5 WEDNESDAY
- ☽ ⚹ ♆ **4:09 am** 1:09 am
- ☽ △ ♇ **7:46 am** 4:46 am
- ☽ ☌ ♃ **8:49 am** 5:49 am
- ☽ ☌ ☿ **12:46 pm** 9:46 am

6 THURSDAY
- ☽ ☌ ☉ **8:38 am** 5:38 am
- ☽ ☌ ♀ **9:36 am** 6:36 am
- ☽ □ ♄ **1:19 pm** 10:19 am
- ☽ ⚺ ♅ **10:59 pm** 7:59 pm

7 FRIDAY
- ☽ ⚹ ♂ **6:22 am** 3:22 am
- ☽ □ ♆ **8:16 am** 5:16 am
- ☽ ⚻ ♇ **11:55 am** 8:55 am
- ☽ ⚺ ♃ **2:00 pm** 11:00 am
- ☽ ⚺ ☿ 11:55 pm

8 SATURDAY
- ☽ ⚺ ☿ **2:55 am**
- ♀ □ ♄ **4:25 am** 1:25 am
- ♂ ⚺ ♆ **5:33 pm** 2:33 pm
- ☽ ⚺ ☉ **6:15 pm** 3:15 pm
- ☽ △ ♄ **7:08 pm** 4:08 pm
- ☽ ⚺ ♀ **8:37 pm** 5:37 pm

9 SUNDAY
- ☽ ⚹ ♅ **5:26 am** 2:26 am
- ☉ □ ♄ **6:36 am** 3:36 am
- ☽ △ ♆ **3:05 pm** 12:05 pm
- ☽ □ ♂ **4:24 pm** 1:24 pm
- ☽ ☍ ♇ **6:50 pm** 3:50 pm
- ☽ ⚹ ♃ **10:09 pm** 7:09 pm

10 MONDAY
- ☽ ⚹ ☿ **10:35 pm** 7:35 pm

11 TUESDAY
- ☽ ⚻ ♄ **4:14 am** 1:14 am
- ☽ ⚹ ☉ **7:58 am** 4:58 am
- ♂ □ ♇ **9:21 am** 6:21 am
- ☽ ⚹ ♀ **12:02 pm** 9:02 am
- ☽ □ ♅ **3:16 pm** 12:16 pm
- ☽ ⚻ ♆ 10:17 pm

12 WEDNESDAY
- ☽ ⚻ ♆ **1:17 am**
- ☽ ⚻ ♇ **5:07 am** 2:07 am
- ☽ △ ♂ **6:26 am** 3:26 am
- ☿ □ ♄ **6:47 am** 3:47 am
- ☽ □ ♃ **9:49 am** 6:49 am
- ♀ ⚺ ♅ **9:24 pm** 6:24 pm

13 THURSDAY
- ☽ ☍ ♄ **4:18 pm** 1:18 pm
- ☽ □ ☿ **11:51 pm** 8:51 pm
- ☽ □ ☉ 10:18 pm

14 FRIDAY
- ☽ □ ☉ **1:18 am**
- ☽ △ ♅ **3:50 am** 12:50 am
- ☽ □ ♀ **7:13 am** 4:13 am
- ☉ ☌ ☿ **12:33 pm** 9:33 am
- ☽ ☍ ♆ **1:54 pm** 10:54 am
- ☽ △ ♇ **5:39 pm** 2:39 pm
- ☿ ⚺ ♅ **9:41 pm** 6:41 pm
- ☽ ⚻ ♂ **11:08 pm** 8:08 pm
- ☽ △ ♃ **11:44 pm** 8:44 pm

15 SATURDAY
- ☉ ⚺ ♅ **10:16 am** 7:16 am
- ♂ ⚺ ♃ **12:37 pm** 9:37 am

16 SUNDAY
- ☽ ⚻ ♄ **5:14 am** 2:14 am
- ☽ ⚻ ♅ **4:45 pm** 1:45 pm
- ☽ △ ☉ **7:14 pm** 4:14 pm
- ♀ □ ♆ **11:46 pm** 8:46 pm
- ☽ △ ☿ 11:05 pm
- ☽ ⚻ ♆ 11:22 pm
- ☽ △ ♀ 11:40 pm

17 MONDAY
- ☽ △ ☿ **2:05 am**
- ☽ ⚻ ♆ **2:22 am**
- ☽ △ ♀ **2:40 am**
- ☿ □ ♆ **3:41 am** 12:41 am
- ☽ □ ♇ **5:54 am** 2:54 am
- ☿ ☌ ♀ **8:43 am** 5:43 am
- ☽ ⚻ ♃ **1:02 pm** 10:02 am
- ☽ ☍ ♂ **3:10 pm** 12:10 pm
- ☿ ⚻ ♇ **11:13 pm** 8:13 pm

18 TUESDAY
- ♀ ⚻ ♇ **10:12 am** 7:12 am
- ☽ △ ♄ **4:19 pm** 1:19 pm

19 WEDNESDAY
- ☽ ☍ ♅ **3:24 am** 12:24 am
- ☽ ⚻ ☉ **10:15 am** 7:15 am
- ☽ △ ♆ **12:19 pm** 9:19 am
- ☽ ⚹ ♇ **3:32 pm** 12:32 pm
- ☽ ⚻ ♀ **6:41 pm** 3:41 pm
- ☿ ⚺ ♃ **9:40 pm** 6:40 pm
- ☽ ☍ ♃ **11:22 pm** 8:22 pm
- ☽ ⚻ ☿ **11:40 pm** 8:40 pm

20 THURSDAY
- ☽ ⚻ ♂ **3:47 am** 12:47 am
- ☉ □ ♆ **2:12 pm** 11:12 am
- ☽ □ ♄ 9:08 pm

21 FRIDAY
- ☽ □ ♄ **12:08 am**
- ☽ ⚻ ♅ **10:44 am** 7:44 am
- ☿ ⚹ ♂ **12:23 pm** 9:23 am
- ☽ □ ♆ **6:58 pm** 3:58 pm
- ☽ ☍ ☉ **9:08 pm** 6:08 pm
- ☽ ⚺ ♇ **9:55 pm** 6:55 pm

22 SATURDAY
- ♀ ⚺ ♃ **5:56 am** 2:56 am
- ☽ ⚻ ♃ **6:18 am** 3:18 am
- ☽ ☍ ♀ **6:20 am** 3:20 am
- ☉ ⚻ ♇ **8:01 am** 5:01 am
- ☽ △ ♂ **12:37 pm** 9:37 am
- ☽ ☍ ☿ **3:25 pm** 12:25 pm

23 SUNDAY
- ☽ ⚹ ♄ **5:02 am** 2:02 am
- ☽ △ ♅ **3:20 pm** 12:20 pm
- ☽ ⚹ ♆ **11:05 pm** 8:05 pm
- ☽ ☌ ♇ 10:50 pm

24 MONDAY
- ☽ ☌ ♇ **1:50 am**
- ☽ ⚻ ☉ **4:57 am** 1:57 am
- ☽ △ ♃ **10:52 am** 7:52 am
- ☽ ⚻ ♀ **3:00 pm** 12:00 pm
- ☽ □ ♂ **6:58 pm** 3:58 pm

25 TUESDAY
- ☽ ⚻ ☿ **3:27 am** 12:27 am
- ☽ ⚺ ♄ **8:14 am** 5:14 am
- ☽ □ ♅ **6:30 pm** 3:30 pm
- ☽ ⚺ ♆ 11:00 pm

26 WEDNESDAY
- ☽ ⚺ ♆ **2:00 am**
- ☽ ⚺ ♇ **4:37 am** 1:37 am
- ☽ △ ☉ **11:26 am** 8:26 am
- ☿ △ ♄ **2:10 pm** 11:10 am
- ☽ □ ♃ **2:27 pm** 11:27 am
- ☽ △ ♀ **10:33 pm** 7:33 pm
- ☽ ⚹ ♂ 9:26 pm

27 THURSDAY
- ☽ ⚹ ♂ **12:26 am**
- ☽ ☌ ♄ **10:57 am** 7:57 am
- ☽ △ ☿ **2:11 pm** 11:11 am
- ☽ ⚹ ♅ **9:23 pm** 6:23 pm

28 FRIDAY
- ☽ ☌ ♆ **4:45 am** 1:45 am
- ☽ ⚹ ♇ **7:18 am** 4:18 am
- ☽ □ ☉ **5:53 pm** 2:53 pm
- ☽ ⚹ ♃ **6:03 pm** 3:03 pm
- ☉ ⚺ ♃ **8:54 pm** 5:54 pm
- ♀ ⚹ ♂ 9:49 pm

29 SATURDAY
- ♀ ⚹ ♂ **12:49 am**
- ☽ ⚺ ♂ **6:04 am** 3:04 am
- ☽ □ ♀ **6:16 am** 3:16 am
- ☽ ⚺ ♄ **1:55 pm** 10:55 am
- ☿ ⚹ ♅ **10:20 pm** 7:20 pm
- ☽ ⚺ ♅ 9:37 pm
- ☽ □ ☿ 9:56 pm

30 SUNDAY
- ☽ ⚺ ♅ **12:37 am**
- ☽ □ ☿ **12:56 am**
- ☽ ⚺ ♆ **7:53 am** 4:53 am
- ☽ □ ♇ **10:23 am** 7:23 am
- ☽ ⚺ ♃ **10:09 pm** 7:09 pm
- ☽ ⚹ ☉ 9:57 pm

Eastern time in bold type
Pacific time in medium type

JUNE 2024

DATE	SID.TIME	SUN	MOON	NODE	MERCURY	VENUS	MARS	JUPITER	SATURN	URANUS	NEPTUNE	PLUTO	CERES	PALLAS	JUNO	VESTA	CHIRON
1 Sa	16 39 53	11 ♊ 00 04	27 ♊ 57	14 ♈ 02	25 ♉ 02	10 ♊ 01	23 ♉ 53	1 ♊ 25	18 ♓ 45	24 ♉ 10	29 ♓ 40	1 ♒ 55 R	20 ♑ 41 R	25 ♏ 30 R	10 ♏ 34	22 ♋ 01	22 ♈ 16
2 Su	16 43 49	11 57 35	12 ♋ 11	14 03 R	27 26	11 15	24 38	1 39	18 48	24 14	29 41	1 54	20 35	25 13	10 46	22 25	22 18
3 M	16 47 46	12 55 05	26 29	14 02	29 23	12 28	25 23	1 53	18 50	24 17	29 42	1 53	20 28	24 57	10 58	22 50	22 21
4 T	16 51 42	13 52 34	10 ♌ 45	14 00	1 ♊ 21	13 42	26 08	2 07	18 53	24 20	29 43	1 52	20 22	24 41	11 11	23 15	22 23
5 W	16 55 39	14 50 02	24 57	13 55	3 22	14 56	26 53	2 21	18 55	24 24	29 44	1 51	20 14	24 26	11 23	23 40	22 26
6 Th	16 59 35	15 47 29	8 ♍ 59	13 47	5 24	16 10	27 37	2 35	18 58	24 27	29 45	1 50	20 07	24 11	11 36	24 05	22 28
7 F	17 3 32	16 44 56	22 49	13 37	7 28	17 23	28 22	2 49	19 00	24 30	29 45	1 50	19 59	23 56	11 49	24 30	22 31
8 Sa	17 7 29	17 42 22	6 ♎ 21	13 27	9 34	18 37	29 07	3 03	19 02	24 34	29 46	1 49	19 50	23 42	12 02	24 55	22 33
9 Su	17 11 25	18 39 47	19 32	13 17	11 42	19 51	29 51	3 17	19 04	24 37	29 47	1 48	19 42	23 27	12 15	25 21	22 35
10 M	17 15 22	19 37 10	2 ♏ 24	13 07	13 51	21 04	0 ♊ 36	3 30	19 06	24 40	29 48	1 47	19 33	23 14	12 28	25 46	22 37
11 T	17 19 18	20 34 33	14 55	13 00	16 01	22 18	1 21	3 44	19 08	24 43	29 48	1 46	19 24	23 00	12 42	26 11	22 40
12 W	17 23 15	21 31 55	27 09	12 55	18 12	23 32	2 05	3 58	19 10	24 47	29 49	1 45	19 14	22 47	12 56	26 37	22 42
13 Th	17 27 11	22 29 16	9 ♐ 10	12 52	20 23	24 46	2 49	4 12	19 12	24 50	29 50	1 44	19 04	22 35	13 09	27 02	22 44
14 F	17 31 8	23 26 35	21 02	12 51 D	22 35	25 59	3 34	4 25	19 13	24 53	29 50	1 43	18 54	22 23	13 24	27 28	22 46
15 Sa	17 35 4	24 23 54	2 ♑ 51	12 52 R	24 47	27 13	4 18	4 39	19 15	24 56	29 51	1 42	18 44	22 11	13 38	27 53	22 48
16 Su	17 39 1	25 21 12	14 42	12 52	26 59	28 27	5 02	4 53	19 16	24 59	29 52	1 41	18 34	22 00	13 52	28 19	22 50
17 M	17 42 58	26 18 29	26 40	12 52	29 11	29 41	5 46	5 06	19 18	25 02	29 52	1 40	18 23	21 49	14 07	28 45	22 52
18 T	17 46 54	27 15 46	8 ♒ 50	12 48	1 ♋ 21	0 ♋ 54	6 30	5 20	19 19	25 05	29 53	1 39	18 12	21 38	14 22	29 10	22 54
19 W	17 50 51	28 13 01	21 16	12 43	3 31	2 08	7 14	5 34	19 20	25 08	29 53	1 37	18 00	21 28	14 37	29 36	22 56
20 Th	17 54 47	29 10 16	4 ♓ 00	12 36	5 39	3 22	7 58	5 47	19 21	25 12	29 54	1 36	17 49	21 19	14 52	0 ♌ 02	22 58
21 F	17 58 44	0 ♋ 07 31	17 05	12 26	7 46	4 35	8 42	6 01	19 22	25 15	29 54	1 35	17 37	21 10	15 07	0 28	23 00
22 Sa	18 2 40	1 04 45	0 ♈ 29	12 14	9 52	5 49	9 26	6 14	19 23	25 18	29 54	1 34	17 25	21 01	15 22	0 54	23 01
23 Su	18 6 37	2 01 58	14 11	12 03	11 56	7 03	10 10	6 27	19 23	25 23	29 54	1 33	17 13	20 53	15 38	1 20	23 03
24 M	18 10 34	2 59 12	28 06	11 52	13 58	8 17	10 54	6 41	19 24	25 26	29 55	1 32	17 01	20 46	15 53	1 46	23 05
25 T	18 14 30	3 56 25	12 ♉ 12	11 43	15 59	9 30	11 37	6 54	19 25	25 29	29 55	1 30	16 49	20 38	16 09	2 12	23 06
26 W	18 18 27	4 53 37	26 22	11 36	17 57	10 44	12 21	7 07	19 25	25 32	29 55	1 29	16 36	20 32	16 25	2 38	23 08
27 Th	18 22 23	5 50 50	10 ♊ 35	11 32	19 53	11 58	13 04	7 21	19 26	25 35	29 56	1 28	16 24	20 26	16 41	3 05	23 09
28 F	18 26 20	6 48 03	24 46	11 31 D	21 48	13 11	13 48	7 34	19 26	25 38	29 56	1 27	16 11	20 20	16 57	3 31	23 11
29 Sa	18 30 16	7 45 15	8 ♋ 55	11 31	23 40	14 25	14 31	7 47	19 26 R	25 41	29 56	1 25	15 58	20 14	17 13	3 57	23 12
30 Su	18 34 13	8 42 28	22 59	11 30	25 30	15 39	15 14	8 00	19 26	25 40	29 56	1 24	15 45	20 10	17 30	4 24	23 14

EPHEMERIS CALCULATED FOR 12 MIDNIGHT GREENWICH MEAN TIME. ALL OTHER DATA AND FACING ASPECTARIAN PAGE IN **EASTERN TIME (BOLD)** AND PACIFIC TIME (REGULAR).

JULY 2024

Eastern time in bold type
Pacific time in medium type

JULY 2024

DATE	SID.TIME	SUN	MOON	NODE	MERCURY	VENUS	MARS	JUPITER	SATURN	URANUS	NEPTUNE	PLUTO	CERES	PALLAS	JUNO	VESTA	CHIRON
1 M	18 38 9	9♋39 41	6♉59	11♈29R	27♋18	16♋53	15♉58	8♊13	19♓26R	25♉43	29♓56	1♒23R	15♍32R	20♍05R	17♍46	4♋50	23♈15
2 T	18 42 6	10 36 55	20 53	11 25	29 04	18 06	16 41	8 26	19 25	25 46	29 56R	1 22	15 19	20 01	18 03	5 16	23 16
3 W	18 46 3	11 34 08	4♊41	11 19	0♌48	19 20	17 24	8 39	19 25	25 49	29 56	1 20	15 06	19 58	18 20	5 43	23 18
4 Th	18 49 59	12 31 22	18 18	11 10	2 30	20 34	18 07	8 52	19 25	25 51	29 56	1 19	14 52	19 55	18 37	6 10	23 19
5 F	18 53 56	13 28 35	1♋45	10 59	4 09	21 47	18 50	9 05	19 24	25 54	29 56	1 18	14 39	19 53	18 54	6 36	23 20
6 Sa	18 57 52	14 25 49	14 57	10 46	5 47	23 01	19 33	9 17	19 24	25 56	29 56	1 16	14 26	19 50	19 11	7 03	23 21
7 Su	19 1 49	15 23 03	27 54	10 34	7 22	24 15	20 16	9 30	19 23	25 59	29 56	1 15	14 13	19 49	19 28	7 30	23 22
8 M	19 5 45	16 20 17	10♌35	10 22	8 55	25 29	20 58	9 43	19 22	26 02	29 55	1 14	13 59	19 47	19 45	7 56	23 23
9 T	19 9 42	17 17 30	22 59	10 13	10 26	26 42	21 41	9 55	19 21	26 04	29 55	1 12	13 46	19 47	20 03	8 23	23 24
10 W	19 13 38	18 14 44	5♍09	10 06	11 55	27 56	22 23	10 08	19 21	26 06	29 55	1 11	13 33	19 46D	20 20	8 50	23 25
11 Th	19 17 35	19 11 58	17 07	10 02	13 22	29 10	23 06	10 20	19 19	26 09	29 55	1 09	13 20	19 47	20 38	9 17	23 26
12 F	19 21 32	20 09 11	28 58	10 00D	14 46	0♌24	23 48	10 33	19 18	26 11	29 54	1 08	13 07	19 47	20 56	9 44	23 26
13 Sa	19 25 28	21 06 24	10♎46	10 00R	16 08	1 37	24 30	10 45	19 17	26 14	29 54	1 07	12 54	19 48	21 14	10 11	23 27
14 Su	19 29 25	22 03 38	22 36	10 00	17 28	2 51	25 13	10 57	19 16	26 16	29 54	1 05	12 41	19 50	21 32	10 38	23 28
15 M	19 33 21	23 00 51	4♏34	10 00	18 45	4 05	25 55	11 09	19 14	26 18	29 53	1 04	12 28	19 52	21 50	11 05	23 29
16 T	19 37 18	23 58 05	16 46	9 58	20 00	5 19	26 37	11 21	19 13	26 20	29 53	1 02	12 16	19 54	22 08	11 32	23 29
17 W	19 41 14	24 55 19	29 15	9 53	21 13	6 32	27 19	11 33	19 11	26 23	29 52	1 01	12 04	19 57	22 26	11 59	23 30
18 Th	19 45 11	25 52 33	12♐07	9 47	22 23	7 46	28 01	11 45	19 09	26 25	29 52	1 00	11 52	20 00	22 44	12 26	23 30
19 F	19 49 7	26 49 47	25 22	9 38	23 31	9 00	28 42	11 57	19 08	26 27	29 51	0 58	11 40	20 03	23 03	12 53	23 31
20 Sa	19 53 4	27 47 02	9♑01	9 27	24 36	10 13	29 24	12 09	19 06	26 29	29 51	0 57	11 28	20 07	23 21	13 21	23 31
21 Su	19 57 1	28 44 17	23 03	9 17	25 38	11 27	0♊06	12 21	19 04	26 31	29 50	0 55	11 16	20 11	23 40	13 48	23 31
22 M	20 0 57	29 41 32	7♒21	9 07	26 37	12 41	0 47	12 32	19 02	26 33	29 50	0 54	11 04	20 16	23 58	14 15	23 32
23 T	20 4 54	0♌38 48	21 52	8 58	27 33	13 55	1 29	12 44	18 59	26 35	29 49	0 53	10 53	20 21	24 17	14 42	23 32
24 W	20 8 50	1 36 04	6♓27	8 52	28 26	15 08	2 10	12 55	18 57	26 37	29 48	0 51	10 42	20 27	24 36	15 10	23 32
25 Th	20 12 47	2 33 22	21 01	8 49	29 16	16 22	2 51	13 07	18 55	26 39	29 48	0 50	10 31	20 32	24 55	15 37	23 32
26 F	20 16 43	3 30 40	5♈29	8 48D	0♍02	17 36	3 32	13 18	18 52	26 40	29 47	0 48	10 21	20 39	25 14	16 05	23 32R
27 Sa	20 20 40	4 27 59	19 46	8 48	0 45	18 49	4 13	13 29	18 50	26 42	29 46	0 47	10 10	20 45	25 33	16 32	23 32
28 Su	20 24 36	5 25 19	3♉52	8 48R	1 25	20 03	4 54	13 40	18 47	26 44	29 46	0 45	10 00	20 52	25 52	17 00	23 32
29 M	20 28 33	6 22 40	17 45	8 48	2 00	21 17	5 35	13 51	18 44	26 46	29 45	0 44	9 51	20 59	26 11	17 27	23 32
30 T	20 32 30	7 20 03	1♊26	8 46	2 32	22 30	6 16	14 02	18 42	26 47	29 44	0 43	9 41	21 07	26 30	17 55	23 32
31 W	20 36 26	8 17 26	14 55	8 41	2 59	23 44	6 57	14 13	18 39	26 49	29 43	0 41	9 32	21 15	26 50	18 22	23 32

EPHEMERIS CALCULATED FOR 12 MIDNIGHT GREENWICH MEAN TIME. ALL OTHER DATA AND FACING ASPECTARIAN PAGE IN **EASTERN TIME (BOLD)** AND PACIFIC TIME (REGULAR).

AUGUST 2024

☽ Last Aspect day	ET / hr:mn / PT		asp	☽ Ingress sign	day	ET / hr:mn / PT	
3	**6:31 am**	3:31 am	△♆	♌	3	**7:10 am**	4:10 am
5	**11:16 am**	8:16 am	□♅	♍	5	**5:17 pm**	2:17 pm
8	**4:40 am**	1:40 am	☍♆	♎	8	**5:31 am**	2:31 am
9	**5:45 pm**	2:45 pm	⚹☉	♏	10	**6:34 pm**	3:34 pm
13	**5:01 am**	2:01 am	△♆	♐	13	**6:01 am**	3:01 am
15	**12:52 pm**	9:52 am	△☿	♑	15	**1:51 pm**	10:51 am
17	**4:43 pm**	1:43 pm	⚹♆	♒	17	**5:45 pm**	2:45 pm
19	**2:26 pm**	11:26 am	☍☉	♓	19	**6:52 pm**	3:52 pm
21	**5:54 pm**	2:54 pm	☌♆	♈	21	**7:02 pm**	4:02 pm
23	**8:44 am**	5:44 am	△☿	♉	23	**8:00 pm**	5:00 pm
25	**9:40 pm**	6:40 pm	⚹♆	♊	25	**11:04 pm**	8:04 pm
28	**3:14 am**	12:14 am	□♆	♋	28	**4:47 am**	1:47 am
30	**11:24 am**	8:24 am	△♆	♌	30	**1:09 pm**	10:09 am

☽ Phases & Eclipses phase	day	ET / hr:mn / PT	
New Moon	4	**7:13 am**	4:13 am
2nd Quarter	12	**11:19 am**	8:19 am
Full Moon	19	**2:26 pm**	11:26 am
4th Quarter	25	**5:26 am**	2:26 am

Planet Ingress	day	ET / hr:mn / PT	
♀ ♍	4	**10:23 pm**	7:23 pm
⚵ ♎	9	**12:35 pm**	9:35 am
☿ ♌	14	**8:16 pm**	5:16 pm
☉ ♍	22	**10:55 am**	7:55 am
⚶ ♍	24	**7:38 pm**	4:38 pm
♀ ♎	29	**9:23 am**	6:23 am

Planetary Motion	day	ET / hr:mn / PT	
☿ ℞	4		9:56 pm
☿ ℞	5	**12:56 am**	
⚷ D	26	**3:37 am**	12:37 am
☿ D	28	**5:14 pm**	2:14 pm

1 THURSDAY
☽ ⚻ ♇ **12:31 am**
☽ ⚹ ☿ **5:43 am** 2:43 am
☽ ⚺ ♂ **2:15 pm** 11:15 am
☽ ⚺ ☉ **5:55 pm** 2:55 pm
☽ ⚺ ♃ 11:16 pm

2 FRIDAY
☽ ⚺ ♃ **2:16 am**
♀ □ ♅ **9:27 am** 6:27 am
☽ △ ♄ **9:32 am** 6:32 am
☽ ⚹ ♅ 10:17 pm
☽ ⚺ ♀ 11:57 pm

3 SATURDAY
☽ ⚹ ♅ **1:17 am**
☽ ⚺ ♀ **2:57 am**
☽ △ ♆ **6:31 am** 3:31 am
☽ ☍ ♇ **8:19 am** 5:19 am
☽ ⚺ ☿ **2:48 pm** 11:48 am
☽ ⚹ ♂ 10:54 pm

4 SUNDAY
☽ ⚹ ♂ **1:54 am**
☽ ☌ ☉ **7:13 am** 4:13 am
☽ ⚹ ♃ **12:01 pm** 9:01 am
♀ ⚻ ♆ **3:24 pm** 12:24 pm
☽ ⚻ ♄ **6:31 pm** 3:31 pm

5 MONDAY
♀ ⚻ ♇ **9:18 am** 6:18 am
☽ □ ♅ **11:16 am** 8:16 am
☽ ⚻ ♆ **4:32 pm** 1:32 pm
☽ ⚻ ♇ **6:22 pm** 3:22 pm
☽ ☌ ♀ **7:24 pm** 4:24 pm
☽ ☌ ☿ 10:19 pm

6 TUESDAY
☽ ☌ ☿ **1:19 am**
☽ □ ♂ **4:15 pm** 1:15 pm
☽ ⚺ ☉ **11:27 pm** 8:27 pm
☽ □ ♃ 9:08 pm

7 WEDNESDAY
☽ □ ♃ **12:08 am**
☽ ☍ ♄ **5:44 am** 2:44 am
☉ ⚹ ♃ **9:37 am** 6:37 am
☿ ☌ ♀ **11:12 pm** 8:12 pm
☽ △ ♅ **11:27 pm** 8:27 pm

8 THURSDAY
☽ ☍ ♆ **4:40 am** 1:40 am
☽ △ ♇ **6:32 am** 3:32 am
☽ ⚺ ☿ **12:47 pm** 9:47 am
☽ ⚺ ♀ **2:43 pm** 11:43 am

9 FRIDAY
☽ △ ♂ **8:40 am** 5:40 am
☽ △ ♃ **1:55 pm** 10:55 am
☽ ⚹ ☉ **5:45 pm** 2:45 pm
☽ ⚻ ♄ **6:24 pm** 3:24 pm
☉ ⚻ ♄ 10:26 pm

10 SATURDAY
☉ ⚻ ♄ **1:26 am**
☽ ⚻ ♅ **12:36 pm** 9:36 am
☽ ⚻ ♆ **5:37 pm** 2:37 pm
☽ □ ♇ **7:27 pm** 4:27 pm
☽ ⚹ ☿ **11:42 pm** 8:42 pm

11 SUNDAY
☽ ⚹ ♀ **10:40 am** 7:40 am
☽ ⚻ ♂ 9:48 pm

12 MONDAY
☽ ⚻ ♂ **12:48 am**
☽ ⚻ ♃ **3:14 am** 12:14 am
☽ △ ♄ **6:29 am** 3:29 am
☽ □ ☉ **11:19 am** 8:19 am
☽ ☍ ♅ 9:24 pm

13 TUESDAY
☽ ☍ ♅ **12:24 am**
☽ △ ♆ **5:01 am** 2:01 am
☽ ⚹ ♇ **6:45 am** 3:45 am
☽ □ ☿ **8:09 am** 5:09 am

14 WEDNESDAY
☽ □ ♀ **3:33 am** 12:33 am
☿ ⚻ ♇ **9:03 am** 6:03 am
♂ ☌ ♃ **11:22 am** 8:22 am
☽ ☍ ♃ **1:35 pm** 10:35 am
☽ ☍ ♂ **1:40 pm** 10:40 am
☽ □ ♄ **3:38 pm** 12:38 pm
☽ △ ☉ 9:57 pm

15 THURSDAY
☽ △ ☉ **12:57 am**
☽ ⚻ ♅ **8:42 am** 5:42 am
☽ □ ♆ **12:50 pm** 9:50 am
☽ △ ☿ **12:52 pm** 9:52 am
☿ ⚻ ♆ **1:19 pm** 10:19 am
☽ ⚺ ♇ **2:27 pm** 11:27 am
♂ □ ♄ 10:30 pm

16 FRIDAY
♂ □ ♄ **1:30 am**
☽ △ ♀ **3:08 pm** 12:08 pm
☽ ⚻ ♃ **7:45 pm** 4:45 pm
☽ ⚹ ♄ **8:49 pm** 5:49 pm
☽ ⚻ ♂ **9:51 pm** 6:51 pm

17 SATURDAY
☽ ⚻ ☉ **9:33 am** 6:33 am
☽ △ ♅ **12:59 pm** 9:59 am
☽ ⚻ ☿ **1:57 pm** 10:57 am
☽ ⚹ ♆ **4:43 pm** 1:43 pm
☽ ☌ ♇ **6:13 pm** 3:13 pm

18 SUNDAY
☿ □ ♅ **5:47 am** 2:47 am
☉ ☌ ☿ **9:58 pm** 6:58 pm
☽ ⚻ ♀ **10:05 pm** 7:05 pm
☽ △ ♃ **10:22 pm** 7:22 pm
☽ ⚺ ♄ **10:38 pm** 7:38 pm
♀ □ ♃ 10:53 pm
☽ △ ♂ 11:08 pm

19 MONDAY
♀ □ ♃ **1:53 am**
☽ △ ♂ **2:08 am**
♀ ☍ ♄ **4:30 am** 1:30 am
☽ ☍ ☿ **12:32 pm** 9:32 am
☉ □ ♅ **12:45 pm** 9:45 am
☽ □ ♅ **2:19 pm** 11:19 am
☽ ☍ ☉ **2:26 pm** 11:26 am
♃ □ ♄ **5:46 pm** 2:46 pm
☽ ⚺ ♆ **5:48 pm** 2:48 pm
☽ ⚺ ♇ **7:15 pm** 4:15 pm

20 TUESDAY
☽ ☌ ♄ **10:45 pm** 7:45 pm
☽ □ ♃ **11:10 pm** 8:10 pm
☽ ☍ ♀ 11:44 pm

21 WEDNESDAY
☽ ☍ ♀ **2:44 am**
☽ □ ♂ **4:34 am** 1:34 am
☽ ⚻ ☿ **10:15 am** 7:15 am
☽ ⚹ ♅ **2:32 pm** 11:32 am
☉ ⚻ ♆ **5:29 pm** 2:29 pm
☽ ☌ ♆ **5:54 pm** 2:54 pm
☽ ⚻ ☉ **5:56 pm** 2:56 pm
☽ ⚹ ♇ **7:21 pm** 4:21 pm

22 THURSDAY
☉ ⚻ ♇ **3:34 pm** 12:34 pm
☽ ⚺ ♄ **10:58 pm** 7:58 pm
♀ □ ♂ **11:20 pm** 8:20 pm
☽ ⚹ ♃ 9:05 pm

23 FRIDAY
☽ ⚹ ♃ **12:05 am**
☽ ⚹ ♂ **7:21 am** 4:21 am
☽ ⚻ ♀ **7:43 am** 4:43 am
☽ △ ☿ **8:44 am** 5:44 am
☽ ⚺ ♅ **3:24 pm** 12:24 pm
☿ ⚺ ♀ **4:15 pm** 1:15 pm
☽ ⚺ ♆ **6:46 pm** 3:46 pm
☽ □ ♇ **8:17 pm** 5:17 pm
☽ △ ☉ **10:22 pm** 7:22 pm
☿ ⚹ ♂ 9:31 pm

24 SATURDAY
☿ ⚹ ♂ **12:31 am**
☽ ⚹ ♄ 9:46 pm
☽ ⚺ ♃ 11:40 pm

25 SUNDAY
☽ ⚹ ♄ **12:46 am**
☽ ⚺ ♃ **2:40 am**
☽ □ ☿ **9:25 am** 6:25 am
☽ ⚺ ♂ **12:12 pm** 9:12 am
☽ △ ♀ **3:03 pm** 12:03 pm
☽ ☌ ♅ **6:15 pm** 3:15 pm
☽ ⚹ ♆ **9:40 pm** 6:40 pm
☽ △ ♇ **11:17 pm** 8:17 pm

26 MONDAY
☽ □ ☉ **5:26 am** 2:26 am

27 TUESDAY
♀ △ ♅ **3:24 am** 12:24 am
☽ □ ♄ **5:02 am** 2:02 am
☽ ☌ ♃ **7:50 am** 4:50 am
☽ ⚹ ☿ **1:17 pm** 10:17 am
☽ ☌ ♂ **8:00 pm** 5:00 pm
☽ ⚺ ♅ **11:45 pm** 8:45 pm
☽ □ ♀ 10:50 pm

28 WEDNESDAY
☽ □ ♀ **1:50 am**
☽ □ ♆ **3:14 am** 12:14 am
☽ ⚻ ♇ **4:56 am** 1:56 am
☽ ⚹ ☉ **3:50 pm** 12:50 pm
♀ ☍ ♆ **4:25 pm** 1:25 pm

29 THURSDAY
♀ △ ♇ **10:32 am** 7:32 am
☽ △ ♄ **11:57 am** 8:57 am
☽ ⚺ ♃ **3:46 pm** 12:46 pm
☽ ⚺ ☿ **8:56 pm** 5:56 pm

30 FRIDAY
☽ ⚺ ♂ **6:52 am** 3:52 am
☽ ⚹ ♅ **7:54 am** 4:54 am
☽ △ ♆ **11:24 am** 8:24 am
☽ ☍ ♇ **1:14 pm** 10:14 am
☽ ⚹ ♀ **4:10 pm** 1:10 pm

31 SATURDAY
♂ ⚺ ♅ **3:52 am** 12:52 am
☽ ⚺ ☉ **5:30 am** 2:30 am
☽ ⚻ ♄ **9:18 pm** 6:18 pm
☽ ⚹ ♃ 11:10 pm

Eastern time in bold type
Pacific time in medium type

AUGUST 2024

DATE	SID.TIME	SUN	MOON	NODE	MERCURY	VENUS	MARS	JUPITER	SATURN	URANUS	NEPTUNE	PLUTO	CERES	PALLAS	JUNO	VESTA	CHIRON
1 Th	20 40 23	9♌14 51	28♊11	8♉34R	3♍22	24♌58	7♊37	14♊24	18♓36R	26♉51	29♓42R	0♒40R	9♍23R	21♏23	27♍09	18♌50	23♈31R
2 F	20 44 19	10 12 16	11♋15	8 25	3 40	26 12	8 18	14 35	18 33	26 52	29 41	0 38	9 14	21 31	27 28	19 18	23 31
3 Sa	20 48 16	11 09 43	24 06	8 15	3 54	27 25	8 58	14 46	18 30	26 53	29 40	0 37	9 06	21 40	27 48	19 45	23 31
4 Su	20 52 12	12 07 10	6♌44	8 05	4 03	28 39	9 39	14 56	18 27	26 55	29 39	0 36	8 58	21 49	28 07	20 13	23 30
5 M	20 56 9	13 04 38	19 09	7 56	4 06R	29 53	10 19	15 06	18 23	26 56	29 38	0 34	8 50	21 59	28 27	20 41	23 30
6 T	21 0 6	14 02 08	1♍23	7 48	4 05	1♍06	10 59	15 16	18 20	26 58	29 37	0 33	8 43	22 09	28 47	21 08	23 29
7 W	21 4 2	14 59 38	13 25	7 43	3 58	2 20	11 39	15 27	18 17	26 59	29 36	0 32	8 36	22 19	29 07	21 36	23 29
8 Th	21 7 59	15 57 09	25 19	7 40	3 46	3 34	12 19	15 37	18 13	27 00	29 35	0 30	8 29	22 29	29 26	22 04	23 28
9 F	21 11 55	16 54 41	7♎07	7 39D	3 28	4 47	12 58	15 47	18 10	27 01	29 34	0 29	8 23	22 40	29 46	22 32	23 27
10 Sa	21 15 52	17 52 14	18 53	7 40	3 05	6 01	13 38	15 56	18 06	27 03	29 33	0 27	8 17	22 51	0♎06	23 00	23 27
11 Su	21 19 48	18 49 47	0♏43	7 41	2 37	7 15	14 18	16 06	18 02	27 04	29 32	0 26	8 11	23 02	0 26	23 28	23 26
12 M	21 23 45	19 47 22	12 40	7 42R	2 05	8 28	14 57	16 16	17 59	27 05	29 31	0 25	8 06	23 14	0 46	23 56	23 26
13 T	21 27 41	20 44 58	24 50	7 42	1 27	9 42	15 36	16 25	17 55	27 06	29 29	0 23	8 01	23 26	1 06	24 23	23 24
14 W	21 31 38	21 42 34	7♐19	7 41	0 46	10 56	16 15	16 35	17 51	27 07	29 28	0 22	7 56	23 38	1 26	24 51	23 23
15 Th	21 35 35	22 40 12	20 10	7 38	0 01	12 09	16 55	16 44	17 47	27 08	29 27	0 21	7 52	23 50	1 47	25 19	23 22
16 F	21 39 31	23 37 50	3♑27	7 33	29♌13	13 23	17 33	16 53	17 43	27 08	29 26	0 20	7 48	24 03	2 07	25 47	23 21
17 Sa	21 43 28	24 35 30	17 11	7 27	29 06	14 37	18 12	17 02	17 39	27 09	29 25	0 18	7 45	24 15	2 27	26 15	23 20
18 Su	21 47 24	25 33 10	1♒21	7 20	27 31	15 50	18 51	17 11	17 35	27 10	29 23	0 17	7 42	24 28	2 47	26 44	23 19
19 M	21 51 21	26 30 52	15 54	7 14	26 40	17 04	19 30	17 20	17 31	27 11	29 22	0 16	7 39	24 42	3 08	27 12	23 18
20 T	21 55 17	27 28 35	0♓43	7 09	25 49	18 17	20 08	17 28	17 27	27 12	29 21	0 15	7 36	24 55	3 28	27 40	23 17
21 W	21 59 14	28 26 19	15 40	7 06	25 00	19 31	20 47	17 37	17 23	27 12	29 19	0 13	7 34	25 09	3 49	28 08	23 15
22 Th	22 3 10	29 24 05	0♈36	7 04D	24 14	20 44	21 25	17 45	17 19	27 13	29 18	0 12	7 33	25 23	4 09	28 36	23 14
23 F	22 7 7	0♍21 52	15 25	7 04	23 32	21 58	22 03	17 53	17 14	27 13	29 16	0 11	7 31	25 37	4 30	29 04	23 13
24 Sa	22 11 3	1 19 42	0♉00	7 05	22 54	23 11	22 41	18 02	17 10	27 14	29 15	0 10	7 30	25 52	4 50	29 32	23 11
25 Su	22 15 0	2 17 32	14 17	7 07	22 23	24 25	23 19	18 10	17 06	27 14	29 14	0 09	7 30	26 06	5 11	0♍00	23 10
26 M	22 18 57	3 15 25	28 14	7 08R	21 57	25 39	23 56	18 17	17 01	27 15	29 12	0 08	7 29D	26 21	5 31	0 29	23 08
27 T	22 22 53	4 13 20	11♊52	7 08	21 39	26 52	24 34	18 25	16 57	27 15	29 11	0 06	7 29	26 36	5 52	0 57	23 07
28 W	22 26 50	5 11 16	25 12	7 06	21 28D	28 06	25 12	18 33	16 53	27 15	29 09	0 05	7 30	26 52	6 13	1 25	23 05
29 Th	22 30 46	6 09 14	8♋14	7 03	21 25	29 19	25 49	18 40	16 48	27 15	29 06	0 04	7 31	27 07	6 34	1 53	23 04
30 F	22 34 43	7 07 14	21 00	6 59	21 30	0♎33	26 26	18 47	16 44	27 15	29 06	0 03	7 32	27 23	6 54	2 22	23 02
31 Sa	22 38 39	8 05 16	3♌33	6 54	21 43	1 46	27 03	18 54	16 39	27 14	29 05	0 02	7 33	27 39	7 15	2 50	23 00

EPHEMERIS CALCULATED FOR 12 MIDNIGHT GREENWICH MEAN TIME. ALL OTHER DATA AND FACING ASPECTARIAN PAGE IN **EASTERN TIME (BOLD)** AND PACIFIC TIME (REGULAR).

SEPTEMBER 2024

☽ Last Aspect day	ET / hr:mn / PT		asp	☽ Ingress sign	day	ET / hr:mn / PT	
1	**8:25 pm**	5:25 pm	✶♂	♍	1	**11:48 pm**	8:48 pm
4	**12:06 pm**	9:06 am	△♇	♎	4	**12:12 pm**	9:12 am
6		10:08 pm	□♇	♏	6		10:18 pm
7	**1:08 am**		□♇	♏	7	**1:18 am**	
9	**1:11 pm**	10:11 am	✶♇	♐	9	**1:26 pm**	10:26 am
11	**8:21 pm**	5:21 pm	□♆	♑	11	**10:38 pm**	7:38 pm
14	**3:35 am**	12:35 am	☌♇	♒	14	**3:53 am**	12:53 am
15		10:04 pm	□♅	♓	16	**5:39 am**	2:39 am
16	**1:04 am**		□♅	♓	16	**5:39 am**	2:39 am
18	**5:02 am**	2:02 am	✶♇	♈	18	**5:24 am**	2:24 am
20	**4:39 am**	1:39 am	□♇	♉	20	**5:03 am**	2:03 am
22	**6:14 am**	3:14 am	△☉	♊	22	**6:24 am**	3:24 am
24	**7:59 am**	4:59 am	□♆	♋	24	**10:50 am**	7:50 am
26	**6:12 pm**	3:12 pm	☍♇	♌	26	**6:47 pm**	3:47 pm
28	**11:36 pm**	8:36 pm	□♅	♍	29	**5:42 am**	2:42 am

☽ Phases & Eclipses phase	day	ET / hr:mn / PT	
New Moon	2	**9:56 pm**	6:56 pm
2nd Quarter	10		11:06 pm
2nd Quarter	11	**2:06 am**	
Full Moon	17	**10:34 pm**	7:34 pm
☍	17	25° ♓ 41'	
4th Quarter	24	**2:50 pm**	11:50 am

Planet Ingress	day	ET / hr:mn / PT	
♇ ♑	1	**8:10 pm**	5:10 pm
♂ ♋	4	**3:46 pm**	12:46 pm
♀ ♐	8	**6:29 am**	3:29 am
☿ ♍	8		11:50 pm
☿ ♍	9	**2:50 am**	
☉ ♎	22	**8:44 am**	5:44 am
♀ ♏	22	**10:36 pm**	7:36 pm
☿ ♎	26	**4:09 am**	1:09 am

Planetary Motion	day	ET / hr:mn / PT	
♅ ℞	1	**11:18 am**	8:18 am

1 SUNDAY
☽ ✶ ♃ **2:10 am**
☽ ☌ ☿ **8:36 am** 5:36 am
☽ □ ♅ **6:22 pm** 3:22 pm
☽ ✶ ♂ **8:25 pm** 5:25 pm
☽ ⚻ ♆ **9:52 pm** 6:52 pm
☽ ⚻ ♇ **11:48 pm** 8:48 pm

2 MONDAY
☽ ⚺ ♀ **9:35 am** 6:35 am
☽ ☌ ☉ **9:56 pm** 6:56 pm
♂ □ ♆ 9:10 pm

3 TUESDAY
♂ □ ♆ **12:10 am**
☽ ☍ ♄ **8:37 am** 5:37 am
☽ □ ♃ **2:34 pm** 11:34 am
☽ ⚺ ☿ 9:17 pm

4 WEDNESDAY
☽ ⚺ ☿ **12:17 am**
☽ △ ♅ **6:37 am** 3:37 am
☽ ☍ ♆ **10:05 am** 7:05 am
☽ □ ♂ **12:00 pm** 9:00 am
☽ △ ♇ **12:06 pm** 9:06 am
♂ ⚻ ♇ **1:59 pm** 10:59 am

5 Thursday
☽ ☌ ♀ **5:12 am** 2:12 am
☽ ⚺ ☉ **4:12 pm** 1:12 pm
☽ ⚻ ♄ **9:11 pm** 6:11 pm

6 FRIDAY
☽ △ ♃ **4:08 am** 1:08 am
☽ ✶ ☿ **7:11 pm** 4:11 pm
☽ ⚻ ♅ **7:42 pm** 4:42 pm
☽ ⚻ ♆ **11:04 pm** 8:04 pm
☿ □ ♅ 9:21 pm
☽ □ ♇ 10:08 pm

7 SATURDAY
☿ □ ♅ **12:21 am**
☽ □ ♇ **1:08 am**
☽ △ ♂ **4:24 am** 1:24 am
☉ ☍ ♄ 9:35 pm
☽ ⚺ ♀ 10:14 pm

8 SUNDAY
☉ ☍ ♄ **12:35 am**
☽ ⚺ ♀ **1:14 am**
☿ ⚻ ♆ **6:52 am** 3:52 am
☽ △ ♄ **9:37 am** 6:37 am
☽ ✶ ☉ **10:29 am** 7:29 am
☽ ⚻ ♃ **5:20 pm** 2:20 pm
☿ ⚻ ♇ 9:55 pm

9 MONDAY
☿ ⚻ ♇ **12:55 am**
☽ ☍ ♅ **7:58 am** 4:58 am
☽ △ ♆ **11:07 am** 8:07 am
☽ ✶ ♇ **1:11 pm** 10:11 am
☽ □ ☿ **2:50 pm** 11:50 am
☽ ⚻ ♂ **7:28 pm** 4:28 pm

10 TUESDAY
☽ ✶ ♀ **6:48 pm** 3:48 pm
☽ □ ♄ **8:02 pm** 5:02 pm
☽ □ ☉ 11:06 pm

11 WEDNESDAY
☽ □ ☉ **2:06 am**
☽ ☍ ♃ **4:07 am** 1:07 am
♀ ⚻ ♄ **6:52 am** 3:52 am
☽ ⚻ ♅ **5:28 pm** 2:28 pm
☽ □ ♆ **8:21 pm** 5:21 pm
☽ ⚺ ♇ **10:21 pm** 7:21 pm
☿ ✶ ♂ **11:42 pm** 8:42 pm

12 THURSDAY
☉ □ ♃ **6:53 am** 3:53 am
☽ ☍ ♂ **6:56 am** 3:56 am
☽ △ ☿ **7:36 am** 4:36 am
☽ ✶ ♄ 11:53 pm

13 FRIDAY
☽ ✶ ♄ **2:53 am**
☽ □ ♀ **7:30 am** 4:30 am
☽ ⚻ ♃ **11:02 am** 8:02 am
☽ △ ☉ **1:01 pm** 10:01 am
☽ △ ♅ **11:04 pm** 8:04 pm
☽ ✶ ♆ 10:40 pm

14 SATURDAY
☽ ✶ ♆ **1:40 am**
☽ ☌ ♇ **3:35 am** 12:35 am
☽ ⚻ ♂ **1:52 pm** 10:52 am
☽ ⚻ ☿ **7:21 pm** 4:21 pm
♀ △ ♃ 10:34 pm

15 SUNDAY
♀ △ ♃ **1:34 am**
☽ ⚺ ♄ **5:55 am** 2:55 am
☽ △ ♃ **2:05 pm** 11:05 am
☽ △ ♀ **3:09 pm** 12:09 pm
☽ ⚻ ☉ **7:15 pm** 4:15 pm
☽ □ ♅ 10:04 pm

16 MONDAY
☽ □ ♅ **1:04 am**
☽ ⚺ ♆ **3:27 am** 12:27 am
☽ ⚺ ♇ **5:19 am** 2:19 am
☽ △ ♂ **5:03 pm** 2:03 pm
☽ ☍ ☿ 11:55 pm

17 TUESDAY
☽ ☍ ☿ **2:55 am**
☽ ☌ ♄ **6:11 am** 3:11 am
☽ □ ♃ **2:30 pm** 11:30 am
☽ ⚻ ♀ **7:31 pm** 4:31 pm
☽ ☍ ☉ **10:34 pm** 7:34 pm
☽ ✶ ♅ 9:53 pm

18 WEDNESDAY
☽ ✶ ♅ **12:53 am**
☽ ☌ ♆ **3:10 am** 12:10 am
☿ ☍ ♄ **4:50 am** 1:50 am
☽ ✶ ♇ **5:02 am** 2:02 am
☽ □ ♂ **6:27 pm** 3:27 pm

19 THURSDAY
☽ ⚺ ♄ **5:24 am** 2:24 am
☽ ⚻ ☿ **8:57 am** 5:57 am
☉ △ ♅ **10:04 am** 7:04 am
☽ ✶ ♃ **2:11 pm** 11:11 am
☽ ☍ ♀ **11:14 pm** 8:14 pm
☽ ⚺ ♅ 9:25 pm
☽ ⚻ ☉ 10:26 pm
☽ ⚺ ♆ 11:41 pm

20 FRIDAY
☽ ⚺ ♅ **12:25 am**
☽ ⚻ ☉ **1:26 am**
☽ ⚺ ♆ **2:41 am**
☽ □ ♇ **4:39 am** 1:39 am
♀ ⚻ ♅ **1:36 pm** 10:36 am
☉ ☍ ♆ **8:17 pm** 5:17 pm
☽ ✶ ♂ **8:18 pm** 5:18 pm

21 SATURDAY
☿ □ ♃ **4:50 am** 1:50 am
☽ ✶ ♄ **5:28 am** 2:28 am
☽ ⚺ ♃ **3:03 pm** 12:03 pm
☽ △ ☿ **4:30 pm** 1:30 pm
♀ ⚻ ♆ **4:53 pm** 1:53 pm
☽ ☌ ♅ 10:29 pm
☉ △ ♇ 11:12 pm

22 SUNDAY
☽ ☌ ♅ **1:29 am**
☉ △ ♇ **2:12 am**
☽ ✶ ♆ **3:50 am** 12:50 am
☽ ⚻ ♀ **4:53 am** 1:53 am
☽ △ ♇ **5:57 am** 2:57 am
☽ △ ☉ **6:14 am** 3:14 am
♀ □ ♇ **5:15 pm** 2:15 pm
☽ ⚺ ♂ 9:37 pm

23 MONDAY
☽ ⚺ ♂ **12:37 am**
☽ □ ♄ **7:58 am** 4:58 am
☽ ☌ ♃ **6:39 pm** 3:39 pm

24 TUESDAY
☽ □ ☿ **4:13 am** 1:13 am
☽ ⚺ ♅ **5:31 am** 2:31 am
☽ □ ♆ **7:59 am** 4:59 am
☽ ⚻ ♇ **10:19 am** 7:19 am
☿ △ ♅ **1:27 pm** 10:27 am
☽ △ ♀ **2:30 pm** 11:30 am
☽ □ ☉ **2:50 pm** 11:50 am

25 WEDNESDAY
☿ ☍ ♆ **7:07 am** 4:07 am
☉ ⚺ ♀ **7:27 am** 4:27 am
☽ ☌ ♂ **8:40 am** 5:40 am
☽ △ ♄ **1:52 pm** 10:52 am
☿ △ ♇ 9:14 pm
☽ ⚺ ♃ 10:45 pm

26 THURSDAY
☿ △ ♇ **12:14 am**
☽ ⚺ ♃ **1:45 am**
☽ ✶ ♅ **1:02 pm** 10:02 am
☽ △ ♆ **3:38 pm** 12:38 pm
☽ ☍ ♇ **6:12 pm** 3:12 pm
☽ ✶ ☿ **9:18 pm** 6:18 pm

27 FRIDAY
☽ ✶ ☉ **3:51 am** 12:51 am
☽ □ ♀ **4:47 am** 1:47 am
☽ ⚺ ♂ **8:33 pm** 5:33 pm
☽ ⚻ ♄ **11:04 pm** 8:04 pm

28 SATURDAY
☽ ✶ ♃ **12:05 pm** 9:05 am
☽ □ ♅ **11:36 pm** 8:36 pm
☽ ⚻ ♆ 11:16 pm

29 SUNDAY
☽ ⚻ ♆ **2:16 am**
☽ ⚻ ♇ **5:03 am** 2:03 am
☽ ⚺ ☿ **6:48 pm** 3:48 pm
☽ ⚺ ☉ **8:25 pm** 5:25 pm
☽ ✶ ♀ **10:49 pm** 7:49 pm
♂ △ ♄ 9:06 pm

30 MONDAY
♂ △ ♄ **12:06 am**
☽ ☍ ♄ **10:38 am** 7:38 am
☽ ✶ ♂ **11:11 am** 8:11 am
☉ ☌ ☿ **5:09 pm** 2:09 pm
☽ □ ♃ 9:30 pm

Eastern time in bold type
Pacific time in medium type

SEPTEMBER 2024

DATE	SID.TIME	SUN	MOON	NODE	MERCURY	VENUS	MARS	JUPITER	SATURN	URANUS	NEPTUNE	PLUTO	CERES	PALLAS	JUNO	VESTA	CHIRON
1 Su	22 42 36	9♍03 20	15♌54	6♈50R	22♌05	2♎59	27♊40	19♊01	16♓35R	27♉15R	29♓03R	0♒01R	7♑35	27♍55	7♎36	3♈47	22♈58R
2 M	22 46 33	10 01 25	28 05	6 45	22 35	4 13	28 17	19 08	16 30	27 15	29 02	0 00	7 37	28 11	7 57	4 15	22 57
3 T	22 50 29	10 59 32	10♍07	6 42	23 13	5 26	28 54	19 15	16 25	27 15	29 00	29♑59	7 40	28 28	8 18	4 43	22 55
4 W	22 54 26	11 57 40	22 01	6 40	23 59	6 40	29 30	19 21	16 21	27 15	28 59	29 58	7 43	28 44	8 39	5 12	22 53
5 Th	22 58 22	12 55 51	3♎50	6 39D	24 53	7 53	0♋06	19 28	16 16	27 15	28 57	29 57	7 46	29 01	9 00	5 40	22 51
6 F	23 2 19	13 54 02	15 37	6 39	25 54	9 07	0 43	19 34	16 12	27 15	28 55	29 56	7 49	29 18	9 21	6 09	22 49
7 Sa	23 6 15	14 52 16	27 23	6 40	27 02	10 20	1 19	19 40	16 07	27 15	28 54	29 55	7 53	29 35	9 42	6 37	22 47
8 Su	23 10 12	15 50 31	9♏14	6 42	28 16	11 33	1 54	19 46	16 03	27 14	28 52	29 54	7 57	29 52	10 03	7 05	22 45
9 M	23 14 8	16 48 47	21 12	6 44	29 36	12 47	2 30	19 52	15 58	27 14	28 50	29 53	8 02	0♎10	10 24	7 34	22 43
10 T	23 18 5	17 47 06	3♐21	6 45	1♍02	14 00	3 06	19 57	15 53	27 14	28 49	29 53	8 07	0 28	10 45	8 02	22 41
11 W	23 22 1	18 45 25	15 48	6 45R	2 32	15 13	3 41	20 03	15 49	27 13	28 47	29 52	8 12	0 45	11 06	8 31	22 39
12 Th	23 25 58	19 43 47	28 35	6 44	4 07	16 27	4 16	20 08	15 44	27 13	28 46	29 51	8 17	1 03	11 27	8 59	22 37
13 F	23 29 55	20 42 10	11♑46	6 43	5 45	17 40	4 51	20 13	15 40	27 12	28 44	29 51	8 23	1 21	11 48	9 28	22 34
14 Sa	23 33 51	21 40 34	25 25	6 43	7 27	18 53	5 26	20 18	15 35	27 12	28 43	29 49	8 29	1 40	12 09	9 56	22 32
15 Su	23 37 48	22 39 00	9♒31	6 41	9 11	20 07	6 01	20 23	15 30	27 11	28 41	29 49	8 36	1 58	12 31	10 25	22 30
16 M	23 41 44	23 37 28	24 03	6 39	10 57	21 20	6 35	20 27	15 26	27 10	28 39	29 48	8 42	2 17	12 52	10 53	22 28
17 T	23 45 41	24 35 57	8♓56	6 37D	12 45	22 33	7 10	20 32	15 21	27 09	28 38	29 47	8 49	2 35	13 13	11 22	22 25
18 W	23 49 37	25 34 28	24 03	6 37	14 35	23 46	7 44	20 36	15 17	27 08	28 36	29 47	8 57	2 54	13 34	11 50	22 23
19 Th	23 53 34	26 33 01	9♈15	6 37	16 25	25 00	8 18	20 40	15 12	27 08	28 34	29 46	9 04	3 13	13 55	12 19	22 20
20 F	23 57 30	27 31 36	24 21	6 38	18 16	26 13	8 52	20 44	15 08	27 07	28 33	29 45	9 12	3 32	14 17	12 47	22 18
21 Sa	0 1 27	28 30 13	9♉15	6 38	20 07	27 26	9 26	20 47	15 04	27 06	28 31	29 45	9 20	3 51	14 38	13 16	22 16
22 Su	0 5 24	29 28 53	23 49	6 38	21 59	28 39	9 59	20 51	14 59	27 05	28 29	29 44	9 29	4 10	14 59	13 16	22 13
23 M	0 9 20	0♎27 34	7♊58	6 39	23 50	29 52	10 32	20 54	14 55	27 04	28 28	29 44	9 37	4 30	15 21	13 44	22 11
24 T	0 13 17	1 26 18	21 43	6 39R	25 42	1♏05	11 05	20 57	14 51	27 03	28 26	29 43	9 46	4 50	15 42	14 13	22 08
25 W	0 17 13	2 25 05	5♋03	6 39	27 32	2 18	11 38	21 00	14 46	27 02	28 24	29 43	9 56	5 09	16 03	14 41	22 06
26 Th	0 21 10	3 23 53	18 00	6 39	29 23	3 31	12 11	21 03	14 42	27 01	28 23	29 42	10 05	5 29	16 24	15 10	22 03
27 F	0 25 6	4 22 44	0♌38	6 39	1♎12	4 44	12 43	21 05	14 38	27 00	28 21	29 42	10 15	5 49	16 46	15 38	22 00
28 Sa	0 29 3	5 21 37	13 00	6 39	3 01	5 57	13 16	21 08	14 34	26 58	28 19	29 41	10 25	6 09	17 07	16 07	21 58
29 Su	0 32 59	6 20 32	25 08	6 39D	4 50	7 10	13 48	21 10	14 30	26 57	28 18	29 41	10 35	6 29	17 29	16 35	21 55
30 M	0 36 56	7 19 29	7♍08	6 39	6 37	8 23	14 19	21 12	14 26	26 56	28 16	29 41	10 46	6 49	17 50	17 04	21 53

EPHEMERIS CALCULATED FOR 12 MIDNIGHT GREENWICH MEAN TIME. ALL OTHER DATA AND FACING ASPECTARIAN PAGE IN **EASTERN TIME (BOLD)** AND PACIFIC TIME (REGULAR).

OCTOBER 2024

☽ Last Aspect day	ET	PT	asp	☽ Ingress sign	day	ET	PT
1	**5:39 pm**	2:39 pm	△♇	♎	1	**6:20 pm**	3:20 pm
4	**6:40 am**	3:40 am	□♇	♏	4	**7:22 am**	4:22 am
6	**6:52 pm**	3:52 pm	⚹♇	♐	6	**7:34 pm**	4:34 pm
8		10:54 pm	□♆	♑	9	**5:38 am**	2:38 am
9	**1:54 am**		□♆	♑	9	**5:38 am**	2:38 am
11	**11:53 am**	8:53 am	☌♇	♒	11	**12:31 pm**	9:31 am
13	**10:11 am**	7:11 am	□♅	♓	13	**3:55 pm**	12:55 pm
15	**4:00 pm**	1:00 pm	⚹♇	♈	15	**4:34 pm**	1:34 pm
17	**3:26 pm**	12:26 pm	□♇	♉	17	**4:00 pm**	1:00 pm
19	**3:33 pm**	12:33 pm	△♇	♊	19	**4:07 pm**	1:07 pm

☽ Last Aspect day	ET	PT	asp	☽ Ingress sign	day	ET	PT
21	**5:00 pm**	2:00 pm	△☉	♋	21	**6:50 pm**	3:50 pm
23		9:47 pm	☍♇	♌	23		10:24 pm
24	**12:47 am**		☍♇	♌	24	**1:24 am**	
26	**4:04 am**	1:04 am	□♅	♍	26	**11:47 am**	8:47 am
28	**11:54 pm**	8:54 pm	△♇	♎	28		9:30 pm
28	**11:54 pm**	8:54 pm	△♇	♎	29	**12:30 am**	
31	**12:57 pm**	9:57 am	□♇	♏	31	**1:29 pm**	10:29 am

☽ Phases & Eclipses phase	day	ET	PT
New Moon	2	**2:49 pm**	11:49 am
●	2	10° ♎ 04′	
2nd Quarter	10	**2:55 pm**	11:55 am
Full Moon	17	**7:26 am**	4:26 am
4th Quarter	24	**4:03 am**	1:03 am

Planet Ingress	day	ET	PT
☿ ♏	13	**3:23 pm**	12:23 pm
♀ ♐	17	**3:28 pm**	12:28 pm
☉ ♏	22	**6:15 pm**	3:15 pm
⚶ ♎	26		11:35 pm
⚶ ♎	27	**2:35 am**	

Planetary Motion	day	ET	PT
♃ ℞	9	**3:05 am**	12:05 am
♇ D	11	**8:34 pm**	5:34 pm

1 TUESDAY
☽ □ ♃ **12:30 am**
☽ △ ♅ **12:00 pm** 9:00 am
☽ ☍ ♆ **2:42 pm** 11:42 am
☽ △ ♇ **5:39 pm** 2:39 pm

2 WEDNESDAY
☽ ☌ ☉ **2:49 pm** 11:49 am
☽ ☌ ☿ **6:22 pm** 3:22 pm
☽ ⚺ ♀ **6:43 pm** 3:43 pm
☽ ⚻ ♄ **11:17 pm** 8:17 pm
☿ ⚺ ♀ 10:26 pm

3 THURSDAY
☿ ⚺ ♀ **1:26 am**
☽ □ ♂ **3:00 am** 12:00 am
☽ △ ♃ **1:40 pm** 10:40 am
☽ ⚻ ♅ 9:56 pm
☿ ⚻ ♄ 11:46 pm

4 FRIDAY
☽ ⚻ ♅ **12:56 am**
☿ ⚻ ♄ **2:46 am**
☿ ⚻ ♆ **3:37 am** 12:37 am
☽ □ ♇ **6:40 am** 3:40 am
♀ △ ♄ **1:04 pm** 10:04 am

5 SATURDAY
☽ ⚺ ☉ **9:13 am** 6:13 am
☽ △ ♄ **11:46 am** 8:46 am
☽ ☌ ♀ **2:28 pm** 11:28 am
☽ ⚺ ☿ **5:30 pm** 2:30 pm

☽ △ ♂ **6:27 pm** 3:27 pm
☽ ⚻ ♃ 11:19 pm
☿ □ ♂ 11:37 pm

6 SUNDAY
☽ ⚻ ♃ **2:19 am**
☿ □ ♂ **2:37 am**
☽ ☍ ♅ **1:09 pm** 10:09 am
☉ ⚻ ♄ **2:28 pm** 11:28 am
☽ △ ♆ **3:47 pm** 12:47 pm
☽ ⚹ ♇ **6:52 pm** 3:52 pm

7 MONDAY
☽ □ ♄ **10:50 pm** 7:50 pm
☽ ⚹ ☉ 10:49 pm

8 TUESDAY
☽ ⚹ ☉ **1:49 am**
♀ △ ♂ **6:22 am** 3:22 am
☽ ⚻ ♂ **8:02 am** 5:02 am
☽ ⚺ ♀ **8:09 am** 5:09 am
☿ △ ♃ **8:23 am** 5:23 am
☽ ☍ ♃ **1:10 pm** 10:10 am
☽ ⚹ ☿ **1:54 pm** 10:54 am
☽ ⚻ ♅ **11:23 pm** 8:23 pm
☽ □ ♆ 10:54 pm

9 WEDNESDAY
☽ □ ♆ **1:54 am**
☽ ⚺ ♇ **4:58 am** 1:58 am

10 THURSDAY
☽ ⚹ ♄ **7:16 am** 4:16 am
♀ ⚻ ♃ **11:44 am** 8:44 am

☽ □ ☉ **2:55 pm** 11:55 am
☽ ☍ ♂ **6:22 pm** 3:22 pm
☽ ⚻ ♃ **9:02 pm** 6:02 pm
☽ ⚹ ♀ **9:58 pm** 6:58 pm

11 FRIDAY
☽ □ ☿ **5:35 am** 2:35 am
☽ △ ♅ **6:31 am** 3:31 am
☽ ⚹ ♆ **8:54 am** 5:54 am
☽ ☌ ♇ **11:53 am** 8:53 am
☿ ⚻ ♅ **1:11 pm** 10:11 am

12 SATURDAY
☿ ⚻ ♆ **8:41 am** 5:41 am
☽ ⚺ ♄ **12:19 pm** 9:19 am
☽ △ ☉ **11:39 pm** 8:39 pm
☽ ⚻ ♂ 9:44 pm
☽ △ ♃ 10:22 pm

13 SUNDAY
☽ ⚻ ♂ **12:44 am**
☽ △ ♃ **1:22 am**
☽ □ ♀ **7:08 am** 4:08 am
☿ □ ♇ **10:03 am** 7:03 am
☽ □ ♅ **10:11 am** 7:11 am
☽ ⚺ ♆ **12:26 pm** 9:26 am
☽ ⚺ ♇ **3:19 pm** 12:19 pm
☽ △ ☿ **3:59 pm** 12:59 pm
♂ ⚺ ♃ **7:08 pm** 4:08 pm
☉ △ ♃ **11:52 pm** 8:52 pm

14 MONDAY
☉ □ ♂ **4:15 am** 1:15 am
☽ ☌ ♄ **2:09 pm** 11:09 am

♀ ☍ ♅ **6:22 pm** 3:22 pm
☽ □ ♃ 11:38 pm

15 TUESDAY
☽ □ ♃ **2:38 am**
☽ △ ♂ **3:41 am** 12:41 am
☽ ⚻ ☉ **4:34 am** 1:34 am
☽ ⚹ ♅ **10:59 am** 7:59 am
☽ △ ♀ **12:28 pm** 9:28 am
☽ ☌ ♆ **1:09 pm** 10:09 am
☽ ⚹ ♇ **4:00 pm** 1:00 pm
♀ △ ♆ **8:49 pm** 5:49 pm
☽ ⚻ ☿ **10:22 pm** 7:22 pm

16 WEDNESDAY
☽ ⚺ ♄ **1:52 pm** 10:52 am
☽ ⚹ ♃ 11:09 pm

17 THURSDAY
☽ ⚹ ♃ **2:09 am**
☽ □ ♂ **4:44 am** 1:44 am
☽ ☍ ☉ **7:26 am** 4:26 am
♀ ⚹ ♇ **8:30 am** 5:30 am
☽ ⚺ ♅ **10:21 am** 7:21 am
☽ ⚺ ♆ **12:32 pm** 9:32 am
☽ □ ♇ **3:26 pm** 12:26 pm
☽ ⚻ ♀ **4:02 pm** 1:02 pm

18 FRIDAY
☽ ☍ ☿ **3:15 am** 12:15 am
☽ ⚹ ♄ **1:13 pm** 10:13 am
☽ ⚺ ♃ 10:46 pm
☉ ⚻ ♅ 11:40 pm

19 SATURDAY
☽ ⚺ ♃ **1:46 am**
☉ ⚻ ♅ **2:40 am**
☽ ⚹ ♂ **6:00 am** 3:00 am
☽ ⚼ ♅ **10:11 am** 7:11 am
☽ ⚻ ☉ **10:44 am** 7:44 am
☽ ⚹ ♆ **12:28 pm** 9:28 am
☽ △ ♇ **3:33 pm** 12:33 pm
☽ ☍ ♀ **8:30 pm** 5:30 pm

20 SUNDAY
☽ ⚻ ☿ **9:39 am** 6:39 am
☉ ⚻ ♆ **11:44 am** 8:44 am
☽ □ ♄ **2:07 pm** 11:07 am

21 MONDAY
☽ ⚼ ♃ **3:25 am** 12:25 am
☽ ⚺ ♂ **9:39 am** 6:39 am
☽ ⚺ ♅ **12:22 pm** 9:22 am
☽ □ ♆ **2:50 pm** 11:50 am
☽ △ ☉ **5:00 pm** 2:00 pm
☽ ⚻ ♇ **6:15 pm** 3:15 pm
☿ △ ♄ 11:35 pm

22 TUESDAY
☿ △ ♄ **2:35 am**
☽ ⚻ ♀ **4:30 am** 1:30 am
☉ □ ♇ **10:15 am** 7:15 am
☽ △ ♄ **6:17 pm** 3:17 pm
☽ △ ☿ **8:22 pm** 5:22 pm

23 WEDNESDAY
☽ ⚺ ♃ **8:36 am** 5:36 am
☽ ⚼ ♂ **5:20 pm** 2:20 pm
☽ ⚹ ♅ **6:16 pm** 3:16 pm

☽ △ ♆ **9:00 pm** 6:00 pm
☽ ☍ ♇ 9:47 pm

24 THURSDAY
☽ ☍ ♇ **12:47 am**
☽ □ ☉ **4:03 am** 1:03 am
☽ △ ♀ **5:43 pm** 2:43 pm
♂ ⚹ ♅ **8:13 pm** 5:13 pm
☽ ⚻ ♄ 11:27 pm

25 FRIDAY
☽ ⚻ ♄ **2:27 am**
☽ □ ☿ **12:41 pm** 9:41 am
☽ ⚹ ♃ **5:42 pm** 2:42 pm

26 SATURDAY
☽ □ ♅ **4:04 am** 1:04 am
☽ ⚺ ♂ **5:16 am** 2:16 am
☽ ⚻ ♆ **7:02 am** 4:02 am
☽ ⚻ ♇ **11:11 am** 8:11 am
☽ ⚹ ☉ **7:54 pm** 4:54 pm

27 SUNDAY
☿ ⚻ ♃ **4:50 am** 1:50 am
☽ □ ♀ **11:39 am** 8:39 am
☽ ☍ ♄ **1:56 pm** 10:56 am

28 MONDAY
☽ □ ♃ **5:37 am** 2:37 am
♂ △ ♆ **8:31 am** 5:31 am
☽ ⚹ ☿ **9:16 am** 6:16 am
♀ □ ♄ **9:35 am** 6:35 am
☽ △ ♅ **4:23 pm** 1:23 pm
☽ ☍ ♆ **7:31 pm** 4:31 pm

☽ ⚹ ♂ **7:55 pm** 4:55 pm
☽ △ ♇ **11:54 pm** 8:54 pm

29 TUESDAY
☽ ⚺ ☉ **2:24 pm** 11:24 am
☽ ⚻ ♄ 11:50 pm

30 WEDNESDAY
☽ ⚻ ♄ **2:50 am**
☽ ⚹ ♀ **7:39 am** 4:39 am
☿ ☍ ♅ **6:15 pm** 3:15 pm
☽ △ ♃ **6:22 pm** 3:22 pm

31 THURSDAY
☽ ⚻ ♅ **5:15 am** 2:15 am
☽ ⚺ ☿ **6:47 am** 3:47 am
☽ ⚻ ♆ **8:27 am** 5:27 am
☽ □ ♂ **10:57 am** 7:57 am
☽ □ ♇ **12:57 pm** 9:57 am
☿ △ ♆ **8:33 pm** 5:33 pm

Eastern time in bold type
Pacific time in medium type

OCTOBER 2024

DATE	SID. TIME	SUN	MOON	NODE	MERCURY	VENUS	MARS	JUPITER	SATURN	URANUS	NEPTUNE	PLUTO	CERES	PALLAS	JUNO	VESTA	CHIRON
1 T	0 40 53	8≏18 28	19♍01	6Υ39	8≏24	9♍36	14♋51	21Ⅱ13	14♓22R	26♉54R	28♓14R	29♑40R	10♑57	7♐10	18≏11	17♍33	21Υ50R
2 W	0 44 49	9 17 30	0≏49	6 39R	10 10	10 49	15 22	21 15	14 18	26 53	28 13	29 40	11 08	7 30	18 33	18 01	21 47
3 Th	0 48 46	10 16 33	12 36	6 39	11 55	12 02	15 53	21 16	14 14	26 52	28 11	29 40	11 20	7 51	18 54	18 30	21 45
4 F	0 52 42	11 15 39	24 24	6 39	13 39	13 15	16 24	21 17	14 10	26 50	28 10	29 39	11 31	8 11	19 15	18 58	21 42
5 Sa	0 56 39	12 14 46	6♏14	6 38	15 23	14 28	16 55	21 18	14 06	26 48	28 08	29 39	11 42	8 32	19 37	19 27	21 39
6 Su	1 0 35	13 13 56	18 10	6 37	17 06	15 41	17 25	21 19	14 02	26 47	28 06	29 39	11 54	8 53	19 58	19 55	21 37
7 M	1 4 32	14 13 07	0♐13	6 36	18 47	16 54	17 56	21 20	13 59	26 45	28 05	29 39	12 07	9 14	20 19	20 24	21 34
8 T	1 8 28	15 12 21	12 27	6 35	20 28	18 07	18 25	21 20	13 55	26 43	28 03	29 39	12 19	9 35	20 41	20 52	21 31
9 W	1 12 25	16 11 36	24 55	6 34	22 09	19 20	18 55	21 20R	13 52	26 42	28 02	29 39	12 32	9 56	21 02	21 21	21 28
10 Th	1 16 22	17 10 53	7♑40	6 34D	23 48	20 32	19 24	21 20	13 48	26 40	28 00	29 39D	12 45	10 17	21 24	21 49	21 26
11 F	1 20 18	18 10 12	20 46	6 34	25 27	21 45	19 53	21 20	13 45	26 38	27 59	29 39	12 58	10 39	21 45	22 18	21 23
12 Sa	1 24 15	19 09 32	4≈15	6 34	27 05	22 58	20 22	21 20	13 41	26 36	27 57	29 39	13 11	11 00	22 06	22 46	21 20
13 Su	1 28 11	20 08 54	18 09	6 35	28 42	24 11	20 51	21 19	13 38	26 35	27 56	29 39	13 25	11 22	22 28	23 15	21 17
14 M	1 32 8	21 08 18	2♓28	6 36	0♏18	25 23	21 19	21 18	13 35	26 33	27 54	29 39	13 38	11 43	22 49	23 43	21 15
15 T	1 36 4	22 07 44	17 10	6 37	1 54	26 36	21 47	21 17	13 32	26 31	27 53	29 39	13 52	12 05	23 10	24 12	21 12
16 W	1 40 1	23 07 11	2Υ09	6 38R	3 29	27 49	22 15	21 16	13 29	26 29	27 51	29 39	14 07	12 26	23 32	24 40	21 09
17 Th	1 43 57	24 06 41	17 20	6 37	5 04	29 02	22 42	21 14	13 26	26 27	27 50	29 39	14 21	12 48	23 53	25 09	21 06
18 F	1 47 54	25 06 12	2♉32	6 36	6 38	0♐14	23 09	21 13	13 23	26 25	27 48	29 39	14 35	13 10	24 14	25 37	21 03
19 Sa	1 51 51	26 05 46	17 35	6 34	8 11	1 26	23 36	21 11	13 20	26 23	27 47	29 39	14 50	13 32	24 35	26 05	21 01
20 Su	1 55 47	27 05 21	2Ⅱ22	6 32	9 44	2 39	24 02	21 09	13 18	26 21	27 45	29 40	15 05	13 54	24 57	26 34	20 58
21 M	1 59 44	28 04 59	16 45	6 29	11 16	3 51	24 29	21 07	13 15	26 19	27 44	29 40	15 20	14 16	25 18	27 02	20 56
22 T	2 3 40	29 04 40	0♋40	6 26	12 47	5 04	24 54	21 04	13 13	26 17	27 43	29 40	15 35	14 38	25 39	27 31	20 53
23 W	2 7 37	0♏04 22	14 07	6 24	14 18	6 16	25 20	21 01	13 10	26 14	27 40	29 40	15 51	15 00	26 01	27 59	20 50
24 Th	2 11 33	1 04 07	27 08	6 23D	15 48	7 28	25 45	20 59	13 08	26 12	27 40	29 41	16 06	15 22	26 22	28 27	20 47
25 F	2 15 30	2 03 54	9♌45	6 23	17 18	8 41	26 10	20 56	13 06	26 10	27 39	29 41	16 22	15 45	26 43	28 56	20 45
26 Sa	2 19 26	3 03 43	22 03	6 24	18 47	9 53	26 34	20 52	13 04	26 08	27 37	29 41	16 38	16 07	27 04	29 24	20 42
27 Su	2 23 23	4 03 34	4♍06	6 26	20 15	11 05	26 58	20 49	13 01	26 06	27 36	29 42	16 54	16 30	27 25	29 52	20 39
28 M	2 27 20	5 03 28	16 00	6 28	21 43	12 18	27 22	20 45	13 00	26 03	27 35	29 42	17 11	16 52	27 46	0≏21	20 37
29 T	2 31 16	6 03 21	27 48	6 29R	23 10	13 30	27 45	20 42	12 58	26 01	27 34	29 43	17 27	17 15	28 07	0 49	20 34
30 W	2 35 13	7 03 21	9≏34	6 28	24 37	14 42	28 08	20 38	12 56	25 59	27 32	29 43	17 44	17 37	28 28	1 17	20 31
31 Th	2 39 9	8 03 20	21 22	6 28	26 03	15 54	28 31	20 34	12 54	25 56	27 31	29 44	18 01	18 00	28 49	1 45	20 29

EPHEMERIS CALCULATED FOR 12 MIDNIGHT GREENWICH MEAN TIME. ALL OTHER DATA AND FACING ASPECTARIAN PAGE IN **EASTERN TIME (BOLD)** AND PACIFIC TIME (REGULAR).

NOVEMBER 2024

☽ Last Aspect day	ET / hr:mn / PT	asp	☽ Ingress sign	day	ET / hr:mn / PT
2	9:51 pm	⚹♇	♐	2	10:19 pm
3	**12:51 am**	⚹♇	♐	3	**1:19 am**
5	**5:23 am** 2:23 am	□♆	♑	5	**10:17 am** 7:17 am
7	**5:38 pm** 2:38 pm	☌♇	♒	7	**5:58 pm** 2:58 pm
9	**7:23 pm** 4:23 pm	⚹♀	♓	9	**11:00 pm** 8:00 pm
11	10:13 pm	⚹♇	♈	11	10:26 pm
12	**1:13 am**	⚹♇	♈	12	**1:26 am**
13	10:50 pm	□♇	♉	13	10:59 pm
14	**1:50 am**	□♇	♉	14	**1:59 am**
15	11:03 pm	△♇	♊	15	11:09 pm
16	**2:03 am**	△♇	♊	16	**2:09 am**
17	**11:09 pm** 8:09 pm	□♆	♋	18	**3:50 am** 12:50 am
20	**6:20 am** 3:20 am	△☉	♌	20	**8:51 am** 5:51 am
22	**8:15 am** 5:15 am	□♅	♍	22	**6:01 pm** 3:01 pm
24	9:35 pm	☍♆	♎	25	**6:20 am** 3:20 am
25	**12:35 am**	☍♆	♎	25	**6:20 am** 3:20 am
27	**4:14 am** 1:14 am	⚹☿	♏	27	**7:21 pm** 4:21 pm
29	10:19 pm	△♆	♐	30	**6:53 am** 3:53 am
30	**1:19 am**	△♆	♐	30	**6:53 am** 3:53 am

☽ Phases & Eclipses phase	day	ET / hr:mn / PT
New Moon	1	**8:47 am** 5:47 am
2nd Quarter	8	9:55 pm
2nd Quarter	9	**12:55 am**
Full Moon	15	**4:28 pm** 1:28 pm
4th Quarter	22	**8:28 pm** 5:28 pm
New Moon	30	10:21 pm
New Moon	12/1	**1:21 am**

Planet Ingress		day	ET / hr:mn / PT
☿	♐	2	**3:18 pm** 12:18 pm
✱	♏	3	**3:35 am** 1:35 am
♂	♌	3	**11:10 pm** 8:10 pm
♀	♑	11	**1:26 pm** 10:26 am
♇	♒	19	**3:29 pm** 12:29 pm
☉	♐	21	**2:56 pm** 11:56 am
♀	♑	30	**5:37 pm** 2:37 pm

Planetary Motion		day	ET / hr:mn / PT
♄	D	15	**9:20 am** 6:20 am
☿	℞	25	**9:42 pm** 6:42 pm

1 FRIDAY
☽ ☌ ☉ **8:47 am** 5:47 am
☽ △ ♄ **3:20 pm** 12:20 pm
☽ ⚺ ♀ 11:53 pm

2 SATURDAY
☽ ⚺ ♀ **2:53 am**
☿ △ ♂ **4:21 am** 1:21 am
☽ ⚻ ♃ **6:18 am** 3:18 am
☿ ⚹ ♇ **11:03 am** 8:03 am
☽ ☍ ♅ **5:06 pm** 2:06 pm
☽ △ ♆ **8:20 pm** 5:20 pm
☽ △ ♂ 9:40 pm
☽ ⚹ ♇ 9:51 pm
☽ ☌ ☿ 11:37 pm

3 SUNDAY
☽ △ ♂ **12:40 am**
☽ ⚹ ♇ **12:51 am**
☽ ☌ ☿ **1:37 am**
♂ ☍ ♇ **6:37 am** 3:37 am
♀ ☍ ♃ **10:25 am** 7:25 am
☽ ⚺ ☉ 9:18 pm
☽ □ ♄ 10:19 pm

4 MONDAY
☽ ⚺ ☉ **12:18 am**
☽ □ ♄ **1:19 am**
☉ △ ♄ **12:36 pm** 9:36 am
☽ ☍ ♃ **3:32 pm** 12:32 pm
☽ ☌ ♀ **6:51 pm** 3:51 pm
☽ ⚻ ♅ 11:10 pm

5 TUESDAY
☽ ⚻ ♅ **2:10 am**
☽ □ ♆ **5:23 am** 2:23 am
☽ ⚺ ♇ **9:53 am** 6:53 am
☽ ⚻ ♂ **11:15 am** 8:15 am
☽ ⚺ ☿ **6:30 pm** 3:30 pm

6 WEDNESDAY
☽ ⚹ ♄ **10:17 am** 7:17 am
☽ ⚹ ☉ **2:11 pm** 11:11 am
☽ ⚻ ♃ **11:38 pm** 8:38 pm

7 THURSDAY
☽ ⚺ ♀ **8:51 am** 5:51 am
☽ △ ♅ **10:01 am** 7:01 am
☽ ⚹ ♆ **1:12 pm** 10:12 am
☽ ☌ ♇ **5:38 pm** 2:38 pm
☽ ☍ ♂ **8:15 pm** 5:15 pm
♀ ⚻ ♅ **9:20 pm** 6:20 pm

8 FRIDAY
☽ ⚹ ☿ **7:52 am** 4:52 am
☽ ⚺ ♄ **4:48 pm** 1:48 pm
☽ □ ☉ 9:55 pm

9 SATURDAY
☽ □ ☉ **12:55 am**
☽ △ ♃ **5:12 am** 2:12 am
♀ □ ♆ **8:15 am** 5:15 am
☽ □ ♅ **3:17 pm** 12:17 pm
☽ ⚺ ♆ **6:25 pm** 3:25 pm
☽ ⚹ ♀ **7:23 pm** 4:23 pm

☽ ⚺ ♇ **10:44 pm** 7:44 pm
☽ ⚻ ♂ 11:21 pm

10 SUNDAY
☽ ⚻ ♂ **2:21 am**
☽ □ ☿ **5:20 pm** 2:20 pm
☽ ☌ ♄ **8:39 pm** 5:39 pm

11 MONDAY
☉ ⚻ ♃ **6:08 am** 3:08 am
☽ □ ♃ **8:07 am** 5:07 am
☽ △ ☉ **8:17 am** 5:17 am
♀ ⚺ ♇ **10:44 am** 7:44 am
☽ ⚹ ♅ **5:56 pm** 2:56 pm
☽ ☌ ♆ **9:01 pm** 6:01 pm
☽ ⚹ ♇ 10:13 pm
☽ □ ♀ 11:29 pm

12 TUESDAY
☽ ⚹ ♇ **1:13 am**
☽ □ ♀ **2:29 am**
☽ △ ♂ **5:37 am** 2:37 am
☿ □ ♄ **8:22 am** 5:22 am
☽ ⚺ ♄ **10:08 pm** 7:08 pm
☽ △ ☿ **11:19 pm** 8:19 pm

13 WEDNESDAY
☽ ⚹ ♃ **8:51 am** 5:51 am
☽ ⚻ ☉ **12:54 pm** 9:54 am
☽ ⚺ ♅ **6:34 pm** 3:34 pm
☽ ⚺ ♆ **9:38 pm** 6:38 pm
☽ □ ♇ 10:50 pm

14 THURSDAY
☽ □ ♇ **1:50 am**
♀ ⚻ ♂ **3:02 am** 12:02 am
☽ □ ♂ **6:57 am** 3:57 am
☽ △ ♀ **7:13 am** 4:13 am
☽ ⚹ ♄ **10:18 pm** 7:18 pm

15 FRIDAY
☽ ⚻ ☿ **3:20 am** 12:20 am
☽ ⚺ ♃ **8:36 am** 5:36 am
☽ ☍ ☉ **4:28 pm** 1:28 pm
☽ ☌ ♅ **6:32 pm** 3:32 pm
☽ ⚹ ♆ **9:43 pm** 6:43 pm
☽ △ ♇ 11:03 pm

16 SATURDAY
☽ △ ♇ **2:03 am**
☽ ⚹ ♂ **8:00 am** 5:00 am
☽ ⚻ ♀ **11:41 am** 8:41 am
☉ ☍ ♅ **9:45 pm** 6:45 pm
☽ □ ♄ **10:52 pm** 7:52 pm

17 SUNDAY
☽ ☍ ☿ **7:41 am** 4:41 am
☽ ☌ ♃ **9:07 am** 6:07 am
☽ ⚺ ♅ **7:42 pm** 4:42 pm
☽ ⚻ ☉ **9:27 pm** 6:27 pm
☽ □ ♆ **11:09 pm** 8:09 pm

18 MONDAY
☽ ⚻ ♇ **3:47 am** 12:47 am
☿ ☍ ♃ **3:55 am** 12:55 am
☽ ⚺ ♂ **10:49 am** 7:49 am
☽ ☍ ♀ **6:35 pm** 3:35 pm

☉ △ ♆ **9:07 pm** 6:07 pm
☽ △ ♄ 10:48 pm

19 TUESDAY
☽ △ ♄ **1:48 am**
☽ ⚺ ♃ **12:17 pm** 9:17 am
☽ ⚻ ☿ **2:43 pm** 11:43 am
☽ ⚹ ♅ **11:56 pm** 8:56 pm

20 WEDNESDAY
☽ △ ♆ **3:46 am** 12:46 am
☽ △ ☉ **6:20 am** 3:20 am
☽ ☍ ♇ **8:52 am** 5:52 am
☽ ⚺ ♂ **5:15 pm** 2:15 pm

21 THURSDAY
☽ ⚻ ♀ **6:20 am** 3:20 am
☽ ⚻ ♄ **8:36 am** 5:36 am
☉ ⚹ ♇ **3:49 pm** 12:49 pm
☽ ⚹ ♃ **7:21 pm** 4:21 pm
☽ △ ☿ 10:36 pm

22 FRIDAY
☽ △ ☿ **1:36 am**
♀ ⚹ ♄ **6:55 am** 3:55 am
☽ □ ♅ **8:15 am** 5:15 am
☽ ⚻ ♆ **12:31 pm** 9:31 am
☽ ⚻ ♇ **6:08 pm** 3:08 pm
☽ □ ☉ **8:28 pm** 5:28 pm

23 SATURDAY
☽ ⚺ ♂ **3:53 am** 12:53 am
☽ ☍ ♄ **7:24 pm** 4:24 pm
☽ △ ♀ **11:21 pm** 8:21 pm

24 SUNDAY
☽ □ ♃ **6:04 am** 3:04 am
☽ □ ☿ **3:10 pm** 12:10 pm
☽ △ ♅ **7:59 pm** 4:59 pm
☽ ☍ ♆ 9:35 pm

25 MONDAY
☽ ☍ ♆ **12:35 am**
☽ △ ♇ **6:33 am** 3:33 am
☽ ⚹ ☉ **2:32 pm** 11:32 am
☽ ⚹ ♂ **5:18 pm** 2:18 pm

26 TUESDAY
☽ ⚻ ♄ **8:25 am** 5:25 am
♀ ⚻ ♃ **1:08 pm** 10:08 am
☽ △ ♃ **6:27 pm** 3:27 pm
☽ □ ♀ **7:06 pm** 4:06 pm

27 WEDNESDAY
☉ △ ♂ **3:06 am** 12:06 am
☽ ⚹ ☿ **4:14 am** 1:14 am
☽ ⚻ ♅ **8:51 am** 5:51 am
☽ ⚻ ♆ **1:36 pm** 10:36 am
☽ □ ♇ **7:40 pm** 4:40 pm

28 THURSDAY
☽ □ ♂ **6:49 am** 3:49 am
☽ ⚺ ☉ **9:05 am** 6:05 am
☽ △ ♄ **9:07 pm** 6:07 pm

29 FRIDAY
☽ ⚻ ♃ **6:08 am** 3:08 am
☽ ⚹ ♀ **1:51 pm** 10:51 am
☽ ⚺ ☿ **2:13 pm** 11:13 am
☿ ⚺ ♀ **4:26 pm** 1:26 pm

☽ ☍ ♅ **8:32 pm** 5:32 pm
☽ △ ♆ 10:19 pm

30 SATURDAY
☽ △ ♆ **1:19 am**
☽ ⚹ ♇ **7:18 am** 4:18 am
☽ △ ♂ **6:23 pm** 3:23 pm
☽ ☌ ☉ 10:21 pm

Eastern time in bold type
Pacific time in medium type

NOVEMBER 2024

DATE	SID. TIME	SUN	MOON	NODE	MERCURY	VENUS	MARS	JUPITER	SATURN	URANUS	NEPTUNE	PLUTO	CERES	PALLAS	JUNO	VESTA	CHIRON
1 F	2 43 6	9♏03 22	3♏14	6♈26R	27♏28	17♐06	28♋53	20Ⅱ29R	12♓53R	25♉54R	27♓30R	29♑44	18♑18	18♏23	29♍10	2♎13	20♈26R
2 Sa	2 47 2	10 03 26	15 12	6 21	28 53	18 18	29 14	20 24	12 51	25 52	27 29	29 45	18 35	18 45	29 32	2 41	20 24
3 Su	2 50 59	11 03 31	27 18	6 15	0♐16	19 30	29 36	20 20	12 50	25 49	27 28	29 45	18 52	19 08	29 53	3 10	20 21
4 M	2 54 55	12 03 39	9♐33	6 09	1 39	20 42	29 56	20 15	12 49	25 47	27 27	29 46	19 09	19 31	0♎13	3 38	20 19
5 T	2 58 52	13 03 48	21 59	6 02	3 01	21 54	0♌17	20 10	12 47	25 44	27 26	29 47	19 27	19 54	0 34	4 06	20 16
6 W	3 2 49	14 03 58	4♑37	5 56	4 22	23 06	0 37	20 05	12 46	25 42	27 25	29 47	19 45	20 17	0 55	4 34	20 14
7 Th	3 6 45	15 04 11	17 28	5 51	5 42	24 18	0 56	20 00	12 45	25 40	27 24	29 48	20 02	20 40	1 16	5 02	20 11
8 F	3 10 42	16 04 25	0≈34	5 48	7 01	25 30	1 15	19 54	12 45	25 37	27 23	29 49	20 20	21 03	1 37	5 30	20 09
9 Sa	3 14 38	17 04 40	13 58	5 47D	8 19	26 42	1 34	19 48	12 44	25 35	27 22	29 50	20 38	21 26	1 58	5 58	20 07
10 Su	3 18 35	18 04 57	27 41	5 47	9 35	27 53	1 51	19 42	12 43	25 32	27 21	29 51	20 57	21 49	2 19	6 26	20 04
11 M	3 22 31	19 05 15	11♓44	5 48	10 50	29 05	2 09	19 36	12 43	25 30	27 20	29 51	21 15	22 12	2 39	6 53	20 02
12 T	3 26 28	20 05 34	26 06	5 50R	12 02	0♑18	2 26	19 30	12 42	25 27	27 19	29 52	21 34	22 35	3 00	7 21	19♈57
13 W	3 30 24	21 05 55	10♈46	5 50	13 13	1 28	2 42	19 24	12 42	25 25	27 18	29 52	21 52	22 59	3 21	7 49	19 55
14 Th	3 34 21	22 06 17	25 39	5 50R	14 22	2 40	2 58	19 17	12 42D	25 22	27 18	29 53	22 11	23 22	3 41	8 17	19 53
15 F	3 38 18	23 06 41	10♉38	5 48	15 28	3 51	3 14	19 11	12 42	25 20	27 17	29 54	22 30	23 45	4 02	8 45	19 51
16 Sa	3 42 14	24 07 07	25 35	5 44	16 31	5 02	3 28	19 04	12 42	25 17	27 16	29 55	22 49	24 09	4 22	9 12	19 49
17 Su	3 46 11	25 07 34	10Ⅱ21	5 38	17 31	6 14	3 43	18 57	12 42	25 15	27 15	29 57	23 08	24 32	4 43	9 40	19 46
18 M	3 50 7	26 08 03	24 47	5 31	18 28	7 25	3 56	18 50	12 42	25 12	27 15	29 58	23 27	24 55	5 03	10 07	19 44
19 T	3 54 4	27 08 33	8♋49	5 22	19 20	8 36	4 10	18 43	12 42	25 10	27 14	29 59	23 46	25 19	5 23	10 35	19 42
20 W	3 58 0	28 09 05	22 23	5 14	20 08	9 47	4 22	18 36	12 43	25 07	27 13	0≈00	24 06	25 42	5 44	11 02	19 40
21 Th	4 1 57	29 09 39	5♌29	5 07	20 50	10 58	4 34	18 28	12 43	25 05	27 13	0 01	24 25	26 06	6 04	11 30	19 38
22 F	4 5 53	0♐10 15	18 10	5 02	21 27	12 09	4 45	18 21	12 44	25 02	27 12	0 02	24 45	26 29	6 25	11 57	19 37
23 Sa	4 9 50	1 10 52	0♍30	4 59	21 57	13 20	4 56	18 14	12 44	25 00	27 12	0 04	25 05	26 53	6 45	12 24	19 35
24 Su	4 13 47	2 11 31	12 33	4 59D	22 20	14 30	5 06	18 06	12 45	24 57	27 11	0 05	25 25	27 16	7 05	12 52	19 33
25 M	4 17 43	3 12 12	24 26	4 59	22 34	15 41	5 15	17 59	12 46	24 55	27 11	0 06	25 45	27 40	7 25	13 19	19 31
26 T	4 21 40	4 12 54	6♎13	5 00R	22 40R	16 52	5 24	17 51	12 47	24 52	27 10	0 07	26 05	28 03	7 45	13 46	19 29
27 W	4 25 36	5 13 38	17 59	5 00	22 36	18 02	5 32	17 43	12 48	24 50	27 10	0 08	26 25	28 27	8 05	14 13	19 28
28 Th	4 29 33	6 14 23	29 50	4 56	22 22	19 13	5 39	17 35	12 50	24 47	27 10	0 10	26 45	28 50	8 25	14 40	19 26
29 F	4 33 29	7 15 10	11♏48	4 56	21 57	20 23	5 45	17 27	12 51	24 45	27 09	0 11	27 06	29 14	8 45	15 07	19 26
30 Sa	4 37 26	8 15 58	23 55	4 42	21 21	21 33	5 51	17 19	12 53	24 43	27 09	0 12	27 26	29 38	9 05	15 34	19 24

EPHEMERIS CALCULATED FOR 12 MIDNIGHT GREENWICH MEAN TIME. ALL OTHER DATA AND FACING ASPECTARIAN PAGE IN **EASTERN TIME (BOLD)** AND PACIFIC TIME (REGULAR).

DECEMBER 2024

☽ Last Aspect day	ET / hr:mn / PT		asp	☽ Ingress sign	day	ET / hr:mn / PT	
2	**10:47 am**	7:47 am	□♆	♑	2	**4:09 pm**	1:09 pm
4	**6:34 pm**	3:34 pm	☌♀	♒	4	**11:21 pm**	8:21 pm
6	**7:01 pm**	4:01 pm	□♅	♓	7	**4:49 am**	1:49 am
9	**3:45 am**	12:45 am	☌♆	♈	9	**8:38 am**	5:38 am
10	**5:13 pm**	2:13 pm	△☉	♉	11	**10:55 am**	7:55 am
13	**7:39 am**	4:39 am	⚹♆	♊	13	**12:22 pm**	9:22 am
15	**9:32 am**	6:32 am	□♆	♋	15	**2:21 pm**	11:21 am
17	**1:33 pm**	10:33 am	△♆	♌	17	**6:39 pm**	3:39 pm
19		9:19 pm	△☉	♍	19		11:37 pm
20	**12:19 am**		△☉	♍	20	**2:37 am**	
22	**8:27 am**	5:27 am	☍♆	♎	22	**2:08 pm**	11:08 am
24	**5:44 am**	2:44 am	△♀	♏	25	**3:06 am**	12:06 am
27	**9:24 am**	6:24 am	△♆	♐	27	**2:46 pm**	11:46 am
29	**6:34 pm**	3:34 pm	□♆	♑	29	**11:37 pm**	8:37 pm
31		10:02 pm	⚹♆	♒	1/1	**5:50 am**	2:50 am
1/1	**1:02 am**		⚹♆	♒	1/1	**5:50 am**	2:50 am

☽ Phases & Eclipses phase	day	ET / hr:mn / PT	
New Moon	11/30		10:21 pm
New Moon	1	**1:21 am**	
2nd Quarter	8	**10:27 am**	7:27 am
Full Moon	15	**4:02 am**	1:02 am
4th Quarter	22	**5:18 pm**	2:18 pm
New Moon	30	**5:27 pm**	2:27 pm

Planet Ingress		day	ET / hr:mn / PT	
♀	♒	6		10:13 pm
♀	♒	7	**1:13 am**	
⚳	♒	7	**4:16 am**	1:16 am
☉	♑	21	**4:21 am**	1:21 am

Planetary Motion		day	ET / hr:mn / PT	
♂	℞	6	**6:33 pm**	3:33 pm
♆	D	7	**6:43 pm**	3:43 pm
☿	D	15	**3:56 am**	12:56 pm
⚷	D	29	**4:13 pm**	1:13 pm

1 SUNDAY
☽ ☌ ☉ **1:21 am**
☽ □ ♄ **7:49 am** 4:49 am
☽ ☍ ♃ **3:45 pm** 12:45 pm
☽ ☌ ☿ **8:29 pm** 5:29 pm

2 MONDAY
☽ ⚺ ♀ **5:39 am** 2:39 am
☽ ⚻ ♅ **6:02 am** 3:02 am
♀ △ ♅ **9:43 am** 6:43 am
☽ □ ♆ **10:47 am** 7:47 am
☽ ⚺ ♇ **4:39 pm** 1:39 pm

3 TUESDAY
☽ ⚻ ♂ **3:30 am** 12:30 am
☽ ⚺ ☉ **2:43 pm** 11:43 am
☽ ⚹ ♄ **4:17 pm** 1:17 pm
☽ ⚻ ♃ **11:13 pm** 8:13 pm
☽ ⚺ ☿ **11:43 pm** 8:43 pm

4 WEDNESDAY
☿ ☍ ♃ **5:16 am** 2:16 am
☉ □ ♄ **11:18 am** 8:18 am
☽ △ ♅ **1:24 pm** 10:24 am
♀ ⚹ ♆ **1:52 pm** 10:52 am
☽ ⚹ ♆ **6:09 pm** 3:09 pm
☽ ☌ ♀ **6:34 pm** 3:34 pm
☽ ☌ ♇ **11:56 pm** 8:56 pm

5 THURSDAY
☽ ☍ ♂ **10:28 am** 7:28 am
☉ ☌ ☿ **9:18 pm** 6:18 pm

☽ ⚺ ♄ **10:50 pm** 7:50 pm
☽ ⚹ ☿ 9:56 pm
☽ ⚹ ☉ 10:38 pm

6 FRIDAY
☽ ⚹ ☿ **12:56 am**
☽ ⚹ ☉ **1:38 am**
☽ △ ♃ **4:53 am** 1:53 am
☽ □ ♅ **7:01 pm** 4:01 pm
☿ □ ♄ **8:53 pm** 5:53 pm
☽ ⚺ ♆ **11:46 pm** 8:46 pm

7 SATURDAY
☽ ⚺ ♀ **5:09 am** 2:09 am
☽ ⚺ ♇ **5:29 am** 2:29 am
♀ ☌ ♇ **9:08 am** 6:08 am
☽ ⚻ ♂ **3:36 pm** 12:36 pm
☉ ☍ ♃ **3:58 pm** 12:58 pm
☽ □ ☿ 9:58 pm

8 SUNDAY
☽ □ ☿ **12:58 am**
☽ ☌ ♄ **3:43 am** 12:43 am
☽ □ ♃ **8:56 am** 5:56 am
☽ □ ☉ **10:27 am** 7:27 am
☽ ⚹ ♅ **11:00 pm** 8:00 pm

9 MONDAY
☽ ☌ ♆ **3:45 am** 12:45 am
☽ ⚹ ♇ **9:22 am** 6:22 am
☽ ⚹ ♀ **1:33 pm** 10:33 am
☽ △ ♂ **6:59 pm** 3:59 pm
☽ △ ☿ 9:19 pm

10 TUESDAY
☽ △ ☿ **12:19 am**
☽ ⚺ ♄ **6:59 am** 3:59 am
☽ ⚹ ♃ **11:24 am** 8:24 am
☽ △ ☉ **5:13 pm** 2:13 pm
☽ ⚺ ♅ 10:25 pm

11 WEDNESDAY
☽ ⚺ ♅ **1:25 am**
☽ ⚺ ♆ **6:10 am** 3:10 am
☽ □ ♇ **11:43 am** 8:43 am
☽ □ ♀ **8:01 pm** 5:01 pm
☽ □ ♂ **8:50 pm** 5:50 pm
☽ ⚻ ☿ **11:29 pm** 8:29 pm

12 THURSDAY
♀ ☍ ♂ **5:46 am** 2:46 am
☽ ⚹ ♄ **8:55 am** 5:55 am
☽ ⚺ ♃ **12:39 pm** 9:39 am
☽ ⚻ ☉ **10:34 pm** 7:34 pm
☿ ⚹ ♀ 11:45 pm
☽ ☌ ♅ 11:49 pm

13 FRIDAY
☿ ⚹ ♀ **2:45 am**
☽ ☌ ♅ **2:49 am**
☽ ⚹ ♆ **7:39 am** 4:39 am
☽ △ ♇ **1:15 pm** 10:15 am
☽ ⚹ ♂ **9:58 pm** 6:58 pm
☽ ☍ ☿ **11:20 pm** 8:20 pm
☽ △ ♀ 10:40 pm

14 SATURDAY
☽ △ ♀ **1:40 am**
☽ □ ♄ **10:34 am** 7:34 am
☽ ☌ ♃ **1:43 pm** 10:43 am

15 SUNDAY
☽ ☍ ☉ **4:02 am** 1:02 am
☽ ⚺ ♅ **4:27 am** 1:27 am
☽ □ ♆ **9:32 am** 6:32 am
☉ ⚻ ♅ **9:44 am** 6:44 am
☽ ⚻ ♇ **3:22 pm** 12:22 pm
☽ ⚺ ♂ **11:52 pm** 8:52 pm
☽ ⚻ ☿ 10:16 pm

16 MONDAY
☽ ⚻ ☿ **1:16 am**
☽ ⚻ ♀ **8:34 am** 5:34 am
☽ △ ♄ **1:34 pm** 10:34 am
☽ ⚺ ♃ **4:11 pm** 1:11 pm

17 TUESDAY
☽ ⚹ ♅ **8:02 am** 5:02 am
☽ ⚻ ☉ **11:56 am** 8:56 am
☽ △ ♆ **1:33 pm** 10:33 am
☽ ☍ ♇ **7:50 pm** 4:50 pm

18 WEDNESDAY
☽ ☌ ♂ **4:13 am** 1:13 am
☽ △ ☿ **7:15 am** 4:15 am
☉ □ ♆ **9:29 am** 6:29 am
☽ ☍ ♀ **7:10 pm** 4:10 pm
☽ ⚻ ♄ **7:39 pm** 4:39 pm
☽ ⚹ ♃ **9:40 pm** 6:40 pm
♀ ⚺ ♄ 9:52 pm

19 THURSDAY
♀ ⚺ ♄ **12:52 am**
☽ □ ♅ **3:04 pm** 12:04 pm
☽ ⚻ ♆ **9:10 pm** 6:10 pm
♀ △ ♃ **9:11 pm** 6:11 pm
☽ △ ☉ 9:19 pm

20 FRIDAY
☽ △ ☉ **12:19 am**
☽ ⚻ ♇ **4:01 am** 1:01 am
☽ ⚺ ♂ **12:05 pm** 9:05 am
☽ □ ☿ **6:46 pm** 3:46 pm

21 SATURDAY
☽ ☍ ♄ **5:39 am** 2:39 am
☽ □ ♃ **6:55 am** 3:55 am
☽ ⚻ ♀ **10:45 am** 7:45 am
☉ ⚺ ♇ **10:32 pm** 7:32 pm
☽ △ ♅ 10:50 pm

22 SUNDAY
☽ △ ♅ **1:50 am**
☽ ☍ ♆ **8:27 am** 5:27 am
☽ △ ♇ **3:44 pm** 12:44 pm
☽ □ ☉ **5:18 pm** 2:18 pm
☽ ⚹ ♂ **10:59 pm** 7:59 pm

23 Monday
☽ ⚹ ☿ **11:22 am** 8:22 am
☽ ⚻ ♄ **6:30 pm** 3:30 pm
☽ △ ♃ **6:51 pm** 3:51 pm

24 TUESDAY
☽ △ ♀ **5:44 am** 2:44 am
☽ ⚻ ♅ **2:35 pm** 11:35 am

♃ □ ♄ **4:59 pm** 1:59 pm
☽ ⚻ ♆ **9:28 pm** 6:28 pm
☉ ⚻ ♂ 9:00 pm

25 WEDNESDAY
☉ ⚻ ♂ **12:00 am**
☽ □ ♇ **4:51 am** 1:51 am
☽ □ ♂ **10:44 am** 7:44 am
☽ ⚹ ☉ **12:00 pm** 9:00 am

26 THURSDAY
☽ ⚺ ☿ **5:43 am** 2:43 am
☽ ⚻ ♃ **6:55 am** 3:55 am
☽ △ ♄ **7:31 am** 4:31 am
☿ ☍ ♃ **5:48 pm** 2:48 pm
☽ □ ♀ 9:08 pm
☿ □ ♄ 11:29 pm
☽ ☍ ♅ 11:34 pm

27 FRIDAY
☽ □ ♀ **12:08 am**
☿ □ ♄ **2:29 am**
☽ ☍ ♅ **2:34 am**
☽ △ ♆ **9:24 am** 6:24 am
☽ ⚹ ♇ **4:36 pm** 1:36 pm
☽ △ ♂ **8:50 pm** 5:50 pm
♀ □ ♅ 11:42 pm

28 SATURDAY
♀ □ ♅ **2:42 am**
☽ ⚺ ☉ **4:35 am** 1:35 am
☽ ☍ ♃ **4:50 pm** 1:50 pm
☽ □ ♄ **6:15 pm** 3:15 pm
☽ ☌ ☿ **10:01 pm** 7:01 pm

29 SUNDAY
☽ ⚻ ♅ **11:55 am** 8:55 am
☽ ⚹ ♀ **3:03 pm** 12:03 pm
☽ □ ♆ **6:34 pm** 3:34 pm
☽ ⚺ ♇ 10:29 pm

30 MONDAY
☽ ⚺ ♇ **1:29 am**
☽ ⚻ ♂ **4:07 am** 1:07 am
☽ ☌ ☉ **5:27 pm** 2:27 pm
☽ ⚻ ♃ **11:56 pm** 8:56 pm
☽ ⚹ ♄ 11:03 pm

31 TUESDAY
☽ ⚹ ♄ **2:03 am**
♀ ⚺ ♆ **9:38 am** 6:38 am
☽ ⚺ ☿ **11:00 am** 8:00 am
☽ △ ♅ **6:30 pm** 3:30 pm
☽ ⚹ ♆ 10:02 pm
☽ ⚺ ♀ 11:21 pm

Eastern time in bold type
Pacific time in medium type

DECEMBER 2024

DATE	SID.TIME	SUN	MOON	NODE	MERCURY	VENUS	MARS	JUPITER	SATURN	URANUS	NEPTUNE	PLUTO	CERES	PALLAS	JUNO	VESTA	CHIRON
1 Su	4 41 22	9♐16 48	6♈15	4♈31R	20♐35R	22♑43	5♌56	17Ⅱ11R	12♓54	24♉40R	27♓09R	0♒14	27♐47	0♒01	9Ⅱ25	16♎01	19♈23R
2 M	4 45 19	10 17 39	18 47	4 18	19 37	23 53	6 00	17 03	12 56	24 38	27 08	0 15	28 07	0 25	9 44	16 28	19 21
3 T	4 49 16	11 18 31	1♉31	4 06	18 31	25 03	6 04	16 55	12 58	24 35	27 08	0 16	28 28	0 49	10 04	16 55	19 20
4 W	4 53 12	12 19 24	14 28	3 54	17 17	26 13	6 07	16 47	12 59	24 33	27 08	0 18	28 49	1 12	10 24	17 21	19 18
5 Th	4 57 9	13 20 18	27 36	3 44	15 57	27 23	6 09	16 39	13 01	24 31	27 08	0 19	29 10	1 36	10 43	17 48	19 17
6 F	5 1 5	14 21 12	10♊55	3 37	14 35	28 33	6 10R	16 31	13 04	24 28	27 08	0 21	29 31	2 00	11 03	18 15	19 16
7 Sa	5 5 2	15 22 08	24 25	3 33	13 12	29 42	6 10	16 23	13 06	24 26	27 08D	0 22	29 52	2 24	11 22	18 41	19 15
8 Su	5 8 58	16 23 04	8♋07	3 31D	11 52	0♒51	6 10	16 14	13 08	24 24	27 08	0 23	0♑13	2 47	11 41	19 07	19 13
9 M	5 12 55	17 24 01	22 01	3 31R	10 37	2 01	6 09	16 06	13 10	24 22	27 08	0 25	0 34	3 11	12 01	19 34	19 12
10 T	5 16 51	18 24 58	6♌07	3 31	9 30	3 10	6 07	15 58	13 13	24 19	27 08	0 26	0 56	3 35	12 20	20 00	19 11
11 W	5 20 48	19 25 56	20 25	3 30	8 32	4 19	6 04	15 50	13 15	24 17	27 08	0 28	1 17	3 59	12 39	20 26	19 10
12 Th	5 24 45	20 26 54	4♍53	3 27	7 44	5 27	6 00	15 42	13 18	24 15	27 08	0 30	1 38	4 22	12 58	20 52	19 09
13 F	5 28 41	21 27 54	19 27	3 21	7 08	6 36	5 56	15 34	13 21	24 13	27 08	0 31	2 00	4 46	13 17	21 18	19 08
14 Sa	5 32 38	22 28 54	4♎01	3 12	6 42	7 44	5 50	15 26	13 24	24 11	27 08	0 33	2 21	5 10	13 36	21 44	19 07
15 Su	5 36 34	23 29 54	18 29	3 01	6 28D	8 53	5 44	15 18	13 27	24 09	27 09	0 34	2 43	5 34	13 54	22 10	19 06
16 M	5 40 31	24 30 56	2♏44	2 49	6 30	10 01	5 37	15 10	13 30	24 07	27 09	0 36	3 05	5 57	14 13	22 36	19 05
17 T	5 44 27	25 31 58	16 39	2 36	6 30	11 09	5 29	15 02	13 33	24 05	27 09	0 38	3 27	6 21	14 32	23 01	19 05
18 W	5 48 24	26 33 00	0♐12	2 25	6 45	12 16	5 20	14 54	13 36	24 03	27 10	0 39	3 49	6 45	14 50	23 27	19 04
19 Th	5 52 21	27 34 04	13 19	2 16	7 09	13 24	5 11	14 46	13 40	24 01	27 10	0 41	4 10	7 09	15 09	23 52	19 03
20 F	5 56 17	28 35 08	26 02	2 10	7 40	14 31	5 01	14 38	13 43	23 59	27 10	0 43	4 32	7 32	15 27	24 18	19 03
21 Sa	6 0 14	29 36 13	8♑25	2 07	8 18	15 39	4 49	14 31	13 47	23 57	27 11	0 44	4 55	7 56	15 45	24 43	19 02
22 Su	6 4 10	0♑37 19	20 30	2 06	9 02	16 46	4 37	14 23	13 50	23 55	27 11	0 46	5 17	8 20	16 03	25 08	19 02
23 M	6 8 7	1 38 25	2♒24	2 06	9 51	17 52	4 25	14 15	13 53	23 53	27 12	0 48	5 40	8 43	16 21	25 33	19 01
24 T	6 12 3	2 39 33	14 12	2 05	10 45	18 59	4 11	14 08	13 58	23 51	27 12	0 50	6 01	9 07	16 39	25 58	19 01
25 W	6 16 0	3 40 40	26 00	2 04	11 43	20 05	3 57	14 01	14 02	23 49	27 13	0 51	6 23	9 31	16 57	26 23	19 01
26 Th	6 19 56	4 41 49	7♓53	2 00	12 45	21 11	3 41	13 54	14 06	23 48	27 14	0 53	6 46	9 54	17 15	26 47	19 00
27 F	6 23 53	5 42 58	19 55	1 54	13 50	22 17	3 25	13 47	14 10	23 46	27 14	0 55	7 08	10 18	17 33	27 12	19 00
28 Sa	6 27 50	6 44 07	2♈11	1 45	14 58	23 23	3 09	13 40	14 14	23 44	27 15	0 57	7 30	10 42	17 50	27 37	19 00
29 Su	6 31 46	7 45 17	14 42	1 33	16 09	24 28	2 51	13 33	14 18	23 43	27 16	0 58	7 53	11 05	18 08	28 01	19 00D
30 M	6 35 43	8 46 28	27 30	1 19	17 21	25 33	2 33	13 26	14 23	23 41	27 16	1 00	8 16	11 29	18 25	28 25	19 00
31 T	6 39 39	9 47 38	10♉35	1 06	18 36	26 38	2 14	13 19	14 27	23 40	27 17	1 02	8 38	11 53	18 42	28 49	19 00

JANUARY 2025

☽ Last Aspect day	ET / hr:mn / PT	asp	☽ Ingress sign day	ET / hr:mn / PT
12/31	10:02 pm	⚹♆	♒ 1	**5:50 am** 2:50 am
1	**1:02 am**	⚹♆	♒ 1	**5:50 am** 2:50 am
2	**11:13 pm** 8:13 pm	□♅	♓ 3	**10:21 am** 7:21 am
5	**9:30 am** 6:30 am	☌♆	♈ 5	**2:01 pm** 11:01 am
7	**4:16 pm** 1:16 pm	□♂	♉ 7	**5:11 pm** 2:11 pm
9	**5:50 pm** 2:50 pm	⚹♂	♊ 9	**8:07 pm** 5:07 pm
11	**7:03 pm** 4:03 pm	□♆	♋ 11	**11:24 pm** 8:24 pm
13	**11:46 pm** 8:46 pm	△♆	♌ 14	**4:12 am** 1:12 am
15	**11:10 pm** 8:10 pm	□♅	♍ 16	**11:46 am** 8:46 am
18	**9:01 pm** 6:01 pm	△☉	♎ 18	**10:33 pm** 7:33 pm
20	**11:34 pm** 8:34 pm	□♂	♏ 21	**11:20 am** 8:20 am
23	**7:03 pm** 4:03 pm	△♆	♐ 23	**11:29 pm** 8:29 pm
26	**4:40 am** 1:40 am	□♆	♑ 26	**8:43 am** 5:43 am
28	**10:48 am** 7:48 am	⚹♆	♒ 28	**2:31 pm** 11:31 am
30	**6:29 am** 3:29 am	□♅	♓ 30	**5:52 pm** 2:52 pm

☽ Phases & Eclipses phase	day	ET / hr:mn / PT
2nd Quarter	6	**6:56 pm** 3:56 pm
Full Moon	13	**5:27 pm** 2:27 pm
4th Quarter	21	**3:31 pm** 12:31 pm
New Moon	29	**7:36 am** 4:36 am

Planet Ingress	day	ET / hr:mn / PT
⚵ ♏	2	**6:15 pm** 3:15 pm
♀ ♓	2	**10:24 pm** 7:24 pm
♂ ♋	6	**5:44 am** 2:44 am
☿ ♑	8	**5:30 am** 2:30 am
☉ ♒	19	**3:00 pm** 12:00 pm
☿ ♒	27	**9:53 pm** 6:53 pm

Planetary Motion	day	ET / hr:mn / PT
♅ D	30	**11:22 am** 8:22 am

1 WEDNESDAY
☽ ⚹ ♆ **1:02 am**
☽ ⚺ ♀ **2:21 am**
☽ ☌ ♇ **7:45 am** 4:45 am
☽ ☍ ♂ **8:53 am** 5:53 am

2 THURSDAY
☽ ⚺ ☉ **3:19 am** 12:19 am
☽ △ ♃ **4:51 am** 1:51 am
☽ ⚺ ♄ **7:37 am** 4:37 am
☽ ⚹ ☿ **9:34 pm** 6:34 pm
☉ ⚻ ♃ **10:18 pm** 7:18 pm
☽ □ ♅ **11:13 pm** 8:13 pm
♂ ☍ ♇ 11:21 pm

3 FRIDAY
♂ ☍ ♇ **2:21 am**
☽ ⚺ ♆ **5:44 am** 2:44 am
☽ ☌ ♀ **11:21 am** 8:21 am
☽ ⚻ ♂ **12:05 pm** 9:05 am
☽ ⚺ ♇ **12:21 pm** 9:21 am
☿ ⚻ ♅ **2:19 pm** 11:19 am
♀ ⚻ ♂ **6:41 pm** 3:41 pm
♀ ⚺ ♇ 9:47 pm

4 SATURDAY
♀ ⚺ ♇ **12:47 am**
☽ □ ♃ **8:34 am** 5:34 am
☽ ⚹ ☉ **11:32 am** 8:32 am
☽ ☌ ♄ **11:56 am** 8:56 am
☉ ⚹ ♄ **5:36 pm** 2:36 pm
☽ ⚹ ♅ 11:56 pm

5 SUNDAY
☽ ⚹ ♅ **2:56 am**
☽ □ ☿ **6:57 am** 3:57 am
☽ ☌ ♆ **9:30 am** 6:30 am
☽ △ ♂ **2:25 pm** 11:25 am
☽ ⚹ ♇ **4:06 pm** 1:06 pm
☽ ⚺ ♀ **7:11 pm** 4:11 pm

6 MONDAY
☿ □ ♆ **8:56 am** 5:56 am
☽ ⚹ ♃ **11:38 am** 8:38 am
☽ ⚺ ♄ **3:38 pm** 12:38 pm
☽ □ ☉ **6:56 pm** 3:56 pm

7 TUESDAY
☽ ⚺ ♅ **6:07 am** 3:07 am
☽ ⚺ ♆ **12:46 pm** 9:46 am
☽ △ ☿ **3:49 pm** 12:49 pm
☽ □ ♂ **4:16 pm** 1:16 pm
☽ □ ♇ **7:22 pm** 4:22 pm
☿ ⚻ ♂ **7:28 pm** 4:28 pm
☽ ⚹ ♀ 11:23 pm

8 WEDNESDAY
☽ ⚹ ♀ **2:23 am**
☽ ⚺ ♃ **2:21 pm** 11:21 am
☽ ⚹ ♄ **6:57 pm** 3:57 pm
☽ △ ☉ 10:53 pm

9 THURSDAY
☽ △ ☉ **1:53 am**
☿ ⚺ ♇ **3:48 am** 12:48 am
☽ ☌ ♅ **9:00 am** 6:00 am
☽ ⚹ ♆ **3:46 pm** 12:46 pm
☽ ⚹ ♂ **5:50 pm** 2:50 pm
☽ △ ♇ **10:24 pm** 7:24 pm
☽ ⚻ ☿ 9:28 pm

10 FRIDAY
☽ ⚻ ☿ **12:28 am**
☽ □ ♀ **9:18 am** 6:18 am
☽ ☌ ♃ **5:01 pm** 2:01 pm
☽ □ ♄ **10:15 pm** 7:15 pm

11 SATURDAY
☽ ⚻ ☉ **8:56 am** 5:56 am
☽ ⚺ ♅ **12:04 pm** 9:04 am
☽ □ ♆ **7:03 pm** 4:03 pm
☽ ⚺ ♂ **7:40 pm** 4:40 pm
☽ ⚻ ♇ 10:51 pm

12 SUNDAY
☽ ⚻ ♇ **1:51 am**
☽ ☍ ☿ **9:53 am** 6:53 am
♂ △ ♆ **4:16 pm** 1:16 pm
☽ △ ♀ **4:56 pm** 1:56 pm
☽ ⚺ ♃ **8:28 pm** 5:28 pm
☽ △ ♄ 11:30 pm

13 MONDAY
☽ △ ♄ **2:30 am**
☉ △ ♅ **3:13 am** 12:13 am
☽ ⚹ ♅ **4:22 pm** 1:22 pm
☽ ☍ ☉ **5:27 pm** 2:27 pm
☽ ☌ ♂ **10:48 pm** 7:48 pm
☽ △ ♆ **11:46 pm** 8:46 pm

14 TUESDAY
☽ ☍ ♇ **6:53 am** 3:53 am
♀ □ ♃ **2:48 pm** 11:48 am
☽ ⚻ ☿ **9:56 pm** 6:56 pm
☽ ⚹ ♃ 10:58 pm
☽ ⚻ ♀ 11:57 pm

15 WEDNESDAY
☽ ⚹ ♃ **1:58 am**
☽ ⚻ ♀ **2:57 am**
☽ ⚻ ♄ **8:59 am** 5:59 am
☉ ☍ ♂ **9:39 pm** 6:39 pm
☽ □ ♅ **11:10 pm** 8:10 pm

16 THURSDAY
☽ ⚺ ♂ **4:21 am** 1:21 am
☽ ⚻ ☉ **5:10 am** 2:10 am
☽ ⚻ ♆ **7:09 am** 4:09 am
☿ ⚻ ♃ **7:51 am** 4:51 am
☽ ⚻ ♇ **2:45 pm** 11:45 am

17 FRIDAY
☉ ⚹ ♆ **6:20 am** 3:20 am
☽ □ ♃ **10:33 am** 7:33 am
☽ △ ☿ **2:28 pm** 11:28 am
☽ ☍ ♀ **4:46 pm** 1:46 pm
☽ ☍ ♄ **6:43 pm** 3:43 pm

18 SATURDAY
☽ △ ♅ **9:13 am** 6:13 am
☽ ⚹ ♂ **12:53 pm** 9:53 am
☽ ☍ ♆ **5:48 pm** 2:48 pm
♀ ☌ ♄ **8:26 pm** 5:26 pm
☽ △ ☉ **9:01 pm** 6:01 pm
☽ △ ♇ 10:51 pm
☿ ⚹ ♄ 11:38 pm

19 SUNDAY
☽ △ ♇ **1:51 am**
☿ ⚹ ♄ **2:38 am**
☿ ⚹ ♀ **11:32 am** 8:32 am
☽ △ ♃ **10:06 pm** 7:06 pm

20 MONDAY
☽ ⚻ ♄ **7:21 am** 4:21 am
☽ ⚻ ♀ **10:03 am** 7:03 am
☽ □ ☿ **11:23 am** 8:23 am
☽ ⚻ ♅ **9:43 pm** 6:43 pm
☽ □ ♂ **11:34 pm** 8:34 pm

21 TUESDAY
☽ ⚻ ♆ **6:38 am** 3:38 am
☉ ☌ ♇ **7:29 am** 4:29 am
☽ □ ♇ **2:50 pm** 11:50 am
☽ □ ☉ **3:31 pm** 12:31 pm

22 WEDNESDAY
☽ ⚻ ♃ **10:44 am** 7:44 am
☽ △ ♄ **8:39 pm** 5:39 pm

23 THURSDAY
☽ △ ♀ **3:51 am** 12:51 am
☽ ⚹ ☿ **9:10 am** 6:10 am
♂ ⚹ ♅ **10:08 am** 7:08 am
☽ △ ♂ **10:12 am** 7:12 am
☽ ☍ ♅ **10:13 am** 7:13 am
☿ ☍ ♂ **3:49 pm** 12:49 pm
☿ △ ♅ **5:07 pm** 2:07 pm
☽ △ ♆ **7:03 pm** 4:03 pm

24 FRIDAY
☽ ⚹ ♇ **3:01 am** 12:01 am
☽ ⚹ ☉ **8:55 am** 5:55 am
☽ ☍ ♃ **9:45 pm** 6:45 pm

25 SATURDAY
☽ □ ♄ **7:51 am** 4:51 am
☽ □ ♀ **6:34 pm** 3:34 pm
☽ ⚻ ♂ **6:36 pm** 3:36 pm
♀ △ ♂ **6:54 pm** 3:54 pm
☽ ⚻ ♅ **8:11 pm** 5:11 pm

26 SUNDAY
☽ ⚺ ☿ **3:25 am** 12:25 am
☽ □ ♆ **4:40 am** 1:40 am
☽ ⚺ ♇ **12:11 pm** 9:11 am
☿ ⚹ ♆ **1:33 pm** 10:33 am
♀ ⚹ ♅ **6:11 pm** 3:11 pm
☽ ⚺ ☉ **10:20 pm** 7:20 pm

27 MONDAY
☽ ⚻ ♃ **5:30 am** 2:30 am
☽ ⚹ ♄ **3:33 pm** 12:33 pm
☽ ☍ ♂ **11:52 pm** 8:52 pm
☽ △ ♅ 11:42 pm

28 TUESDAY
☽ △ ♅ **2:42 am**
☽ ⚹ ♀ **4:53 am** 1:53 am
☽ ⚹ ♆ **10:48 am** 7:48 am
☽ ☌ ☿ **4:45 pm** 1:45 pm
☽ ☌ ♇ **5:56 pm** 2:56 pm
☿ ☌ ♇ 11:52 pm

29 WEDNESDAY
☿ ☌ ♇ **2:52 am**
☽ ☌ ☉ **7:36 am** 4:36 am
☽ △ ♃ **10:08 am** 7:08 am
☽ ⚺ ♄ **8:12 pm** 5:12 pm
☽ ⚻ ♂ 11:36 pm

30 THURSDAY
☽ ⚻ ♂ **2:36 am**
☽ □ ♅ **6:29 am** 3:29 am
☽ ⚺ ♀ **11:48 am** 8:48 am
☽ ⚺ ♆ **2:23 pm** 11:23 am
☉ △ ♃ **5:59 pm** 2:59 pm
☽ ⚺ ♇ **9:17 pm** 6:17 pm
☽ ⚺ ☿ 11:43 pm

31 FRIDAY
☽ ⚺ ☿ **2:43 am**
☽ □ ♃ **12:52 pm** 9:52 am
☽ ⚺ ☉ **2:20 pm** 11:20 am
☽ ☌ ♄ **11:09 pm** 8:09 pm

Eastern time in bold type
Pacific time in medium type

JANUARY 2025

DATE	SID.TIME	SUN	MOON	NODE	MERCURY	VENUS	MARS	JUPITER	SATURN	URANUS	NEPTUNE	PLUTO	CERES	PALLAS	JUNO	VESTA	CHIRON
1 W	6 43 36	10♑48 49	23♑55	0♈53R	19♐52	27♒43	1♌55R	13♊13R	14♓31	23♉38R	27♓18	1≈04	9≈01	12♐16	18♏59	29♎13	19♈00
2 Th	6 47 32	11 50 00	7≈27	0 42	21 10	28 47	1 35	13 07	14 36	23 37	27 19	1 06	9 23	12 40	19 16	29 37	19 00
3 F	6 51 29	12 51 10	21 10	0 34	22 29	29 51	1 15	13 00	14 41	23 35	27 20	1 08	9 46	13 03	19 33	0♏00	19 01
4 Sa	6 55 25	13 52 21	5♓00	0 29	23 50	0♓55	0 54	12 54	14 45	23 34	27 20	1 09	10 09	13 27	19 50	0 24	19 01
5 Su	6 59 22	14 53 31	18 55	0 26D	25 12	1 58	0 32	12 49	14 50	23 33	27 21	1 11	10 32	13 50	20 07	0 48	19 01
6 M	7 3 19	15 54 40	2♈55	0 26R	26 35	3 01	0 10	12 43	14 55	23 31	27 22	1 13	10 55	14 14	20 24	1 11	19 01
7 T	7 7 15	16 55 50	16 58	0 26	27 58	4 04	29♋48	12 37	15 00	23 30	27 23	1 15	11 18	14 37	20 40	1 34	19 02
8 W	7 11 12	17 56 59	1♉04	0 26	29 23	5 06	29 25	12 32	15 05	23 29	27 24	1 17	11 40	15 01	20 56	1 57	19 02
9 Th	7 15 8	18 58 07	15 12	0 23	0♑48	6 08	29 02	12 27	15 10	23 28	27 26	1 19	12 03	15 24	21 12	2 20	19 03
10 F	7 19 5	19 59 15	29 21	0 18	2 14	7 09	28 38	12 22	15 15	23 27	27 27	1 21	12 26	15 47	21 28	2 43	19 04
11 Sa	7 23 1	21 00 22	13♊27	0 10	3 41	8 10	28 15	12 17	15 21	23 26	27 28	1 23	12 49	16 11	21 44	3 05	19 04
12 Su	7 26 58	22 01 29	27 27	0 00	5 08	9 11	27 51	12 12	15 26	23 25	27 29	1 25	13 13	16 34	22 00	3 28	19 05
13 M	7 30 55	23 02 36	11♋17	29♓48	6 37	10 11	27 27	12 07	15 31	23 24	27 30	1 27	13 36	16 57	22 15	3 50	19 06
14 T	7 34 51	24 03 42	24 52	29 36	8 05	11 11	27 03	12 03	15 37	23 23	27 31	1 28	13 59	17 21	22 31	4 12	19 06
15 W	7 38 48	25 04 48	8♌10	29 26	9 35	12 10	26 39	11 59	15 42	23 22	27 33	1 30	14 22	17 44	22 46	4 34	19 07
16 Th	7 42 44	26 05 53	21 08	29 18	11 05	13 09	26 15	11 55	15 48	23 21	27 34	1 32	14 45	18 07	23 01	4 55	19 08
17 F	7 46 41	27 06 58	3♍47	29 12	12 35	14 07	25 51	11 51	15 54	23 21	27 35	1 34	15 08	18 30	23 16	5 17	19 09
18 Sa	7 50 37	28 08 03	16 08	29 09	14 06	15 05	25 27	11 48	15 59	23 20	27 37	1 36	15 32	18 53	23 31	5 38	19 10
19 Su	7 54 34	29 09 07	28 14	29 08D	15 38	16 02	25 04	11 44	16 05	23 19	27 38	1 38	15 55	19 16	23 46	5 59	19 11
20 M	7 58 30	0≈10 10	10♎09	29 08	17 10	16 59	24 40	11 41	16 11	23 19	27 39	1 40	16 18	19 39	24 00	6 20	19 12
21 T	8 2 27	1 11 14	21 58	29 09R	18 43	17 55	24 17	11 38	16 17	23 18	27 41	1 42	16 41	20 02	24 15	6 41	19 14
22 W	8 6 24	2 12 17	3♏47	29 09	20 16	18 50	23 54	11 35	16 23	23 18	27 42	1 44	17 05	20 25	24 29	7 02	19 15
23 Th	8 10 20	3 13 19	15 40	29 09	21 50	19 45	23 31	11 32	16 29	23 18	27 44	1 46	17 28	20 48	24 43	7 22	19 16
24 F	8 14 17	4 14 22	27 43	29 05	23 24	20 39	23 09	11 30	16 35	23 17	27 45	1 48	17 51	21 11	24 57	7 42	19 17
25 Sa	8 18 13	5 15 23	10♐02	29 00	24 59	21 33	22 47	11 28	16 41	23 17	27 47	1 50	18 15	21 34	25 11	8 02	19 18
26 Su	8 22 10	6 16 25	22 38	28 53	26 35	22 26	22 25	11 26	16 47	23 16	27 48	1 52	18 38	21 57	25 24	8 22	19 20
27 M	8 26 6	7 17 25	5♑36	28 44	28 11	23 18	22 04	11 24	16 53	23 16	27 50	1 54	19 02	22 19	25 38	8 41	19 21
28 T	8 30 3	8 18 25	18 55	28 35	29 48	24 09	21 44	11 22	17 00	23 16	27 51	1 56	19 25	22 42	25 51	9 01	19 23
29 W	8 33 59	9 19 24	2≈34	28 26	1≈26	24 59	21 24	11 21	17 06	23 16	27 53	1 57	19 49	23 05	26 04	9 20	19 25
30 Th	8 37 56	10 20 22	16 31	28 18	3 04	25 50	21 05	11 20	17 12	23 16D	27 55	1 59	20 12	23 27	26 17	9 38	19 27
31 F	8 41 53	11 21 19	0♓40	28 13	4 43	26 39	20 46	11 19	17 19	23 16	27 56	2 01	20 36	23 50	26 29	9 57	19 28

EPHEMERIS CALCULATED FOR 12 MIDNIGHT GREENWICH MEAN TIME. ALL OTHER DATA AND FACING ASPECTARIAN PAGE IN **EASTERN TIME (BOLD)** AND PACIFIC TIME (REGULAR).

FEBRUARY 2025

☽ Last Aspect day	ET / hr:mn / PT		asp	☽ Ingress sign day	ET / hr:mn / PT	
1	**5:06 pm**	2:06 pm	☌ ♀	♈ 1	**8:10 pm**	5:10 pm
3	**5:19 am**	2:19 am	□ ♂	♉ 3	**10:33 pm**	7:33 pm
5	**10:29 pm**	7:29 pm	⚹ ♆	♊ 5		10:44 pm
5	**10:29 pm**	7:29 pm	⚹ ♆	♊ 6	**1:44 am**	
7		11:52 pm	□ ♆	♋ 8	**6:04 am**	3:04 am
8	**2:52 am**		□ ♆	♋ 8	**6:04 am**	3:04 am
10	**8:49 am**	5:49 am	△ ♆	♌ 10	**12:01 pm**	9:01 am
12	**2:12 pm**	11:12 am	☍ ☿	♍ 12	**8:07 pm**	5:07 pm
15	**3:36 am**	12:36 am	☍ ♆	♎ 15	**6:45 am**	3:45 am
17	**6:24 pm**	3:24 pm	△ ☉	♏ 17	**7:19 pm**	4:19 pm

☽ Last Aspect day	ET / hr:mn / PT		asp	☽ Ingress sign day	ET / hr:mn / PT	
20	**5:06 am**	2:06 am	△ ♆	♐ 20	**7:55 am**	4:55 am
22	**3:38 pm**	12:38 pm	□ ♆	♑ 22	**6:09 pm**	3:09 pm
24	**10:28 pm**	7:28 pm	⚹ ♆	♒ 24		9:40 pm
24	**10:28 pm**	7:28 pm	⚹ ♆	♒ 25	**12:40 am**	
26	**5:04 pm**	2:04 pm	□ ♅	♓ 27	**3:46 am**	12:46 am

☽ Phases & Eclipses phase	day	ET / hr:mn / PT	
2nd Quarter	5	**3:02 am**	12:02 am
Full Moon	12	**8:53 am**	5:53 am
4th Quarter	20	**12:33 pm**	9:33 am
New Moon	27	**7:45 pm**	4:45 pm

Planet Ingress	day	ET / hr:mn / PT	
♀ ♈	3		11:57 pm
♀ ♈	4	**2:57 am**	
☿ ♓	14	**7:06 am**	4:06 am
♀ ♒	16	**2:26 pm**	11:26 am
☉ ♓	18	**5:07 am**	2:07 am
⚵ ♐	19	**10:30 pm**	7:30 pm
⚳ ♓	23	**5:55 pm**	2:55 pm

Planetary Motion		day	ET / hr:mn / PT	
♃	D	4	**4:40 am**	1:40 am
♂	D	23	**9:00 pm**	6:00 pm

1 SATURDAY
☽ △ ♂ **4:02 am** 1:02 am
☽ ⚹ ♅ **8:54 am** 5:54 am
♀ ☌ ♆ **11:33 am** 8:33 am
☽ ☌ ♆ **4:49 pm** 1:49 pm
☽ ☌ ♀ **5:06 pm** 2:06 pm
☽ ⚹ ♇ **11:40 pm** 8:40 pm

2 SUNDAY
☽ ⚹ ☿ **11:35 am** 8:35 am
☽ ⚹ ♃ **3:03 pm** 12:03 pm
☽ ⚹ ☉ **8:23 pm** 5:23 pm
☽ ⚺ ♄ 10:47 pm

3 MONDAY
☽ ⚺ ♄ **1:47 am**
☽ □ ♂ **5:19 am** 2:19 am
☽ ⚺ ♅ **11:12 am** 8:12 am
☿ △ ♃ **4:52 pm** 1:52 pm
☽ ⚺ ♆ **7:16 pm** 4:16 pm
☽ ⚺ ♀ **10:19 pm** 7:19 pm
☽ □ ♇ 11:12 pm

4 TUESDAY
☽ □ ♇ **2:12 am**
☽ ⚺ ♃ **5:41 pm** 2:41 pm
☽ □ ☿ **9:06 pm** 6:06 pm

5 WEDNESDAY
☽ □ ☉ **3:02 am** 12:02 am
☽ ⚹ ♄ **4:59 am** 1:59 am
☽ ⚹ ♂ **7:16 am** 4:16 am
☽ ☌ ♅ **2:10 pm** 11:10 am
☽ ⚹ ♆ **10:29 pm** 7:29 pm

6 THURSDAY
☽ ⚹ ♀ **4:17 am** 1:17 am
☽ △ ♇ **5:34 am** 2:34 am
☉ ⚺ ♄ **9:10 am** 6:10 am
☽ ☌ ♃ **9:16 pm** 6:16 pm

7 FRIDAY
☉ ⚻ ♂ **3:42 am** 12:42 am
♀ ⚹ ♇ **7:14 am** 4:14 am
☽ △ ☿ **8:11 am** 5:11 am
☽ □ ♄ **9:14 am** 6:14 am
☽ ⚺ ♂ **10:18 am** 7:18 am
☽ △ ☉ **10:57 am** 7:57 am
☿ ⚺ ♄ **4:57 pm** 1:57 pm
☽ ⚺ ♅ **6:15 pm** 3:15 pm
☿ ⚻ ♂ **11:15 pm** 8:15 pm
☽ □ ♆ 11:52 pm

8 SATURDAY
☽ □ ♆ **2:52 am**
☽ ⚻ ♇ **10:08 am** 7:08 am
☽ □ ♀ **11:28 am** 8:28 am
☽ ⚺ ♃ 11:12 pm

9 SUNDAY
☽ ⚺ ♃ **2:12 am**
☉ ☌ ☿ **7:08 am** 4:08 am
♂ △ ♄ **8:15 am** 5:15 am
☽ ☌ ♂ **2:48 pm** 11:48 am
☽ △ ♄ **2:57 pm** 11:57 am
☽ ⚻ ☉ **8:39 pm** 5:39 pm
☽ ⚻ ☿ **9:33 pm** 6:33 pm
☽ ⚹ ♅ **11:49 pm** 8:49 pm

10 MONDAY
☽ △ ♆ **8:49 am** 5:49 am
☿ □ ♅ **2:28 pm** 11:28 am
☽ ☍ ♇ **4:21 pm** 1:21 pm
☽ △ ♀ **8:21 pm** 5:21 pm

11 TUESDAY
☽ ⚹ ♃ **8:59 am** 5:59 am
☉ □ ♅ **2:30 pm** 11:30 am
☽ ⚺ ♂ **9:16 pm** 6:16 pm
☽ ⚻ ♄ **10:39 pm** 7:39 pm

12 WEDNESDAY
☽ □ ♅ **7:26 am** 4:26 am
☽ ☍ ☉ **8:53 am** 5:53 am
☽ ☍ ☿ **2:12 pm** 11:12 am
☽ ⚻ ♆ **4:56 pm** 1:56 pm
☽ ⚻ ♇ 9:47 pm

13 THURSDAY
☽ ⚻ ♇ **12:47 am**
☽ ⚻ ♀ **7:34 am** 4:34 am
☿ ⚺ ♆ **9:30 am** 6:30 am
☽ □ ♃ **6:10 pm** 3:10 pm

14 FRIDAY
☽ ⚹ ♂ **6:14 am** 3:14 am
☽ ☍ ♄ **8:53 am** 5:53 am
☽ △ ♅ **5:34 pm** 2:34 pm
☽ ⚻ ☉ 9:20 pm

15 SATURDAY
☽ ⚻ ☉ **12:20 am**
☽ ☍ ♆ **3:36 am** 12:36 am
☽ ⚻ ☿ **11:00 am** 8:00 am
☽ △ ♇ **11:46 am** 8:46 am
☿ ⚺ ♇ **3:58 pm** 12:58 pm
☽ ☍ ♀ **9:19 pm** 6:19 pm

16 SUNDAY
☽ △ ♃ **5:52 am** 2:52 am
☉ ⚺ ♆ **4:38 pm** 1:38 pm
☽ □ ♂ **5:37 pm** 2:37 pm
☽ ⚻ ♄ **9:30 pm** 6:30 pm

17 MONDAY
☽ ⚻ ♅ **5:54 am** 2:54 am
☽ ⚻ ♆ **4:16 pm** 1:16 pm
☽ △ ☉ **6:24 pm** 3:24 pm
☽ □ ♇ 9:34 pm

18 TUESDAY
☽ □ ♇ **12:34 am**
☽ △ ☿ **10:55 am** 7:55 am
☽ ⚻ ♀ **12:28 pm** 9:28 am
☽ ⚻ ♃ **6:57 pm** 3:57 pm
☿ ⚺ ♀ **11:02 pm** 8:02 pm

19 WEDNESDAY
☽ △ ♂ **6:07 am** 3:07 am
☽ △ ♄ **10:59 am** 7:59 am
☽ ☍ ♅ **6:47 pm** 3:47 pm

20 THURSDAY
☽ △ ♆ **5:06 am** 2:06 am
☽ □ ☉ **12:33 pm** 9:33 am
☽ ⚹ ♇ **1:12 pm** 10:12 am
☿ □ ♃ **3:13 pm** 12:13 pm
☉ ⚺ ♇ **8:35 pm** 5:35 pm
☽ △ ♀ 11:28 pm

21 FRIDAY
☽ △ ♀ **2:28 am**
☽ ☍ ♃ **7:09 am** 4:09 am
☽ □ ☿ **9:53 am** 6:53 am
☽ ⚻ ♂ **5:25 pm** 2:25 pm
☽ □ ♄ **10:50 pm** 7:50 pm

22 SATURDAY
☽ ⚻ ♅ **5:48 am** 2:48 am
☽ □ ♆ **3:38 pm** 12:38 pm
☽ ⚺ ♇ **11:15 pm** 8:15 pm

23 SUNDAY
☽ ⚹ ☉ **3:26 am** 12:26 am
☿ △ ♂ **11:58 am** 8:58 am
☽ □ ♀ **12:52 pm** 9:52 am
☽ ⚻ ♃ **4:15 pm** 1:15 pm
☽ ☍ ♂ 10:32 pm

24 MONDAY
☽ ☍ ♂ **1:32 am**
☽ ⚹ ☿ **3:41 am** 12:41 am
☽ ⚹ ♄ **7:10 am** 4:10 am
☽ △ ♅ **1:14 pm** 10:14 am
☽ ⚹ ♆ **10:28 pm** 7:28 pm

25 TUESDAY
☽ ☌ ♇ **5:33 am** 2:33 am
☿ ☌ ♄ **7:02 am** 4:02 am
☽ ⚺ ☉ **1:33 pm** 10:33 am
☽ ⚹ ♀ **6:54 pm** 3:54 pm
☽ △ ♃ **9:33 pm** 6:33 pm

26 WEDNESDAY
☽ ⚻ ♂ **6:03 am** 3:03 am
☽ ⚺ ♄ **11:44 am** 8:44 am
☽ ⚺ ☿ **3:30 pm** 12:30 pm
☽ □ ♅ **5:04 pm** 2:04 pm
☽ ⚺ ♆ 10:50 pm

27 THURSDAY
☽ ⚺ ♆ **1:50 am**
☿ ⚹ ♅ **4:38 am** 1:38 am
☽ ⚺ ♇ **8:30 am** 5:30 am
☽ ☌ ☉ **7:45 pm** 4:45 pm
☽ ⚺ ♀ **9:32 pm** 6:32 pm
☽ □ ♃ **11:54 pm** 8:54 pm

28 FRIDAY
☽ △ ♂ **7:57 am** 4:57 am
☽ ☌ ♄ **1:42 pm** 10:42 am
☽ ⚹ ♅ **6:32 pm** 3:32 pm
☉ ⚺ ♀ **11:08 pm** 8:08 pm
☽ ☌ ☿ **11:19 pm** 8:19 pm

Eastern time in bold type
Pacific time in medium type

FEBRUARY 2025

DATE	SID.TIME	SUN	MOON	NODE	MERCURY	VENUS	MARS	JUPITER	SATURN	URANUS	NEPTUNE	PLUTO	CERES	PALLAS	JUNO	VESTA	CHIRON
1 Sa	8 45 49	12♒22 15	14♓58	28♓10D	6♒23	27♓27	20♋28R	11♊18R	17♓32	23♉16	27♓58	2♒03	20♒59	24♈12	26♏42	10♏15	19♈30
2 Su	8 49 46	13 23 10	29 18	28 09	8 03	28 14	20 10	11 17	17 39	23 16	28 00	2 05	21 23	24 35	26 54	10 33	19 32
3 M	8 53 42	14 24 03	13♈38	28 10	9 44	29 00	19 54	11 17	17 45	23 16	28 02	2 07	21 46	24 57	27 06	10 51	19 34
4 T	8 57 39	15 24 55	27 54	28 11	11 26	29 45	19 38	11 17D	17 52	23 16	28 03	2 09	22 10	25 20	27 18	11 09	19 36
5 W	9 1 35	16 25 46	12♉03	28 12R	13 08	0♈29	19 22	11 17	17 58	23 16	28 05	2 11	22 33	25 42	27 30	11 26	19 38
6 Th	9 5 32	17 26 35	26 05	28 12	14 52	1 13	19 08	11 17	18 05	23 17	28 07	2 13	22 57	26 04	27 41	11 43	19 40
7 F	9 9 28	18 27 22	9♊59	28 10	16 36	1 55	18 54	11 17	18 12	23 17	28 09	2 16	23 20	26 26	27 53	12 00	19 42
8 Sa	9 13 25	19 28 09	23 43	28 06	18 20	2 35	18 41	11 18	18 19	23 18	28 11	2 18	23 44	26 48	28 04	12 17	19 44
9 Su	9 17 22	20 28 53	7♋17	28 01	20 06	3 15	18 29	11 19	18 26	23 18	28 13	2 20	24 08	27 10	28 14	12 33	19 46
10 M	9 21 18	21 29 37	20 39	27 55	21 52	3 53	18 18	11 20	18 33	23 19	28 14	2 22	24 31	27 32	28 25	12 49	19 48
11 T	9 25 15	22 30 18	3♌49	27 48	23 39	4 30	18 07	11 21	18 40	23 19	28 16	2 24	24 55	27 54	28 36	13 04	19 50
12 W	9 29 11	23 30 59	16 44	27 41	25 27	5 06	17 57	11 23	18 46	23 20	28 18	2 26	25 18	28 16	28 46	13 20	19 52
13 Th	9 33 8	24 31 37	29 25	27 38	27 16	5 40	17 48	11 24	18 53	23 21	28 20	2 27	25 42	28 38	28 56	13 35	19 55
14 F	9 37 4	25 32 15	11♍52	27 41R	29 05	6 13	17 40	11 26	19 00	23 22	28 22	2 29	26 05	28 59	29 05	13 50	19 57
15 Sa	9 41 1	26 32 51	24 05	27 34D	0♓54	6 44	17 33	11 28	19 08	23 23	28 24	2 31	26 29	29 21	29 15	14 04	19 59
16 Su	9 44 57	27 33 25	6♎07	27 34	2 45	7 14	17 26	11 30	19 15	23 24	28 26	2 33	26 53	29 43	29 24	14 18	20 02
17 M	9 48 54	28 33 59	18 01	27 36	4 36	7 42	17 20	11 33	19 22	23 25	28 28	2 35	27 16	0♉04	29 33	14 32	20 04
18 T	9 52 51	29 34 31	29 51	27 38	6 27	8 08	17 15	11 35	19 29	23 26	28 30	2 36	27 40	0 25	29 42	14 45	20 07
19 W	9 56 47	0♓35 01	11♏40	27 39	8 18	8 33	17 11	11 38	19 36	23 27	28 32	2 38	28 03	0 47	29 51	14 59	20 09
20 Th	10 0 44	1 35 31	23 33	27 41R	10 10	8 56	17 07	11 41	19 43	23 28	28 34	2 40	28 27	1 08	29 59	15 11	20 12
21 F	10 4 40	2 35 59	5♐35	27 41	12 01	9 17	17 04	11 44	19 50	23 29	28 36	2 42	28 50	1 29	0♐07	15 24	20 15
22 Sa	10 8 37	3 36 26	17 52	27 40	13 53	9 36	17 03	11 48	19 58	23 30	28 39	2 43	29 14	1 50	0 15	15 36	20 17
23 Su	10 12 33	4 36 52	0♑27	27 38	15 43	9 53	17 01	11 51	20 05	23 31	28 41	2 45	29 38	2 11	0 22	15 48	20 20
24 M	10 16 30	5 37 16	13 25	27 35	17 33	10 07	17 01D	11 55	20 12	23 33	28 43	2 47	0♓01	2 32	0 29	15 59	20 23
25 T	10 20 26	6 37 39	26 47	27 32	19 22	10 20	17 01	11 59	20 19	23 34	28 45	2 48	0 25	2 53	0 36	16 10	20 25
26 W	10 24 23	7 38 00	10♒34	27 29	21 09	10 31	17 02	12 03	20 27	23 35	28 47	2 50	0 48	3 14	0 43	16 21	20 28
27 Th	10 28 20	8 38 20	24 44	27 27	22 54	10 39	17 04	12 07	20 34	23 37	28 49	2 52	1 12	3 35	0 50	16 31	20 31
28 F	10 32 16	9 38 38	9♓13	27 25	24 37	10 45	17 07	12 12	20 41	23 39	28 51	2 54	1 35	3 55	0 56	16 41	20 34

EPHEMERIS CALCULATED FOR 12 MIDNIGHT GREENWICH MEAN TIME. ALL OTHER DATA AND FACING ASPECTARIAN PAGE IN **EASTERN TIME (BOLD)** AND PACIFIC TIME (REGULAR).

MARCH 2025

☽ Last Aspect day	ET / hr:mn / PT		asp	☽ Ingress sign	day	ET / hr:mn / PT	
1	**3:05 am**	12:05 am	☌ ♆	♈	1	**4:52 am**	1:52 am
2	**8:52 am**	5:52 am	□ ♂	♉	3	**5:37 am**	2:37 am
5	**5:53 am**	2:53 am	⚹ ♆	♊	5	**7:29 am**	4:29 am
7	**9:57 am**	6:57 am	□ ♆	♋	7	**11:29 am**	8:29 am
9	**5:32 pm**	2:32 pm	△ ♆	♌	9	**6:59 pm**	3:59 pm
11	**4:16 pm**	1:16 pm	□ ♅	♍	12	**3:56 am**	12:56 am
14	**1:47 pm**	10:47 am	☍ ♆	♎	14	**2:59 pm**	11:59 am
16	**5:53 am**	2:53 am	□ ♂	♏	17	**3:30 am**	12:30 am
19	**3:28 pm**	12:28 pm	△ ♆	♐	19	**4:17 pm**	1:17 pm
21		11:53 pm	□ ♆	♑	22	**3:29 am**	12:29 am
22	**2:53 am**		□ ♆	♑	22	**3:29 am**	12:29 am
24	**11:01 am**	8:01 am	⚹ ♆	♒	24	**11:25 am**	8:25 am
26	**6:15 am**	3:15 am	□ ♅	♓	26	**3:31 pm**	12:31 pm
28	**4:30 pm**	1:30 pm	☌ ♆	♈	28	**4:36 pm**	1:36 pm
30	**5:18 am**	2:18 am	□ ♂	♉	30	**4:16 pm**	1:16 pm

☽ Phases & Eclipses phase	day	ET / hr:mn / PT	
2nd Quarter	6	**11:32 am**	8:32 am
Full Moon	13		11:55 pm
Full Moon	14	**2:55 am**	
●	14	23° ♍ 57'	
4th Quarter	22	**7:29 am**	4:29 am
New Moon	29	**6:58 am**	3:58 am
●	29	9° ♈ 00'	

Planet Ingress		day	ET / hr:mn / PT	
☿	♈	3	**4:04 am**	1:04 am
☉	♈	20	**5:01 am**	2:01 am
♀	♓	27	**4:41 am**	1:41 am
☿	♓	29	**10:18 pm**	7:18 pm
♆	♈	30	**8:00 am**	5:00 am

Planetary Motion		day	ET / hr:mn / PT	
♀	℞	1	**7:36 pm**	4:36 pm
☿	℞	14		11:46 pm
☿	℞	15	**2:46 am**	
⚵	℞	19	**2:00 pm**	11:00 am
⚶	℞	21	**6:10 am**	3:10 am

1 SATURDAY
☽ ☌ ♆ **3:05 am** 12:05 am
☽ ⚹ ♇ **9:34 am** 6:34 am
☽ ☌ ♀ **10:26 pm** 7:26 pm
☽ ⚺ ☉ 9:06 pm
☽ ⚹ ♃ 9:55 pm

2 SUNDAY
☽ ⚺ ☉ **12:06 am**
☽ ⚹ ♃ **12:55 am**
☽ □ ♂ **8:52 am** 5:52 am
☿ ☌ ♆ **11:22 am** 8:22 am
☉ □ ♃ **1:19 pm** 10:19 am
☽ ⚺ ♄ **2:47 pm** 11:47 am
☽ ⚺ ♅ **7:18 pm** 4:18 pm

3 MONDAY
☽ ⚺ ♆ **3:57 am** 12:57 am
☽ ⚺ ☿ **5:47 am** 2:47 am
☽ □ ♇ **10:27 am** 7:27 am
☽ ⚺ ♀ **11:16 pm** 8:16 pm
☽ ⚺ ♃ 11:16 pm

4 TUESDAY
☽ ⚺ ♃ **2:16 am**
☽ ⚹ ☉ **4:47 am** 1:47 am
☽ ⚹ ♂ **10:25 am** 7:25 am
☽ ⚹ ♄ **4:37 pm** 1:37 pm
☽ ☌ ♅ **8:56 pm** 5:56 pm

5 WEDNESDAY
☽ ⚹ ♆ **5:53 am** 2:53 am
☿ ⚹ ♇ **8:13 am** 5:13 am
☽ △ ♇ **12:36 pm** 9:36 am
☽ ⚹ ☿ **1:01 pm** 10:01 am
☽ ⚹ ♀ 10:21 pm

6 THURSDAY
☽ ⚹ ♀ **1:21 am**
☽ ☌ ♃ **5:17 am** 2:17 am
☽ □ ☉ **11:32 am** 8:32 am
☽ ⚺ ♂ **1:52 pm** 10:52 am
☽ □ ♄ **8:23 pm** 5:23 pm
☽ ⚺ ♅ 9:33 pm

7 FRIDAY
☽ ⚺ ♅ **12:33 am**
☽ □ ♆ **9:57 am** 6:57 am
☽ ⚻ ♇ **4:56 pm** 1:56 pm
☽ □ ☿ **10:05 pm** 7:05 pm
☉ △ ♂ 9:13 pm

8 SATURDAY
☉ △ ♂ **12:13 am**
☽ □ ♀ **5:20 am** 2:20 am
☽ ⚺ ♃ **10:43 am** 7:43 am
☽ ☌ ♂ **7:52 pm** 4:52 pm
☽ △ ☉ **9:16 pm** 6:16 pm
☽ △ ♄ 11:40 pm

9 SUNDAY
☽ △ ♄ **3:40 am**
☽ ⚹ ♅ **7:39 am** 4:39 am
☽ △ ♆ **5:32 pm** 2:32 pm
☽ ☍ ♇ 9:48 pm

10 MONDAY
☽ ☍ ♇ **12:48 am**
☽ △ ☿ **9:56 am** 6:56 am
☽ △ ♀ **12:21 pm** 9:21 am
☽ ⚹ ♃ **7:46 pm** 4:46 pm

11 TUESDAY
☽ ⚺ ♂ **5:35 am** 2:35 am
☽ ⚻ ☉ **11:10 am** 8:10 am
☽ ⚻ ♄ **12:32 pm** 9:32 am
☽ □ ♅ **4:16 pm** 1:16 pm
☿ ☌ ♀ **6:55 pm** 3:55 pm
☽ ⚻ ♆ 11:36 pm

12 WEDNESDAY
☽ ⚻ ♆ **2:36 am**
☉ ☌ ♄ **6:29 am** 3:29 am
☽ ⚻ ♇ **10:05 am** 7:05 am
☽ ⚻ ♀ **8:10 pm** 5:10 pm
☽ ⚻ ☿ **9:55 pm** 6:55 pm

13 THURSDAY
☽ □ ♃ **6:13 am** 3:13 am
☽ ⚹ ♂ **4:45 pm** 1:45 pm
☽ ☍ ♄ **11:40 pm** 8:40 pm
☽ ☍ ☉ 11:55 pm

14 FRIDAY
☽ ☍ ☉ **2:55 am**
☽ △ ♅ **3:06 am** 12:06 am
☉ ⚹ ♅ **5:16 am** 2:16 am
☽ ☍ ♆ **1:47 pm** 10:47 am
☽ △ ♇ **9:27 pm** 6:27 pm

15 SATURDAY
☽ ☍ ♀ **5:24 am** 2:24 am
☽ ☍ ☿ **10:12 am** 7:12 am
☽ △ ♃ **6:38 pm** 3:38 pm

16 SUNDAY
☽ □ ♂ **5:53 am** 2:53 am
☽ ⚻ ♄ **12:32 pm** 9:32 am
☽ ⚻ ♅ **3:35 pm** 12:35 pm
☽ ⚻ ☉ **8:45 pm** 5:45 pm
☽ ⚻ ♆ 11:29 pm

17 MONDAY
☽ ⚻ ♆ **2:29 am**
☽ □ ♇ **10:11 am** 7:11 am
☽ ⚻ ♀ **3:25 pm** 12:25 pm
☽ ⚻ ☿ **9:54 pm** 6:54 pm

18 TUESDAY
☽ ⚻ ♃ **8:06 am** 5:06 am
☽ △ ♂ **7:56 pm** 4:56 pm
☽ △ ♄ 11:03 pm

19 WEDNESDAY
☽ △ ♄ **2:03 am**
☽ ☍ ♅ **4:38 am** 1:38 am
☽ △ ☉ **3:08 pm** 12:08 pm
☽ △ ♆ **3:28 pm** 12:28 pm
☉ ☌ ♆ **7:25 pm** 4:25 pm
☽ ⚹ ♇ **10:59 pm** 7:59 pm
☽ △ ♀ 10:09 pm

20 THURSDAY
☽ △ ♀ **1:09 am**
☽ △ ☿ **7:56 am** 4:56 am
☽ ☍ ♃ **9:01 pm** 6:01 pm

21 FRIDAY
☽ ⚻ ♂ **9:06 am** 6:06 am
☽ □ ♄ **2:23 pm** 11:23 am
☽ ⚻ ♅ **4:29 pm** 1:29 pm
♀ ⚹ ♇ **5:32 pm** 2:32 pm
☽ □ ♆ 11:53 pm

22 SATURDAY
☽ □ ♆ **2:53 am**
☽ □ ☉ **7:29 am** 4:29 am
☽ □ ♀ **9:10 am** 6:10 am
☽ ⚺ ♇ **9:59 am** 6:59 am
☽ □ ☿ **3:13 pm** 12:13 pm
☉ ☌ ♀ **9:07 pm** 6:07 pm

23 SUNDAY
☽ ⚻ ♃ **7:25 am** 4:25 am
☉ ⚹ ♇ **3:32 pm** 12:32 pm
☽ ☍ ♂ **7:23 pm** 4:23 pm
☽ ⚹ ♄ **11:41 pm** 8:41 pm
☽ △ ♅ 10:18 pm

24 MONDAY
☽ △ ♅ **1:18 am**
☽ ⚹ ♆ **11:01 am** 8:01 am
☽ ⚹ ♀ **2:15 pm** 11:15 am
☉ ☌ ☿ **3:48 pm** 12:48 pm
☽ ☌ ♇ **5:34 pm** 2:34 pm
☽ ⚹ ☿ **7:06 pm** 4:06 pm
☽ ⚹ ☉ **7:36 pm** 4:36 pm

25 TUESDAY
☽ △ ♃ **2:01 pm** 11:01 am
☿ ⚹ ♇ **6:02 pm** 3:02 pm
☽ ⚻ ♂ 10:40 pm

26 WEDNESDAY
☽ ⚻ ♂ **1:40 am**
☽ ⚺ ♄ **5:04 am** 2:04 am
☽ □ ♅ **6:15 am** 3:15 am
☽ ⚺ ♆ **3:17 pm** 12:17 pm
☽ ⚺ ♀ **4:03 pm** 1:03 pm
☽ ⚺ ☿ **7:44 pm** 4:44 pm
☽ ⚺ ♇ **9:20 pm** 6:20 pm
☽ ⚺ ☉ 11:58 pm

27 THURSDAY
☽ ⚺ ☉ **2:58 am**
♀ ☌ ♆ **9:13 am** 6:13 am
☽ □ ♃ **4:56 pm** 1:56 pm

28 FRIDAY
☽ △ ♂ **4:27 am** 1:27 am
☽ ☌ ♄ **7:03 am** 4:03 am
☽ ⚹ ♅ **7:55 am** 4:55 am
☽ ☌ ♀ **3:17 pm** 12:17 pm
☽ ☌ ♆ **4:30 pm** 1:30 pm
☽ ☌ ☿ **6:02 pm** 3:02 pm
☽ ⚹ ♇ **10:12 pm** 7:12 pm

29 SATURDAY
☽ ☌ ☉ **6:58 am** 3:58 am
☽ ⚹ ♃ **5:32 pm** 2:32 pm
☿ ☌ ♆ **10:47 pm** 7:47 pm

30 SUNDAY
☽ □ ♂ **5:18 am** 2:18 am
☽ ⚺ ♄ **7:14 am** 4:14 am
☽ ⚺ ♅ **7:50 am** 4:50 am
☽ ⚺ ♀ **1:20 pm** 10:20 am
☽ ⚺ ☿ **3:28 pm** 12:28 pm
☽ ⚺ ♆ **4:17 pm** 1:17 pm
☽ □ ♇ **9:53 pm** 6:53 pm

31 MONDAY
☽ ⚺ ☉ **9:55 am** 6:55 am
☽ ⚺ ♃ **5:42 pm** 2:42 pm

Eastern time in bold type
Pacific time in medium type

MARCH 2025

DATE	SID.TIME	SUN	MOON	NODE	MERCURY	VENUS	MARS	JUPITER	SATURN	URANUS	NEPTUNE	PLUTO	CERES	PALLAS	JUNO	VESTA	CHIRON
1 Sa	10 36 13	10♓38 54	23♒55	27♈24	26♓17	10♈49	17♋10	12Ⅱ16	20♓41	23♉38	28♓54	2≈53	1♓59	4≈16	1♐02	16♍50	20♈37
2 Su	10 40 9	11 39 08	8♓43	27 24	27 54	10 50R	17 14	12 21	20 49	23 40	28 56	2 55	2 22	4 36	1 07	16 59	20 40
3 M	10 44 6	12 39 21	23 30	27 25	29 26	10 49	17 18	12 26	20 56	23 41	28 58	2 56	2 45	4 57	1 13	17 08	20 43
4 T	10 48 2	13 39 31	8♈09	27 26	0♈54	10 45	17 24	12 31	21 03	23 43	29 00	2 58	3 09	5 17	1 18	17 16	20 45
5 W	10 51 59	14 39 40	22 35	27 27	2 17	10 39	17 29	12 37	21 11	23 45	29 02	2 59	3 32	5 37	1 22	17 24	20 48
6 Th	10 55 55	15 39 46	6♉46	27 28R	3 34	10 31	17 36	12 42	21 18	23 46	29 05	3 01	3 56	5 57	1 27	17 31	20 52
7 F	10 59 52	16 39 50	20 39	27 28	4 45	10 19	17 43	12 48	21 26	23 48	29 07	3 03	4 19	6 17	1 31	17 38	20 55
8 Sa	11 3 49	17 39 52	4Ⅱ13	27 28	5 49	10 06	17 51	12 54	21 33	23 50	29 09	3 04	4 42	6 37	1 35	17 45	20 58
9 Su	11 7 45	18 39 52	17 31	27 27	6 46	9 49	18 00	13 00	21 40	23 52	29 11	3 05	5 06	6 57	1 38	17 51	21 01
10 M	11 11 42	19 39 50	0♋33	27 26	7 35	9 31	18 09	13 06	21 48	23 54	29 14	3 07	5 29	7 17	1 42	17 56	21 04
11 T	11 15 38	20 39 45	13 20	27 25	8 16	9 10	18 18	13 12	21 55	23 56	29 16	3 08	5 52	7 36	1 47	18 02	21 07
12 W	11 19 35	21 39 39	25 54	27 24	8 49	8 46	18 28	13 19	22 03	23 58	29 18	3 10	6 15	7 56	1 50	18 06	21 10
13 Th	11 23 31	22 39 30	8♌16	27 24	9 13	8 21	18 39	13 26	22 10	24 00	29 20	3 11	6 39	8 15	1 52	18 11	21 13
14 F	11 27 28	23 39 19	20 28	27 23D	9 28	7 53	18 51	13 32	22 17	24 02	29 23	3 13	7 02	8 34	1 52	18 14	21 17
15 Sa	11 31 24	24 39 07	2♍31	27 23	9 35R	7 24	19 02	13 39	22 25	24 04	29 25	3 14	7 25	8 53	1 53	18 18	21 20
16 Su	11 35 21	25 38 52	14 27	27 23	9 33	6 52	19 15	13 46	22 32	24 06	29 27	3 15	7 48	9 12	1 55	18 21	21 23
17 M	11 39 18	26 38 35	26 18	27 23R	9 23	6 20	19 28	13 54	22 40	24 08	29 29	3 16	8 11	9 31	1 56	18 23	21 27
18 T	11 43 14	27 38 17	8♎07	27 23	9 05	5 45	19 41	14 01	22 47	24 10	29 32	3 18	8 34	9 50	1 56	18 25	21 30
19 W	11 47 11	28 37 57	19 57	27 23	8 39	5 10	19 55	14 09	22 54	24 13	29 34	3 19	8 57	10 09	1 57R	18 26	21 33
20 Th	11 51 7	29 37 35	1♏51	27 23	8 07	4 33	20 09	14 16	23 02	24 15	29 36	3 20	9 20	10 27	1 57	18 27	21 37
21 F	11 55 4	0♈37 12	13 53	27 23	7 29	3 56	20 24	14 24	23 09	24 17	29 38	3 21	9 43	10 46	1 57	18 28R	21 40
22 Sa	11 59 0	1 36 46	26 08	27 23D	6 46	3 19	20 40	14 32	23 16	24 20	29 41	3 23	10 06	11 04	1 56	18 28	21 43
23 Su	12 2 57	2 36 19	8♐39	27 23	5 58	2 41	20 55	14 40	23 24	24 22	29 43	3 24	10 29	11 22	1 55	18 27	21 47
24 M	12 6 53	3 35 50	21 32	27 23	5 08	2 03	21 12	14 48	23 31	24 24	29 45	3 25	10 52	11 40	1 54	18 26	21 50
25 T	12 10 50	4 35 20	4♑48	27 24	4 16	1 26	21 28	14 57	23 39	24 27	29 48	3 26	11 15	11 58	1 52	18 25	21 54
26 W	12 14 47	5 34 47	18 31	27 24	3 23	0 49	21 45	15 05	23 46	24 30	29 50	3 27	11 38	12 16	1 50	18 23	21 57
27 Th	12 18 43	6 34 13	2≈40	27 25	2 30	0 13	22 03	15 14	23 53	24 32	29 52	3 28	12 01	12 34	1 48	18 20	22 00
28 F	12 22 40	7 33 37	17 14	27 26R	1 39	29♓04	22 21	15 22	24 00	24 35	29 54	3 29	12 23	12 51	1 46	18 17	22 04
29 Sa	12 26 36	8 32 59	2♓07	27 26	0 50	29 04	22 39	15 31	24 08	24 37	29 57	3 30	12 46	13 09	1 43	18 13	22 07
30 Su	12 30 33	9 32 19	17 13	27 25	0 04	28 32	22 58	15 40	24 15	24 40	29 59	3 31	13 09	13 26	1 39	18 09	22 11
31 M	12 34 29	10 31 37	2♈21	27 24	29♓22	28 01	23 17	15 49	24 22	24 43	0♈01	3 32	13 31	13 43	1 36	18 05	22 14

EPHEMERIS CALCULATED FOR 12 MIDNIGHT GREENWICH MEAN TIME. ALL OTHER DATA AND FACING ASPECTARIAN PAGE IN **EASTERN TIME (BOLD)** AND PACIFIC TIME (REGULAR).

APRIL 2025

☽ Last Aspect day	ET / hr:mn	PT	asp	☽ Ingress sign	day	ET / hr:mn	PT
1	1:43 pm	10:43 am	⚹☿	♊	1	4:26 pm	1:26 pm
3	2:26 pm	11:26 am	□☿	♋	3	6:50 pm	3:50 pm
5	6:54 pm	3:54 pm	△☿	♌	5		9:34 pm
5	6:54 pm	3:54 pm	△☿	♌	6	12:34 am	
7		9:08 pm	□♅	♍	8	9:40 am	6:40 am
8	12:08 am		□♅	♍	8	9:40 am	6:40 am
10	3:49 pm	12:49 pm	☍☿	♎	10	9:12 pm	6:12 pm
13	6:01 am	3:01 am	□♂	♏	13	9:54 am	6:54 am
15	10:24 pm	7:24 pm	△☿	♐	15	10:37 pm	7:37 pm
18	7:38 am	4:38 am	△☉	♑	18	10:12 am	7:12 am
20	1:21 pm	10:21 am	⚹♄	♒	20	7:22 pm	4:22 pm
22	5:55 pm	2:55 pm	□♅	♓	22		10:07 pm
22	5:55 pm	2:55 pm	□♅	♓	23	1:07 am	
24	10:57 pm	7:57 pm	☌♀	♈	25	3:24 am	12:24 am
26	12:18 pm	9:18 am	⚹♃	♉	27	3:17 am	12:17 am
28		10:18 pm	⚹♀	♊	28		11:34 pm
29	1:18 am		⚹♀	♊	29	2:34 am	
30	11:49 pm	8:49 pm	□♄	♋	5/1	3:23 am	12:23 am

☽ Phases & Eclipses phase	day	ET / hr:mn	PT
2nd Quarter	4	10:15 pm	7:15 pm
Full Moon	12	8:22 pm	5:22 pm
4th Quarter	20	9:36 pm	6:36 pm
New Moon	27	3:31 pm	12:31 pm

Planet Ingress	day	ET / hr:mn	PT
⚵ ♏	14		11:30 pm
⚵ ♏	15	2:30 am	
☿ ♈	15		11:25 pm
☿ ♈	16	2:25 am	
♂ ♌	17		9:21 pm
♂ ♌	18	12:21 am	
☉ ♉	19	3:56 pm	12:56 pm
♀ ♈	30	1:16 pm	10:16 am

Planetary Motion		day	ET / hr:mn	PT
☿	D	7	7:08 am	4:08 am
♀	D	12	9:02 pm	6:02 pm

1 TUESDAY
☽⚹♂ 6:15 am 3:15 am
☽⚹♄ 7:33 am 4:33 am
☽☌♅ 7:56 am 4:56 am
☽⚹♀ 11:54 am 8:54 am
☽⚹☿ 1:43 pm 10:43 am
☽⚹♆ 4:34 pm 1:34 pm
☽△♇ 10:17 pm 7:17 pm

2 WEDNESDAY
☽⚹☉ 2:20 pm 11:20 am
☽☌♃ 7:25 pm 4:25 pm

3 THURSDAY
☽⚺♂ 9:17 am 6:17 am
☽□♄ 9:52 am 6:52 am
☽⚺♅ 10:01 am 7:01 am
☽□♀ 12:37 pm 9:37 am
☽□☿ 2:26 pm 11:26 am
☽□♆ 7:07 pm 4:07 pm
☽⚻♇ 10:06 pm

4 FRIDAY
☽⚻♇ 1:06 am
♄⚹♅ 12:21 pm 9:21 am
♂⚹♅ 7:05 pm 4:05 pm
♂△♄ 9:08 pm 6:08 pm
☽□☉ 10:15 pm 7:15 pm
☽⚺♃ 9:12 pm

5 SATURDAY
☽⚺♃ 12:12 am
☽⚹♅ 3:20 pm 12:20 pm
☽△♄ 3:29 pm 12:29 pm
☽☌♂ 3:49 pm 12:49 pm
☽△♀ 4:36 pm 1:36 pm
☽△☿ 6:54 pm 3:54 pm
☽△♆ 10:02 pm

6 SUNDAY
☽△♆ 1:02 am
☉⚹♃ 5:44 am 2:44 am
☽☍♇ 7:19 am 4:19 am
♀△♂ 8:13 am 5:13 am

7 MONDAY
♀☌♄ 7:01 am 4:01 am
☽⚹♃ 8:37 am 5:37 am
☽△☉ 10:31 am 7:31 am
☽□♅ 9:08 pm
☽⚻♀ 9:09 pm
☽⚻♄ 9:37 pm
♀⚹♅ 9:48 pm
☽⚺♂ 11:07 pm

8 TUESDAY
☽□♅ 12:08 am
☽⚻♀ 12:09 am
☽⚻♄ 12:37 am
♀⚹♅ 12:48 am
☽⚺♂ 2:07 am
☽⚻☿ 3:33 am 12:33 am
☽⚻♆ 10:19 am 7:19 am
☽⚻♇ 4:50 pm 1:50 pm

9 WEDNESDAY
☽□♃ 8:04 pm 5:04 pm
☽⚻☉ 11:26 pm

10 THURSDAY
☽⚻☉ 2:26 am
☽☍♀ 10:39 am 7:39 am
☽△♅ 11:36 am 8:36 am
☽☍♄ 12:26 pm 9:26 am
☽⚹♂ 3:19 pm 12:19 pm
☽☍☿ 3:49 pm 12:49 pm
☽☍♆ 10:03 pm 7:03 pm

11 FRIDAY
☽△♇ 4:38 am 1:38 am

12 SATURDAY
☽△♃ 9:20 am 6:20 am
☽☍☉ 8:22 pm 5:22 pm
☽⚻♀ 11:00 pm 8:00 pm
☽⚻♅ 9:28 pm
☽⚻♄ 10:38 pm

13 SUNDAY
☽⚻♅ 12:28 am
☽⚻♄ 1:38 am
☽□♂ 6:01 am 3:01 am
☽⚻☿ 6:32 am 3:32 am
☽⚻♆ 10:57 am 7:57 am
☽□♇ 5:27 pm 2:27 pm

14 MONDAY
☉⚺♀ 4:52 am 1:52 am
☽⚻♃ 11:06 pm 8:06 pm
☉⚺♅ 9:20 pm

15 TUESDAY
☉⚺♅ 12:20 am
☽△♀ 12:04 pm 9:04 am
☽☍♅ 1:31 pm 10:31 am
☽⚻☉ 2:38 pm 11:38 am
☽△♄ 3:00 pm 12:00 pm
☉⚺♄ 7:32 pm 4:32 pm
☽△♂ 8:52 pm 5:52 pm
☽△☿ 10:24 pm 7:24 pm
☽△♆ 11:50 pm 8:50 pm

16 WEDNESDAY
☽⚹♇ 6:08 am 3:08 am
☿☌♆ 9:11 pm

17 THURSDAY
☿☌♆ 12:11 am
☽☍♃ 12:11 pm 9:11 am
☽□♀ 9:40 pm
☽⚻♅ 10:37 pm

18 FRIDAY
☽□♀ 12:40 am
☽⚻♅ 1:37 am
☽□♄ 3:21 am 12:21 am
☽△☉ 7:38 am 4:38 am
☽⚻♂ 10:33 am 7:33 am
☽□♆ 11:33 am 8:33 am
☽□☿ 1:50 pm 10:50 am
☽⚺♇ 5:31 pm 2:31 pm

19 SATURDAY
♂△♆ 6:53 pm 3:53 pm
☽⚻♃ 11:16 pm 8:16 pm

20 SUNDAY
☉⚺♆ 10:35 am 7:35 am
☽⚹♀ 11:23 am 8:23 am
☽△♅ 11:27 am 8:27 am
☽⚹♄ 1:21 pm 10:21 am
♀⚹♅ 2:21 pm 11:21 am
☿⚹♇ 5:40 pm 2:40 pm
☽⚹♆ 8:48 pm 5:48 pm
☉□♂ 9:34 pm 6:34 pm
☽☍♂ 9:35 pm 6:35 pm
☽□☉ 9:36 pm 6:36 pm
☽☌♇ 11:20 pm

21 MONDAY
☽☌♇ 2:20 am
☽⚹☿ 3:00 am 12:00 am

22 TUESDAY
☽△♃ 7:04 am 4:04 am
☽□♅ 5:55 pm 2:55 pm
☽⚺♀ 6:56 pm 3:56 pm
☽⚺♄ 7:55 pm 4:55 pm
☽⚺♆ 11:35 pm

23 WEDNESDAY
☽⚺♆ 2:35 am
☽⚻♂ 4:54 am 1:54 am
☽⚹☉ 7:14 am 4:14 am
☽⚺♇ 7:38 am 4:38 am
☽⚺☿ 12:24 pm 9:24 am
☉□♇ 1:10 pm 10:10 am

24 THURSDAY
☽□♃ 11:10 am 8:10 am
♀☌♄ 8:02 pm 5:02 pm
☽⚹♅ 8:50 pm 5:50 pm
☽☌♄ 10:54 pm 7:54 pm
☽☌♀ 10:57 pm 7:57 pm

25 FRIDAY
☽☌♆ 4:53 am 1:53 am
☽△♂ 8:29 am 5:29 am
☽⚹♇ 9:34 am 6:34 am
☽⚺☉ 12:40 pm 9:40 am
☽☌☿ 6:04 pm 3:04 pm

26 SATURDAY
☽⚹♃ 12:18 pm 9:18 am
♂☍♇ 9:05 pm 6:05 pm
☽⚺♅ 9:07 pm 6:07 pm
☽⚺♄ 11:16 pm 8:16 pm
☽⚺♀ 9:25 pm

27 SUNDAY
☽⚺♀ 12:25 am
☽⚺♆ 4:49 am 1:49 am
☽□♇ 9:16 am 6:16 am
☽□♂ 9:38 am 6:38 am
☽☌☉ 3:31 pm 12:31 pm
☽⚺☿ 9:39 pm 6:39 pm

28 MONDAY
☽⚺♃ 12:10 pm 9:10 am
☽☌♅ 8:33 pm 5:33 pm
☽⚹♄ 10:51 pm 7:51 pm
☽⚹♀ 10:18 pm

29 TUESDAY
☽⚹♀ 1:18 am
☽⚹♆ 4:14 am 1:14 am
☽△♇ 8:39 am 5:39 am
☽⚹♂ 10:29 am 7:29 am
☽⚺☉ 6:19 pm 3:19 pm
☽⚹☿ 10:50 pm

30 WEDNESDAY
☽⚹☿ 1:50 am
☽☌♃ 12:58 pm 9:58 am
☽⚺♅ 9:15 pm 6:15 pm
☽□♄ 11:49 pm 8:49 pm

Eastern time in bold type
Pacific time in medium type

APRIL 2025

DATE	SID.TIME	SUN	MOON	NODE	MERCURY	VENUS	MARS	JUPITER	SATURN	URANUS	NEPTUNE	PLUTO	CERES	PALLAS	JUNO	VESTA	CHIRON
1 T	12 38 26	11♈30 53	17♋23	27♈22R	28♓45R	27♓32R	23♋36	15♊59	24♓29	24♉45	0♈03	3≈33	13♊54	14≏00	1♐32R	18♍00R	22♈18
2 W	12 42 22	12 30 06	2♌11	27 21	28 12	27 05	23 56	16 08	24 37	24 48	0 06	3 34	14 16	14 17	1 28	17 54	22 22
3 Th	12 46 19	13 29 18	16 38	27 19	27 45	26 40	24 16	16 18	24 44	24 51	0 08	3 35	14 39	14 33	1 23	17 48	22 25
4 F	12 50 15	14 28 27	0♍40	27 18	27 25	26 17	24 36	16 27	24 51	24 54	0 10	3 36	15 01	14 50	1 18	17 42	22 29
5 Sa	12 54 12	15 27 34	14 18	27 17D	27 06	25 56	24 57	16 37	24 58	24 57	0 12	3 37	15 24	15 06	1 13	17 35	22 32
6 Su	12 58 9	16 26 38	27 31	27 18	26 55	25 38	25 19	16 47	25 05	25 00	0 14	3 38	15 46	15 23	1 07	17 28	22 36
7 M	13 2 5	17 25 40	10♎24	27 19	26 50D	25 22	25 40	16 56	25 12	25 02	0 17	3 38	16 08	15 39	1 01	17 20	22 39
8 T	13 6 2	18 24 40	22 58	27 20	26 50	25 08	26 02	17 07	25 19	25 05	0 19	3 39	16 30	15 55	0 55	17 11	22 43
9 W	13 9 58	19 23 37	5♏17	27 21	26 56	24 57	26 24	17 17	25 26	25 08	0 21	3 40	16 53	16 10	0 48	17 03	22 46
10 Th	13 13 55	20 22 32	17 25	27 22	27 07	24 49	26 46	17 27	25 33	25 11	0 23	3 41	17 15	16 26	0 41	16 53	22 50
11 F	13 17 51	21 21 25	29 24	27 23R	27 22	24 43	27 09	17 37	25 40	25 14	0 25	3 41	17 37	16 41	0 34	16 44	22 54
12 Sa	13 21 48	22 20 16	11♐18	27 22	27 43	24 39	27 32	17 48	25 47	25 17	0 28	3 42	17 59	16 57	0 27	16 34	22 57
13 Su	13 25 44	23 19 05	23 09	27 20	28 08	24 37 D	27 55	17 58	25 54	25 20	0 30	3 42	18 21	17 12	0 19	16 23	23 01
14 M	13 29 41	24 17 52	4♑59	27 17	28 38	24 39	28 19	18 09	26 01	25 24	0 32	3 43	18 43	17 27	0 11	16 13	23 04
15 T	13 33 38	25 16 37	16 49	27 12	29 11	24 42	28 43	18 19	26 08	25 27	0 34	3 44	19 04	17 41	0 02	16 02	23 08
16 W	13 37 34	26 15 20	28 42	27 07	29 49	24 48	29 07	18 30	26 14	25 30	0 36	3 44	19 26	17 56	29♏54	15 50	23 11
17 Th	13 41 31	27 14 02	10♒40	27 02	0♈31	24 56	29 31	18 41	26 21	25 33	0 38	3 45	19 48	18 10	29 45	15 38	23 15
18 F	13 45 27	28 12 41	22 46	26 57	1 16	25 06	29 56	18 52	26 28	25 36	0 40	3 45	20 10	18 25	29 35	15 26	23 19
19 Sa	13 49 24	29 11 19	5♓02	26 54	2 05	25 18	0♌20	19 03	26 34	25 39	0 42	3 46	20 31	18 39	29 26	15 13	23 22
20 Su	13 53 20	0♉09 56	17 33	26 51	2 57	25 33	0 45	19 14	26 41	25 43	0 44	3 46	20 53	18 52	29 16	15 01	23 26
21 M	13 57 17	1 08 30	0♈21	26 51D	3 52	25 49	1 11	19 26	26 48	25 46	0 46	3 46	21 14	19 06	29 06	14 48	23 29
22 T	14 1 13	2 07 03	13 30	26 51	4 50	26 07	1 36	19 37	26 54	25 49	0 48	3 47	21 36	19 19	28 55	14 34	23 33
23 W	14 5 10	3 05 35	27 03	26 52	5 51	26 27	2 02	19 48	27 01	25 52	0 50	3 47	21 57	19 33	28 45	14 21	23 36
24 Th	14 9 7	4 04 04	11♉03	26 54	6 55	26 50	2 28	20 00	27 07	25 56	0 52	3 48	22 18	19 46	28 34	14 07	23 40
25 F	14 13 3	5 02 32	25 28	26 55R	8 01	27 13	2 54	20 11	27 14	25 59	0 54	3 48	22 39	19 59	28 23	13 53	23 43
26 Sa	14 17 0	6 00 59	10♊17	26 54	9 10	27 39	3 20	20 23	27 20	26 02	0 56	3 48	23 00	20 11	28 12	13 38	23 47
27 Su	14 20 56	6 59 24	25 23	26 52	10 22	28 06	3 47	20 35	27 26	26 06	0 58	3 48	23 21	20 24	28 00	13 24	23 50
28 M	14 24 53	7 57 47	10♋38	26 47	11 36	28 35	4 14	20 46	27 32	26 09	1 00	3 48	23 42	20 36	27 48	13 10	23 54
29 T	14 28 49	8 56 08	25 51	26 41	12 51	29 05	4 41	20 58	27 39	26 12	1 02	3 49	24 03	20 48	27 36	12 55	23 57
30 W	14 32 46	9 54 27	10♌53	26 35	14 10	29 36	5 08	21 10	27 45	26 16	1 04	3 49	24 24	21 00	27 24	12 40	24 01

EPHEMERIS CALCULATED FOR 12 MIDNIGHT GREENWICH MEAN TIME. ALL OTHER DATA AND FACING ASPECTARIAN PAGE IN **EASTERN TIME (BOLD)** AND PACIFIC TIME (REGULAR).

☽ Last Aspect / ☽ Ingress

day	ET / hr:mn / PT		asp	sign	day	ET / hr:mn / PT	
4/30	**11:49 pm**	8:49 pm	□ ♄	♋	1	**3:23 am**	12:23 am
3	**4:02 am**	1:02 am	△ ♄	♌	3	**7:29 am**	4:29 am
5	**9:03 am**	6:03 am	□ ♅	♍	5	**3:40 pm**	12:40 pm
7		9:11 pm	☍ ♄	♎	8	**3:06 am**	12:06 am
8	**12:11 am**		☍ ♄	♎	8	**3:06 am**	12:06 am
9		11:17 pm	△ ♃	♏	10	**3:58 pm**	12:58 pm
10	**2:17 am**		△ ♃	♏	10	**3:58 pm**	12:58 pm
12		11:37 pm	△ ♄	♐	13	**4:35 am**	1:35 am
13	**2:37 am**		△ ♄	♐	13	**4:35 am**	1:35 am
15	**2:29 pm**	11:29 am	□ ♄	♑	15	**3:58 pm**	12:58 pm
17		9:27 pm	⚹ ♄	♒	17		10:29 pm
18	**12:27 am**		⚹ ♄	♒	18	**1:29 am**	
20	**7:59 am**	4:59 am	□ ☉	♓	20	**8:28 am**	5:28 am
22	**12:06 pm**	9:06 am	☌ ♄	♈	22	**12:26 pm**	9:26 am
24	**7:44 am**	4:44 am	⚹ ♃	♉	24	**1:38 pm**	10:38 am
26	**9:52 am**	6:52 am	☌ ♅	♊	26	**1:21 pm**	10:21 am
28	**9:01 am**	6:01 am	☌ ♃	♋	28	**1:33 pm**	10:33 am
30	**12:50 pm**	9:50 am	⚹ ♅	♌	30	**4:17 pm**	1:17 pm

☽ Phases & Eclipses

phase	day	ET / hr:mn / PT	
2nd Quarter	4	**9:52 am**	6:52 am
Full Moon	12	**12:56 pm**	9:56 am
4th Quarter	20	**7:59 am**	4:59 am
New Moon	26	**11:02 pm**	8:02 pm

Planet Ingress

		day	ET / hr:mn / PT	
☿	♉	10	**8:15 am**	5:15 am
⚳	♈	16	**2:23 pm**	11:23 am
☉	♊	20	**2:55 pm**	11:55 am
♄	♈	24	**11:35 pm**	8:35 pm
☿	♊	25	**8:59 pm**	5:59 pm

Planetary Motion

		day	ET / hr:mn / PT	
♇	℞	4	**11:27 am**	8:27 am

1 THURSDAY
☽ □ ♀ **3:57 am** 12:57 am
☽ □ ♆ **5:14 am** 2:14 am
☽ ⚻ ♇ **9:48 am** 6:48 am
☽ ⚺ ♂ **1:22 pm** 10:22 am
☽ ⚹ ☉ **11:45 pm** 8:45 pm

2 FRIDAY
☽ □ ☿ **9:38 am** 6:38 am
♀ ☌ ♆ **1:07 pm** 10:07 am
☽ ⚺ ♃ **4:45 pm** 1:45 pm
☽ ⚹ ♅ 10:06 pm

3 SATURDAY
☽ ⚹ ♅ **1:06 am**
☽ △ ♄ **4:02 am** 1:02 am
☽ △ ♆ **9:37 am** 6:37 am
☽ △ ♀ **10:33 am** 7:33 am
☽ ☍ ♇ **2:25 pm** 11:25 am
☽ ☌ ♂ **8:13 pm** 5:13 pm

4 SUNDAY
☽ □ ☉ **9:52 am** 6:52 am
☽ △ ☿ **11:14 pm** 8:14 pm
☽ ⚹ ♃ 9:43 pm

5 MONDAY
☽ ⚹ ♃ **12:43 am**
☽ □ ♅ **9:03 am** 6:03 am
☽ ⚻ ♄ **12:24 pm** 9:24 am
☿ ⚹ ♃ **1:21 pm** 10:21 am
☽ ⚻ ♆ **6:04 pm** 3:04 pm
☽ ⚻ ♀ **10:01 pm** 7:01 pm
☽ ⚻ ♇ **11:05 pm** 8:05 pm

6 TUESDAY
☽ ⚺ ♂ **7:34 am** 4:34 am
♀ ⚹ ♇ **5:31 pm** 2:31 pm
☽ △ ☉ 9:50 pm

7 WEDNESDAY
☽ △ ☉ **12:50 am**
☽ □ ♃ **12:30 pm** 9:30 am
☽ ⚻ ☿ **6:38 pm** 3:38 pm
☽ △ ♅ **8:30 pm** 5:30 pm
☽ ☍ ♄ 9:11 pm

8 THURSDAY
☽ ☍ ♄ **12:11 am**
☽ ☍ ♆ **5:45 am** 2:45 am
☿ ⚺ ♅ **8:56 am** 5:56 am
☽ △ ♇ **10:48 am** 7:48 am
☽ ☍ ♀ **1:22 pm** 10:22 am
☽ ⚹ ♂ **10:07 pm** 7:07 pm

9 FRIDAY
☿ ⚺ ♄ **1:31 pm** 10:31 am
☽ ⚻ ☉ **6:43 pm** 3:43 pm
☽ △ ♃ 11:17 pm

10 SATURDAY
☽ △ ♃ **2:17 am**
☽ ⚻ ♅ **9:36 am** 6:36 am
☽ ⚻ ♄ **1:31 pm** 10:31 am
☽ ☍ ☿ **5:15 pm** 2:15 pm
☽ ⚻ ♆ **6:47 pm** 3:47 pm
☽ □ ♇ **11:42 pm** 8:42 pm

11 SUNDAY
☿ ⚺ ♆ **4:01 am** 1:01 am
☽ ⚻ ♀ **6:18 am** 3:18 am
☽ □ ♂ **1:39 pm** 10:39 am

12 MONDAY
☽ ☍ ☉ **12:56 pm** 9:56 am
☿ □ ♇ **1:23 pm** 10:23 am
☽ ⚻ ♃ **4:09 pm** 1:09 pm
☽ ☍ ♅ **10:35 pm** 7:35 pm
☽ △ ♄ 11:37 pm

13 TUESDAY
☽ △ ♄ **2:37 am**
☽ △ ♆ **7:29 am** 4:29 am
☽ ⚹ ♇ **12:11 pm** 9:11 am
☽ ⚻ ☿ **4:08 pm** 1:08 pm
☽ △ ♀ **10:48 pm** 7:48 pm

14 WEDNESDAY
☽ △ ♂ **4:28 am** 1:28 am
☉ ⚺ ♃ **3:09 pm** 12:09 pm

15 THURSDAY
☽ ☍ ♃ **4:54 am** 1:54 am
☽ ⚻ ☉ **5:49 am** 2:49 am
☽ ⚻ ♅ **10:24 am** 7:24 am
☽ □ ♄ **2:29 pm** 11:29 am
☽ □ ♆ **6:55 pm** 3:55 pm
☽ ⚺ ♇ **11:20 pm** 8:20 pm

16 FRIDAY
☽ △ ☿ **1:29 pm** 10:29 am
☽ □ ♀ **1:45 pm** 10:45 am
☿ ⚺ ♀ **4:24 pm** 1:24 pm
☽ ⚻ ♂ **5:37 pm** 2:37 pm

17 SATURDAY
☽ ⚻ ♃ **3:50 pm** 12:50 pm
☉ ☌ ♅ **7:32 pm** 4:32 pm
☽ △ ♅ **8:24 pm** 5:24 pm
☽ △ ☉ **8:28 pm** 5:28 pm
☽ ⚹ ♄ 9:27 pm
☿ □ ♂ 9:36 pm

18 SUNDAY
☽ ⚹ ♄ **12:27 am**
☿ □ ♂ **12:36 am**
☽ ⚹ ♆ **4:27 am** 1:27 am
☽ ☌ ♇ **8:34 am** 5:34 am
☽ ⚹ ♀ 11:18 pm

19 MONDAY
☽ ⚹ ♀ **2:18 am**
☽ ☍ ♂ **4:23 am** 1:23 am
☽ □ ☿ **8:00 am** 5:00 am
☽ △ ♃ 9:13 pm

20 TUESDAY
☽ △ ♃ **12:13 am**
☽ □ ♅ **3:53 am** 12:53 am
☉ ⚹ ♄ **5:38 am** 2:38 am
☽ ⚺ ♄ **7:49 am** 4:49 am
☽ □ ☉ **7:59 am** 4:59 am
☽ ⚺ ♆ **11:23 am** 8:23 am
☽ ⚺ ♇ **3:09 pm** 12:09 pm

21 WEDNESDAY
☽ ⚺ ♀ **11:32 am** 8:32 am
☽ ⚻ ♂ **11:58 am** 8:58 am
☽ ⚹ ☿ **10:21 pm** 7:21 pm

22 THURSDAY
♀ △ ♂ **3:42 am** 12:42 am
☽ □ ♃ **5:27 am** 2:27 am
☽ ⚹ ♅ **8:19 am** 5:19 am
☉ ⚹ ♆ **8:40 am** 5:40 am
☽ ☌ ♄ **12:06 pm** 9:06 am
☽ ☌ ♆ **3:15 pm** 12:15 pm
☽ ⚹ ☉ **3:43 pm** 12:43 pm
☽ ⚹ ♇ **6:42 pm** 3:42 pm

23 FRIDAY
☽ △ ♂ **4:13 pm** 1:13 pm
☽ ☌ ♀ **5:13 pm** 2:13 pm

24 SATURDAY
☿ ⚺ ♃ **3:16 am** 12:16 am
☽ ⚹ ♃ **7:44 am** 4:44 am
☽ ⚺ ☿ **8:23 am** 5:23 am
☽ ⚺ ♅ **9:54 am** 6:54 am
☉ △ ♇ **11:55 am** 8:55 am
☽ ⚺ ♄ **1:35 pm** 10:35 am
☽ ⚺ ♆ **4:24 pm** 1:24 pm
☿ ☌ ♅ **7:15 pm** 4:15 pm
☽ □ ♇ **7:36 pm** 4:36 pm
☽ ⚺ ☉ **8:08 pm** 5:08 pm

25 SUNDAY
☽ □ ♂ **6:06 pm** 3:06 pm
☽ ⚺ ♀ **8:25 pm** 5:25 pm
☿ ⚹ ♄ **9:46 pm** 6:46 pm

26 MONDAY
☽ ⚺ ♃ **8:15 am** 5:15 am
☽ ☌ ♅ **9:52 am** 6:52 am
☽ ⚹ ♄ **1:33 pm** 10:33 am
☽ ☌ ☿ **4:05 pm** 1:05 pm
☽ ⚹ ♆ **4:10 pm** 1:10 pm
☿ ⚹ ♆ **4:37 pm** 1:37 pm
☽ △ ♇ **7:14 pm** 4:14 pm
☽ ☌ ☉ **11:02 pm** 8:02 pm

27 TUESDAY
☿ △ ♇ **1:56 pm** 10:56 am
☽ ⚹ ♂ **7:35 pm** 4:35 pm
☽ ⚹ ♀ **11:21 pm** 8:21 pm

28 WEDNESDAY
☽ ☌ ♃ **9:01 am** 6:01 am
☽ ⚺ ♅ **10:08 am** 7:08 am
☽ □ ♄ **1:59 pm** 10:59 am
☽ □ ♆ **4:31 pm** 1:31 pm
☽ ⚻ ♇ **7:36 pm** 4:36 pm
☽ ⚺ ☿ 9:54 pm

29 THURSDAY
☽ ⚺ ☿ **12:54 am**
☽ ⚺ ☉ **3:02 am** 12:02 am
☽ ⚺ ♂ **11:05 pm** 8:05 pm
☉ ☌ ☿ 9:13 pm

30 FRIDAY
☉ ☌ ☿ **12:13 am**
☽ □ ♀ **4:45 am** 1:45 am
☽ ⚺ ♃ **12:16 pm** 9:16 am
☽ ⚹ ♅ **12:50 pm** 9:50 am
☽ △ ♄ **5:00 pm** 2:00 pm
☽ △ ♆ **7:31 pm** 4:31 pm
☽ ☍ ♇ **10:43 pm** 7:43 pm

31 SATURDAY
☽ ⚹ ☉ **10:46 am** 7:46 am
☽ ⚹ ☿ **2:38 pm** 11:38 am

Eastern time in bold type
Pacific time in medium type

MAY 2025

DATE	SID.TIME	SUN	MOON	NODE	MERCURY	VENUS	MARS	JUPITER	SATURN	URANUS	NEPTUNE	PLUTO	CERES	PALLAS	JUNO	VESTA	CHIRON
1 Th	14 36 42	10♉52 45	25♊34	26♈29R	15♈31	0♈09	5♋36	21♊22	27♓51	26♉19	1♈06	3♒49	24♓45	21♒11	27♏12R	12♎25R	24♈04
2 F	14 40 39	11 51 01	9♋49	26 23	16 54	0 44	6 03	21 34	27 57	26 22	1 08	3 49	25 05	21 23	27 00	12 10	24 08
3 Sa	14 44 36	12 49 14	23 35	26 20	18 18	1 20	6 31	21 47	28 03	26 26	1 09	3 49	25 26	21 34	26 47	11 56	24 11
4 Su	14 48 32	13 47 25	6♌52	26 18D	19 45	1 56	6 59	21 59	28 09	26 29	1 11	3 49R	25 47	21 45	26 34	11 41	24 15
5 M	14 52 29	14 45 35	19 44	26 19	21 14	2 34	7 27	22 11	28 15	26 33	1 13	3 49	26 07	21 55	26 21	11 26	24 18
6 T	14 56 25	15 43 42	2♍14	26 20R	22 45	3 13	7 55	22 23	28 21	26 36	1 15	3 49	26 27	22 06	26 08	11 11	24 21
7 W	15 0 22	16 41 48	14 27	26 21	24 18	3 53	8 24	22 35	28 26	26 40	1 16	3 49	26 47	22 16	25 55	10 56	24 25
8 Th	15 4 18	17 39 51	26 28	26 20	25 53	4 34	8 53	22 48	28 32	26 43	1 18	3 49	27 08	22 26	25 42	10 42	24 28
9 F	15 8 15	18 37 53	8≏21	26 20	27 30	5 17	9 21	23 00	28 38	26 47	1 20	3 49	27 28	22 35	25 29	10 27	24 31
10 Sa	15 12 11	19 35 53	20 11	26 17	29 09	6 00	9 50	23 13	28 43	26 50	1 22	3 49	27 48	22 45	25 16	10 13	24 35
11 Su	15 16 8	20 33 51	1♏59	26 12	0♉50	6 44	10 20	23 26	28 49	26 53	1 23	3 49	28 07	22 54	25 02	9 59	24 38
12 M	15 20 5	21 31 48	13 49	26 04	2 32	7 29	10 49	23 38	28 54	26 57	1 25	3 48	28 27	23 03	24 49	9 45	24 41
13 T	15 24 1	22 29 43	25 43	25 55	4 17	8 15	11 18	23 51	29 00	27 00	1 26	3 48	28 47	23 11	24 35	9 31	24 45
14 W	15 27 58	23 27 36	7♐43	25 44	6 04	9 02	11 48	24 04	29 05	27 04	1 28	3 48	29 06	23 20	24 22	9 17	24 48
15 Th	15 31 54	24 25 28	19 50	25 33	7 53	9 49	12 18	24 16	29 10	27 07	1 28	3 48	29 26	23 28	24 08	9 04	24 51
16 F	15 35 51	25 23 19	2♑04	25 23	9 44	10 38	12 48	24 29	29 16	27 11	1 30	3 47	29 45	23 36	23 55	8 51	24 54
17 Sa	15 39 47	26 21 09	14 29	25 15	11 37	11 27	13 18	24 42	29 21	27 14	1 31	3 47	0♈04	23 43	23 43	8 38	24 57
18 Su	15 43 44	27 18 57	27 05	25 08	13 31	12 17	13 48	24 55	29 26	27 18	1 34	3 47	0 24	23 51	23 28	8 25	25 01
19 M	15 47 40	28 16 44	9≈56	25 05	15 28	13 07	14 18	25 08	29 31	27 21	1 36	3 46	0 43	23 58	23 14	8 13	25 04
20 T	15 51 37	29 14 30	23 03	25 03D	17 27	13 58	14 48	25 21	29 36	27 25	1 37	3 46	1 02	24 04	23 01	8 01	25 07
21 W	15 55 34	0♊12 15	6♓30	25 03	19 27	14 49	15 19	25 34	29 41	27 28	1 38	3 45	1 20	24 11	22 47	7 49	25 10
22 Th	15 59 30	1 09 58	20 19	25 03R	21 29	15 43	15 50	25 47	29 45	27 32	1 40	3 45	1 39	24 17	22 34	7 38	25 13
23 F	16 3 27	2 07 41	4♈31	25 03	23 33	16 36	16 20	26 00	29 50	27 35	1 41	3 45	1 58	24 23	22 21	7 27	25 16
24 Sa	16 7 23	3 05 23	19 06	25 01	25 39	17 29	16 51	26 13	29 55	27 39	1 42	3 44	2 16	24 28	22 08	7 17	25 19
25 Su	16 11 20	4 03 04	3♉58	24 57	27 46	18 23	17 23	26 27	29 59	27 42	1 44	3 43	2 35	24 34	21 55	7 07	25 22
26 M	16 15 16	5 00 43	19 03	24 50	29 55	19 18	17 54	26 40	0♈04	27 46	1 45	3 43	2 53	24 39	21 42	6 57	25 25
27 T	16 19 13	5 58 22	4♊11	24 41	2♊04	20 14	18 25	26 53	0 08	27 49	1 46	3 42	3 11	24 43	21 29	6 48	25 28
28 W	16 23 9	6 55 59	19 12	24 30	4 15	21 09	18 57	27 06	0 13	27 53	1 47	3 42	3 29	24 48	21 17	6 39	25 31
29 Th	16 27 6	7 53 36	3♋56	24 21	6 26	22 05	19 28	27 20	0 17	27 56	1 49	3 41	3 47	24 52	21 04	6 30	25 34
30 F	16 31 3	8 51 11	18 16	24 11	8 38	23 01	20 00	27 33	0 21	28 00	1 50	3 40	4 05	24 55	20 52	6 22	25 36
31 Sa	16 34 59	9 48 44	2♌07	24 04	10 50	23 58	20 32	27 47	0 25	28 03	1 51	3 40	4 22	24 59	20 40	6 15	25 39

EPHEMERIS CALCULATED FOR 12 MIDNIGHT GREENWICH MEAN TIME. ALL OTHER DATA AND FACING ASPECTARIAN PAGE IN **EASTERN TIME (BOLD)** AND PACIFIC TIME (REGULAR).

JUNE 2025

☽ Last Aspect day	ET / hr:mn / PT	asp	☽ Ingress sign day	ET / hr:mn / PT
1	**7:38 pm** 4:38 pm	⚹ ♃	♍ 1	**11:00 pm** 8:00 pm
4	**7:11 am** 4:11 am	□ ♃	♎ 4	**9:38 am** 6:38 am
6	**9:04 pm** 6:04 pm	△ ♃	♏ 6	**10:23 pm** 7:23 pm
9	**8:06 am** 5:06 am	☍ ♅	♐ 9	**10:56 am** 7:56 am
11	**3:58 pm** 12:58 pm	△ ♂	♑ 11	**9:55 pm** 6:55 pm
14	**4:52 am** 1:52 am	△ ♅	♒ 14	**7:00 am** 4:00 am
16	**1:31 pm** 10:31 am	☍ ♂	♓ 16	**2:09 pm** 11:09 am
18	**5:34 pm** 2:34 pm	⚹ ♅	♈ 18	**7:08 pm** 4:08 pm
20	**9:49 pm** 6:49 pm	⚹ ☉	♉ 20	**9:53 pm** 6:53 pm
22	**9:50 pm** 6:50 pm	☌ ♅	♊ 22	**10:57 pm** 7:57 pm
23	**4:26 am** 1:26 am	□ ♂	♋ 24	**11:44 pm** 8:44 pm
26	10:16 pm	⚹ ♅	♌ 26	11:05 pm
27	**1:16 am**	⚹ ♅	♌ 27	**2:05 am**
29	**7:03 am** 4:03 am	□ ♅	♍ 29	**7:44 am** 4:44 am

☽ Phases & Eclipses phase	day	ET / hr:mn / PT
2nd Quarter	2	**11:41 pm** 8:41 pm
Full Moon	11	**3:44 am** 12:44 am
4th Quarter	18	**3:19 pm** 12:19 pm
New Moon	25	**6:32 am** 3:32 am

Planet Ingress	day	ET / hr:mn / PT
♀ ♉	5	9:43 pm
♀ ♉	6	**12:43 am**
☿ ♋	8	**6:58 pm** 3:58 pm
♃ ♋	9	**5:02 pm** 2:02 pm
♂ ♍	17	**4:35 am** 1:35 am
☉ ♋	20	**10:42 pm** 7:42 pm
☿ ♌	26	**3:09 pm** 12:09 pm

Planetary Motion	day	ET / hr:mn / PT
⚳ ℞	9	**5:40 am** 2:40 am
⚶ D	14	**2:00 pm** 11:00 am

1 SUNDAY
- ☽ ☌ ♂ **6:41 am** 3:41 am
- ♃ ⚺ ♅ **11:48 am** 8:48 am
- ☽ △ ♀ **2:52 pm** 11:52 am
- ☽ □ ♅ **7:32 pm** 4:32 pm
- ☽ ⚹ ♃ **7:38 pm** 4:38 pm
- ☽ ⚻ ♄ 9:04 pm
- ☽ ⚻ ♆ 11:35 pm

2 MONDAY
- ☽ ⚻ ♄ **12:04 am**
- ☽ ⚻ ♆ **2:35 am**
- ☽ ⚻ ♇ **5:55 am** 2:55 am
- ☽ □ ☉ **11:41 pm** 8:41 pm

3 TUESDAY
- ☽ □ ☿ **11:23 am** 8:23 am
- ☽ ⚺ ♂ **6:58 pm** 3:58 pm

4 WEDNESDAY
- ☽ ⚻ ♀ **6:08 am** 3:08 am
- ☽ △ ♅ **6:15 am** 3:15 am
- ☽ □ ♃ **7:11 am** 4:11 am
- ♀ ⚺ ♅ **7:33 am** 4:33 am
- ☽ ☍ ♄ **11:04 am** 8:04 am
- ☽ ☍ ♆ **1:30 pm** 10:30 am
- ☽ △ ♇ **4:52 pm** 1:52 pm
- ♀ ⚹ ♃ **10:32 pm** 7:32 pm

5 THURSDAY
- ☽ △ ☉ **4:46 pm** 1:46 pm
- ☿ ⚹ ♂ **6:10 pm** 3:10 pm

6 FRIDAY
- ☽ ⚹ ♂ **10:19 am** 7:19 am
- ☽ △ ☿ **12:56 pm** 9:56 am
- ☽ ⚻ ♅ **7:13 pm** 4:13 pm
- ☽ △ ♃ **9:04 pm** 6:04 pm
- ♀ ⚺ ♄ **9:32 pm** 6:32 pm
- ☽ ⚻ ♄ 9:09 pm
- ☽ ☍ ♀ 9:22 pm
- ☽ ⚻ ♆ 11:23 pm

7 SATURDAY
- ☽ ⚻ ♄ **12:09 am**
- ☽ ☍ ♀ **12:22 am**
- ☽ ⚻ ♆ **2:23 am**
- ☽ □ ♇ **5:37 am** 2:37 am
- ♀ ⚺ ♆ 9:23 pm
- ☿ ⚺ ♅ 10:32 pm

8 SUNDAY
- ♀ ⚺ ♆ **12:23 am**
- ☿ ⚺ ♅ **1:32 am**
- ☽ ⚻ ☉ **10:59 am** 7:59 am
- ☿ ☌ ♃ **4:12 pm** 1:12 pm
- ☽ □ ♂ 10:57 pm

9 MONDAY
- ☽ □ ♂ **1:57 am**
- ☿ □ ♄ **6:48 am** 3:48 am
- ☽ ☍ ♅ **8:06 am** 5:06 am
- ☽ ⚻ ♃ **10:48 am** 7:48 am
- ☽ △ ♄ **12:56 pm** 9:56 am
- ♀ □ ♇ **1:20 pm** 10:20 am
- ☽ ⚻ ☿ **2:08 pm** 11:08 am
- ☽ △ ♆ **2:55 pm** 11:55 am
- ☽ ⚹ ♇ **5:58 pm** 2:58 pm
- ☽ ⚻ ♀ **6:23 pm** 3:23 pm
- ☿ □ ♆ **6:54 pm** 3:54 pm

10 TUESDAY
- ☿ ⚻ ♇ **1:13 pm** 10:13 am

11 WEDNESDAY
- ☽ ☍ ☉ **3:44 am** 12:44 am
- ☿ ⚹ ♀ **3:41 pm** 12:41 pm
- ☽ △ ♂ **3:58 pm** 12:58 pm
- ☽ ⚻ ♅ **7:27 pm** 4:27 pm
- ☽ ☍ ♃ **10:54 pm** 7:54 pm
- ☽ □ ♄ 9:07 pm
- ☽ □ ♆ 10:51 pm

12 THURSDAY
- ☽ □ ♄ **12:07 am**
- ☽ □ ♆ **1:51 am**
- ☽ ⚺ ♇ **4:39 am** 1:39 am
- ☽ △ ♀ **10:22 am** 7:22 am
- ☽ ☍ ☿ **11:56 am** 8:56 am

13 FRIDAY
- ☽ ⚻ ☉ **6:06 pm** 3:06 pm

14 SATURDAY
- ☽ ⚻ ♂ **3:50 am** 12:50 am
- ☽ △ ♅ **4:52 am** 1:52 am
- ☽ ⚻ ♃ **8:59 am** 5:59 am
- ☽ ⚹ ♄ **9:21 am** 6:21 am
- ☽ ⚹ ♆ **10:52 am** 7:52 am
- ☽ ☌ ♇ **1:27 pm** 10:27 am
- ☽ □ ♀ **11:57 pm** 8:57 pm

15 SUNDAY
- ♂ □ ♅ **5:47 am** 2:47 am
- ☽ ⚻ ☿ **5:55 am** 2:55 am
- ♃ □ ♄ **10:36 am** 7:36 am

16 MONDAY
- ☽ △ ☉ **6:02 am** 3:02 am
- ☽ □ ♅ **12:18 pm** 9:18 am
- ☽ ☍ ♂ **1:31 pm** 10:31 am
- ☽ ⚺ ♄ **4:35 pm** 1:35 pm
- ☽ △ ♃ **5:01 pm** 2:01 pm
- ☽ ⚺ ♆ **5:54 pm** 2:54 pm
- ☽ ⚺ ♇ **8:17 pm** 5:17 pm

17 TUESDAY
- ☽ ⚹ ♀ **11:02 am** 8:02 am
- ☽ △ ☿ **8:09 pm** 5:09 pm

18 WEDNESDAY
- ☽ □ ☉ **3:19 pm** 12:19 pm
- ☽ ⚹ ♅ **5:34 pm** 2:34 pm
- ☽ ⚻ ♂ **8:45 pm** 5:45 pm
- ☽ ☌ ♄ **9:38 pm** 6:38 pm
- ☽ □ ♃ **10:46 pm** 7:46 pm
- ☽ ☌ ♆ **10:46 pm** 7:46 pm
- ♃ □ ♆ **11:16 pm** 8:16 pm
- ☽ ⚹ ♇ 9:57 pm

19 THURSDAY
- ☽ ⚹ ♇ **12:57 am**
- ☽ ⚺ ♀ **7:19 pm** 4:19 pm
- ♂ ⚻ ♄ **8:08 pm** 5:08 pm
- ☉ ⚺ ♅ 10:47 pm

20 FRIDAY
- ☉ ⚺ ♅ **1:47 am**
- ☽ □ ☿ **6:32 am** 3:32 am
- ☽ ⚺ ♅ **8:34 pm** 5:34 pm
- ☽ ⚹ ☉ **9:49 pm** 6:49 pm
- ♂ ⚻ ♆ **11:14 pm** 8:14 pm
- ☽ ⚺ ♄ 9:25 pm
- ☽ ⚺ ♆ 10:24 pm
- ☽ △ ♂ 10:29 pm
- ☽ ⚹ ♃ 11:10 pm

21 SATURDAY
- ☽ ⚺ ♄ **12:25 am**
- ☽ ⚺ ♆ **1:24 am**
- ☽ △ ♂ **1:29 am**
- ☽ ⚹ ♃ **2:10 am**
- ☽ □ ♇ **3:24 am** 12:24 am
- ☽ ☌ ♀ 10:02 pm

22 SUNDAY
- ☽ ☌ ♀ **1:02 am**
- ♂ ⚹ ♃ **6:32 am** 3:32 am
- ☽ ⚹ ☿ **1:44 pm** 10:44 am
- ☉ □ ♄ **2:36 pm** 11:36 am
- ☽ ☌ ♅ **9:50 pm** 6:50 pm
- ♂ ⚻ ♇ 10:00 pm
- ☽ ⚹ ♄ 10:33 pm
- ☽ ⚺ ☉ 11:17 pm
- ☽ ⚹ ♆ 11:25 pm

23 MONDAY
- ♂ ⚻ ♇ **1:00 am**
- ☽ ⚹ ♄ **1:33 am**
- ☽ ⚺ ☉ **2:17 am**
- ☽ ⚹ ♆ **2:25 am**
- ☽ ⚺ ♃ **3:55 am** 12:55 am
- ☽ △ ♇ **4:18 am** 1:18 am
- ☽ □ ♂ **4:26 am** 1:26 am
- ☉ □ ♆ **4:29 am** 1:29 am
- ♃ ⚻ ♇ 11:16 pm

24 TUESDAY
- ♃ ⚻ ♇ **2:16 am**
- ☽ ⚺ ♀ **5:32 am** 2:32 am
- ☉ ⚻ ♇ **8:59 am** 5:59 am
- ☉ ☌ ♃ **11:17 am** 8:17 am
- ☽ ⚺ ☿ **7:44 pm** 4:44 pm
- ☽ ⚺ ♅ **10:47 pm** 7:47 pm
- ☽ □ ♄ 11:28 pm

25 WEDNESDAY
- ☽ □ ♄ **2:28 am**
- ☽ □ ♆ **3:16 am** 12:16 am
- ☽ ⚻ ♇ **5:05 am** 2:05 am
- ☽ ☌ ♃ **5:33 am** 2:33 am
- ☽ ☌ ☉ **6:32 am** 3:32 am
- ☽ ⚹ ♂ **7:17 am** 4:17 am

26 THURSDAY
- ☿ ⚹ ♅ **5:45 am** 2:45 am
- ☉ ⚹ ♂ **10:11 am** 7:11 am
- ☽ ⚹ ♀ **11:08 am** 8:08 am
- ☽ ⚹ ♅ 10:16 pm

27 FRIDAY
- ☽ ⚹ ♅ **1:16 am**
- ☽ ☌ ☿ **3:13 am** 12:13 am
- ☽ △ ♄ **5:04 am** 2:04 am
- ☽ △ ♆ **5:50 am** 2:50 am
- ☽ ☍ ♇ **7:39 am** 4:39 am
- ☽ ⚺ ♃ **9:04 am** 6:04 am
- ☽ ⚺ ♂ **12:15 pm** 9:15 am
- ☽ ⚺ ☉ **1:02 pm** 10:02 am
- ☿ △ ♄ **11:53 pm** 8:53 pm

28 SATURDAY
- ☿ △ ♆ **7:58 am** 4:58 am
- ☽ □ ♀ **8:23 pm** 5:23 pm

29 SUNDAY
- ☿ ☍ ♇ **3:57 am** 12:57 am
- ☽ □ ♅ **7:03 am** 4:03 am
- ☽ ⚻ ♄ **11:02 am** 8:02 am
- ☽ ⚻ ♆ **11:45 am** 8:45 am
- ☽ ⚻ ♇ **1:37 pm** 10:37 am
- ☽ ⚺ ☿ **2:37 pm** 11:37 am
- ☽ ⚹ ♃ **4:13 pm** 1:13 pm
- ☽ ☌ ♂ **9:14 pm** 6:14 pm
- ☽ ⚹ ☉ **11:54 pm** 8:54 pm

30 MONDAY
- ☿ ⚺ ♃ **12:16 pm** 9:16 am

Eastern time in bold type
Pacific time in medium type

JUNE 2025

DATE	SID.TIME	SUN	MOON	NODE	MERCURY	VENUS	MARS	JUPITER	SATURN	URANUS	NEPTUNE	PLUTO	CERES	PALLAS	JUNO	VESTA	CHIRON
1 Su	16 38 56	10♊46 17	15♌30	23♓59R	13♊02	24♈56	21♌03	28♊00	0♈33	28♉07	1♈52	3♒38R	4♈40	25♒04	20♊16R	6♏08R	25♈42
2 M	16 42 52	11 43 48	28 25	23 57	15 14	25 53	21 36	28 13	0 37	28 10	1 53	3 38	4 57	25 07	20 05	6 01	25 45
3 T	16 46 49	12 41 17	10♍57	23 57D	17 25	26 52	22 08	28 27	0 41	28 13	1 54	3 37	5 14	25 09	19 53	5 55	25 47
4 W	16 50 45	13 38 45	23 10	23 56	19 35	27 50	22 40	28 40	0 44	28 17	1 55	3 37	5 31	25 10	19 42	5 50	25 50
5 Th	16 54 42	14 36 13	5♎10	23 54	21 44	28 49	23 12	28 54	0 48	28 20	1 56	3 36	5 48	25 12	19 31	5 45	25 53
6 F	16 58 39	15 33 38	17 01	23 54	23 52	29 48	23 45	29 07	0 52	28 24	1 57	3 35	6 05	25 13	19 21	5 40	25 55
7 Sa	17 2 35	16 31 03	28 50	23 50	25 58	0♉48	24 17	29 21	0 55	28 27	1 58	3 34	6 22	25 13	19 10	5 36	25 58
8 Su	17 6 32	17 28 27	10♏39	23 44	28 03	1 48	24 50	29 35	0 58	28 30	1 59	3 33	6 38	25 13	19 00	5 33	26 00
9 M	17 10 28	18 25 50	22 33	23 34	0♋05	2 48	25 22	29 48	1 02	28 34	2 00	3 33	6 55	25 14R	18 50	5 29	26 03
10 T	17 14 25	19 23 12	4♐33	23 22	2 06	3 49	25 55	0♋02	1 05	28 37	2 00	3 32	7 11	25 14	18 41	5 27	26 05
11 W	17 18 21	20 20 33	16 42	23 09	4 04	4 50	26 28	0 15	1 08	28 40	2 01	3 31	7 27	25 13	18 31	5 25	26 08
12 Th	17 22 18	21 17 53	29 01	22 56	5 51	5 51	27 01	0 29	1 11	28 44	2 02	3 30	7 43	25 13	18 22	5 23	26 10
13 F	17 26 14	22 15 13	11♑29	22 43	7 55	6 52	27 35	0 43	1 14	28 47	2 03	3 29	7 58	25 12	18 14	5 22	26 12
14 Sa	17 30 11	23 12 32	24 08	22 33	9 46	7 54	28 08	0 56	1 17	28 50	2 03	3 28	8 14	25 10	18 05	5 21D	26 15
15 Su	17 34 8	24 09 50	6♒58	22 24	11 36	8 56	28 41	1 10	1 19	28 53	2 04	3 27	8 29	25 08	17 57	5 21	26 17
16 M	17 38 4	25 07 08	20 00	22 19	13 22	9 58	29 15	1 24	1 22	28 57	2 05	3 26	8 45	25 06	17 49	5 22	26 19
17 T	17 42 1	26 04 26	3♓15	22 16	15 07	11 01	29 48	1 37	1 24	29 00	2 05	3 25	9 00	25 04	17 41	5 23	26 21
18 W	17 45 57	27 01 43	16 45	22 16	16 49	12 04	0♍22	1 51	1 27	29 03	2 06	3 24	9 14	25 01	17 34	5 24	26 23
19 Th	17 49 54	27 59 00	0♈30	22 16	18 29	13 07	0 55	2 05	1 29	29 06	2 06	3 23	9 29	24 57	17 27	5 26	26 25
20 F	17 53 50	28 56 16	14 33	22 15	20 06	14 10	1 29	2 18	1 31	29 09	2 07	3 22	9 44	24 54	17 20	5 28	26 27
21 Sa	17 57 47	29 53 33	28 52	22 13	21 41	15 14	2 03	2 32	1 34	29 12	2 07	3 20	9 58	24 50	17 14	5 31	26 29
22 Su	18 1 43	0♋50 49	13♉26	22 08	23 13	16 17	2 37	2 46	1 36	29 16	2 08	3 19	10 12	24 45	17 08	5 34	26 31
23 M	18 5 40	1 48 06	28 11	22 01	24 43	17 21	3 11	2 59	1 38	29 19	2 08	3 18	10 26	24 41	17 01	5 38	26 33
24 T	18 9 37	2 45 22	12♊59	21 52	26 11	18 26	3 45	3 13	1 39	29 22	2 09	3 17	10 40	24 35	16 57	5 42	26 35
25 W	18 13 33	3 42 38	27 43	21 41	27 34	19 30	4 19	3 27	1 41	29 25	2 09	3 16	10 53	24 30	16 52	5 47	26 37
26 Th	18 17 30	4 39 54	12♋15	21 30	28 56	20 35	4 53	3 41	1 43	29 28	2 09	3 15	11 07	24 24	16 47	5 52	26 39
27 F	18 21 26	5 37 09	26 28	21 20	0♌16	21 39	5 28	3 54	1 44	29 31	2 10	3 14	11 20	24 18	16 43	5 57	26 40
28 Sa	18 25 23	6 34 24	10♌16	21 12	1 33	22 44	6 02	4 08	1 46	29 34	2 10	3 13	11 33	24 11	16 40	6 03	26 42
29 Su	18 29 19	7 31 38	23 38	21 07	2 47	23 49	6 37	4 22	1 47	29 37	2 10	3 11	11 46	24 04	16 38	6 10	26 44
30 M	18 33 16	8 28 52	6♍34	21 05	3 58	24 55	7 11	4 35	1 48	29 40	2 10	3 10	11 58	23 57	16 35	6 17	26 45

EPHEMERIS CALCULATED FOR 12 MIDNIGHT GREENWICH MEAN TIME. ALL OTHER DATA AND FACING ASPECTARIAN PAGE IN **EASTERN TIME (BOLD)** AND PACIFIC TIME (REGULAR).

JULY 2025

☽ Last Aspect day	ET / hr:mn / PT	asp	☽ Ingress sign	day	ET / hr:mn / PT
1	**4:47 pm** 1:47 pm	△♅	♎	1	**5:16 pm** 2:16 pm
2	**3:30 pm** 12:30 pm	□☉	♏	4	**5:33 am** 2:33 am
6	**6:04 pm** 3:04 pm	☍♅	♐	6	**6:06 pm** 3:06 pm
7	**5:29 pm** 2:29 pm	□♂	♑	9	**4:55 am** 1:55 am
10	**4:37 pm** 1:37 pm	☍☉	♒	11	**1:21 pm** 10:21 am
12	**3:45 pm** 12:45 pm	☍☿	♓	13	**7:45 pm** 4:45 pm
15	**1:10 pm** 10:10 am	△☉	♈	15	9:32 pm
15	**1:10 pm** 10:10 am	△☉	♈	16	**12:32 am**
17	**8:38 pm** 5:38 pm	□☉	♉	18	**3:59 am** 12:59 am
19	11:43 pm	⚹☉	♊	20	**6:22 am** 3:22 am
20	**2:43 am**	⚹☉	♊	20	**6:22 am** 3:22 am
21	**3:52 pm** 12:52 pm	□♂	♋	22	**8:26 am** 5:26 am
23	**8:42 pm** 5:42 pm	⚹♂	♌	24	**11:28 am** 8:28 am
26	**7:02 am** 4:02 am	⚹♀	♍	26	**4:55 pm** 1:55 pm
28	**8:57 pm** 5:57 pm	□♀	♎	28	10:43 pm
28	**8:57 pm** 5:57 pm	□♀	♎	29	**1:43 am**
29	**11:59 pm** 8:59 pm	□♃	♏	31	**1:25 pm** 10:25 am

☽ Phases & Eclipses phase	day	ET / hr:mn / PT
2nd Quarter	2	**3:30 pm** 12:30 pm
Full Moon	10	**4:37 pm** 1:37 pm
4th Quarter	17	**8:38 pm** 5:38 pm
New Moon	24	**3:11 pm** 12:11 pm

Planet Ingress	day	ET / hr:mn / PT
♀ ♊	4	**11:31 am** 8:31 am
♅ ♊	7	**3:45 am** 12:45 am
☉ ♌	22	**9:29 am** 6:29 am
♀ ♋	30	**11:57 pm** 8:57 pm

Planetary Motion		day	ET / hr:mn / PT
♆	℞	4	**5:34 pm** 2:34 pm
⚵	D	10	9:01 pm
⚵	D	11	**12:01 am**
♄	℞	12	9:07 pm
♄	℞	13	**12:07 am**
☿	℞	17	9:45 pm
☿	℞	18	**12:45 am**
⚷	℞	30	**10:42 am** 7:42 am

1 TUESDAY
☽△♀ **10:43 am** 7:43 am
☽△♅ **4:47 pm** 1:47 pm
☽☍♄ **8:54 pm** 5:54 pm
☽☍♆ **9:34 pm** 6:34 pm
☽△♇ **11:27 pm** 8:27 pm

2 WEDNESDAY
☽□♃ **3:25 am** 12:25 am
☽⚹☿ **6:29 am** 3:29 am
☽⊻♂ **10:34 am** 7:34 am
☽□☉ **3:30 pm** 12:30 pm

4 FRIDAY
☽⊼♀ **4:56 am** 1:56 am
☽⊼♅ **5:17 am** 2:17 am
♀☌♅ **8:45 am** 5:45 am
☽⊼♄ **9:21 am** 6:21 am
☽⊼♆ **9:58 am** 6:58 am
☽□♇ **11:46 am** 8:46 am
☽△♃ **5:06 pm** 2:06 pm
☽□☿ 9:29 pm
☽⚹♂ 11:20 pm

5 SATURDAY
☽□☿ **12:29 am**
☽⚹♂ **2:20 am**
☽△☉ **9:29 am** 6:29 am

6 SUNDAY
♀⚹♄ **4:43 am** 1:43 am
♀⚹♆ **10:47 am** 7:47 am
☽☍♅ **6:04 pm** 3:04 pm
☽△♄ **9:54 pm** 6:54 pm
☽△♆ **10:26 pm** 7:26 pm
☽☍♀ **11:37 pm** 8:37 pm
☽⚹♇ 9:06 pm

7 MONDAY
☽⚹♇ **12:06 am**
♀△♇ **4:44 am** 1:44 am
☽⊼♃ **6:36 am** 3:36 am
☽△☿ **5:00 pm** 2:00 pm
☽□♂ **5:29 pm** 2:29 pm
☽⊼☉ 11:28 pm

8 TUESDAY
☽⊼☉ **2:28 am**

9 WEDNESDAY
☽⊼♅ **5:05 am** 2:05 am
☽□♄ **8:36 am** 5:36 am
☽□♆ **9:04 am** 6:04 am
☽⊻♇ **10:34 am** 7:34 am
☽⊼♀ **3:54 pm** 12:54 pm
☽☍♃ **5:59 pm** 2:59 pm

10 THURSDAY
☽⊼☿ **6:06 am** 3:06 am
☽△♂ **6:11 am** 3:11 am
☽☍☉ **4:37 pm** 1:37 pm
♀⊻♃ **8:53 pm** 5:53 pm

11 FRIDAY
☽△♅ **1:42 pm** 10:42 am
☽⚹♄ **4:55 pm** 1:55 pm
☽⚹♆ **5:20 pm** 2:20 pm
☽☌♇ **6:42 pm** 3:42 pm
☽⊼♃ 11:54 pm

12 SATURDAY
☽⊼♃ **2:54 am**
☽△♀ **5:07 am** 2:07 am
☽☍☿ **3:45 pm** 12:45 pm
☽⊼♂ **4:15 pm** 1:15 pm

13 SUNDAY
☽⊼☉ **3:58 am** 12:58 am
☽□♅ **8:15 pm** 5:15 pm
☽⊻♄ **11:12 pm** 8:12 pm
☽⊻♆ **11:35 pm** 8:35 pm
☽⊻♇ 9:49 pm

14 MONDAY
☽⊻♇ **12:49 am**
☽△♃ **9:46 am** 6:46 am
☽□♀ **3:53 pm** 12:53 pm
☽⊼☿ **10:40 pm** 7:40 pm
☽☍♂ 9:16 pm

15 TUESDAY
☽☍♂ **12:16 am**
☽△☉ **1:10 pm** 10:10 am
☽⚹♅ 10:11 pm

16 WEDNESDAY
☽⚹♅ **1:11 am**
☽☌♄ **3:53 am** 12:53 am
☽☌♆ **4:15 am** 1:15 am
☽⚹♇ **5:23 am** 2:23 am
☽□♃ **3:02 pm** 12:02 pm
☽⚹♀ 9:44 pm

17 THURSDAY
☽⚹♀ **12:44 am**
☽△☿ **3:21 am** 12:21 am
☽⊼♂ **6:37 am** 3:37 am
☽□☉ **8:38 pm** 5:38 pm

18 FRIDAY
☽⊻♅ **4:45 am** 1:45 am
☽⊻♄ **7:13 am** 4:13 am
☽⊻♆ **7:35 am** 4:35 am
☽□♇ **8:38 am** 5:38 am
☿⚹♀ **9:37 am** 6:37 am
☽⚹♃ **6:57 pm** 3:57 pm

19 SATURDAY
☽□☿ **6:08 am** 3:08 am
☽⊻♀ **8:00 am** 5:00 am
☽△♂ **11:36 am** 8:36 am
☽⚹☉ 11:43 pm

20 SUNDAY
☽⚹☉ **2:43 am**
☽☌♅ **7:16 am** 4:16 am
☽⚹♄ **9:31 am** 6:31 am
☽⚹♆ **9:53 am** 6:53 am
☽△♇ **10:52 am** 7:52 am
☽⊻♃ **9:56 pm** 6:56 pm

21 MONDAY
☽⚹☿ **7:36 am** 4:36 am
☽☌♀ **2:23 pm** 11:23 am
☽□♂ **3:52 pm** 12:52 pm

22 TUESDAY
☽⊻☉ **8:22 am** 5:22 am
☽⊻♅ **9:28 am** 6:28 am
☽□♄ **11:33 am** 8:33 am
☽□♆ **11:57 am** 8:57 am
☽⊼♇ **12:53 pm** 9:53 am
☽☌♃ 9:56 pm
☉⚹♅ 10:32 pm

23 WEDNESDAY
☽☌♃ **12:56 am**
☉⚹♅ **1:32 am**
♀□♂ **4:23 am** 1:23 am
☽⊻☿ **8:47 am** 5:47 am
☽⚹♂ **8:42 pm** 5:42 pm
☽⊻♀ **9:23 pm** 6:23 pm

24 THURSDAY
☉△♄ **7:23 am** 4:23 am
☽⚹♅ **12:40 pm** 9:40 am
☉△♆ **1:31 pm** 10:31 am
☽△♄ **2:38 pm** 11:38 am
☽△♆ **3:04 pm** 12:04 pm
☽☌☉ **3:11 pm** 12:11 pm
☽☍♇ **4:00 pm** 1:00 pm
☉☍♇ 11:33 pm

25 FRIDAY
☉☍♇ **2:33 am**
☽⊻♃ **5:28 am** 2:28 am
☽☌☿ **10:58 am** 7:58 am

26 SATURDAY
☽⊻♂ **3:51 am** 12:51 am
☽⚹♀ **7:02 am** 4:02 am
☽□♅ **6:20 pm** 3:20 pm
☽⊼♄ **8:11 pm** 5:11 pm
☽⊼♆ **8:41 pm** 5:41 pm
☽⊼♇ **9:37 pm** 6:37 pm
☽⊻☉ 10:07 pm

27 SUNDAY
☽⊻☉ **1:07 am**
☽⚹♃ **12:57 pm** 9:57 am
☽⊻☿ **3:18 pm** 12:18 pm

28 MONDAY
☽☌♂ **2:43 pm** 11:43 am
☽□♀ **8:57 pm** 5:57 pm
☿⊻♃ **11:43 pm** 8:43 pm

29 TUESDAY
☽△♅ **3:21 am** 12:21 am
☽☍♄ **5:04 am** 2:04 am
☽☍♆ **5:39 am** 2:39 am
☽△♇ **6:35 am** 3:35 am
☽⚹☉ **3:17 pm** 12:17 pm
☽⚹☿ **10:12 pm** 7:12 pm
☽□♃ **11:59 pm** 8:59 pm

31 THURSDAY
☽⊻♂ **5:11 am** 2:11 am
☽△♀ **2:52 pm** 11:52 am
☽⊼♅ **3:16 pm** 12:16 pm
☽⊼♄ **4:44 pm** 1:44 pm
☽⊼♆ **5:26 pm** 2:26 pm
☽□♇ **6:20 pm** 3:20 pm
♀⊻♅ **7:03 pm** 4:03 pm
☉☌☿ **7:41 pm** 4:41 pm

Eastern time in bold type
Pacific time in medium type

JULY 2025

DATE	SID. TIME	SUN	MOON	NODE	MERCURY	VENUS	MARS	JUPITER	SATURN	URANUS	NEPTUNE	PLUTO	CERES	PALLAS	JUNO	VESTA	CHIRON
1 T	18 37 13	9♋26 06	19♍08	21♓04D	5♋06	26♊00	7♍46	4♋49	1♈49	29♉42	2♈10	3≈08R	12♈11	23≈49R	16♈31R	6♏24	26♈47
2 W	18 41 9	10 23 19	1≏23	21 04R	6 12	27 06	8 21	5 03	1 50	29 45	2 10	3 07	12 23	23 41	16 28	6 32	26 48
3 Th	18 45 6	11 20 32	13 24	21 04	7 14	28 11	8 56	5 16	1 51	29 48	2 10	3 06	12 35	23 33	16 25	6 40	26 50
4 F	18 49 2	12 17 44	25 17	21 03	8 14	29 17	9 31	5 30	1 52	29 51	2 11R	3 05	12 46	23 24	16 23	6 49	26 51
5 Sa	18 52 59	13 14 56	7♏07	21 01	9 10	0♋23	10 06	5 44	1 53	29 54	2 11	3 03	12 58	23 15	16 21	6 58	26 53
6 Su	18 56 55	14 12 08	18 59	20 56	10 03	1 30	10 41	5 57	1 53	29 56	2 11	3 02	13 09	23 05	16 19	7 07	26 54
7 M	19 0 52	15 09 20	0♐57	20 48	10 52	2 36	11 16	6 11	1 54	29 59	2 11	3 01	13 20	22 56	16 17	7 17	26 55
8 T	19 4 48	16 06 32	13 04	20 39	11 38	3 43	11 51	6 24	1 55	0♊02	2 10	2 59	13 31	22 46	16 16	7 28	26 56
9 W	19 8 45	17 03 44	25 23	20 28	12 21	4 49	12 26	6 38	1 55	0 04	2 10	2 58	13 41	22 35	16 16	7 38	26 57
10 Th	19 12 42	18 00 55	7♑54	20 17	12 59	5 56	13 02	6 51	1 56	0 07	2 10	2 57	13 51	22 24	16 15	7 49	26 59
11 F	19 16 38	18 58 07	20 39	20 07	13 34	7 03	13 37	7 05	1 56	0 10	2 10	2 55	14 01	22 13	16 15D	8 01	27 00
12 Sa	19 20 35	19 55 19	3≈37	19 58	14 04	8 10	14 13	7 19	1 56	0 12	2 10	2 54	14 11	22 02	16 15	8 12	27 01
13 Su	19 24 31	20 52 32	16 47	19 51	14 31	9 17	14 48	7 32	1 56R	0 15	2 09	2 53	14 20	21 50	16 15	8 25	27 02
14 M	19 28 28	21 49 44	0♓09	19 47	14 52	10 25	15 24	7 45	1 56	0 17	2 09	2 51	14 30	21 38	16 16	8 37	27 02
15 T	19 32 24	22 46 57	13 41	19 46	15 10	11 32	16 00	7 59	1 56	0 20	2 09	2 50	14 39	21 26	16 17	8 50	27 03
16 W	19 36 21	23 44 11	27 23	19 46	15 23	12 40	16 36	8 12	1 56	0 22	2 09	2 48	14 47	21 14	16 18	9 03	27 04
17 Th	19 40 17	24 41 25	11♈16	19 47R	15 34R	13 48	17 11	8 26	1 55	0 24	2 08	2 47	14 56	21 01	16 20	9 17	27 05
18 F	19 44 14	25 38 40	25 18	19 46	15 33	14 56	17 47	8 39	1 55	0 27	2 08	2 46	15 04	20 48	16 22	9 31	27 06
19 Sa	19 48 11	26 35 55	9♉29	19 44	15 27	16 04	18 23	8 52	1 54	0 29	2 07	2 44	15 12	20 35	16 24	9 45	27 06
20 Su	19 52 7	27 33 12	23 48	19 44	15 15	17 12	18 59	9 06	1 54	0 31	2 07	2 43	15 19	20 21	16 27	9 59	27 07
21 M	19 56 4	28 30 29	8♊11	19 39	14 59	18 20	19 36	9 19	1 53	0 34	2 06	2 41	15 26	20 07	16 29	10 14	27 07
22 T	20 0 0	29 27 47	22 34	19 33	14 39	19 28	20 12	9 32	1 52	0 36	2 06	2 40	15 34	19 53	16 33	10 29	27 08
23 W	20 3 57	0♌25 06	6♋53	19 25	14 14	20 37	20 48	9 46	1 51	0 38	2 05	2 39	15 40	19 39	16 36	10 45	27 08
24 Th	20 7 53	1 22 25	21 01	19 18	13 44	21 46	21 25	9 59	1 50	0 40	2 05	2 37	15 47	19 25	16 40	11 01	27 09
25 F	20 11 50	2 19 46	4♌54	19 11	13 12	22 54	22 01	10 12	1 49	0 42	2 04	2 36	15 53	19 10	16 44	11 17	27 09
26 Sa	20 15 46	3 17 06	18 28	19 05	12 54	24 03	22 38	10 25	1 48	0 44	2 03	2 34	15 59	18 56	16 48	11 33	27 09
27 Su	20 19 43	4 14 27	1♍40	19 02	12 34	25 12	23 14	10 38	1 46	0 46	2 03	2 33	16 04	18 41	16 53	11 50	27 09
28 M	20 23 40	5 11 49	14 32	19 00D	11 55	26 21	23 51	10 51	1 45	0 48	2 02	2 31	16 10	18 26	16 58	12 07	27 10
29 T	20 27 36	6 09 11	27 04	19 01	11 13	27 30	24 27	11 04	1 43	0 50	2 01	2 30	16 14	18 11	17 03	12 24	27 10
30 W	20 31 33	7 06 34	9≏19	19 02	10 29	28 39	25 04	11 17	1 42	0 52	2 01	2 29	16 19	17 55	17 08	12 42	27 10R
31 Th	20 35 29	8 03 57	21 21	19 03	9 45	29 49	25 41	11 30	1 40	0 54	2 00	2 27	16 23	17 40	17 14	12 59	27 10

EPHEMERIS CALCULATED FOR 12 MIDNIGHT GREENWICH MEAN TIME. ALL OTHER DATA AND FACING ASPECTARIAN PAGE IN **EASTERN TIME (BOLD)** AND PACIFIC TIME (REGULAR).

AUGUST 2025

☽ Last Aspect day	ET / hr:mn	PT	asp	☽ Ingress sign	day	ET / hr:mn	PT
2	9:07 pm	6:07 pm	✶♂	♐	2		11:00 pm
2	9:07 pm	6:07 pm	✶♂	♐	3	2:00 am	
5	11:29 am	8:29 am	□♂	♑	5	1:04 pm	10:04 am
6	1:40 pm	10:40 am	☍♃	♒	7	9:18 pm	6:18 pm
9	3:55 am	12:55 am	☍☉	♓	9		11:50 pm
9	3:55 am	12:55 am	☍☉	♓	10	2:50 am	
10		11:55 pm	△♃	♈	12	6:33 am	3:33 am
11	2:55 am		△♃	♈	12	6:33 am	3:33 am
13	6:54 pm	3:54 pm	△☉	♉	14	9:22 am	6:22 am
15		10:12 pm	□☉	♊	16	12:01 pm	9:01 am
16	1:12 am		□☉	♊	16	12:01 pm	9:01 am
18	7:53 am	4:53 am	✶☉	♋	18	3:05 pm	12:05 pm
20	8:27 am	5:27 am	☌♀	♌	20	7:17 pm	4:17 pm
21	2:13 pm	11:13 am	☌☿	♍	22		10:24 pm
21	2:13 pm	11:13 am	☌☿	♍	23	1:24 am	
25	9:53 am	6:53 am	✶♀	♎	25	10:08 am	7:08 am
26	10:06 pm	7:06 pm	✶☿	♏	27	9:27 pm	6:27 pm
29	8:47 pm	5:47 pm	□☿	♐	30	10:04 am	7:04 am

☽ Phases & Eclipses phase	day	ET / hr:mn	PT
2nd Quarter	1	8:41 am	5:41 am
Full Moon	9	3:55 am	12:55 am
4th Quarter	15		10:12 pm
4th Quarter	16	1:12 am	
New Moon	22		11:07 pm
New Moon	23	2:07 am	
2nd Quarter	30		11:25 pm
2nd Quarter	31	2:25 am	

Planet Ingress	day	ET / hr:mn	PT
♂ ♎	6	7:23 pm	4:23 pm
☉ ♍	22	4:34 pm	1:34 pm
♀ ♌	25	12:27 pm	9:27 am

Planetary Motion		day	ET / hr:mn	PT
☿	D	11	3:30 am	12:30 am
⚷	℞	11	5:36 pm	2:36 pm

1 FRIDAY
☽ □ ☿ **6:56 am** 3:56 am
☽ □ ☉ **8:41 am** 5:41 am
♀ □ ♄ **9:34 am** 6:34 am
☽ △ ♃ **1:25 pm** 10:25 am
♀ □ ♆ **4:49 pm** 1:49 pm
♀ ⚻ ♇ 10:46 pm

2 SATURDAY
♀ ⚻ ♇ **1:46 am**
☽ ✶ ♂ **9:07 pm** 6:07 pm

3 SUNDAY
☽ ☍ ♅ **3:59 am** 12:59 am
☽ △ ♄ **5:08 am** 2:08 am
☽ △ ♆ **5:55 am** 2:55 am
☽ ✶ ♇ **6:46 am** 3:46 am
☽ ⚻ ♀ **9:56 am** 6:56 am
☽ △ ☿ **4:00 pm** 1:00 pm
☽ △ ☉ 11:12 pm
☽ ⚻ ♃ 11:44 pm

4 MONDAY
☽ △ ☉ **2:12 am**
☽ ⚻ ♃ **2:44 am**
☉ ⚺ ♃ **10:43 am** 7:43 am

5 TUESDAY
☿ ⚺ ♀ **5:09 am** 2:09 am
☽ □ ♂ **11:29 am** 8:29 am
☽ ⚻ ♅ **3:06 pm** 12:06 pm
☽ □ ♄ **3:54 pm** 12:54 pm
☽ □ ♆ **4:44 pm** 1:44 pm
☽ ⚺ ♇ **5:31 pm** 2:31 pm
☽ ⚻ ☿ **11:52 pm** 8:52 pm
☽ ☍ ♀ 11:38 pm

6 WEDNESDAY
☽ ☍ ♀ **2:38 am**
☽ ☍ ♃ **1:40 pm** 10:40 am
☽ ⚻ ☉ **4:53 pm** 1:53 pm

7 THURSDAY
☽ △ ♂ **10:35 pm** 7:35 pm
☽ △ ♅ **11:20 pm** 8:20 pm
☽ ✶ ♄ **11:49 pm** 8:49 pm
☽ ✶ ♆ 9:43 pm
☽ ☌ ♇ 10:26 pm

8 FRIDAY
☽ ✶ ♆ **12:43 am**
☽ ☌ ♇ **1:26 am**
☽ ☍ ☿ **5:52 am** 2:52 am
♂ △ ♅ **2:45 pm** 11:45 am
☽ ⚻ ♀ **3:31 pm** 12:31 pm
☽ ⚻ ♃ **9:31 pm** 6:31 pm
♂ ☍ ♄ **10:52 pm** 7:52 pm

9 SATURDAY
☽ ☍ ☉ **3:55 am** 12:55 am
♂ ☍ ♆ **6:13 pm** 3:13 pm

10 SUNDAY
☽ □ ♅ **4:52 am** 1:52 am
☽ ⚺ ♄ **5:05 am** 2:05 am
☽ ⚺ ♆ **6:02 am** 3:02 am
☽ ⚻ ♂ **6:37 am** 3:37 am
☽ ⚺ ♇ **6:42 am** 3:42 am
♂ △ ♇ **8:29 am** 5:29 am
☽ ⚻ ☿ **10:18 am** 7:18 am
☽ △ ♀ 10:12 pm
☽ △ ♃ 11:55 pm

11 MONDAY
☽ △ ♀ **1:12 am**
☽ △ ♃ **2:55 am**
☽ ⚻ ☉ **12:10 pm** 9:10 am
♄ ✶ ♅ **11:32 pm** 8:32 pm
♀ ☌ ♃ 10:30 pm

12 TUESDAY
♀ ☌ ♃ **1:30 am**
☽ ☌ ♄ **8:34 am** 5:34 am
☽ ✶ ♅ **8:36 am** 5:36 am
☽ ☌ ♆ **9:36 am** 6:36 am
☽ ✶ ♇ **10:14 am** 7:14 am
☽ ☍ ♂ **12:38 pm** 9:38 am
☽ △ ☿ **1:59 pm** 10:59 am

13 WEDNESDAY
☽ □ ♃ **6:51 am** 3:51 am
☽ □ ♀ **9:03 am** 6:03 am
☽ △ ☉ **6:54 pm** 3:54 pm

14 THURSDAY
☽ ⚺ ♄ **11:11 am** 8:11 am
☽ ⚺ ♅ **11:28 am** 8:28 am
☽ ⚺ ♆ **12:19 pm** 9:19 am
☽ □ ♇ **12:57 pm** 9:57 am
☽ ⚻ ♂ **5:45 pm** 2:45 pm
☽ □ ☿ **5:49 pm** 2:49 pm
☿ ✶ ♂ **10:05 pm** 7:05 pm

15 FRIDAY
☽ ✶ ♃ **10:14 am** 7:14 am
☽ ✶ ♀ **4:16 pm** 1:16 pm
☽ □ ☉ 10:12 pm

16 SATURDAY
☽ □ ☉ **1:12 am**
☽ ✶ ♄ **1:39 pm** 10:39 am
☽ ☌ ♅ **2:11 pm** 11:11 am
☽ ✶ ♆ **2:54 pm** 11:54 am
☽ △ ♇ **3:31 pm** 12:31 pm
☽ ✶ ☿ **10:33 pm** 7:33 pm
☽ △ ♂ **10:47 pm** 7:47 pm

17 SUNDAY
☽ ⚺ ♃ **1:45 pm** 10:45 am
☽ ⚺ ♀ **11:46 pm** 8:46 pm
☿ ✶ ♂ 10:33 pm

18 MONDAY
☿ ✶ ♂ **1:33 am**
☽ ✶ ☉ **7:53 am** 4:53 am
☽ □ ♄ **4:33 pm** 1:33 pm
☽ ⚺ ♅ **5:21 pm** 2:21 pm
☽ □ ♆ **5:57 pm** 2:57 pm
☽ ⚻ ♇ **6:34 pm** 3:34 pm

19 TUESDAY
☽ □ ♂ **4:30 am** 1:30 am
☽ ⚺ ☿ **5:00 am** 2:00 am
☽ ☌ ♃ **6:02 pm** 3:02 pm

20 WEDNESDAY
☽ ☌ ♀ **8:27 am** 5:27 am
☽ ⚺ ☉ **3:49 pm** 12:49 pm
☽ △ ♄ **8:34 pm** 5:34 pm
☽ ✶ ♅ **9:40 pm** 6:40 pm
☽ △ ♆ **10:08 pm** 7:08 pm
☽ ☍ ♇ **10:47 pm** 7:47 pm

21 THURSDAY
☽ ✶ ♂ **11:44 am** 8:44 am
☽ ☌ ☿ **2:13 pm** 11:13 am
☽ ⚺ ♃ **11:55 pm** 8:55 pm

22 FRIDAY
☽ ⚺ ♀ **7:28 pm** 4:28 pm
☽ ☌ ☉ 11:07 pm
☽ ⚻ ♄ 11:30 pm

23 SATURDAY
☽ ☌ ☉ **2:07 am**
☽ ⚻ ♄ **2:30 am**
☽ □ ♅ **3:57 am** 12:57 am
☽ ⚻ ♆ **4:18 am** 1:18 am
☽ ⚻ ♇ **4:59 am** 1:59 am
☉ ⚻ ♄ **7:05 am** 4:05 am
☽ ⚺ ♂ **9:29 pm** 6:29 pm

24 SUNDAY
☉ □ ♅ **3:15 am** 12:15 am
☽ ⚺ ☿ **3:35 am** 12:35 am
☉ ⚻ ♆ **6:58 am** 3:58 am
☽ ✶ ♃ **8:14 am** 5:14 am
☉ ⚻ ♇ **4:06 pm** 1:06 pm

25 MONDAY
☽ ✶ ♀ **9:53 am** 6:53 am
☽ ☍ ♄ **11:00 am** 8:00 am
☽ △ ♅ **12:52 pm** 9:52 am
☽ ☍ ♆ **1:04 pm** 10:04 am
☽ △ ♇ **1:48 pm** 10:48 am
☽ ⚺ ☉ **3:41 pm** 12:41 pm
♀ △ ♄ **8:56 pm** 5:56 pm
☿ ⚺ ♃ **11:27 pm** 8:27 pm

26 TUESDAY
☽ ☌ ♂ **10:26 am** 7:26 am
♀ ✶ ♅ **4:58 pm** 1:58 pm
♀ △ ♆ **6:18 pm** 3:18 pm
☽ □ ♃ **7:23 pm** 4:23 pm
☽ ✶ ☿ **10:06 pm** 7:06 pm
♀ ☍ ♇ 10:54 pm

27 WEDNESDAY
♀ ☍ ♇ **1:54 am**
☽ ⚻ ♄ **10:02 pm** 7:02 pm
☽ ⚻ ♅ 9:20 pm
☽ ⚻ ♆ 9:23 pm
☽ □ ♇ 10:10 pm

28 THURSDAY
☽ ⚻ ♅ **12:20 am**
☽ ⚻ ♆ **12:23 am**
☽ □ ♇ **1:10 am**
☽ □ ♀ **3:48 am** 12:48 am
☽ ✶ ☉ **8:27 am** 5:27 am
♅ ✶ ♆ **8:09 pm** 5:09 pm
☽ ⚺ ♂ 10:58 pm

29 FRIDAY
☽ ⚺ ♂ **1:58 am**
☽ △ ♃ **8:38 am** 5:38 am
☽ □ ☿ **8:47 pm** 5:47 pm

30 SATURDAY
☽ △ ♄ **10:19 am** 7:19 am
☽ △ ♆ **12:53 pm** 9:53 am
☽ ☍ ♅ **12:59 pm** 9:59 am
☽ ✶ ♇ **1:42 pm** 10:42 am
☽ △ ♀ **11:12 pm** 8:12 pm
☽ □ ☉ 11:25 pm

31 SUNDAY
☽ □ ☉ **2:25 am**
☽ ✶ ♂ **5:53 pm** 2:53 pm
☽ ⚻ ♃ **9:55 pm** 6:55 pm

Eastern time in bold type
Pacific time in medium type

AUGUST 2025

DATE	SID.TIME	SUN	MOON	NODE	MERCURY	VENUS	MARS	JUPITER	SATURN	URANUS	NEPTUNE	PLUTO	CERES	PALLAS	JUNO	VESTA	CHIRON
1 F	20 39 26	9♌01 21	3♏15	19♓04R	9♌00R	0♋58	26♍18	11♋43	1♈38R	0♊55	1♈59R	2≈26R	16♉27	17≈24R	17♏20	13♍17	27♈10R
2 Sa	20 43 22	9 58 45	15 07	19 04	8 16	2 07	26 55	11 56	1 36	0 57	1 58	2 25	16 31	17 09	17 26	13 36	27 10
3 Su	20 47 19	10 56 10	27 01	19 03	7 34	3 17	27 32	12 08	1 34	0 59	1 57	2 23	16 34	16 53	17 33	13 54	27 09
4 M	20 51 15	11 53 36	9♐01	19 00	6 53	4 27	28 09	12 21	1 32	1 00	1 56	2 22	16 37	16 38	17 39	14 13	27 09
5 T	20 55 12	12 51 03	21 12	18 56	6 16	5 37	28 46	12 34	1 30	1 02	1 55	2 20	16 39	16 22	17 46	14 32	27 09
6 W	20 59 9	13 48 30	3♑37	18 50	5 43	6 46	29 24	12 46	1 28	1 03	1 54	2 19	16 42	16 06	17 54	14 52	27 09
7 Th	21 3 5	14 45 58	16 18	18 45	5 14	7 56	0♎01	12 59	1 26	1 05	1 53	2 18	16 44	15 51	18 01	15 11	27 08
8 F	21 7 2	15 43 27	29 17	18 39	4 51	9 06	0 38	13 11	1 23	1 06	1 52	2 16	16 45	15 35	18 09	15 31	27 08
9 Sa	21 10 58	16 40 57	12♒34	18 35	4 33	10 17	1 16	13 23	1 21	1 08	1 51	2 15	16 46	15 19	18 17	15 51	27 07
10 Su	21 14 55	17 38 28	26 06	18 32	4 21	11 27	1 53	13 36	1 18	1 09	1 50	2 13	16 47	15 04	18 25	16 11	27 07
11 M	21 18 51	18 36 00	9♓52	18 30D	4♌15D	12 37	2 31	13 49	1 15	1 11	1 49	2 12	16 48R	14 48	18 34	16 32	27 06
12 T	21 22 48	19 33 33	23 49	18 30	4 17	13 48	3 08	14 01	1 12	1 12	1 48	2 11	16 48	14 33	18 42	16 52	27 06
13 W	21 26 44	20 31 07	7♈55	18 31	4 25	14 58	3 46	14 13	1 10	1 13	1 47	2 09	16 48	14 17	18 51	17 13	27 05
14 Th	21 30 41	21 28 43	22 05	18 33	4 40	16 09	4 24	14 25	1 07	1 14	1 46	2 08	16 47	14 02	19 00	17 35	27 04
15 F	21 34 38	22 26 21	6♉18	18 33	5 03	17 19	5 02	14 37	1 04	1 15	1 45	2 07	16 46	13 46	19 10	17 56	27 04
16 Sa	21 38 34	23 24 00	20 32	18 34R	5 32	18 30	5 40	14 49	1 00	1 16	1 44	2 06	16 45	13 31	19 19	18 17	27 03
17 Su	21 42 31	24 21 40	4♊43	18 34	6 09	19 41	6 18	15 01	0 57	1 18	1 42	2 04	16 43	13 16	19 29	18 39	27 02
18 M	21 46 27	25 19 22	18 51	18 31	6 53	20 52	6 56	15 13	0 54	1 19	1 41	2 03	16 41	13 01	19 39	19 01	27 01
19 T	21 50 24	26 17 06	2♋52	18 30	7 44	22 03	7 34	15 25	0 51	1 19	1 40	2 02	16 39	12 47	19 49	19 23	27 00
20 W	21 54 20	27 14 52	16 44	18 27	8 42	23 14	8 12	15 37	0 47	1 20	1 39	2 00	16 36	12 32	20 00	19 45	26 59
21 Th	21 58 17	28 12 39	0♌25	18 24	9 46	24 25	8 50	15 49	0 44	1 21	1 37	1 59	16 33	12 18	20 11	20 08	26 58
22 F	22 2 13	29 10 27	13 52	18 22	10 56	25 37	9 28	16 00	0 40	1 22	1 36	1 58	16 29	12 04	20 22	20 31	26 57
23 Sa	22 6 10	0♍08 17	27 04	18 20	12 13	26 48	10 07	16 12	0 37	1 23	1 35	1 57	16 25	11 50	20 33	20 54	26 56
24 Su	22 10 7	1 06 08	10♍00	18 19D	13 35	27 59	10 45	16 23	0 33	1 23	1 33	1 56	16 21	11 36	20 44	21 17	26 54
25 M	22 14 3	2 04 01	22 40	18 19	15 02	29 11	11 24	16 35	0 29	1 24	1 32	1 54	16 17	11 22	20 55	21 40	26 53
26 T	22 18 0	3 01 55	5♎04	18 19	16 34	0♌23	12 02	16 46	0 25	1 25	1 30	1 53	16 12	11 09	21 07	22 03	26 52
27 W	22 21 56	3 59 50	19 17	18 20	18 11	1 34	12 41	16 57	0 22	1 25	1 29	1 52	16 06	10 56	21 19	22 27	26 50
28 Th	22 25 53	4 57 47	0♏13	18 22	19 51	2 46	13 19	17 09	0 18	1 26	1 28	1 51	16 01	10 43	21 31	22 51	26 49
29 F	22 29 49	5 55 45	11 11	18 23	21 35	3 58	13 58	17 20	0 14	1 26	1 26	1 50	15 55	10 31	21 43	23 14	26 47
30 Sa	22 33 46	6 53 44	23 02	18 24	23 22	5 10	14 37	17 31	0 10	1 27	1 25	1 49	15 48	10 19	21 55	23 38	26 46
31 Su	22 37 42	7♍51 45	4♐56	18 24R	25 11	6 22	15 16	17 42	0♈06	1♊27	1♈23	1≈48	15♉41	10≈07	22♏08	24♍03	26♈44

EPHEMERIS CALCULATED FOR 12 MIDNIGHT GREENWICH MEAN TIME. ALL OTHER DATA AND FACING ASPECTARIAN PAGE IN EASTERN TIME (BOLD) AND PACIFIC TIME (REGULAR).

SEPTEMBER 2025

☽ Last Aspect day	ET / hr:mn / PT		asp	☽ Ingress sign	day	ET / hr:mn / PT	
1	**9:39 pm**	6:39 pm	□ ♄	♑	1	**9:45 pm**	6:45 pm
4	**6:08 am**	3:08 am	⚹ ♄	♒	4	**6:32 am**	3:32 am
5	**4:51 pm**	1:51 pm	△ ♂	♓	6	**11:54 am**	8:54 am
8	**1:44 pm**	10:44 am	☌ ♄	♈	8	**2:37 pm**	11:37 am
9		11:54 pm	☍ ♂	♉	10	**4:03 pm**	1:03 pm
10	**2:54 am**		☍ ♂	♉	10	**4:03 pm**	1:03 pm
12	**4:14 pm**	1:14 pm	⚹ ♄	♊	12	**5:38 pm**	2:38 pm
14	**6:46 pm**	3:46 pm	□ ♄	♋	14	**8:30 pm**	5:30 pm
16	**11:14 pm**	8:14 pm	△ ♄	♌	16		10:20 pm
16	**11:14 pm**	8:14 pm	△ ♄	♌	17	**1:20 am**	
19	**8:21 am**	5:21 am	☌ ♀	♍	19	**8:23 am**	5:23 am
21	**3:54 pm**	12:54 pm	☌ ☉	♎	21	**5:41 pm**	2:41 pm
23	**12:02 pm**	9:02 am	□ ♃	♏	24	**5:00 am**	2:00 am
26	**1:44 pm**	10:44 am	△ ♄	♐	26	**5:37 pm**	2:37 pm
28		10:44 pm	□ ♄	♑	29	**5:55 am**	2:55 am
29	**1:44 am**		□ ♄	♑	29	**5:55 am**	2:55 am

☽ Phases & Eclipses phase	day	ET / hr:mn / PT	
Full Moon	7	**2:09 pm**	11:09 am
●	7	15° ♓ 23'	
4th Quarter	14	**6:33 am**	3:33 am
New Moon	21	**3:54 pm**	12:54 pm
●	21	29° ♍ 05'	
2nd Quarter	29	**7:54 pm**	4:54 pm

Planet Ingress		day	ET / hr:mn / PT	
♄	♓	1	**4:07 am**	1:07 am
☿	♍	2	**9:23 am**	6:23 am
⚶	♐	13	**11:10 pm**	8:10 pm
☿	♎	18	**6:06 am**	3:06 am
♀	♍	19	**8:39 am**	5:39 am
♂	♏	22	**3:54 am**	12:54 am
☉	♎	22	**2:19 pm**	11:19 am

Planetary Motion		day	ET / hr:mn / PT	
♅	℞	5		9:51 pm
♅	℞	6	**12:51 am**	

1 MONDAY
☽ △ ☿ **7:37 pm** 4:37 pm
☽ □ ♄ **9:39 pm** 6:39 pm
☽ □ ♆ 9:20 pm
☽ ⚻ ♅ 9:35 pm
☽ ⚺ ♇ 10:09 pm

2 TUESDAY
☽ □ ♆ **12:20 am**
☽ ⚻ ♅ **12:35 am**
☽ ⚺ ♇ **1:09 am**
☿ ⚻ ♄ **8:21 am** 5:21 am
☽ ⚻ ♀ **4:40 pm** 1:40 pm
☽ △ ☉ **6:23 pm** 3:23 pm
☿ ⚻ ♆ 10:44 pm

3 WEDNESDAY
☿ ⚻ ♆ **1:44 am**
☿ □ ♅ **3:40 am** 12:40 am
☿ ⚻ ♇ **7:05 am** 4:05 am
☽ □ ♂ **7:20 am** 4:20 am
☽ ☍ ♃ **8:50 am** 5:50 am

4 THURSDAY
☽ ⚹ ♄ **6:08 am** 3:08 am
☽ ⚹ ♆ **8:52 am** 5:52 am
☽ △ ♅ **9:13 am** 6:13 am
☽ ☌ ♇ **9:40 am** 6:40 am
☽ ⚻ ☿ **2:17 pm** 11:17 am
♂ □ ♃ **10:59 pm** 7:59 pm

5 FRIDAY
☽ ☍ ♀ **5:49 am** 2:49 am
☽ ⚻ ☉ **6:16 am** 3:16 am
☽ ⚻ ♃ **4:13 pm** 1:13 pm
☽ △ ♂ **4:51 pm** 1:51 pm

6 SATURDAY
☉ ⚺ ♀ **5:38 am** 2:38 am
☽ ⚺ ♄ **11:15 am** 8:15 am
☽ ⚺ ♆ **2:00 pm** 11:00 am
☽ □ ♅ **2:26 pm** 11:26 am
☽ ⚺ ♇ **2:48 pm** 11:48 am

7 SUNDAY
☽ ☍ ☿ **3:41 am** 12:41 am
☽ ☍ ☉ **2:09 pm** 11:09 am
☽ ⚻ ♀ **2:44 pm** 11:44 am
☽ △ ♃ **8:25 pm** 5:25 pm
☽ ⚻ ♂ **10:52 pm** 7:52 pm

8 MONDAY
☽ ☌ ♄ **1:44 pm** 10:44 am
☽ ☌ ♆ **4:33 pm** 1:33 pm
☽ ⚹ ♅ **5:03 pm** 2:03 pm
☽ ⚹ ♇ **5:21 pm** 2:21 pm

9 TUESDAY
☽ ⚻ ☿ **1:31 pm** 10:31 am
☽ ⚻ ☉ **7:35 pm** 4:35 pm
☽ △ ♀ **9:07 pm** 6:07 pm
☽ □ ♃ **10:43 pm** 7:43 pm
☽ ☍ ♂ 11:54 pm

10 WEDNESDAY
☽ ☍ ♂ **2:54 am**
☽ ⚺ ♄ **2:56 pm** 11:56 am
☽ ⚺ ♆ **5:52 pm** 2:52 pm
☽ ⚺ ♅ **6:27 pm** 3:27 pm
☽ □ ♇ **6:43 pm** 3:43 pm
♀ ⚺ ♃ **7:12 pm** 4:12 pm

11 THURSDAY
☽ △ ☿ **10:18 pm** 7:18 pm
☽ △ ☉ 9:29 pm
☽ ⚹ ♃ 9:39 pm
☽ □ ♀ 11:59 pm

12 FRIDAY
☽ △ ☉ **12:29 am**
☽ ⚹ ♃ **12:39 am**
☽ □ ♀ **2:59 am**
☉ ⚹ ♃ **3:30 am** 12:30 am
☽ ⚻ ♂ **6:40 am** 3:40 am
☽ ⚹ ♄ **4:14 pm** 1:14 pm
☿ ⚹ ♃ **5:53 pm** 2:53 pm
☽ ⚹ ♆ **7:23 pm** 4:23 pm
☽ ☌ ♅ **8:03 pm** 5:03 pm
☽ △ ♇ **8:17 pm** 5:17 pm

13 SATURDAY
☉ ☌ ☿ **6:52 am** 3:52 am

14 SUNDAY
☽ ⚺ ♃ **3:34 am** 12:34 am
☽ □ ☉ **6:33 am** 3:33 am
☽ □ ☿ **8:17 am** 5:17 am
☽ ⚹ ♀ **10:10 am** 7:10 am
☽ △ ♂ **11:41 am** 8:41 am
☽ □ ♄ **6:46 pm** 3:46 pm
☽ □ ♆ **10:13 pm** 7:13 pm
☽ ⚺ ♅ **10:58 pm** 7:58 pm
☽ ⚻ ♇ **11:12 pm** 8:12 pm

15 MONDAY
☿ ⚺ ♀ **10:59 pm** 7:59 pm
☿ ⚺ ♂ **11:01 pm** 8:01 pm
♀ ⚹ ♂ **11:04 pm** 8:04 pm

16 TUESDAY
☽ ☌ ♃ **8:18 am** 5:18 am
☽ ⚹ ☉ **2:53 pm** 11:53 am
☽ □ ♂ **6:53 pm** 3:53 pm
☽ ⚺ ♀ **7:47 pm** 4:47 pm
☽ ⚹ ☿ **8:52 pm** 5:52 pm
☽ △ ♄ **11:14 pm** 8:14 pm

17 WEDNESDAY
☽ △ ♆ **3:00 am** 12:00 am
☽ ⚹ ♅ **3:52 am** 12:52 am
☽ ☍ ♇ **4:05 am** 1:05 am
☿ ☍ ♄ **1:47 pm** 10:47 am

18 THURSDAY
♀ ⚻ ♄ **7:34 am** 4:34 am
☽ ⚺ ♃ **3:17 pm** 12:17 pm
☿ ☍ ♆ **6:01 pm** 3:01 pm
☿ △ ♅ 9:52 pm
☽ ⚺ ☉ 10:58 pm
☿ △ ♇ 11:27 pm

19 FRIDAY
☿ △ ♅ **12:52 am**
☽ ⚺ ☉ **1:58 am**
☿ △ ♇ **2:27 am**
☽ ⚹ ♂ **4:40 am** 1:40 am
☽ ⚻ ♄ **5:52 am** 2:52 am
☽ ☌ ♀ **8:21 am** 5:21 am
☽ ⚻ ♆ **10:01 am** 7:01 am
☽ □ ♅ **10:59 am** 7:59 am
☽ ⚻ ♇ **11:12 am** 8:12 am
☽ ⚺ ☿ **12:37 pm** 9:37 am
♀ ⚻ ♆ 10:20 pm
♂ ⚻ ♄ 10:24 pm

20 SATURDAY
♀ ⚻ ♆ **1:20 am**
♂ ⚻ ♄ **1:24 am**
♀ □ ♅ **11:42 am** 8:42 am
♀ ⚻ ♇ **1:59 pm** 10:59 am
☽ ⚹ ♃ 9:34 pm
☉ ☍ ♄ 10:46 pm

21 SUNDAY
☽ ⚹ ♃ **12:34 am**
☉ ☍ ♄ **1:46 am**
☽ ☍ ♄ **2:42 pm** 11:42 am
☽ ☌ ☉ **3:54 pm** 12:54 pm
☽ ⚺ ♂ **5:05 pm** 2:05 pm
☽ ☍ ♆ **7:14 pm** 4:14 pm
☽ △ ♅ **8:20 pm** 5:20 pm
☽ △ ♇ **8:34 pm** 5:34 pm
☽ ⚺ ♀ **11:58 pm** 8:58 pm

22 MONDAY
☽ ☌ ☿ **7:36 am** 4:36 am

23 TUESDAY
♂ ⚻ ♆ **7:01 am** 4:01 am
☉ ☍ ♆ **8:53 am** 5:53 am
☽ □ ♃ **12:02 pm** 9:02 am
☉ ⚺ ♂ **1:10 pm** 10:10 am
☉ △ ♅ **10:55 pm** 7:55 pm
☽ ⚻ ♄ 10:33 pm
☉ △ ♇ 11:05 pm

24 WEDNESDAY
☽ ⚻ ♄ **1:33 am**
☉ △ ♇ **2:05 am**
♂ ⚻ ♅ **3:15 am** 12:15 am
☽ ⚻ ♆ **6:29 am** 3:29 am
☽ ⚻ ♅ **7:40 am** 4:40 am
♂ □ ♇ **7:52 am** 4:52 am
☽ □ ♇ **7:56 am** 4:56 am
☽ ☌ ♂ **7:56 am** 4:56 am
☽ ⚺ ☉ **8:27 am** 5:27 am
☽ ⚹ ♀ **6:18 pm** 3:18 pm

25 THURSDAY
☽ ⚺ ☿ **5:15 am** 2:15 am
☽ △ ♃ 10:06 pm

26 FRIDAY
☽ △ ♃ **1:06 am**
☽ △ ♄ **1:44 pm** 10:44 am
☽ △ ♆ **6:58 pm** 3:58 pm
☽ ☍ ♅ **8:13 pm** 5:13 pm
☽ ⚹ ♇ **8:32 pm** 5:32 pm
☽ ⚺ ♂ 9:14 pm
☽ ⚹ ☉ 11:34 pm

27 SATURDAY
☽ ⚺ ♂ **12:14 am**
☽ ⚹ ☉ **2:34 am**
☽ □ ♀ **2:00 pm** 11:00 am

28 SUNDAY
☽ ⚹ ☿ **3:43 am** 12:43 am
☽ ⚻ ♃ **2:21 pm** 11:21 am
☽ □ ♄ 10:44 pm

29 MONDAY
☽ □ ♄ **1:44 am**
☽ □ ♆ **7:05 am** 4:05 am
☽ ⚻ ♅ **8:22 am** 5:22 am
☽ ⚺ ♇ **8:43 am** 5:43 am
☽ ⚹ ♂ **3:55 pm** 12:55 pm
☽ □ ☉ **7:54 pm** 4:54 pm

30 TUESDAY
☽ △ ♀ **8:20 am** 5:20 am
☽ □ ☿ **11:39 pm** 8:39 pm
☽ ☍ ♃ 10:40 pm

Eastern time in bold type
Pacific time in medium type

SEPTEMBER 2025

DATE	SID.TIME	SUN	MOON	NODE	MERCURY	VENUS	MARS	JUPITER	SATURN	URANUS	NEPTUNE	PLUTO	CERES	PALLAS	JUNO	VESTA	CHIRON
1 M	22 41 39	8♍49 47	16♐55	18♓24R	27♌03	7♋34	15♎55	17♋52	0♈01R	1♊27	11♈22R	1♒47R	15♈34R	9♒55R	22♏21	24♏27	26♈43R
2 T	22 45 36	9 47 51	29 06	18 23	28 56	8 46	16 34	18 03	29♓57	1 27	1 20	1 46	15 27	9 44	22 34	24 52	26 41
3 W	22 49 32	10 45 56	11♑33	18 23	0♍51	9 58	17 13	18 14	29 53	1 28	1 19	1 44	15 19	9 33	22 47	25 16	26 39
4 Th	22 53 29	11 44 02	24 18	18 22	2 46	11 10	17 52	18 24	29 49	1 28	1 17	1 43	15 11	9 22	23 00	25 41	26 38
5 F	22 57 25	12 42 10	7♒24	18 21	4 42	12 22	18 31	18 35	29 44	1 28	1 16	1 42	15 03	9 11	23 14	26 06	26 36
6 Sa	23 1 22	13 40 19	20 52	18 20	6 39	13 35	19 10	18 45	29 40	1 28R	1 14	1 41	14 54	9 01	23 27	26 31	26 34
7 Su	23 5 18	14 38 30	4♓42	18 20D	8 35	14 47	19 50	18 55	29 36	1 28	1 12	1 41	14 45	8 52	23 41	26 56	26 32
8 M	23 9 15	15 36 43	18 51	18 20	10 31	16 00	20 29	19 05	29 31	1 28	1 11	1 40	14 35	8 42	23 55	27 22	26 30
9 T	23 13 11	16 34 57	3♈15	18 20	12 27	17 12	21 08	19 16	29 27	1 28	1 09	1 39	14 26	8 33	24 09	27 47	26 28
10 W	23 17 8	17 33 13	17 48	18 20R	14 22	18 25	21 48	19 25	29 22	1 27	1 08	1 38	14 16	8 24	24 23	28 13	26 26
11 Th	23 21 5	18 31 31	2♉24	18 20	16 17	19 37	22 27	19 35	29 18	1 27	1 06	1 37	14 06	8 16	24 38	28 39	26 24
12 F	23 25 1	19 29 51	16 58	18 20	18 11	20 50	23 07	19 45	29 13	1 27	1 04	1 36	13 55	8 08	24 52	29 04	26 22
13 Sa	23 28 58	20 28 14	1♊25	18 20	20 04	22 03	23 47	19 55	29 09	1 27	1 03	1 35	13 44	8 00	25 07	29 30	26 20
14 Su	23 32 54	21 26 38	15 40	18 20D	21 56	23 16	24 26	20 04	29 04	1 26	1 01	1 34	13 33	7 52	25 22	29 57	26 18
15 M	23 36 51	22 25 05	29 42	18 20	23 47	24 29	25 06	20 14	29 00	1 26	1 00	1 34	13 22	7 45	25 37	0♐23	26 16
16 T	23 40 47	23 23 34	13♋30	18 20	25 37	25 42	25 46	20 23	28 55	1 25	0 58	1 33	13 11	7 39	25 52	0 49	26 14
17 W	23 44 44	24 22 05	27 02	18 21	27 27	26 55	26 26	20 32	28 50	1 25	0 56	1 32	12 59	7 32	26 07	1 16	26 12
18 Th	23 48 40	25 20 38	10♌19	18 21	29 15	28 08	27 06	20 41	28 46	1 24	0 55	1 31	12 47	7 26	26 22	1 42	26 09
19 F	23 52 37	26 19 13	23 21	18 22	1♎02	29 21	27 46	20 50	28 41	1 24	0 53	1 31	12 35	7 21	26 38	2 09	26 07
20 Sa	23 56 33	27 17 50	6♍11	18 23R	2 48	0♍35	28 26	20 59	28 36	1 23	0 51	1 30	12 22	7 16	26 54	2 36	26 05
21 Su	0 0 30	28 16 30	18 47	18 23	4 33	1 48	29 06	21 08	28 32	1 22	0 50	1 29	12 10	7 11	27 09	3 02	26 02
22 M	0 4 27	29 15 11	1♎25	18 22	6 17	3 01	29 47	21 16	28 27	1 22	0 48	1 29	11 57	7 06	27 25	3 30	26 00
23 T	0 8 23	0♎13 54	13 25	18 20	8 00	4 15	0♏27	21 25	28 22	1 21	0 46	1 28	11 44	7 02	27 41	3 57	25 58
24 W	0 12 20	1 12 39	25 30	18 20	9 43	5 28	1 07	21 33	28 18	1 20	0 45	1 27	11 31	6 58	27 58	4 24	25 55
25 Th	0 16 16	2 11 26	7♏27	18 18	11 24	6 42	1 48	21 41	28 13	1 19	0 43	1 27	11 18	6 55	28 14	4 52	25 53
26 F	0 20 13	3 10 14	19 20	18 16	13 04	7 55	2 28	21 49	28 08	1 18	0 41	1 27	11 05	6 52	28 30	5 19	25 50
27 Sa	0 24 9	4 09 05	1♐11	18 14	14 43	9 09	3 09	21 57	28 04	1 17	0 40	1 26	10 51	6 49	28 47	5 47	25 48
28 Su	0 28 6	5 07 57	13 03	18 12	16 22	10 23	3 50	22 05	27 59	1 16	0 38	1 26	10 38	6 47	29 04	6 14	25 45
29 M	0 32 2	6 06 52	25 01	18 10D	17 59	11 37	4 30	22 13	27 55	1 15	0 36	1 25	10 25	6 45	29 20	6 42	25 43
30 T	0 35 59	7 05 48	7♐09	18 10	19 34	12 50	5 11	22 20	27 50	1 14	0 35	1 25	10 11	6 43	29 37	7 10	25 40

EPHEMERIS CALCULATED FOR 12 MIDNIGHT GREENWICH MEAN TIME. ALL OTHER DATA AND FACING ASPECTARIAN PAGE IN **EASTERN TIME (BOLD)** AND PACIFIC TIME (REGULAR).

OCTOBER 2025

☽ Last Aspect day	ET / hr:mn / PT	asp	☽ Ingress sign	day	ET / hr:mn / PT
1	**11:33 am** 8:33 am	✶ ♄	♒	1	**3:52 pm** 12:52 pm
3	**2:15 pm** 11:15 am	△ ☿	♓	3	**10:07 pm** 7:07 pm
5	**8:30 pm** 5:30 pm	☌ ♄	♈	5	9:48 pm
5	**8:30 pm** 5:30 pm	☌ ♄	♈	6	**12:48 am**
7	**2:24 pm** 11:24 am	□ ♃	♉	7	10:12 pm
7	**2:24 pm** 11:24 am	□ ♃	♉	8	**1:12 am**
9	**8:31 pm** 5:31 pm	✶ ♄	♊	9	10:12 pm
9	**8:31 pm** 5:31 pm	✶ ♄	♊	10	**1:12 am**
11	**10:56 pm** 7:56 pm	□ ♀	♋	11	11:37 pm
11	**10:56 pm** 7:56 pm	□ ♀	♋	12	**2:37 am**
13	10:05 pm	△ ♄	♌	14	**6:47 am** 3:47 am
14	**1:05 am**	△ ♄	♌	14	**6:47 am** 3:47 am
15	10:06 pm	✶ ☉	♍	16	**2:06 pm** 11:06 am
16	**1:06 am**	✶ ☉	♍	16	**2:06 pm** 11:06 am
18	**5:10 pm** 2:10 pm	☍ ♄	♎	18	9:01 pm
18	**5:10 pm** 2:10 pm	☍ ♄	♎	19	**12:01 am**
21	**8:25 am** 5:25 am	☌ ☉	♏	21	**11:42 am** 8:42 am
23	9:14 pm	△ ♆	♐	23	9:19 pm
24	**12:14 am**	△ ♆	♐	24	**12:19 am**
26	**12:42 pm** 9:42 am	□ ♆	♑	26	**12:53 pm** 9:53 am
28	**11:38 pm** 8:38 pm	✶ ♆	♒	28	**11:55 pm** 8:55 pm
30	11:15 pm	□ ♂	♓	31	**7:46 am** 4:46 am
31	**2:15 am**	□ ♂	♓	31	**7:46 am** 4:46 am

☽ Phases & Eclipses phase	day	ET / hr:mn / PT
Full Moon	6	**11:48 pm** 8:48 pm
4th Quarter	13	**2:13 pm** 11:13 am
New Moon	21	**8:25 am** 5:25 am
2nd Quarter	29	**12:21 pm** 9:21 am

Planet Ingress	day	ET / hr:mn / PT
⚵ ♐	1	**3:55 am** 12:55 am
☿ ♏	6	**12:41 pm** 9:41 am
♀ ♎	13	**5:19 pm** 2:19 pm
♆ ♓	22	**5:48 am** 2:48 am
☉ ♏	22	**11:51 pm** 8:51 pm
☿ ♐	29	**7:02 am** 4:02 am

Planetary Motion		day	ET / hr:mn / PT
⚴	D	4	**3:17 am** 12:17 am
♇	D	13	**10:54 pm** 7:54 pm

1 WEDNESDAY
☽ ☍ ♃ **1:40 am**
☽ ✶ ♄ **11:33 am** 8:33 am
☽ ✶ ♆ **4:51 pm** 1:51 pm
☿ □ ♃ **4:59 pm** 1:59 pm
☽ △ ♅ **6:05 pm** 3:05 pm
☽ ☌ ♇ **6:29 pm** 3:29 pm

2 THURSDAY
☽ □ ♂ **4:29 am** 1:29 am
☽ △ ☉ **9:41 am** 6:41 am
☽ ⚻ ♀ **10:28 pm** 7:28 pm

3 FRIDAY
☽ ⚻ ♃ **9:23 am** 6:23 am
☽ △ ☿ **2:15 pm** 11:15 am
☽ ⚺ ♄ **5:49 pm** 2:49 pm
☽ ⚺ ♆ **10:56 pm** 7:56 pm
☽ □ ♅ 9:06 pm
☽ ⚺ ♇ 9:32 pm

4 SATURDAY
☽ □ ♅ **12:06 am**
☽ ⚺ ♇ **12:32 am**
☽ △ ♂ **12:36 pm** 9:36 am
☽ ⚻ ☉ **6:42 pm** 3:42 pm
☿ ⚻ ♄ **8:32 pm** 5:32 pm

5 SUNDAY
☽ ☍ ♀ **7:34 am** 4:34 am
☽ △ ♃ **1:15 pm** 10:15 am
☽ ☌ ♄ **8:30 pm** 5:30 pm
☽ ⚻ ☿ **11:26 pm** 8:26 pm
☽ ☌ ♆ 10:28 pm
☽ ✶ ♅ 11:35 pm

6 MONDAY
☽ ☌ ♆ **1:28 am**
☽ ✶ ♅ **2:35 am**
☽ ✶ ♇ **3:04 am** 12:04 am
☽ ⚻ ♂ **4:54 pm** 1:54 pm
☿ ⚻ ♆ **6:53 pm** 3:53 pm
☽ ☍ ☉ **11:48 pm** 8:48 pm

7 TUESDAY
☿ ⚻ ♅ **5:41 am** 2:41 am
☿ □ ♇ **10:41 am** 7:41 am
☽ ⚻ ♀ **12:58 pm** 9:58 am
☽ □ ♃ **2:24 pm** 11:24 am
☽ ⚺ ♄ **8:48 pm** 5:48 pm
☽ ⚺ ♆ 10:46 pm
☽ ⚺ ♅ 11:52 pm

8 WEDNESDAY
☽ ⚺ ♆ **1:46 am**
☽ ⚺ ♅ **2:52 am**
☽ □ ♇ **3:24 am** 12:24 am
☽ ☍ ☿ **5:15 am** 2:15 am
♀ ✶ ♃ **7:41 am** 4:41 am
☽ ☍ ♂ **7:16 pm** 4:16 pm

9 THURSDAY
☽ ⚻ ☉ **3:08 am** 12:08 am
☽ ✶ ♃ **2:39 pm** 11:39 am
☽ △ ♀ **5:12 pm** 2:12 pm
☽ ✶ ♄ **8:31 pm** 5:31 pm
☽ ✶ ♆ 10:41 pm
☽ ☌ ♅ 11:48 pm

10 FRIDAY
☽ ✶ ♆ **1:41 am**
☽ ☌ ♅ **2:48 am**
☽ △ ♇ **3:25 am** 12:25 am
☽ ⚻ ☿ **10:36 am** 7:36 am
☽ ⚻ ♂ **9:59 pm** 6:59 pm

11 SATURDAY
♀ ☍ ♄ **7:11 am** 4:11 am
☽ △ ☉ **7:14 am** 4:14 am
☽ ⚺ ♃ **3:57 pm** 12:57 pm
☽ □ ♄ **9:30 pm** 6:30 pm
☽ □ ♀ **10:56 pm** 7:56 pm

12 SUNDAY
☽ □ ♆ **3:02 am** 12:02 am
☽ ⚺ ♅ **4:12 am** 1:12 am
☽ ⚻ ♇ **4:56 am** 1:56 am
☽ △ ☿ **6:10 pm** 3:10 pm

13 MONDAY
☽ △ ♂ **3:07 am** 12:07 am
☽ □ ☉ **2:13 pm** 11:13 am
☽ ☌ ♃ **7:49 pm** 4:49 pm
♀ ☍ ♆ **9:16 pm** 6:16 pm
☽ △ ♄ 10:05 pm

14 TUESDAY
☽ △ ♄ **1:05 am**
☽ △ ♆ **7:08 am** 4:08 am
☽ ✶ ♀ **8:10 am** 5:10 am
☽ ✶ ♅ **8:21 am** 5:21 am
☽ ☍ ♇ **9:14 am** 6:14 am
♀ △ ♅ **10:10 am** 7:10 am
♀ △ ♇ **7:45 pm** 4:45 pm

15 WEDNESDAY
☽ □ ☿ **5:41 am** 2:41 am
☽ □ ♂ **11:50 am** 8:50 am
☽ ✶ ☉ 10:06 pm
☽ ⚺ ♃ 11:52 pm

16 THURSDAY
☽ ✶ ☉ **1:06 am**
☽ ⚺ ♃ **2:52 am**
☽ ⚻ ♄ **7:47 am** 4:47 am
☽ ⚻ ♆ **2:21 pm** 11:21 am
☽ □ ♅ **3:37 pm** 12:37 pm
☽ ⚻ ♇ **4:41 pm** 1:41 pm
☽ ⚺ ♀ **9:35 pm** 6:35 pm
☉ □ ♃ 10:43 pm

17 FRIDAY
☉ □ ♃ **1:43 am**
☽ ✶ ☿ **9:10 pm** 6:10 pm
☽ ✶ ♂ 9:01 pm

18 SATURDAY
☽ ✶ ♂ **12:01 am**
☽ ✶ ♃ **12:43 pm** 9:43 am
☽ ⚺ ☉ **3:33 pm** 12:33 pm
☽ ☍ ♄ **5:10 pm** 2:10 pm
☽ ☍ ♆ 9:11 pm
☽ △ ♅ 10:27 pm
☽ △ ♇ 11:44 pm

19 SUNDAY
☽ ☍ ♆ **12:11 am**
☽ △ ♅ **1:27 am**
☽ △ ♇ **2:44 am**
☉ ⚻ ♄ **10:31 am** 7:31 am
☽ ☌ ♀ **2:26 pm** 11:26 am
☿ ☌ ♂ 11:52 pm

20 MONDAY
☿ ☌ ♂ **2:52 am**
☽ ⚺ ♂ **2:44 pm** 11:44 am
☽ ⚺ ☿ **3:24 pm** 12:24 pm
☽ □ ♃ 9:29 pm

21 TUESDAY
☽ □ ♃ **12:29 am**
☽ ⚻ ♄ **4:24 am** 1:24 am
☽ ☌ ☉ **8:25 am** 5:25 am
☽ ⚻ ♆ **11:44 am** 8:44 am
☽ ⚻ ♅ **1:00 pm** 10:00 am
☽ □ ♇ **2:29 pm** 11:29 am

22 WEDNESDAY
☽ ⚺ ♀ **9:25 am** 6:25 am
☉ ⚻ ♆ **11:26 pm** 8:26 pm

23 THURSDAY
☽ ☌ ♂ **6:55 am** 3:55 am
☽ ☌ ☿ **10:57 am** 7:57 am
☽ △ ♃ **1:19 pm** 10:19 am
☉ ⚻ ♅ **1:47 pm** 10:47 am
☽ △ ♄ **4:38 pm** 1:38 pm
☽ △ ♆ 9:14 pm
☽ ☍ ♅ 10:27 pm
☽ ⚺ ☉ 11:34 pm

24 FRIDAY
☽ △ ♆ **12:14 am**
☽ ☍ ♅ **1:27 am**
☽ ⚺ ☉ **2:34 am**
☽ ✶ ♇ **3:08 am** 12:08 am
☉ □ ♇ **9:25 am** 6:25 am
☿ △ ♃ **11:08 am** 8:08 am

25 SATURDAY
☽ ✶ ♀ **5:17 am** 2:17 am
☿ △ ♄ **5:17 pm** 2:17 pm
☽ ⚺ ♂ **11:27 pm** 8:27 pm
☽ ⚻ ♃ 11:16 pm

26 SUNDAY
☽ ⚻ ♃ **2:16 am**
☽ □ ♄ **5:01 am** 2:01 am
☽ ⚺ ☿ **6:19 am** 3:19 am
☽ □ ♆ **12:42 pm** 9:42 am
☽ ⚻ ♅ **1:50 pm** 10:50 am
☽ ⚺ ♇ **3:42 pm** 12:42 pm
☽ ✶ ☉ **8:35 pm** 5:35 pm

27 MONDAY
☽ □ ♀ 9:11 pm
♂ △ ♃ 11:19 pm

28 TUESDAY
☽ □ ♀ **12:11 am**
♂ △ ♃ **2:19 am**
☽ ☍ ♃ **1:57 pm** 10:57 am
☽ ✶ ♂ **2:36 pm** 11:36 am
☽ ✶ ♄ **4:06 pm** 1:06 pm
☽ ✶ ☿ **11:17 pm** 8:17 pm
☽ ✶ ♆ **11:38 pm** 8:38 pm
☽ △ ♅ 9:39 pm
☽ ☌ ♇ 11:39 pm

29 WEDNESDAY
☽ △ ♅ **12:39 am**
☽ ☌ ♇ **2:39 am**
☿ △ ♆ **3:26 am** 12:26 am
☽ □ ☉ **12:21 pm** 9:21 am
♂ △ ♄ **3:05 pm** 12:05 pm
☿ ☍ ♅ **3:36 pm** 12:36 pm

30 THURSDAY
☽ △ ♀ **3:35 pm** 12:35 pm
☿ ✶ ♇ **6:06 pm** 3:06 pm
☽ ⚻ ♃ **10:36 pm** 7:36 pm
☽ ⚺ ♄ 9:15 pm
☽ □ ♂ 11:15 pm

31 FRIDAY
☽ ⚺ ♄ **12:15 am**
☽ □ ♂ **2:15 am**
☽ ⚺ ♆ **7:25 am** 4:25 am
☽ □ ♅ **8:18 am** 5:18 am
☽ ⚺ ♇ **10:21 am** 7:21 am
☽ □ ☿ **11:32 am** 8:32 am
☽ △ ☉ **11:42 pm** 8:42 pm

Eastern time in bold type
Pacific time in medium type

OCTOBER 2025

DATE	SID. TIME	SUN	MOON	NODE	MERCURY	VENUS	MARS	JUPITER	SATURN	URANUS	NEPTUNE	PLUTO	CERES	PALLAS	JUNO	VESTA	CHIRON
1 W	0 39 56	8≏04 45	19♉31	18♓10	21≏11	14♍04	5♏52	22♋28	27♓45R	1♊13R	0♈33R	1≈24R	9♍57R	6≈42R	29♏54	7♐38	25♈37R
2 Th	0 43 52	9 03 45	2♊13	18 12	22 46	15 18	6 33	22 35	27 41	1 11	0 31	1 24	9 44	6 41	0♐11	8 06	25 35
3 F	0 47 49	10 02 46	15 17	18 13	24 20	16 32	7 14	22 42	27 36	1 10	0 30	1 23	9 30	6 40	0 29	8 34	25 32
4 Sa	0 51 45	11 01 49	28 47	18 14	25 53	17 46	7 55	22 49	27 32	1 09	0 28	1 23	9 17	6 40D	0 46	9 02	25 30
5 Su	0 55 42	12 00 53	12♋44	18 15R	27 25	19 00	8 36	22 56	27 28	1 07	0 27	1 23	9 03	6 40	1 04	9 30	25 27
6 M	0 59 38	13 00 00	27 05	18 15	28 57	20 14	9 17	23 03	27 23	1 06	0 25	1 23	8 49	6 40	1 21	9 59	25 24
7 T	1 3 35	13 59 08	11♌47	18 14	0♏28	21 28	9 58	23 09	27 19	1 05	0 23	1 23	8 36	6 41	1 39	10 27	25 22
8 W	1 7 31	14 58 19	26 44	18 11	1 57	22 42	10 39	23 15	27 14	1 03	0 22	1 22	8 23	6 42	1 56	10 56	25 19
9 Th	1 11 28	15 57 31	11♍47	18 08	3 27	23 57	11 21	23 22	27 10	1 02	0 20	1 22	8 09	6 43	2 14	11 24	25 16
10 F	1 15 25	16 56 46	26 46	18 03	4 55	25 11	12 02	23 28	27 06	1 00	0 19	1 22	7 56	6 45	2 32	11 53	25 13
11 Sa	1 19 21	17 56 03	11♎34	18 00	6 22	26 25	12 43	23 34	27 02	0 58	0 17	1 22	7 43	6 47	2 50	12 22	25 11
12 Su	1 23 18	18 55 23	26 04	17 57	7 49	27 40	13 25	23 39	26 58	0 57	0 15	1 22	7 30	6 49	3 08	12 50	25 08
13 M	1 27 14	19 54 45	10♏07	17 55D	9 15	28 54	14 06	23 45	26 53	0 55	0 14	1 22	7 17	6 52	3 27	13 19	25 05
14 T	1 31 11	20 54 09	23 57	17 55	10 39	0≏08	14 48	23 50	26 49	0 53	0 12	1 22D	7 04	6 55	3 45	13 48	25 02
15 W	1 35 7	21 53 35	7♐19	17 55	12 03	1 23	15 30	23 56	26 45	0 52	0 11	1 22	6 52	6 58	4 03	14 17	25 00
16 Th	1 39 4	22 53 04	20 22	17 57	13 27	2 37	16 12	24 01	26 41	0 50	0 09	1 22	6 39	7 02	4 22	14 46	24 57
17 F	1 43 0	23 52 35	3♑07	17 59R	14 49	3 52	16 53	24 06	26 38	0 48	0 08	1 22	6 27	7 06	4 40	15 16	24 54
18 Sa	1 46 57	24 52 08	15 38	17 59	16 09	5 06	17 35	24 10	26 34	0 46	0 06	1 22	6 15	7 10	4 59	15 45	24 51
19 Su	1 50 54	25 51 43	27 57	17 57	17 30	6 21	18 17	24 15	26 30	0 44	0 05	1 22	6 03	7 15	5 18	16 14	24 48
20 M	1 54 50	26 51 21	10♒07	17 56	18 49	7 36	18 59	24 19	26 26	0 42	0 03	1 23	5 52	7 20	5 37	16 44	24 46
21 T	1 58 47	27 51 00	22 10	17 52	20 07	8 50	19 41	24 23	26 23	0 40	0 02	1 23	5 40	7 25	5 56	17 13	24 43
22 W	2 2 43	28 50 42	4♓08	17 46	21 23	10 05	20 23	24 28	26 19	0 38	0 01	1 23	5 29	7 30	6 15	17 42	24 40
23 Th	2 6 40	29 50 25	16 01	17 38	22 38	11 20	21 06	24 31	26 16	0 36	29♓59	1 23	5 18	7 36	6 34	18 12	24 37
24 F	2 10 36	0♏50 11	27 52	17 30	23 52	12 35	21 48	24 35	26 12	0 34	29 58	1 23	5 08	7 42	6 53	18 42	24 35
25 Sa	2 14 33	1 49 58	9♈43	17 21	25 04	13 49	22 30	24 39	26 09	0 32	29 56	1 24	4 58	7 48	7 12	19 11	24 32
26 Su	2 18 29	2 49 47	21 36	17 13	26 14	15 04	23 13	24 42	26 06	0 30	29 55	1 24	4 48	7 54	7 32	19 41	24 29
27 M	2 22 26	3 49 39	3♉33	17 07	27 22	16 19	23 55	24 45	26 02	0 28	29 54	1 24	4 38	8 01	7 51	20 11	24 26
28 T	2 26 23	4 49 31	15 39	17 03	28 28	17 34	24 38	24 48	25 59	0 26	29 52	1 25	4 29	8 08	8 10	20 41	24 24
29 W	2 30 19	5 49 26	27 58	17 01D	29 32	18 49	25 20	24 51	25 56	0 23	29 51	1 25	4 20	8 15	8 30	21 11	24 21
30 Th	2 34 16	6 49 22	10♊33	17 01	0♐39	20 04	26 03	24 53	25 53	0 21	29 50	1 26	4 11	8 23	8 49	21 41	24 18
31 F	2 38 12	7 49 19	23 30	17 02	1 31	21 19	26 45	24 56	25 51	0 19	29 49	1 26	4 03	8 31	9 09	22 11	24 16

EPHEMERIS CALCULATED FOR 12 MIDNIGHT GREENWICH MEAN TIME. ALL OTHER DATA AND FACING ASPECTARIAN PAGE IN **EASTERN TIME (BOLD)** AND PACIFIC TIME (REGULAR).

NOVEMBER 2025

☽ Last Aspect day	ET / hr:mn / PT		asp	☽ Ingress sign	day	ET / hr:mn / PT	
2	**10:15 am**	7:15 am	☌ ♆	♈	2	**10:39 am**	7:39 am
4	**6:21 am**	3:21 am	☍ ♀	♉	4	**11:16 am**	8:16 am
6	**9:51 am**	6:51 am	⚹ ♆	♊	6	**10:20 am**	7:20 am
8	**9:32 am**	6:32 am	□ ♆	♋	8	**10:06 am**	7:06 am
10	**12:23 pm**	9:23 am	⚹ ♅	♌	10	**12:34 pm**	9:34 am
12	**6:29 pm**	3:29 pm	□ ♅	♍	12	**6:52 pm**	3:52 pm
15	**4:08 am**	1:08 am	△ ♅	♎	15	**4:44 am**	1:44 am
17	**6:51 am**	3:51 am	□ ♃	♏	17	**4:44 pm**	1:44 pm
20	**4:24 am**	1:24 am	☍ ♅	♐	20	**5:26 am**	2:26 am
22	**4:48 pm**	1:48 pm	□ ♆	♑	22	**5:53 pm**	2:53 pm
25	**4:10 am**	1:10 am	⚹ ♆	♒	25	**5:16 am**	2:16 am
27	**12:53 pm**	9:53 am	□ ♅	♓	27	**2:24 pm**	11:24 am
29	**7:05 pm**	4:05 pm	☌ ♆	♈	29	**8:07 pm**	5:07 pm

☽ Phases & Eclipses phase	day	ET / hr:mn / PT	
Full Moon	5	**8:19 am**	5:19 am
4th Quarter	11		9:28 pm
4th Quarter	12	**12:28 am**	
New Moon	19		10:47 pm
New Moon	20	**1:47 am**	
2nd Quarter	27		10:59 pm
2nd Quarter	28	**1:59 am**	

Planet Ingress		day	ET / hr:mn / PT	
♂	♐	4	**8:01 am**	5:01 am
♀	♏	6	**5:39 pm**	2:39 pm
♅	♉	7	**9:22 pm**	6:22 pm
⚶	♑	15	**5:25 am**	2:25 am
☿	♏	18	**10:20 pm**	7:20 pm
☉	♐	21	**8:36 pm**	5:36 pm
♀	♐	30	**3:14 pm**	12:14 pm

Planetary Motion		day	ET / hr:mn / PT	
☿	℞	9	**2:02 pm**	11:02 am
♃	℞	11	**11:41 am**	8:41 am
⚳	D	21	**6:57 pm**	3:57 pm
♄	D	27	**10:52 pm**	7:52 pm
☿	D	29	**12:38 pm**	9:38 am

1 SATURDAY

☽ ⚻ ♀ 10:47 pm

2 SUNDAY

☽ ⚻ ♀ **1:47 am**
☽ △ ♃ **2:17 am** 12:17 am
☽ ☌ ♄ **3:31 am** 1:31 am
☽ △ ♂ **8:17 am** 5:17 am
☽ ☌ ♆ **10:15 am** 7:15 am
☽ ⚹ ♅ **11:01 am** 8:01 am
☽ ⚹ ♇ **1:05 pm** 10:05 am
☽ △ ☿ **5:18 pm** 2:18 pm
♀ □ ♃ **6:17 pm** 3:17 pm

3 MONDAY

☽ ⚻ ☉ **5:11 am** 2:11 am
♀ ⚻ ♄ **6:57 am** 3:57 am
♂ △ ♆ **10:59 pm** 7:59 pm

4 TUESDAY

☽ □ ♃ **3:25 am** 12:25 am
☽ ⚺ ♄ **4:21 am** 1:21 am
☽ ☍ ♀ **6:21 am** 3:21 am
☽ ⚺ ♆ **10:49 am** 7:49 am
☽ ⚻ ♂ **11:25 am** 8:25 am
☽ ⚺ ♅ **11:28 am** 8:28 am
♂ ☍ ♅ **12:30 pm** 9:30 am
☽ □ ♇ **1:36 pm** 10:36 am
☽ ⚻ ☿ **7:47 pm** 4:47 pm

5 WEDNESDAY

☽ ☍ ☉ **8:19 am** 5:19 am
☽ ⚹ ♃ 11:40 pm

6 THURSDAY

☽ ⚹ ♃ **2:40 am**
☽ ⚹ ♄ **3:24 am** 12:24 am
☽ ⚻ ♀ **9:41 am** 6:41 am
☽ ⚹ ♆ **9:51 am** 6:51 am
♂ ⚹ ♇ **10:11 am** 7:11 am
☽ ☌ ♅ **10:26 am** 7:26 am
♀ ⚻ ♆ **11:37 am** 8:37 am
☽ △ ♇ **12:42 pm** 9:42 am
☽ ☍ ♂ **12:49 pm** 9:49 am
♀ ⚻ ♅ **6:31 pm** 3:31 pm
☽ ☍ ☿ **8:19 pm** 5:19 pm

7 FRIDAY

☽ ⚻ ☉ **10:47 am** 7:47 am
♀ □ ♇ **10:44 pm** 7:44 pm
☽ ⚺ ♃ 11:13 pm
☽ □ ♄ 11:49 pm

8 SATURDAY

☽ ⚺ ♃ **2:13 am**
☽ □ ♄ **2:49 am**
☽ □ ♆ **9:32 am** 6:32 am
☽ ⚺ ♅ **10:04 am** 7:04 am
☽ ⚻ ♇ **12:35 pm** 9:35 am
☽ △ ♀ **1:52 pm** 10:52 am
☽ ⚻ ♂ **3:08 pm** 12:08 pm
☽ ⚻ ☿ **9:17 pm** 6:17 pm

9 SUNDAY

☽ △ ☉ **3:26 pm** 12:26 pm
♀ ⚺ ♂ **11:20 pm** 8:20 pm

10 MONDAY

☽ ☌ ♃ **4:09 am** 1:09 am
☽ △ ♄ **4:39 am** 1:39 am
☽ △ ♆ **11:54 am** 8:54 am
☽ ⚹ ♅ **12:23 pm** 9:23 am
☽ ☍ ♇ **3:16 pm** 12:16 pm
☽ △ ♂ **8:48 pm** 5:48 pm
☽ □ ♀ **9:44 pm** 6:44 pm
☽ △ ☿ 9:21 pm

11 TUESDAY

☽ △ ☿ **12:21 am**
☿ ⚺ ♀ **9:16 pm** 6:16 pm
☽ □ ☉ 9:28 pm

12 WEDNESDAY

☽ □ ☉ **12:28 am**
☽ ⚺ ♃ **9:49 am** 6:49 am
☽ ⚻ ♄ **10:14 am** 7:14 am
☽ ⚻ ♆ **6:05 pm** 3:05 pm
☿ ☌ ♂ **6:15 pm** 3:15 pm
☽ □ ♅ **6:29 pm** 3:29 pm
☽ ⚻ ♇ **9:50 pm** 6:50 pm

13 THURSDAY

☽ □ ☿ **5:49 am** 2:49 am
☽ □ ♂ **7:03 am** 4:03 am
☽ ⚹ ♀ **10:47 am** 7:47 am

14 FRIDAY

☽ ⚹ ☉ **2:20 pm** 11:20 am
☽ ⚹ ♃ **7:09 pm** 4:09 pm
☽ ☍ ♄ **7:30 pm** 4:30 pm

15 SATURDAY

☽ ☍ ♆ **3:50 am** 12:50 am
☽ △ ♅ **4:08 am** 1:08 am
☽ △ ♇ **7:55 am** 4:55 am
☽ ⚹ ☿ **12:40 pm** 9:40 am
☽ ⚹ ♂ **9:16 pm** 6:16 pm

16 SUNDAY

☽ ⚺ ♀ **4:14 am** 1:14 am
☉ △ ♃ 9:08 pm

17 MONDAY

☉ △ ♃ **12:08 am**
☉ △ ♄ **3:56 am** 12:56 am
☽ □ ♃ **6:51 am** 3:51 am
☽ ⚻ ♄ **7:11 am** 4:11 am
☽ ⚺ ☉ **7:29 am** 4:29 am
☿ ⚹ ♇ **3:36 pm** 12:36 pm
☽ ⚻ ♆ **3:46 pm** 12:46 pm
☽ ⚻ ♅ **3:56 pm** 12:56 pm
☽ ⚺ ☿ **7:39 pm** 4:39 pm
☽ □ ♇ **8:05 pm** 5:05 pm

18 TUESDAY

☽ ⚺ ♂ **1:33 pm** 10:33 am
☽ ☌ ♀ **11:49 pm** 8:49 pm

19 WEDNESDAY

☿ ☍ ♅ **6:45 am** 3:45 am
☿ △ ♆ **7:21 am** 4:21 am
☽ △ ♃ **7:23 pm** 4:23 pm
☽ △ ♄ **7:45 pm** 4:45 pm
☽ ☌ ☉ 10:47 pm
☽ ☌ ☿ 11:15 pm

20 THURSDAY

☽ ☌ ☉ **1:47 am**
☽ ☌ ☿ **2:15 am**
☉ ☌ ☿ **4:23 am** 1:23 am
☽ △ ♆ **4:24 am** 1:24 am
☽ ☍ ♅ **4:24 am** 1:24 am
☽ ⚹ ♇ **8:52 am** 5:52 am
♅ ⚹ ♆ **9:39 am** 6:39 am

21 FRIDAY

☽ ☌ ♂ **6:13 am** 3:13 am
☉ ☍ ♅ **7:25 am** 4:25 am
☉ △ ♆ **8:05 am** 5:05 am
☽ ⚺ ♀ **7:38 pm** 4:38 pm

22 SATURDAY

☽ ⚻ ♃ **7:46 am** 4:46 am
☽ □ ♄ **8:13 am** 5:13 am
☽ ⚺ ☿ **8:44 am** 5:44 am
☿ △ ♄ **1:45 pm** 10:45 am
☽ ⚻ ♅ **4:39 pm** 1:39 pm
☽ □ ♆ **4:48 pm** 1:48 pm
☿ △ ♃ **6:37 pm** 3:37 pm
☽ ⚺ ☉ **7:50 pm** 4:50 pm
☽ ⚺ ♇ **9:22 pm** 6:22 pm

23 SUNDAY

☉ ⚹ ♇ **2:20 pm** 11:20 am
☽ ⚺ ♂ **10:14 pm** 7:14 pm

24 MONDAY

☽ ⚹ ♀ **2:24 pm** 11:24 am
☽ ⚹ ☿ **3:28 pm** 12:28 pm
☽ ☍ ♃ **7:12 pm** 4:12 pm
☽ ⚹ ♄ **7:48 pm** 4:48 pm
☿ ☌ ♀ **8:52 pm** 5:52 pm

25 TUESDAY

☽ △ ♅ **3:52 am** 12:52 am
☽ ⚹ ♆ **4:10 am** 1:10 am
☽ ☌ ♇ **8:45 am** 5:45 am
☽ ⚹ ☉ **12:28 pm** 9:28 am

26 WEDNESDAY

♀ △ ♃ **11:31 am** 8:31 am
☽ ⚹ ♂ **12:21 pm** 9:21 am
♀ △ ♄ **6:48 pm** 3:48 pm
☽ □ ☿ **10:12 pm** 7:12 pm

27 THURSDAY

☽ ⚻ ♃ **4:36 am** 1:36 am
☽ ⚺ ♄ **5:23 am** 2:23 am
☽ □ ♀ **6:32 am** 3:32 am
☽ □ ♅ **12:53 pm** 9:53 am
☽ ⚺ ♆ **1:19 pm** 10:19 am
☽ ⚺ ♇ **5:48 pm** 2:48 pm
☽ □ ☉ 10:59 pm

28 FRIDAY

☽ □ ☉ **1:59 am**
☽ □ ♂ **10:58 pm** 7:58 pm

29 SATURDAY

☽ △ ☿ **3:54 am** 12:54 am
☽ △ ♃ **10:45 am** 7:45 am
☽ ☌ ♄ **11:42 am** 8:42 am
☽ △ ♀ **6:13 pm** 3:13 pm
☽ ⚹ ♅ **6:33 pm** 3:33 pm
☽ ☌ ♆ **7:05 pm** 4:05 pm
♀ ☍ ♅ **9:48 pm** 6:48 pm
☽ ⚹ ♇ **11:22 pm** 8:22 pm

30 SUNDAY

♀ △ ♆ **3:48 am** 12:48 am
☽ △ ☉ **11:00 am** 8:00 am

Eastern time in bold type
Pacific time in medium type

NOVEMBER 2025

DATE	SID.TIME	SUN	MOON	NODE	MERCURY	VENUS	MARS	JUPITER	SATURN	URANUS	NEPTUNE	PLUTO	CERES	PALLAS	JUNO	VESTA	CHIRON
		8♏49 18	6♐52	17♓03R	2♐25	22♎34	27♏28	24♋58	25♓48R	0♊17R	29♓48R	1♒27	3♌54R	8♒39	9♏29	22♏41	24♈13R
1 Sa	2 42 9	8♏49 18	6♐52	17♓03R	2♐25	22♎34	27♏28	24♋58	25♓48R	0♊17R	29♓48R	1♒27	3♌54R	8♒39	9♏29	22♏41	24♈13R
2 Su	2 46 5	9 49 19	20 43	17 03R	3 16	23 49	28 11	25 00	25 45	0 14	29 46	1 27	3 47	8 47	9 49	23 11	24 10
3 M	2 50 2	10 49 21	5♈02	17 01	4 03	25 04	28 54	25 02	25 43	0 12	29 45	1 28	3 39	8 56	10 09	23 41	24 08
4 T	2 53 58	11 49 25	19 48	16 58	4 46	26 19	29 37	25 03	25 40	0 10	29 44	1 28	3 32	9 04	10 28	24 11	24 05
5 W	2 57 55	12 49 31	4♉54	16 52	5 23	27 34	0♐20	25 05	25 38	0 07	29 43	1 29	3 26	9 13	10 48	24 42	24 02
6 Th	3 1 52	13 49 39	20 12	16 44	5 54	28 49	1 03	25 06	25 35	0 05	29 42	1 30	3 20	9 23	11 08	25 12	24 00
7 F	3 5 48	14 49 48	5♊31	16 35	6 20	0♏04	1 46	25 07	25 33	0 03	29 41	1 30	3 14	9 32	11 29	25 42	23 57
8 Sa	3 9 45	15 50 00	20 39	16 26	6 38	1 19	2 29	25 08	25 31	0 00	29 40	1 31	3 08	9 42	11 49	26 13	23 55
9 Su	3 13 41	16 50 13	5♋26	16 18	6 49R	2 34	3 12	25 08	25 29	29♉58	29 39	1 32	3 03	9 52	12 09	26 43	23 52
10 M	3 17 38	17 50 29	19 48	16 13	6 52	3 50	3 55	25 09	25 27	29 55	29 38	1 32	2 58	10 02	12 29	27 14	23 50
11 T	3 21 34	18 50 46	3♌41	16 09	6 45	5 05	4 39	25 09R	25 25	29 53	29 37	1 33	2 54	10 12	12 49	27 44	23 47
12 W	3 25 31	19 51 05	17 05	16 08D	6 29	6 20	5 22	25 09	25 23	29 51	29 36	1 34	2 50	10 23	13 10	28 15	23 45
13 Th	3 29 27	20 51 26	0♍04	16 09R	6 03	7 35	6 06	25 09	25 22	29 48	29 35	1 35	2 46	10 33	13 30	28 45	23 43
14 F	3 33 24	21 51 50	12 42	16 09	5 27	8 51	6 49	25 08	25 20	29 46	29 34	1 36	2 43	10 44	13 51	29 16	23 40
15 Sa	3 37 21	22 52 15	25 03	16 09	4 41	10 06	7 33	25 08	25 19	29 43	29 33	1 37	2 40	10 56	14 11	29 47	23 38
16 Su	3 41 17	23 52 41	7♎12	16 06	3 45	11 21	8 16	25 07	25 17	29 41	29 32	1 37	2 37	11 07	14 32	0♐17	23 35
17 M	3 45 14	24 53 10	19 12	16 02	2 41	12 36	9 00	25 06	25 16	29 38	29 32	1 38	2 35	11 18	14 52	0 48	23 33
18 T	3 49 10	25 53 41	1♏07	15 54	1 29	13 52	9 44	25 05	25 15	29 36	29 31	1 39	2 34	11 30	15 13	1 19	23 31
19 W	3 53 7	26 54 13	12 59	15 43	0 11	15 07	10 28	25 04	25 14	29 33	29 30	1 40	2 32	11 42	15 34	1 50	23 29
20 Th	3 57 3	27 54 47	24 51	15 30	28♏50	16 22	11 11	25 02	25 13	29 31	29 29	1 41	2 31	11 54	15 55	2 21	23 27
21 F	4 1 0	28 55 22	6♐43	15 16	27 29	17 38	11 55	25 00	25 12	29 28	29 29	1 42	2 31D	12 07	16 15	2 52	23 24
22 Sa	4 4 56	29 55 59	18 37	15 02	26 10	18 53	12 39	24 58	25 11	29 26	29 28	1 43	2 31	12 19	16 36	3 23	23 22
23 Su	4 8 53	0♐56 37	0♑34	14 49	24 55	20 09	13 23	24 56	25 11	29 23	29 28	1 45	2 31	12 32	16 57	3 54	23 20
24 M	4 12 50	1 57 16	12 36	14 38	23 48	21 24	14 08	24 54	25 10	29 21	29 27	1 46	2 31	12 45	17 18	4 25	23 18
25 T	4 16 46	2 57 57	24 45	14 24	22 49	22 39	14 52	24 51	25 10	29 18	29 26	1 47	2 32	12 58	17 39	4 56	23 16
26 W	4 20 43	3 58 39	7♒05	14 24	22 01	23 55	15 36	24 49	25 10	29 15	29 26	1 48	2 34	13 11	18 00	5 27	23 14
27 Th	4 24 39	4 59 22	19 38	14 21	21 24	25 10	16 20	24 46	25 10	29 13	29 25	1 49	2 35	13 24	18 21	5 58	23 12
28 F	4 28 36	6 00 06	2♓30	14 20	20 59	26 26	17 04	24 43	25 09D	29 11	29 25	1 50	2 37	13 38	18 42	6 29	23 10
29 Sa	4 32 32	7 00 51	15 43	14 20	20 45D	27 41	17 49	24 39	25 09	29 08	29 25	1 52	2 40	13 51	19 03	7 00	23 09
30 Su	4 36 29	8 01 36	29 21	14 20	20 43	28 56	18 33	24 36	25 10	29 06	29 25	1 53	2 43	14 05	19 24	7 31	23 07

EPHEMERIS CALCULATED FOR 12 MIDNIGHT GREENWICH MEAN TIME. ALL OTHER DATA AND FACING ASPECTARIAN PAGE IN **EASTERN TIME (BOLD)** AND PACIFIC TIME (REGULAR).

DECEMBER 2025

☽ Last Aspect day	ET / hr:mn / PT		asp	☽ Ingress sign	day	ET / hr:mn / PT	
1	**1:14 pm**	10:14 am	□♃	♉	1	**10:13 pm**	7:13 pm
3	**8:50 pm**	5:50 pm	✶♆	♊	3	**9:48 pm**	6:48 pm
5	**7:55 pm**	4:55 pm	□♆	♋	5	**8:54 pm**	5:54 pm
7	**8:45 pm**	5:45 pm	△♆	♌	7	**9:48 pm**	6:48 pm
9	**11:56 pm**	8:56 pm	□♅	♍	9		11:20 pm
9	**11:56 pm**	8:56 pm	□♅	♍	10	**2:20 am**	
12	**9:51 am**	6:51 am	☍♆	♎	12	**11:04 am**	8:04 am
14	**10:36 pm**	7:36 pm	✶♂	♏	14	**10:51 pm**	7:51 pm
17	**10:24 am**	7:24 am	△♆	♐	17	**11:38 am**	8:38 am
19	**10:41 pm**	7:41 pm	□♆	♑	19	**11:53 pm**	8:53 pm
22	**9:44 am**	6:44 am	✶♆	♒	22	**10:52 am**	7:52 am
24	**4:42 pm**	1:42 pm	□♅	♓	24	**8:09 pm**	5:09 pm
26		11:03 pm	☌♆	♈	27	**3:02 am**	12:02 am
27	**2:03 am**		☌♆	♈	27	**3:02 am**	12:02 am
28	**9:13 pm**	6:13 pm	△☿	♉	29	**6:57 am**	3:57 am
31	**7:25 am**	4:25 am	✶♆	♊	31	**8:13 am**	5:13 am

☽ Phases & Eclipses phase	day	ET / hr:mn / PT	
Full Moon	4	**3:14 pm**	3:14 pm
4th Quarter	11	**3:52 pm**	12:52 pm
New Moon	19	**3:43 pm**	5:43 pm
2nd Quarter	27	**2:10 pm**	11:10 am

Planet Ingress	day	ET / hr:mn / PT	
☿ ♐	11	**5:40 pm**	2:40 pm
♂ ♑	14		11:34 pm
♂ ♑	15	**2:34 am**	
☉ ♑	21	**10:03 am**	7:03 am
♀ ♑	24	**11:26 am**	8:26 am
⚵ ♑	29	**9:35 am**	6:35 am

Planetary Motion	day	ET / hr:mn / PT	
♆ D	10	**7:21 am**	4:21 am

1 MONDAY
- ☽△♂ **5:14 am** 2:14 am
- ☽⚻☿ **7:29 am** 4:29 am
- ☽□♃ **1:14 pm** 10:14 am
- ☽⚺♄ **2:22 pm** 11:22 am
- ☽⚺♅ **8:36 pm** 5:36 pm
- ☽⚺♆ **9:14 pm** 6:14 pm
- ☽⚻♀ 10:05 pm
- ☽□♇ 10:20 pm

2 TUESDAY
- ☽⚻♀ **1:05 am**
- ☽□♇ **1:20 am**
- ♀✶♇ **4:07 am** 1:07 am
- ☽⚻☉ **3:45 pm** 12:45 pm

3 WEDNESDAY
- ☽⚻♂ **7:58 am** 4:58 am
- ☽☍☿ **9:06 am** 6:06 am
- ☽✶♃ **12:57 pm** 9:57 am
- ☽✶♄ **2:15 pm** 11:15 am
- ☽☌♅ **8:07 pm** 5:07 pm
- ☽✶♆ **8:50 pm** 5:50 pm
- ☽△♇ 9:53 pm

4 THURSDAY
- ☽△♇ **12:53 am**
- ☽☍♀ **4:49 am** 1:49 am
- ☽☍☉ **6:14 pm** 3:14 pm

5 FRIDAY
- ☽☍♂ **9:23 am** 6:23 am
- ☽⚻☿ **10:24 am** 7:24 am
- ☽⚺♃ **11:44 am** 8:44 am
- ☽□♄ **1:19 pm** 10:19 am
- ☽⚺♅ **7:05 pm** 4:05 pm
- ☽□♆ **7:55 pm** 4:55 pm
- ☽⚻♇ 9:07 pm

6 SATURDAY
- ☽⚻♇ **12:07 am**
- ☿△♃ **8:05 am** 5:05 am
- ☽⚻♀ **8:22 am** 5:22 am
- ☽⚻☉ **9:21 pm** 6:21 pm

7 SUNDAY
- ♂⚻♃ **4:55 am** 1:55 am
- ☽☌♃ **11:51 am** 8:51 am
- ☿△♄ **11:58 am** 8:58 am
- ☽⚻♂ **12:16 pm** 9:16 am
- ☽△♄ **1:50 pm** 10:50 am
- ☽△☿ **1:59 pm** 10:59 am
- ☽✶♅ **7:44 pm** 4:44 pm
- ☽△♆ **8:45 pm** 5:45 pm
- ☽☍♇ 10:18 pm

8 MONDAY
- ☽☍♇ **1:18 am**
- ☽△♀ **2:56 pm** 11:56 am
- ♂□♄ **7:16 pm** 4:16 pm

9 TUESDAY
- ☽△☉ **4:00 am** 1:00 am
- ☽⚺♃ **3:14 pm** 12:14 pm
- ☽⚻♄ **5:47 pm** 2:47 pm
- ☽△♂ **7:06 pm** 4:06 pm
- ☽□☿ **10:26 pm** 7:26 pm
- ☽□♅ **11:56 pm** 8:56 pm
- ☽⚻♆ 10:12 pm

10 WEDNESDAY
- ☽⚻♆ **1:12 am**
- ☽⚻♇ **6:13 am** 3:13 am
- ☿☍♅ **2:59 pm** 11:59 am
- ☽□♀ 11:47 pm

11 THURSDAY
- ☽□♀ **2:47 am**
- ☿△♆ **5:19 am** 2:19 am
- ☽□☉ **3:52 pm** 12:52 pm
- ☽✶♃ **10:44 pm** 7:44 pm
- ☽☍♄ 11:00 pm

12 FRIDAY
- ☽☍♄ **2:00 am**
- ☽□♂ **6:56 am** 3:56 am
- ☽△♅ **8:20 am** 5:20 am
- ☽☍♆ **9:51 am** 6:51 am
- ☽✶☿ **1:02 pm** 10:02 am
- ☽△♇ **3:20 pm** 12:20 pm

13 SATURDAY
- ♂⚻♅ **4:44 am** 1:44 am
- ☿✶♇ **11:32 am** 8:32 am
- ☽✶♀ **7:54 pm** 4:54 pm

14 SUNDAY
- ♂□♆ **6:44 am** 3:44 am
- ☽✶☉ **8:20 am** 5:20 am
- ☽□♃ **9:34 am** 6:34 am
- ☽⚻♄ **1:35 pm** 10:35 am
- ☽⚻♅ **7:49 pm** 4:49 pm
- ☉⚻♃ **9:30 pm** 6:30 pm
- ☽⚻♆ **9:36 pm** 6:36 pm
- ☽✶♂ **10:36 pm** 7:36 pm

15 MONDAY
- ☽□♇ **3:24 am** 12:24 am
- ☽⚺☿ **8:18 am** 5:18 am

16 TUESDAY
- ☽⚺♀ **3:42 pm** 12:42 pm
- ☽△♃ **9:46 pm** 6:46 pm
- ☉□♄ **11:34 pm** 8:34 pm
- ☽△♄ 11:30 pm
- ☽⚺☉ 11:46 pm

17 WEDNESDAY
- ☽△♄ **2:30 am**
- ☽⚺☉ **2:46 am**
- ☽☍♅ **8:25 am** 5:25 am
- ☽△♆ **10:24 am** 7:24 am
- ☽⚺♂ **3:31 pm** 12:31 pm
- ☽✶♇ **4:19 pm** 1:19 pm

18 THURSDAY
- ♂⚺♇ **4:32 am** 1:32 am
- ☽☌☿ **5:02 am** 2:02 am
- ♀⚻♃ **8:45 pm** 5:45 pm

19 FRIDAY
- ☽⚻♃ **9:40 am** 6:40 am
- ☽☌♀ **11:19 am** 8:19 am
- ☽□♄ **3:04 pm** 12:04 pm
- ☉⚻♅ **6:34 pm** 3:34 pm
- ☽⚻♅ **8:32 pm** 5:32 pm
- ☽☌☉ **8:43 pm** 5:43 pm
- ☽□♆ **10:41 pm** 7:41 pm

20 SATURDAY
- ☽⚺♇ **4:37 am** 1:37 am
- ☽☌♂ **7:42 am** 4:42 am
- ☉□♆ **8:02 pm** 5:02 pm
- ♀□♄ 9:09 pm
- ☽⚺☿ 9:54 pm

21 SUNDAY
- ♀□♄ **12:09 am**
- ☽⚺☿ **12:54 am**
- ☽☍♃ **8:26 pm** 5:26 pm
- ☽✶♄ 11:27 pm

22 MONDAY
- ☽✶♄ **2:27 am**
- ☽⚺♀ **5:21 am** 2:21 am
- ☽△♅ **7:26 am** 4:26 am
- ☽✶♆ **9:44 am** 6:44 am
- ☽⚺☉ **1:05 pm** 10:05 am
- ☽☌♇ **3:37 pm** 12:37 pm
- ☽⚺♂ **10:20 pm** 7:20 pm
- ♀⚻♅ 10:22 pm

23 TUESDAY
- ♀⚻♅ **1:22 am**
- ☽✶☿ **6:54 pm** 3:54 pm
- ☉⚺♇ **8:37 pm** 5:37 pm
- ♀□♆ 9:31 pm

24 WEDNESDAY
- ♀□♆ **12:31 am**
- ☽⚻♃ **5:40 am** 2:40 am
- ☽⚺♄ **12:14 pm** 9:14 am
- ☽□♅ **4:42 pm** 1:42 pm
- ☽⚺♆ **7:05 pm** 4:05 pm
- ☽✶♀ **9:06 pm** 6:06 pm
- ☽⚺♇ 9:52 pm

25 THURSDAY
- ☽⚺♇ **12:52 am**
- ☽✶☉ **3:13 am** 12:13 am
- ☽✶♂ **10:45 am** 7:45 am

26 FRIDAY
- ☽□☿ **10:02 am** 7:02 am
- ♀⚺♇ **12:17 pm** 9:17 am
- ☽△♃ **12:43 pm** 9:43 am
- ☽☌♄ **7:41 pm** 4:41 pm
- ☽✶♅ **11:37 pm** 8:37 pm
- ☽☌♆ 11:03 pm

27 SATURDAY
- ☽☌♆ **2:03 am**
- ☽✶♇ **7:37 am** 4:37 am
- ☿⚻♃ **8:16 am** 5:16 am
- ☽□♀ **9:33 am** 6:33 am
- ☽□☉ **2:10 pm** 11:10 am
- ☽□♂ **8:05 pm** 5:05 pm

28 SUNDAY
- ☽□♃ **4:59 pm** 1:59 pm
- ☽△☿ **9:13 pm** 6:13 pm
- ☽⚺♄ 9:13 pm

29 MONDAY
- ☽⚺♄ **12:13 am**
- ☽⚺♅ **3:37 am** 12:37 am
- ☽⚺♆ **6:04 am** 3:04 am
- ☽□♇ **11:24 am** 8:24 am
- ☽△♀ **6:03 pm** 3:03 pm
- ☽△☉ **9:22 pm** 6:22 pm
- ☽△♂ 10:54 pm
- ☿□♄ 11:15 pm

30 TUESDAY
- ☽△♂ **1:54 am**
- ☿□♄ **2:15 am**
- ☽✶♃ **6:27 pm** 3:27 pm
- ☽✶♄ 10:58 pm

31 WEDNESDAY
- ☽✶♄ **1:58 am**
- ☽⚻☿ **4:34 am** 1:34 am
- ☽☌♅ **4:56 am** 1:56 am
- ☽✶♆ **7:25 am** 4:25 am
- ☿⚻♅ **8:08 am** 5:08 am
- ☽△♇ **12:35 pm** 9:35 am
- ☽⚻♀ **11:21 pm** 8:21 pm
- ☽⚻☉ 10:37 pm

Eastern time in bold type
Pacific time in medium type

DECEMBER 2025

DATE	SID.TIME	SUN	MOON	NODE	MERCURY	VENUS	MARS	JUPITER	SATURN	URANUS	NEPTUNE	PLUTO	CERES	PALLAS	JUNO	VESTA	CHIRON
1 M	4 40 26	9✗02 23	13♈27	14♈18R	20♏51	0✗12	19✗18	24♋32R	25♓10	29♉03R	29♓24R	1♒54	2♈46	14♒19	19✗46	8♋02	23♈05R
2 T	4 44 22	10 03 11	28 01	14 13	21 08	1 27	20 02	24 28	25 10	29 01	29 24	1 55	2 49	14 33	20 07	8 34	23 03
3 W	4 48 19	11 04 00	12♉59	14 05	21 35	2 43	20 47	24 24	25 11	28 58	29 23	1 57	2 53	14 47	20 28	9 05	23 02
4 Th	4 52 15	12 04 49	28 13	13 55	22 10	3 58	21 31	24 20	25 11	28 56	29 23	1 58	2 57	15 02	20 49	9 36	23 00
5 F	4 56 12	13 05 40	13♊33	13 43	22 52	5 14	22 16	24 15	25 12	28 53	29 23	1 59	3 02	15 16	21 11	10 07	22 59
6 Sa	5 0 8	14 06 32	28 48	13 32	23 40	6 29	23 01	24 11	25 13	28 51	29 23	2 01	3 07	15 31	21 32	10 39	22 57
7 Su	5 4 5	15 07 25	13♋46	13 21	24 33	7 45	23 46	24 06	25 14	28 49	29 23	2 02	3 12	15 46	21 53	11 10	22 56
8 M	5 8 1	16 08 19	28 20	13 13	25 32	9 00	24 30	24 01	25 15	28 46	29 22	2 04	3 18	16 01	22 15	11 41	22 54
9 T	5 11 58	17 09 15	12♌24	13 08	26 35	10 16	25 15	23 56	25 16	28 44	29 22	2 05	3 24	16 16	22 36	12 13	22 53
10 W	5 15 55	18 10 11	25 57	13 05	27 42	11 31	26 00	23 51	25 17	28 41	29 22D	2 07	3 30	16 31	22 57	12 44	22 52
11 Th	5 19 51	19 11 09	9♍02	13 05	28 51	12 47	26 45	23 45	25 18	28 39	29 22	2 08	3 37	16 47	23 19	13 15	22 50
12 F	5 23 48	20 12 08	21 42	13 05	0✗04	14 02	27 30	23 40	25 20	28 37	29 22	2 10	3 44	17 02	23 40	13 47	22 49
13 Sa	5 27 44	21 13 07	4♎03	13 04	1 19	15 18	28 15	23 34	25 21	28 35	29 22	2 11	3 51	17 18	24 02	14 18	22 48
14 Su	5 31 41	22 14 08	16 09	13 02	2 36	16 33	29 01	23 28	25 23	28 32	29 23	2 13	3 58	17 33	24 23	14 50	22 47
15 M	5 35 37	23 15 08	28 06	12 57	3 56	17 49	29 46	23 22	25 25	28 30	29 23	2 14	4 06	17 48	24 45	15 21	22 46
16 T	5 39 34	24 16 13	9♏57	12 49	5 16	19 04	0♑31	23 16	25 27	28 28	29 23	2 16	4 14	18 05	25 06	15 52	22 45
17 W	5 43 30	25 17 17	21 47	12 39	6 38	20 20	1 16	23 10	25 29	28 26	29 23	2 17	4 23	18 21	25 28	16 24	22 44
18 Th	5 47 27	26 18 22	3✗38	12 26	8 01	21 35	2 02	23 03	25 31	28 24	29 23	2 19	4 32	18 38	25 49	16 55	22 43
19 F	5 51 24	27 19 27	15 33	12 12	9 26	22 51	2 47	22 57	25 33	28 21	29 24	2 21	4 41	18 54	26 11	17 27	22 42
20 Sa	5 55 20	28 20 34	27 33	12 01	10 51	24 06	3 32	22 50	25 35	28 19	29 24	2 22	4 50	19 10	26 32	17 58	22 41
21 Su	5 59 17	29 21 40	9♑39	11 44	12 17	25 22	4 18	22 43	25 37	28 17	29 24	2 24	5 00	19 27	26 54	18 30	22 40
22 M	6 3 13	0♑22 48	21 51	11 33	13 44	26 37	5 04	22 36	25 40	28 15	29 25	2 26	5 10	19 44	27 16	19 02	22 40
23 T	6 7 10	1 23 55	4♒12	11 24	15 11	27 53	5 49	22 29	25 42	28 13	29 25	2 27	5 20	20 00	27 37	19 33	22 39
24 W	6 11 6	2 25 03	16 42	11 18	16 39	29 08	6 35	22 22	25 45	28 11	29 26	2 29	5 31	20 17	27 59	20 05	22 39
25 Th	6 15 3	3 26 11	29 23	11 16D	18 08	0♑24	7 20	22 15	25 48	28 09	29 26	2 31	5 41	20 34	28 20	20 36	22 38
26 F	6 18 59	4 27 19	12♓19	11 15	19 37	1 39	8 06	22 07	25 51	28 08	29 27	2 32	5 52	20 51	28 42	21 08	22 38
27 Sa	6 22 56	5 28 27	25 31	11 15R	21 06	2 55	8 52	22 00	25 54	28 06	29 27	2 34	6 04	21 08	29 04	21 39	22 37
28 Su	6 26 53	6 29 35	9♈03	11 16	22 36	4 10	9 38	21 52	25 57	28 04	29 28	2 36	6 15	21 26	29 25	22 11	22 37
29 M	6 30 49	7 30 43	22 56	11 15	24 06	5 26	10 24	21 45	26 00	28 02	29 28	2 38	6 27	21 43	29 47	22 42	22 37
30 T	6 34 46	8 31 51	7♉02	11 11	25 37	6 41	11 09	21 37	26 03	28 00	29 29	2 40	6 39	22 00	0♑08	23 14	22 36
31 W	6 38 42	9 32 59	21 50	11 06	27 08	7 57	11 55	21 29	26 07	27 59	29 30	2 41	6 52	22 18	0 30	23 46	22 36

EPHEMERIS CALCULATED FOR 12 MIDNIGHT GREENWICH MEAN TIME. ALL OTHER DATA AND FACING ASPECTARIAN PAGE IN **EASTERN TIME (BOLD)** AND PACIFIC TIME (REGULAR).

JANUARY 2026

☽ Last Aspect day	ET / hr:mn / PT	asp	☽ Ingress sign day	ET / hr:mn / PT
2	**7:24 am** 4:24 am	□♆	♋ 2	**8:09 am** 5:09 am
4	**7:59 am** 4:59 am	△♆	♌ 4	**8:44 am** 5:44 am
6	**8:05 am** 5:05 am	□♅	♍ 6	**11:57 am** 8:57 am
8	**6:23 pm** 3:23 pm	☍♆	♎ 8	**7:06 pm** 4:06 pm
10	**12:54 pm** 9:54 am	□♀	♏ 11	**5:55 am** 2:55 am
13	**5:59 pm** 2:59 pm	△♆	♐ 13	**6:34 pm** 3:34 pm
16	**6:19 am** 3:19 am	□♆	♑ 16	**6:47 am** 3:47 am
18	**4:57 pm** 1:57 pm	✶♆	♒ 18	**5:18 pm** 2:18 pm
20	**9:16 pm** 6:16 pm	□♅	♓ 20	10:50 pm
20	**9:16 pm** 6:16 pm	□♅	♓ 21	**1:50 am**
23	**8:17 am** 5:17 am	☌♆	♈ 23	**8:26 am** 5:26 am
24	**4:36 pm** 1:36 pm	□♃	♉ 25	**1:05 pm** 10:05 am
27	**12:58 pm** 9:58 am	✶♄	♊ 27	**3:55 pm** 12:55 pm
29	**2:57 pm** 11:57 am	□♄	♋ 29	**5:32 pm** 2:32 pm
31	**4:52 pm** 1:52 pm	△♄	♌ 31	**7:09 pm** 4:09 pm

☽ Phases & Eclipses phase	day	ET / hr:mn / PT
Full Moon	3	**5:03 am** 2:03 am
4th Quarter	10	**13:48 am** 7:48 am
New Moon	18	**2:52 pm** 11:52 am
2nd Quarter	25	**11:47 pm** 8:47 pm

Planet Ingress	day	ET / hr:mn / PT
☿ ♑	1	**4:11 pm** 1:11 pm
⚶ ♒	11	**3:40 pm** 12:40 pm
♀ ♒	17	**7:43 am** 4:43 am
☉ ♒	19	**8:45 pm** 5:45 pm
☿ ♒	20	**11:41 am** 8:41 am
♂ ♒	23	**4:17 am** 1:17 am
♀ ♓	24	**8:33 pm** 5:33 pm
♆ ♈	26	**12:37 pm** 9:37 am

Planetary Motion	day	ET / hr:mn / PT
⚷ D	2	**9:38 am** 6:38 am

1 THURSDAY
☽ ⚻ ☉ **1:37 am**
☽ ⚻ ♂ **5:04 am** 2:04 am
☿ □ ♆ **8:33 am** 5:33 am
☽ ⚺ ♃ **6:10 pm** 3:10 pm
☽ □ ♄ 11:09 pm

2 FRIDAY
☽ □ ♄ **2:09 am**
☽ ⚺ ♅ **4:49 am** 1:49 am
☽ □ ♆ **7:24 am** 4:24 am
☽ ☍ ☿ **9:58 am** 6:58 am
☽ ⚻ ♇ **12:35 pm** 9:35 am

3 SATURDAY
☽ ☍ ♀ **3:40 am** 12:40 am
☽ ☍ ☉ **5:03 am** 2:03 am
☽ ☍ ♂ **7:37 am** 4:37 am
☿ ⚺ ♇ **11:56 am** 8:56 am
☽ ☌ ♃ **5:54 pm** 2:54 pm
☽ △ ♄ 11:45 pm

4 SUNDAY
☽ △ ♄ **2:45 am**
☽ ✶ ♅ **5:12 am** 2:12 am
☽ △ ♆ **7:59 am** 4:59 am
☽ ☍ ♇ **1:25 pm** 10:25 am
☽ ⚻ ☿ **4:25 pm** 1:25 pm

5 MONDAY
☽ ⚻ ♀ **9:56 am** 6:56 am
☽ ⚻ ☉ **10:24 am** 7:24 am
☽ ⚻ ♂ **12:08 pm** 9:08 am
☽ ⚺ ♃ **7:40 pm** 4:40 pm

6 TUESDAY
☽ ⚻ ♄ **5:48 am** 2:48 am
☽ □ ♅ **8:05 am** 5:05 am
☽ ⚻ ♆ **11:13 am** 8:13 am
☉ ☌ ♀ **11:36 am** 8:36 am
☽ ⚻ ♇ **5:06 pm** 2:06 pm

7 WEDNESDAY
☽ △ ☿ **3:02 am** 12:02 am
☽ △ ☉ **8:04 pm** 5:04 pm
☽ △ ♀ **8:44 pm** 5:44 pm
☽ △ ♂ **8:46 pm** 5:46 pm
♀ ☌ ♂ **9:43 pm** 6:43 pm
☽ ✶ ♃ 9:59 pm

8 THURSDAY
☽ ✶ ♃ **12:59 am**
☽ ☍ ♄ **12:46 pm** 9:46 am
☽ △ ♅ **2:50 pm** 11:50 am
☽ ☍ ♆ **6:23 pm** 3:23 pm
☽ △ ♇ 9:47 pm

9 FRIDAY
☽ △ ♇ **12:47 am**
☉ ☌ ♂ **6:41 am** 3:41 am
♀ ☍ ♃ **12:35 pm** 9:35 am
☽ □ ☿ **7:34 pm** 4:34 pm

10 SATURDAY
☉ ☍ ♃ **3:42 am** 12:42 am
♂ ☍ ♃ **9:25 am** 6:25 am
☽ □ ♃ **10:08 am** 7:08 am
☽ □ ♂ **10:12 am** 7:12 am
☽ □ ☉ **10:48 am** 7:48 am
☽ □ ♀ **12:54 pm** 9:54 am
☽ ⚻ ♄ **11:36 pm** 8:36 pm
☽ ⚻ ♅ 10:20 pm

11 SUNDAY
☽ ⚻ ♅ **1:20 am**
☽ ⚻ ♆ **5:15 am** 2:15 am
☽ □ ♇ **12:03 pm** 9:03 am

12 MONDAY
☽ ✶ ☿ **4:44 pm** 1:44 pm
☽ △ ♃ **9:46 pm** 6:46 pm
☽ ✶ ♂ 11:43 pm

13 TUESDAY
☽ ✶ ♂ **2:43 am**
☽ ✶ ☉ **4:48 am** 1:48 am
☽ ✶ ♀ **8:27 am** 5:27 am
☽ △ ♄ **12:33 pm** 9:33 am
☽ ☍ ♅ **1:49 pm** 10:49 am
☽ △ ♆ **5:59 pm** 2:59 pm
☽ ✶ ♇ 9:54 pm

14 WEDNESDAY
☽ ✶ ♇ **12:54 am**
☿ ☍ ♃ **3:17 am** 12:17 am
♀ ✶ ♄ 10:19 pm

15 THURSDAY
♀ ✶ ♄ **1:19 am**
☽ ⚻ ♃ **9:40 am** 6:40 am
♀ △ ♅ **10:22 am** 7:22 am
☽ ⚺ ☿ **2:48 pm** 11:48 am
☽ ⚺ ♂ **7:23 pm** 4:23 pm
☽ ⚺ ☉ **10:52 pm** 7:52 pm
☽ □ ♄ 10:17 pm
☽ ⚻ ♅ 11:03 pm

16 FRIDAY
☽ □ ♄ **1:17 am**
☽ ⚻ ♅ **2:03 am**
☽ ⚺ ♀ **3:53 am** 12:53 am
☽ □ ♆ **6:19 am** 3:19 am
☽ ⚺ ♇ **1:08 pm** 10:08 am

17 SATURDAY
♀ ✶ ♆ **3:33 am** 12:33 am
☉ ✶ ♄ **5:41 am** 2:41 am
☉ △ ♅ **11:59 am** 8:59 am
☽ ☍ ♃ **8:14 pm** 5:14 pm
☿ ☌ ♂ 11:40 pm

18 SUNDAY
☿ ☌ ♂ **2:40 am**
☽ ☌ ♂ **10:11 am** 7:11 am
☽ ☌ ☿ **10:48 am** 7:48 am
☽ ✶ ♄ **12:22 pm** 9:22 am
☽ △ ♅ **12:39 pm** 9:39 am
☽ ☌ ☉ **2:52 pm** 11:52 am
☽ ✶ ♆ **4:57 pm** 1:57 pm
☽ ☌ ♀ **9:03 pm** 6:03 pm
☿ ✶ ♄ **11:09 pm** 8:09 pm
☽ ☌ ♇ **11:35 pm** 8:35 pm
☿ △ ♅ 9:38 pm

19 MONDAY
☿ △ ♅ **12:38 am**
☉ ✶ ♆ **4:55 pm** 1:55 pm
♀ ☌ ♇ **11:04 pm** 8:04 pm
♄ ✶ ♅ 9:19 pm
♂ △ ♅ 9:56 pm
♂ ✶ ♄ 10:02 pm

20 TUESDAY
♄ ✶ ♅ **12:19 am**
♂ △ ♅ **12:56 am**
♂ ✶ ♄ **1:02 am**
☽ ⚻ ♃ **4:54 am** 1:54 am
☿ ✶ ♆ **9:34 am** 6:34 am
☽ □ ♅ **9:16 pm** 6:16 pm
☽ ⚺ ♄ **9:26 pm** 6:26 pm
☽ ⚺ ♂ **10:36 pm** 7:36 pm
☽ ⚺ ♆ 10:35 pm

21 WEDNESDAY
☽ ⚺ ♆ **1:35 am**
☽ ⚺ ☿ **3:55 am** 12:55 am
☽ ⚺ ☉ **4:18 am** 1:18 am
☽ ⚺ ♇ **8:03 am** 5:03 am
☉ ☌ ☿ **10:49 am** 7:49 am
☽ ⚺ ♀ **11:29 am** 8:29 am

22 THURSDAY
☽ △ ♃ **11:41 am** 8:41 am
☿ ☌ ♇ **12:15 pm** 9:15 am
♂ ✶ ♆ 10:39 pm

23 FRIDAY
♂ ✶ ♆ **1:39 am**
☽ ✶ ♅ **3:59 am** 12:59 am
☽ ☌ ♄ **4:33 am** 1:33 am
☉ ☌ ♇ **5:28 am** 2:28 am
☽ ☌ ♆ **8:17 am** 5:17 am
☽ ✶ ♂ **8:41 am** 5:41 am
☽ ✶ ♇ **2:33 pm** 11:33 am
☽ ✶ ☉ **3:17 pm** 12:17 pm
☽ ✶ ☿ **6:16 pm** 3:16 pm
☽ ✶ ♀ **11:18 pm** 8:18 pm

24 SATURDAY
☽ □ ♃ **4:36 pm** 1:36 pm

25 SUNDAY
☽ ⚺ ♅ **8:46 am** 5:46 am
☽ ⚺ ♄ **9:42 am** 6:42 am
☽ ⚺ ♆ **1:03 pm** 10:03 am
☽ □ ♂ **4:27 pm** 1:27 pm
☽ □ ♇ **7:07 pm** 4:07 pm
☽ □ ☉ **11:47 pm** 8:47 pm

26 MONDAY
☽ □ ☿ **5:50 am** 2:50 am
☽ □ ♀ **8:31 am** 5:31 am
☽ ✶ ♃ **7:41 pm** 4:41 pm

27 TUESDAY
☽ ☌ ♅ **11:43 am** 8:43 am
☽ ✶ ♄ **12:58 pm** 9:58 am
☽ ✶ ♆ **3:58 pm** 12:58 pm
♂ ☌ ♇ **6:02 pm** 3:02 pm
☽ △ ♇ **9:52 pm** 6:52 pm
☽ △ ♂ **10:05 pm** 7:05 pm

28 WEDNESDAY
☽ △ ☉ **6:06 am** 3:06 am
☽ △ ☿ **3:01 pm** 12:01 pm
☽ △ ♀ **3:32 pm** 12:32 pm
☽ ⚺ ♃ **9:15 pm** 6:15 pm

29 THURSDAY
☿ ☌ ♀ **5:17 am** 2:17 am
☽ ⚺ ♅ **1:22 pm** 10:22 am
☽ □ ♄ **2:57 pm** 11:57 am
☽ □ ♆ **5:40 pm** 2:40 pm
☽ ⚻ ♇ **11:31 pm** 8:31 pm
☽ ⚻ ♂ 11:25 pm

30 FRIDAY
☽ ⚻ ♂ **2:25 am**
☽ ⚻ ☉ **11:17 am** 8:17 am
☿ ⚻ ♃ **3:58 pm** 12:58 pm
☽ ⚻ ♀ **9:39 pm** 6:39 pm
☽ ☌ ♃ **10:18 pm** 7:18 pm
☽ ⚻ ☿ **11:14 pm** 8:14 pm

31 SATURDAY
♀ ⚻ ♃ **4:39 am** 1:39 am
☽ ✶ ♅ **2:55 pm** 11:55 am
☽ △ ♄ **4:52 pm** 1:52 pm
☽ △ ♆ **7:23 pm** 4:23 pm
☽ ☍ ♇ 10:21 pm

Eastern time in bold type
Pacific time in medium type

JANUARY 2026

DATE	SID. TIME	SUN	MOON	NODE	MERCURY	VENUS	MARS	JUPITER	SATURN	URANUS	NEPTUNE	PLUTO	CERES	PALLAS	JUNO	VESTA	CHIRON
1 Th	6 42 39	10♑34 07	6Ⅱ43	10♓58R	28♐39	9♑12	12♑41	21♋21R	26♓10	27♉57R	29♓30	2♒43	7♈04	22♒35	0♌52	24♑17	22♈36R
2 F	6 46 35	11 35 15	21 45	10 48	0♑11	10 28	13 27	21 14	26 14	27 55	29 31	2 45	7 17	22 53	1 13	24 49	22 36D
3 Sa	6 50 32	12 36 23	6♋47	10 39	1 43	11 43	14 13	21 06	26 17	27 54	29 32	2 47	7 30	23 11	1 35	25 20	22 36
4 Su	6 54 29	13 37 31	21 38	10 30	3 15	12 59	14 59	20 58	26 21	27 52	29 33	2 49	7 43	23 29	1 57	25 52	22 36
5 M	6 58 25	14 38 39	6♌11	10 23	4 48	14 14	15 46	20 50	26 25	27 51	29 34	2 50	7 57	23 47	2 18	26 23	22 36
6 T	7 2 22	15 39 46	20 18	10 19	6 21	15 30	16 32	20 42	26 29	27 49	29 35	2 52	8 11	24 04	2 40	26 55	22 36
7 W	7 6 18	16 40 54	3♍58	10 17	7 55	16 45	17 18	20 34	26 33	27 48	29 35	2 54	8 25	24 23	3 01	27 27	22 37
8 Th	7 10 15	17 42 02	17 10	10 17	9 29	18 01	18 04	20 26	26 37	27 46	29 36	2 56	8 39	24 41	3 23	27 58	22 37
9 F	7 14 11	18 43 10	29 57	10 18	11 03	19 16	18 50	20 18	26 41	27 45	29 37	2 58	8 53	24 59	3 45	28 30	22 37
10 Sa	7 18 8	19 44 18	12♎23	10 19R	12 38	20 32	19 37	20 09	26 45	27 44	29 38	3 00	9 08	25 17	4 06	29 01	22 37
11 Su	7 22 4	20 45 26	24 32	10 20	14 13	21 47	20 23	20 01	26 50	27 43	29 39	3 02	9 23	25 35	4 28	29 33	22 38
12 M	7 26 1	21 46 35	6♏30	10 18	15 48	23 03	21 09	19 53	26 54	27 41	29 41	3 04	9 38	25 54	4 49	0♒04	22 38
13 T	7 29 58	22 47 43	18 22	10 15	17 24	24 18	21 56	19 45	26 58	27 40	29 42	3 05	9 53	26 12	5 11	0 36	22 39
14 W	7 33 54	23 48 51	0♐13	10 09	19 01	25 34	22 42	19 37	27 03	27 39	29 43	3 07	10 08	26 31	5 32	1 07	22 40
15 Th	7 37 51	24 49 59	12 06	10 02	20 38	26 49	23 29	19 29	27 08	27 38	29 44	3 09	10 24	26 50	5 54	1 39	22 40
16 F	7 41 47	25 51 06	24 04	9 53	22 15	28 05	24 15	19 21	27 12	27 37	29 45	3 11	10 40	27 08	6 15	2 11	22 41
17 Sa	7 45 44	26 52 14	6♑11	9 45	23 53	29 20	25 02	19 13	27 17	27 36	29 46	3 13	10 56	27 27	6 37	2 42	22 42
18 Su	7 49 40	27 53 21	18 27	9 36	25 32	0♒35	25 49	19 05	27 22	27 35	29 48	3 15	11 12	27 46	6 58	3 14	22 43
19 M	7 53 37	28 54 27	0♒53	9 29	27 11	1 51	26 35	18 57	27 27	27 34	29 49	3 17	11 28	28 05	7 20	3 45	22 43
20 T	7 57 33	29 55 33	13 31	9 25	28 50	3 06	27 22	18 49	27 32	27 34	29 50	3 19	11 45	28 23	7 41	4 17	22 44
21 W	8 1 30	0♒56 38	26 19	9 22	0♒31	4 22	28 08	18 41	27 37	27 33	29 52	3 21	12 02	28 42	8 02	4 48	22 45
22 Th	8 5 27	1 57 42	9♓19	9 21D	2 11	5 37	28 55	18 34	27 43	27 32	29 53	3 23	12 19	29 01	8 24	5 20	22 46
23 F	8 9 23	2 58 46	22 31	9 21	3 53	6 53	29 42	18 26	27 48	27 31	29 54	3 25	12 36	29 20	8 45	5 51	22 48
24 Sa	8 13 20	3 59 48	5♈56	9 21	5 34	8 08	0♒29	18 19	27 53	27 31	29 56	3 26	12 53	29 40	9 07	6 22	22 49
25 Su	8 17 16	5 00 50	19 34	9 25	7 17	9 23	1 15	18 11	27 59	27 30	29 57	3 28	13 10	29 59	9 28	6 54	22 50
26 M	8 21 13	6 01 50	3♉26	9 25R	9 00	10 39	2 02	18 04	28 04	27 30	29 59	3 30	13 28	0♓18	9 49	7 25	22 51
27 T	8 25 9	7 02 49	17 32	9 25	10 43	11 54	2 49	17 57	28 10	27 29	0♈00	3 32	13 46	0 37	10 10	7 57	22 53
28 W	8 29 6	8 03 48	1Ⅱ51	9 23	12 27	13 09	3 36	17 49	28 15	27 29	0 02	3 34	14 04	0 57	10 31	8 28	22 54
29 Th	8 33 2	9 04 45	16 20	9 20	14 12	14 25	4 23	17 42	28 21	27 28	0 04	3 36	14 22	1 16	10 53	8 59	22 55
30 F	8 36 59	10 05 41	0♋54	9 16	15 57	15 40	5 10	17 35	28 27	27 28	0 05	3 38	14 40	1 35	11 14	9 31	22 57
31 Sa	8 40 56	11 06 35	15 28	9 11	17 43	16 55	5 57	17 28	28 33	27 28	0 07	3 40	14 58	1 55	11 35	10 02	22 58

EPHEMERIS CALCULATED FOR 12 MIDNIGHT GREENWICH MEAN TIME. ALL OTHER DATA AND FACING ASPECTARIAN PAGE IN **EASTERN TIME (BOLD)** AND PACIFIC TIME (REGULAR).

FEBRUARY 2026

☽ Last Aspect day	ET / hr:mn / PT	asp	☽ Ingress sign day	ET / hr:mn / PT
2	**5:55 pm** 2:55 pm	□ ♅	♍ 2	**10:21 pm** 7:21 pm
4	11:49 pm	☍ ♄	♎ 5	**4:33 am** 1:33 am
5	**2:49 am**	☍ ♄	♎ 5	**4:33 am** 1:33 am
7	**6:59 am** 3:59 am	△ ♀	♏ 7	**2:13 pm** 11:13 am
9	11:01 pm	□ ♀	♐ 9	11:22 pm
10	**2:01 am**	□ ♀	♐ 10	**2:22 am**
12	**2:29 pm** 11:29 am	□ ♄	♑ 12	**2:44 pm** 11:44 am
14	**8:31 pm** 5:31 pm	△ ♅	♒ 14	10:17 pm
14	**8:31 pm** 5:31 pm	△ ♅	♒ 15	**1:17 am**
17	**7:01 am** 4:01 am	☌ ☉	♓ 17	**9:09 am** 6:09 am
19	**10:23 am** 7:23 am	⚹ ♅	♈ 19	**2:39 pm** 11:39 am
21	**6:11 am** 3:11 am	⚹ ♂	♉ 21	**6:31 pm** 3:31 pm
23	**5:29 pm** 2:29 pm	☌ ♅	♊ 23	**9:29 pm** 6:29 pm
25	**6:00 pm** 3:00 pm	△ ♂	♋ 25	9:11 pm
25	**6:00 pm** 3:00 pm	△ ♂	♋ 26	**12:11 am**
27	**11:21 pm** 8:21 pm	⚹ ♅	♌ 28	**3:17 am** 12:17 am

☽ Phases & Eclipses phase	day	ET / hr:mn / PT
Full Moon	1	**5:09 pm** 2:09 pm
4th Quarter	9	**7:43 am** 4:43 am
New Moon	17	**7:01 am** 4:01 am
●	17	28° ♒ 50'
2nd Quarter	24	**7:28 am** 4:28 am

Planet Ingress	day	ET / hr:mn / PT
☿ ♓	6	**5:48 pm** 2:48 pm
♀ ♓	10	**5:19 am** 2:19 am
♄ ♈	13	**7:11 pm** 4:11 pm
☉ ♓	18	**10:52 am** 7:52 am

Planetary Motion	day	ET / hr:mn / PT
♅ D	3	**9:33 pm** 6:33 pm
☿ ℞	25	10:48 pm
☿ ℞	26	**1:48 am**

1 SUNDAY
☽ ☍ ♇ **1:21 am**
☽ ☍ ♂ **7:06 am** 4:06 am
☽ ☍ ☉ **5:09 pm** 2:09 pm
☽ ⚺ ♃ 9:15 pm

2 MONDAY
☽ ⚺ ♃ **12:15 am**
☽ ☍ ♀ **4:56 am** 1:56 am
☽ ☍ ☿ **8:55 am** 5:55 am
☽ □ ♅ **5:55 pm** 2:55 pm
☽ ⚻ ♄ **8:20 pm** 5:20 pm
☽ ⚻ ♆ **10:42 pm** 7:42 pm

3 TUESDAY
☽ ⚻ ♇ **4:59 am** 1:59 am
☽ ⚻ ♂ **2:06 pm** 11:06 am
☽ ⚻ ☉ 10:50 pm

4 WEDNESDAY
☽ ⚻ ☉ **1:50 am**
☽ ⚹ ♃ **4:37 am** 1:37 am
☽ ⚻ ♀ **3:37 pm** 12:37 pm
☽ ⚻ ☿ **10:39 pm** 7:39 pm
☽ △ ♅ **11:49 pm** 8:49 pm
☽ ☍ ♄ 11:49 pm

5 THURSDAY
☽ ☍ ♄ **2:49 am**
☽ ☍ ♆ **5:02 am** 2:02 am
☿ □ ♅ **7:14 am** 4:14 am
☉ ⚻ ♃ **11:09 am** 8:09 am
☽ △ ♇ **11:45 am** 8:45 am
☽ △ ♂ 10:00 pm

6 FRIDAY
☽ △ ♂ **1:00 am**
☿ ⚺ ♄ **6:50 am** 3:50 am
☽ □ ♃ **12:21 pm** 9:21 am
☽ △ ☉ **2:49 pm** 11:49 am
☿ ⚺ ♆ **10:08 pm** 7:08 pm

7 SATURDAY
☽ △ ♀ **6:59 am** 3:59 am
☽ ⚻ ♅ **9:13 am** 6:13 am
☽ ⚻ ♄ **12:53 pm** 9:53 am
☽ ⚻ ♆ **2:53 pm** 11:53 am
☽ △ ☿ **5:39 pm** 2:39 pm
☽ □ ♇ **9:59 pm** 6:59 pm

8 SUNDAY
♀ □ ♅ **4:49 am** 1:49 am
☽ □ ♂ **3:53 pm** 12:53 pm
☽ △ ♃ **11:10 pm** 8:10 pm
☿ ⚺ ♇ 9:23 pm

9 MONDAY
☿ ⚺ ♇ **12:23 am**
☽ □ ☉ **7:43 am** 4:43 am
♀ ⚺ ♄ **9:10 pm** 6:10 pm
☽ ☍ ♅ **9:16 pm** 6:16 pm
☽ △ ♄ 10:33 pm
☽ □ ♀ 11:01 pm

10 TUESDAY
☽ △ ♄ **1:33 am**
☽ □ ♀ **2:01 am**
☽ △ ♆ **3:12 am** 12:12 am
☽ ⚹ ♇ **10:27 am** 7:27 am
♀ ⚺ ♆ **1:30 pm** 10:30 am
☽ □ ☿ **4:02 pm** 1:02 pm

11 WEDNESDAY
☽ ⚹ ♂ **8:43 am** 5:43 am
☽ ⚻ ♃ **11:18 am** 8:18 am
☽ ⚹ ☉ 10:53 pm

12 THURSDAY
☽ ⚹ ☉ **1:53 am**
☽ ⚻ ♅ **9:44 am** 6:44 am
☽ □ ♄ **2:29 pm** 11:29 am
☽ □ ♆ **3:43 pm** 12:43 pm
♂ ⚻ ♃ **8:15 pm** 5:15 pm
☽ ⚹ ♀ **9:23 pm** 6:23 pm
☽ ⚺ ♇ **10:50 pm** 7:50 pm

13 FRIDAY
♀ ⚺ ♇ **11:44 am** 8:44 am
☽ ⚹ ☿ **1:17 pm** 10:17 am
☽ ☍ ♃ **10:28 pm** 7:28 pm
☽ ⚺ ♂ 9:26 pm

14 SATURDAY
☽ ⚺ ♂ **12:26 am**
☽ ⚺ ☉ **6:08 pm** 3:08 pm
☽ △ ♅ **8:31 pm** 5:31 pm
☽ ⚹ ♄ 10:33 pm
☽ ⚹ ♆ 11:22 pm

15 SUNDAY
☽ ⚹ ♄ **1:33 am**
☽ ⚹ ♆ **2:22 am**
☽ ☌ ♇ **9:10 am** 6:10 am
☽ ⚺ ♀ **2:01 pm** 11:01 am
☉ □ ♅ 9:02 pm

16 MONDAY
☉ □ ♅ **12:02 am**
☽ ⚺ ☿ **6:08 am** 3:08 am
☽ ⚻ ♃ **7:15 am** 4:15 am
☽ ☌ ♂ **1:09 pm** 10:09 am
☿ △ ♃ **4:31 pm** 1:31 pm

17 TUESDAY
☽ □ ♅ **4:40 am** 1:40 am
☽ ☌ ☉ **7:01 am** 4:01 am
☽ ⚺ ♄ **9:53 am** 6:53 am
☽ ⚺ ♆ **10:20 am** 7:20 am
☽ ⚺ ♇ **4:48 pm** 1:48 pm

18 WEDNESDAY
☽ ☌ ♀ **3:02 am** 12:02 am
☽ △ ♃ **1:31 pm** 10:31 am
☽ ☌ ☿ **6:09 pm** 3:09 pm
☽ ⚺ ♂ **10:47 pm** 7:47 pm
☉ ⚺ ♄ 9:48 pm

19 THURSDAY
☉ ⚺ ♄ **12:48 am**
☉ ⚺ ♆ **3:41 am** 12:41 am
☽ ⚹ ♅ **10:23 am** 7:23 am
☽ ☌ ♄ **3:48 pm** 12:48 pm
☽ ☌ ♆ **3:55 pm** 12:55 pm
☽ ⚺ ☉ **4:51 pm** 1:51 pm
☽ ⚹ ♇ **10:08 pm** 7:08 pm

20 FRIDAY
♄ ☌ ♆ **11:53 am** 8:53 am
☽ ⚺ ♀ **1:09 pm** 10:09 am
☽ □ ♃ **5:49 pm** 2:49 pm
☽ ⚺ ☿ 11:20 pm

21 SATURDAY
☽ ⚺ ☿ **2:20 am**
☽ ⚹ ♂ **6:11 am** 3:11 am
☽ ⚺ ♅ **2:24 pm** 11:24 am
☽ ⚺ ♆ **7:53 pm** 4:53 pm
☽ ⚺ ♄ **8:04 pm** 5:04 pm
☽ ⚹ ☉ 9:40 pm
☽ □ ♇ 10:56 pm

22 SUNDAY
☽ ⚹ ☉ **12:40 am**
☽ □ ♇ **1:56 am**
♀ △ ♃ **3:02 pm** 12:02 pm
☉ ⚺ ♇ **6:49 pm** 3:49 pm
☽ ⚹ ♃ **8:56 pm** 5:56 pm
☽ ⚹ ♀ **9:32 pm** 6:32 pm

23 MONDAY
☽ ⚹ ☿ **7:51 am** 4:51 am
☽ □ ♂ **12:19 pm** 9:19 am
☽ ☌ ♅ **5:29 pm** 2:29 pm
☽ ⚹ ♆ **10:57 pm** 7:57 pm
☽ ⚹ ♄ **11:26 pm** 8:26 pm

24 TUESDAY
☽ △ ♇ **4:56 am** 1:56 am
☽ □ ☉ **7:28 am** 4:28 am
☽ ⚺ ♃ **11:31 pm** 8:31 pm

25 WEDNESDAY
☽ □ ♀ **5:10 am** 2:10 am
☽ □ ☿ **11:34 am** 8:34 am
☽ △ ♂ **6:00 pm** 3:00 pm
☽ ⚺ ♅ **8:15 pm** 5:15 pm
☽ □ ♆ 10:47 pm
☽ □ ♄ 11:34 pm

26 THURSDAY
☽ □ ♆ **1:47 am**
☽ □ ♄ **2:34 am**
☽ ⚻ ♇ **7:45 am** 4:45 am
☽ △ ☉ **2:04 pm** 11:04 am
☽ ☌ ♃ 11:11 pm

27 FRIDAY
☽ ☌ ♃ **2:11 am**
♂ □ ♅ **11:21 am** 8:21 am
☽ △ ♀ **12:59 pm** 9:59 am
☽ △ ☿ **2:13 pm** 11:13 am
☽ ⚹ ♅ **11:21 pm** 8:21 pm
☽ ⚻ ♂ 9:03 pm
☿ ☌ ♀ 9:35 pm

28 SATURDAY
☽ ⚻ ♂ **12:03 am**
☿ ☌ ♀ **12:35 am**
☽ △ ♆ **5:02 am** 2:02 am
☽ △ ♄ **6:08 am** 3:08 am
☽ ☍ ♇ **11:04 am** 8:04 am
☽ ⚻ ☉ **9:24 pm** 6:24 pm

Eastern time in bold type
Pacific time in medium type

FEBRUARY 2026

DATE	SID.TIME	SUN	MOON	NODE	MERCURY	VENUS	MARS	JUPITER	SATURN	URANUS	NEPTUNE	PLUTO	CERES	PALLAS	JUNO	VESTA	CHIRON
1 Su	8 44 52	12≈07 29	29♋55	9♓07R	19≈15	18≈11	6♑44	17♋22R	28♓38	27♉28R	0♈08	3≈42	15♈17	2♉14	11♑56	10≈33	23♈00
2 M	8 48 49	13 08 21	14♌09	9 04	21 15	19 26	7 31	17 15	28 44	27 28	0 10	3 44	15 35	2 34	12 17	11 05	23 02
3 T	8 52 45	14 09 13	28 05	9 03D	24 47	20 41	8 18	17 09	28 50	27 28	0 12	3 46	15 54	2 53	12 38	11 36	23 03
4 W	8 56 42	15 10 03	11♍39	9 02	26 34	21 56	9 05	17 02	28 56	27 28D	0 13	3 48	16 13	3 13	12 59	12 07	23 05
5 Th	9 0 38	16 10 52	24 51	9 03	28 34	23 12	9 52	16 56	29 03	27 28	0 15	3 49	16 32	3 32	13 20	12 38	23 07
6 F	9 4 35	17 11 40	7♎41	9 04	0♓05	24 27	10 39	16 50	29 09	27 28	0 17	3 51	16 51	3 52	13 41	13 10	23 09
7 Sa	9 8 31	18 12 28	20 11	9 06	1 50	25 42	11 26	16 44	29 15	27 28	0 19	3 53	17 11	4 12	14 01	13 41	23 10
8 Su	9 12 28	19 13 14	2♏25	9 07	3 34	26 57	12 13	16 38	29 21	27 28	0 21	3 55	17 30	4 31	14 22	14 12	23 12
9 M	9 16 25	20 14 00	14 27	9 08R	5 17	28 13	13 00	16 32	29 28	27 29	0 22	3 57	17 50	4 51	14 43	14 43	23 14
10 T	9 20 21	21 14 44	26 21	9 08	6 58	29 28	13 47	16 27	29 34	27 29	0 24	3 59	18 09	5 11	15 04	15 14	23 16
11 W	9 24 18	22 15 27	8♐14	9 07	8 37	0♓43	14 34	16 22	29 40	27 29	0 26	4 01	18 29	5 30	15 24	15 45	23 18
12 Th	9 28 14	23 16 10	20 08	9 06	10 13	1 58	15 21	16 16	29 47	27 29	0 28	4 02	18 49	5 50	15 45	16 16	23 20
13 F	9 32 11	24 16 51	2♑08	9 04	11 46	3 13	16 09	16 11	29 53	27 30	0 30	4 04	19 09	6 10	16 05	16 47	23 23
14 Sa	9 36 7	25 17 31	14 19	9 02	13 16	4 28	16 56	16 06	0♈00	27 30	0 32	4 06	19 29	6 30	16 26	17 18	23 25
15 Su	9 40 4	26 18 10	26 43	9 00	14 41	5 43	17 43	16 02	0 07	27 31	0 34	4 08	19 50	6 50	16 46	17 49	23 27
16 M	9 44 1	27 18 48	9≈22	8 58	16 01	6 59	18 30	15 57	0 13	27 31	0 36	4 10	20 10	7 10	17 07	18 20	23 29
17 T	9 47 57	28 19 24	22 16	8 57	17 16	8 14	19 17	15 53	0 20	27 32	0 38	4 12	20 30	7 30	17 27	18 51	23 32
18 W	9 51 54	29 19 58	5♓26	8 57D	18 24	9 29	20 05	15 49	0 27	27 33	0 40	4 13	20 51	7 50	17 47	19 22	23 34
19 Th	9 55 50	0♓30 31	18 51	8 57	19 26	10 44	20 52	15 45	0 34	27 33	0 42	4 15	21 12	8 10	18 07	19 53	23 36
20 F	9 59 47	1 21 03	2♈29	8 57	20 19	11 59	21 39	15 41	0 40	27 34	0 44	4 17	21 33	8 30	18 27	20 24	23 39
21 Sa	10 3 43	2 21 32	16 19	8 58	21 05	13 14	22 26	15 37	0 47	27 35	0 46	4 19	21 53	8 50	18 47	20 55	23 41
22 Su	10 7 40	3 22 00	0♉17	8 58	21 41	14 29	23 14	15 34	0 54	27 36	0 48	4 20	22 14	9 10	19 07	21 26	23 44
23 M	10 11 36	4 22 26	14 22	8 59	22 08	15 44	24 01	15 31	1 01	27 37	0 50	4 22	22 36	9 30	19 27	21 56	23 46
24 T	10 15 33	5 22 50	28 32	8 59R	22 26	16 59	24 48	15 28	1 08	27 38	0 52	4 24	22 57	9 50	19 47	22 27	23 49
25 W	10 19 29	6 23 13	12♊44	8 59	22 34R	18 13	25 36	15 25	1 15	27 39	0 54	4 25	23 18	10 10	20 07	22 58	23 52
26 Th	10 23 26	7 23 33	26 56	8 59	22 31	19 28	26 23	15 22	1 22	27 40	0 56	4 27	23 39	10 30	20 27	23 28	23 54
27 F	10 27 23	8 23 51	11♋06	8 59D	22 31	20 43	27 10	15 20	1 29	27 41	0 58	4 29	24 01	10 50	20 46	23 59	23 57
28 Sa	10 31 19	9 24 07	25 10	8 59	22 20	21 58	27 57	15 17	1 36	27 43	1 00	4 30	24 22	11 10	21 06	24 29	24 00

EPHEMERIS CALCULATED FOR 12 MIDNIGHT GREENWICH MEAN TIME. ALL OTHER DATA AND FACING ASPECTARIAN PAGE IN **EASTERN TIME (BOLD)** AND PACIFIC TIME (REGULAR).

MARCH 2026

D Last Aspect / D Ingress

D Last Aspect			D Ingress		
day	ET / hr:mn / PT	asp	sign	day	ET / hr:mn / PT
20	5:23 am 2:23 am	♂ ♀	♍ 20		11:35 pm
20	5:23 am 2:23 am	□ ♀	♏ 21		
22	10:40 pm		⧫ 23		2:35 am
			⧫ 23		4:19 am 1:19 am
24	1:40 am	♂ ⅄	⧫ 23		4:19 am 1:19 am
24	6:37 am 3:37 am	□ ⅄	♒ 25		6:33 am 3:33 am
27	7:40 am 4:40 am	△ ⅄	⅄ 27		10:10 am 7:10 am
29	1:26 pm 10:26 am	△ ♂	⅄ 29		3:33 pm 12:33 pm
31	8:31 pm 5:31 pm	△ ♀	⅄ 31		10:51 pm 7:51 pm

D Phases & Eclipses

phase		day	ET / hr:mn / PT
Full Moon	3	E:38 am	3:38 am
	3	12° ♍ 54'	
4th Quarter	11	5:38 am	2:38 am
New Moon	18	9:23 am	6:23 am
2nd Quarter	25	3:16 pm	12:18 pm

Planet Ingress

	day	ET / hr:mn / PT
⅄ ⅄	2	9:16 am 6:16 am
♀ ⅄	6	5:46 am 2:46 am
♀ ⅄	10	5:26 pm 2:26 pm
⅄ ⅄	14	10:16 am
⅄ ⅄	15	1:16 am
⊙ ⅄	20	10:46 am 7:46 am
⅄ ⅄	29	4:49 pm 1:49 pm
⅄ ⅄	30	12:01 pm 9:01 am

Planetary Motion

	day	ET / hr:mn / PT
⅄ D	10	11:30 pm 8:30 pm
♀ D	20	3:33 pm 12:33 pm

---

1 SUNDAY

	ET / hr:mn / PT	
D ∠ ⅄	5:38 am	2:38 am
⅄ △ ♀	4:38 am	1:38 am
D ★ ♀	10:03 pm	7:03 pm

2 MONDAY

D ⅄ ♀	3:36 am	12:36 am
⅄ ⅄ ♀	7:27 am	4:27 am
D △ ⅄	9:31 am	6:31 am
D ⅄ ⅄	10:58 am	7:58 am
D ∠ ♀	3:43 pm	12:43 pm

3 TUESDAY

D ★ ♀	6:38 am	3:38 am
D □ ♀	10:45 am	7:45 am
D ⅄ ⅄	7:39 pm	4:39 pm
D ⅄ ⅄	8:26 pm	5:26 pm

4 WEDNESDAY

D ∠ ⅄	9:42 am	6:42 am
⅄ ⅄ ⅄	9:53 am	6:53 am
D □ ♀	11:41 am	8:41 am
D △ ⅄	4:08 pm	1:08 pm
D ∠ ⅄	5:21 pm	2:21 pm
D ⅄ ⅄	6:01 pm	3:01 pm
D ∠ ⅄	10:35 pm	7:35 pm

5 THURSDAY

⅄ ⅄ ⅄	3:07 am	
⊙ △ ⅄	9:14 am	
⅄ ⅄ ♀	3:22 am	
D □ ♀	3:55 pm	
D ∠ ♀	6:55 pm	

6 FRIDAY

D ⅄ ♀	12:04 am	
		3:53 am
D ★ ⅄	6:53 pm	9:58 am
D ★ ♀		10:30

7 SATURDAY

D ⅄ ⅄	12:58 am	
D ⅄ ♀	1:30 am	12:53
⅄ ⅄ ⅄	3:53 am	3:02 am
D □ ⅄	6:02 am	3:27 am
D ⅄ ♀	6:33 am	3:33 am
D ⅄ ♀	8:14 am	5:14 am

8 SUNDAY

D ⅄ ♀	5:46 am	1:46 am
D ⅄ ⅄	7:16 am	4:16 am
D ⅄ ⅄	9:40 am	6:40 am
D △ ⅄	10:23 am	7:23 am
⅄ ⅄ ♀	11:42 am	8:42 am
D ∠ ♀		10:23

9 MONDAY

⅄ ⅄ ⅄	1:23 am	4:28
D ⅄ ♀	7:28 am	4:28 am
D ∠ ⅄	2:21 pm	11:21
D ⅄ ⅄	2:21 pm	
⅄ ⅄ ⅄	5:15 pm	2:15 pm
D ⅄ ♀	8:34 pm	5:34 pm
D ∠ ♀		8:37
D ★ ⅄	11:37 pm	11:52

10 TUESDAY

⅄ ★ ♀	2:52 am	
D ⅄ ♀	2:59 pm	11:59 pm
D ⅄ ⅄	6:04 pm	3:04 pm

11 WEDNESDAY

D □ ⅄	5:38 am	2:38 am
D △ ♀	8:06 pm	5:06 pm

12 THURSDAY

D ⅄ ♀	3:03 am	12:03 am
D ⅄ ⅄	6:21 am	3:21 am
D ∠ ♀	9:47 am	6:47 am
D ⅄ ⅄	3:59 pm	12:59 pm
D ⅄ ⅄	4:15 pm	1:15 pm
D ⅄ ⅄	10:51 pm	7:51 pm
D ⅄ ⅄	11:08 pm	8:08 pm

13 FRIDAY

D ♂ ♀	6:10 am	3:10 am
D □ ⅄	10:41 am	7:41 am

14 SATURDAY

D △ ⅄	7:33 am	4:33 am
⅄ ⅄ ⅄	11:52 am	
⅄ ★ ♀	2:58 pm	11:58
D ∠ ♀	5:47 pm	2:47 pm
D ∠ ⅄	8:35 pm	5:35 pm

15 SUNDAY

⅄ ⅄ ♀	4:08 am	1:08 am
D □ ♀	6:16 am	3:16 am
D ⅄ ⅄	6:30 am	3:30 am
D ⅄ ⅄	8:42 am	5:42 am
⅄ ★ ⅄	3:54 pm	12:54

16 MONDAY

D ⅄ ⅄	12:08 am	9:08 am
D ⅄ ♀	3:57 pm	12:57 pm
⅄ ★ ⅄		7:13
D ∠ ⅄	10:13 pm	10:57

17 TUESDAY

D ⅄ ⅄	1:57 am	
D ★ ⅄	4:09 am	1:09 am
⅄ ⅄ ⅄	11:25 am	8:25 am
D □ ⅄	4:47 pm	1:47 pm
D ⅄ ♀	8:57 pm	5:57 pm
D ⅄ ⅄	10:18 pm	7:18 pm

18 WEDNESDAY

D ⅄ ⅄	12:09 pm	9:09 am
⅄ ⅄ ♀	4:20 pm	1:20 pm
D ♂ ⅄	9:03 pm	6:03 pm
D ⅄ ⅄	9:23 pm	6:23 pm

19 THURSDAY

D ★ ⅄	3:00 am	12:00
D ⅄ ♀	6:51 am	3:51 am
⅄ ⅄ ⅄	8:34 am	5:34 am
D ⅄ ⅄	2:37 pm	11:37
⅄ □ ⅄	11:32 pm	8:32 pm
		10:53 pm

20 FRIDAY

D △ ⅄	1:53 am	
⊙ ⅄ ♀	5:23 am	2:23 am
D ⅄ ⅄	11:48 pm	8:48 pm

21 SATURDAY

D ⅄ ⊙	3:45 am	12:45
D ⅄ ⅄	5:35 am	2:35 am
D ★ ♀	9:38 am	6:38 am
D △ ⅄		7:56 am
⅄ △ ♀	4:46 pm	1:46 pm
♂ △ ⅄		5:01 pm

22 SUNDAY

D △ ⅄	3:56 am	12:56
D □ ⅄	4:22 am	1:22 am
D ⅄ ♀	7:18 am	4:18 am
D ⅄ ⅄	11:56 am	8:56 am
		10:40

23 MONDAY

D ⅄ ⅄	1:40 am	
D ★ ⅄	7:26 am	4:26 am
D ⅄ ⅄	9:09 am	6:09 am
⅄ ⅄ ⅄	11:48 am	8:48 am
D △ ⅄	12:44 pm	9:44 am
D ⅄ ⅄	7:13 pm	4:13 pm

24 TUESDAY

D ⅄ ♀	5:55 am	2:55 am
⅄ ⅄ ⅄	9:07 am	6:07 am
D ⅄ ♀	8:37 pm	3:37 pm

25 WEDNESDAY

⅄ □ ♀	3:59 am	12:59
D ⅄ ⅄	4:55 am	1:55 am
D ⅄ ⅄	9:53 am	6:53 am
D ★ ⅄	2:16 pm	11:16
⅄ ♂ ⅄	2:39 pm	11:39

26 THURSDAY

D ⅄ ♀	3:13 pm	12:13
D ⅄ ⅄	3:18 pm	12:18
D □ ⅄	11:13 pm	8:13
⅄ ⅄ ⅄	8:58 am	5:58 am
D △ ⅄	3:07 pm	12:07
		11:54

27 FRIDAY

D ♂ ⅄	2:54 am	
D ⅄ ♀	7:40 am	4:40 am
D ⅄ ⅄	7:45 pm	10:45
⅄ ⅄ ⅄	7:01 pm	4:01 pm
D ⅄ ⅄	7:12 pm	4:12
D ⅄ ⅄	11:16 pm	8:16 pm

28 SATURDAY

D ⅄ ⅄	5:35 am	2:35 am
⅄ ⅄ ⅄	9:40 am	10:40
D ⅄ ♀	6:13 pm	3:13 pm
D □ ⅄	11:07 pm	8:07

29 SUNDAY

D ⅄ ⅄	9:52 am	6:52 am
D □ ♀	9:07 am	6:07 am
D △ ⅄	1:28 pm	10:28
D ⅄ ⅄	7:25 pm	4:25 pm
		9:58

30 MONDAY

D ⅄ ⊙	12:58 am	9:58
D ★ ♀	4:55 am	10:14
D ⅄ ⅄	9:30 am	6:30 am

31 TUESDAY

D ⅄ ♀	2:44 pm	11:44
D ★ ⅄	8:17 pm	5:17
D △ ♀	9:20 am	6:20
D □ ⅄	8:31 pm	5:31
		11:34

Eastern time in bold type
Pacific time in medium type

MARCH 2026

DATE	SID.TIME	SUN	MOON	NODE	MERCURY	VENUS	MARS	JUPITER	SATURN	URANUS	NEPTUNE	PLUTO	CERES	PALLAS	JUNO	VESTA	CHIRON
1 Su	10 35 16	10♓24 22	9♌07	8♈59	21♓28	23♓13	28♒45	15♋13R	1♈43	27♉44	1♈03	4♒32	24♈44	11♓30	21♉25	25♒00	24♈03
2 M	10 39 12	11 24 34	22 53	8 59	20 50	24 28	29 32	15 12	1 51	27 45	1 05	4 34	25 06	11 50	21 45	25 31	24 05
3 T	10 43 9	12 24 44	6♍25	8 59R	20 05	25 42	0♓19	15 10	1 58	27 47	1 07	4 35	25 28	12 10	22 04	26 01	24 08
4 W	10 47 5	13 24 53	19 43	8 59	19 15	26 57	1 06	15 09	2 05	27 48	1 09	4 37	25 49	12 30	22 24	26 31	24 11
5 Th	10 51 2	14 25 00	2♎44	8 59	18 19	28 12	1 54	15 08	2 12	27 50	1 11	4 38	26 11	12 50	22 43	27 02	24 14
6 F	10 54 58	15 25 05	15 28	8 58	17 20	29 27	2 41	15 07	2 20	27 51	1 14	4 40	26 33	13 10	23 02	27 32	24 17
7 Sa	10 58 55	16 25 08	27 56	8 57	16 20	0♈41	3 28	15 06	2 27	27 53	1 16	4 41	26 56	13 30	23 21	28 02	24 20
8 Su	11 2 52	17 25 09	10♏10	8 56	15 19	1 56	4 16	15 06	2 34	27 54	1 18	4 43	27 18	13 51	23 40	28 33	24 23
9 M	11 6 48	18 25 10	22 14	8 55	14 19	3 10	5 03	15 05	2 41	27 56	1 20	4 44	27 40	14 11	23 59	29 03	24 26
10 T	11 10 45	19 25 08	4♐10	8 54	13 22	4 25	5 50	15 05	2 49	27 58	1 22	4 46	28 02	14 31	24 17	29 33	24 29
11 W	11 14 41	20 25 05	16 03	8 54D	12 28	5 40	6 37	15 05D	2 56	27 59	1 25	4 47	28 25	14 51	24 36	0♓03	24 32
12 Th	11 18 38	21 25 00	27 57	8 54	11 38	6 54	7 25	15 05	3 04	28 01	1 27	4 49	28 47	15 11	24 55	0 33	24 35
13 F	11 22 34	22 24 54	9♑57	8 54	10 53	8 09	8 12	15 06	3 11	28 03	1 29	4 50	29 10	15 31	25 13	1 03	24 39
14 Sa	11 26 31	23 24 45	22 09	8 55	10 14	9 23	8 59	15 06	3 18	28 05	1 31	4 52	29 32	15 51	25 31	1 33	24 42
15 Su	11 30 27	24 24 35	4♒35	8 57	9 41	10 38	9 46	15 07	3 26	28 07	1 34	4 53	29 55	16 11	25 50	2 03	24 45
16 M	11 34 24	25 24 24	17 19	8 58	9 14	11 52	10 34	15 08	3 33	28 09	1 36	4 54	0♉18	16 31	26 08	2 33	24 48
17 T	11 38 21	26 24 10	0♓25	8 59R	8 54	13 06	11 21	15 09	3 41	28 11	1 38	4 56	0 41	16 51	26 26	3 03	24 51
18 W	11 42 17	27 23 55	13 51	8 59	8 39	14 21	12 08	15 10	3 48	28 13	1 41	4 57	1 03	17 11	26 44	3 33	24 55
19 Th	11 46 14	28 23 37	27 39	8 58	8 31D	15 35	12 55	15 11	3 56	28 15	1 43	4 58	1 26	17 31	27 02	4 03	24 58
20 F	11 50 10	29 23 18	11♈44	8 56	8 30	16 50	13 42	15 13	4 03	28 17	1 45	5 00	1 49	17 52	27 20	4 33	25 01
21 Sa	11 54 7	0♈22 57	26 03	8 54	8 34	18 04	14 29	15 15	4 11	28 19	1 47	5 01	2 12	18 12	27 37	5 02	25 05
22 Su	11 58 3	1 22 33	10♉30	8 50	8 43	19 18	15 17	15 17	4 18	28 21	1 50	5 02	2 35	18 32	27 55	5 32	25 08
23 M	12 2 0	2 22 08	24 59	8 47	8 58	20 32	16 04	15 19	4 25	28 24	1 52	5 03	2 59	18 52	28 12	6 01	25 11
24 T	12 5 56	3 21 40	9♊26	8 45	9 18	21 46	16 51	15 21	4 33	28 26	1 54	5 04	3 22	19 12	28 29	6 31	25 15
25 W	12 9 53	4 21 10	23 45	8 43D	9 44	23 00	17 38	15 24	4 40	28 28	1 56	5 06	3 45	19 32	28 47	7 00	25 18
26 Th	12 13 50	5 20 37	7♋55	8 43	10 13	24 15	18 25	15 27	4 48	28 31	1 59	5 07	4 08	19 51	29 04	7 30	25 22
27 F	12 17 46	6 20 03	21 52	8 44	10 47	25 29	19 12	15 30	4 55	28 33	2 01	5 08	4 32	20 11	29 20	7 59	25 25
28 Sa	12 21 43	7 19 25	5♌36	8 45	11 25	26 43	19 59	15 33	5 03	28 36	2 03	5 09	4 55	20 31	29 37	8 28	25 28
29 Su	12 25 39	8 18 46	19 08	8 47	12 07	27 57	20 46	15 36	5 10	28 38	2 05	5 10	5 19	20 51	29 54	8 58	25 32
30 M	12 29 36	9 18 04	2♍27	8 48R	12 53	29 11	21 33	15 39	5 18	28 41	2 08	5 11	5 42	21 11	0♊10	9 27	25 35
31 T	12 33 32	10 17 20	15 34	8 48	13 41	0♉25	22 20	15 43	5 25	28 43	2 10	5 12	6 06	21 31	0 27	9 56	25 39

EPHEMERIS CALCULATED FOR 12 MIDNIGHT GREENWICH MEAN TIME. ALL OTHER DATA AND FACING ASPECTARIAN PAGE IN EASTERN TIME (**BOLD**) AND PACIFIC TIME (REGULAR).

APRIL 2026

☽ Last Aspect day	ET / hr:mn / PT		asp	☽ Ingress sign	day	ET / hr:mn / PT	
2	**4:55 am**	1:55 am	□♃	♏	3	**8:11 am**	5:11 am
5	**5:29 pm**	2:29 pm	☍♅	♐	5	**7:32 pm**	4:32 pm
8	**5:52 am**	2:52 am	□♂	♑	8	**8:04 am**	5:04 am
10	**6:24 pm**	3:24 pm	△♅	♒	10	**7:55 pm**	4:55 pm
13	**3:42 am**	12:42 am	□♅	♓	13	**4:55 am**	1:55 am
15	**9:07 am**	6:07 am	✶♅	♈	15	**10:04 am**	7:04 am
17	**7:52 am**	4:52 am	☌☉	♉	17	**11:58 am**	8:58 am
19	**11:45 am**	8:45 am	☌♅	♊	19	**12:18 pm**	9:18 am
19		10:17 pm	✶♂	♋	21	**1:00 pm**	10:00 am
20	**1:17 am**		✶♂	♋	21	**1:00 pm**	10:00 am
23	**3:28 pm**	12:28 pm	✶♅	♌	23	**3:41 pm**	12:41 pm
24	**6:21 pm**	3:21 pm	△☿	♍	25	**9:04 pm**	6:04 pm
27	**7:12 am**	4:12 am	✶♃	♎	28	**5:03 am**	2:03 am
30	**4:52 am**	1:52 am	☍☿	♏	30	**3:02 pm**	12:02 pm

☽ Phases & Eclipses phase	day	ET / hr:mn / PT	
Full Moon	1	**10:12 pm**	7:12 pm
4th Quarter	9		9:52 pm
4th Quarter	10	**12:52 am**	
New Moon	17	**7:52 am**	4:52 am
2nd Quarter	23	**10:32 pm**	7:32 pm

Planet Ingress	day	ET / hr:mn / PT	
♂ ♈	9	**3:36 pm**	12:36 pm
☿ ♈	14	**11:21 pm**	8:21 pm
☉ ♉	19	**9:39 pm**	6:39 pm
♀ ♊	23		9:03 pm
♀ ♊	24	**12:03 am**	
♅ ♊	25	**8:50 pm**	5:50 pm
⚳ ♈	25		10:09 pm
⚳ ♈	26	**1:09 am**	

Planetary Motion	day	ET / hr:mn / PT	
☿ ℞	21	**4:35 am**	1:35 am

1 WEDNESDAY
☽ ⚻ ♀ **2:34 am**
☽ ☍ ♆ **3:00 am** 12:00 am
♀ ⚺ ♆ **7:19 am** 4:19 am
☽ △ ♇ **8:41 am** 5:41 am
☽ ☍ ♄ **9:25 am** 6:25 am
☽ ☍ ☉ **10:12 pm** 7:12 pm
☽ ⚻ ☿ 11:56 pm

2 THURSDAY
☽ ⚻ ☿ **2:56 am**
☽ □ ♃ **4:55 am** 1:55 am
☽ ⚻ ♂ **9:59 pm** 6:59 pm

3 FRIDAY
☽ ⚻ ♅ **5:59 am** 2:59 am
☿ △ ♃ **7:28 am** 4:28 am
☽ ⚻ ♆ **12:40 pm** 9:40 am
☽ ☍ ♀ **6:26 pm** 3:26 pm
☽ □ ♇ **6:27 pm** 3:27 pm
♀ □ ♇ **6:38 pm** 3:38 pm
☽ ⚻ ♄ **7:44 pm** 4:44 pm

4 SATURDAY
♀ ⚺ ♄ **8:46 am** 5:46 am
☽ ⚻ ☉ **1:32 pm** 10:32 am
☽ △ ♃ **3:42 pm** 12:42 pm
☽ △ ☿ **6:25 pm** 3:25 pm

5 SUNDAY
☽ △ ♂ **1:07 pm** 10:07 am
☽ ☍ ♅ **5:29 pm** 2:29 pm
☉ □ ♃ **6:23 pm** 3:23 pm
☽ △ ♆ 9:20 pm

6 MONDAY
☽ △ ♆ **12:20 am**
☽ ✶ ♇ **6:10 am** 3:10 am
☽ △ ♄ **8:03 am** 5:03 am
☽ ⚻ ♀ **12:56 pm** 9:56 am

7 TUESDAY
☽ ⚻ ♃ **4:16 am** 1:16 am
☽ △ ☉ **7:05 am** 4:05 am
☽ □ ☿ **12:45 pm** 9:45 am

8 WEDNESDAY
☽ □ ♂ **5:52 am** 2:52 am
☽ ⚻ ♅ **6:15 am** 3:15 am
♂ ✶ ♅ **12:11 pm** 9:11 am
☽ □ ♆ **1:06 pm** 10:06 am
☽ ⚺ ♇ **6:50 pm** 3:50 pm
☽ □ ♄ **9:16 pm** 6:16 pm

9 THURSDAY
☽ △ ♀ **8:27 am** 5:27 am
☽ ☍ ♃ **5:10 pm** 2:10 pm
☽ □ ☉ 9:52 pm

10 FRIDAY
☽ □ ☉ **12:52 am**
☽ ✶ ☿ **7:44 am** 4:44 am
☽ △ ♅ **6:24 pm** 3:24 pm
☽ ✶ ♂ **9:51 pm** 6:51 pm
☽ ✶ ♆ 9:58 pm

11 SATURDAY
☽ ✶ ♆ **12:58 am**
☽ ☌ ♇ **6:22 am** 3:22 am
☽ ✶ ♄ **9:15 am** 6:15 am
☽ □ ♀ 10:43 pm

12 SUNDAY
☽ □ ♀ **1:43 am**
☽ ⚻ ♃ **4:06 am** 1:06 am
☽ ✶ ☉ **3:47 pm** 12:47 pm
☽ ⚺ ☿ **11:55 pm** 8:55 pm
♂ ☌ ♆ 10:30 pm

13 MONDAY
♂ ☌ ♆ **1:30 am**
☽ □ ♅ **3:42 am** 12:42 am
♀ ✶ ♃ **4:21 am** 1:21 am
☽ ⚺ ♆ **9:48 am** 6:48 am
☽ ⚺ ♂ **10:18 am** 7:18 am
☽ ⚺ ♇ **2:45 pm** 11:45 am
☽ ⚺ ♄ **5:55 pm** 2:55 pm

14 TUESDAY
☽ △ ♃ **11:23 am** 8:23 am
☿ ✶ ♅ **1:10 pm** 10:10 am
☽ ✶ ♀ **2:11 pm** 11:11 am
☽ ⚺ ☉ 10:57 pm

15 WEDNESDAY
☽ ⚺ ☉ **1:57 am**
☽ ✶ ♅ **9:07 am** 6:07 am
☽ ☌ ☿ **11:16 am** 8:16 am
☽ ☌ ♆ **2:45 pm** 11:45 am
☽ ☌ ♂ **6:08 pm** 3:08 pm
☽ ✶ ♇ **7:16 pm** 4:16 pm
☽ ☌ ♄ **10:38 pm** 7:38 pm

16 THURSDAY
☽ □ ♃ **2:54 pm** 11:54 am
♂ ✶ ♇ **2:56 pm** 11:56 am
☽ ⚺ ♀ **9:50 pm** 6:50 pm
☿ ☌ ♆ **10:01 pm** 7:01 pm

17 FRIDAY
☽ ☌ ☉ **7:52 am** 4:52 am
☽ ⚺ ♅ **11:14 am** 8:14 am
☽ ⚺ ♆ **4:32 pm** 1:32 pm
☽ ⚺ ☿ **6:33 pm** 3:33 pm
☽ □ ♇ **8:46 pm** 5:46 pm
☽ ⚺ ♂ **10:24 pm** 7:24 pm
☽ ⚺ ♄ 9:22 pm

18 SATURDAY
☽ ⚺ ♄ **12:22 am**
☽ ✶ ♃ **4:01 pm** 1:01 pm
☿ ✶ ♇ **4:34 pm** 1:34 pm
☽ ☌ ♀ 11:44 pm

19 SUNDAY
☽ ☌ ♀ **2:44 am**
☽ ⚺ ☉ **11:38 am** 8:38 am
☽ ☌ ♅ **11:45 am** 8:45 am
☉ ⚺ ♅ **1:22 pm** 10:22 am
☽ ✶ ♆ **4:56 pm** 1:56 pm
♂ ☌ ♄ **6:44 pm** 3:44 pm
☽ △ ♇ **9:03 pm** 6:03 pm
☽ ✶ ☿ 9:19 pm
☽ ✶ ♄ 10:00 pm
☽ ✶ ♂ 10:17 pm

20 MONDAY
☽ ✶ ☿ **12:19 am**
☽ ✶ ♄ **1:00 am**
☽ ✶ ♂ **1:17 am**
☿ ☌ ♄ **7:22 am** 4:22 am
☽ ⚺ ♃ **4:44 pm** 1:44 pm
☿ ☌ ♂ **5:45 pm** 2:45 pm

21 TUESDAY
☽ ⚺ ♀ **7:38 am** 4:38 am
☽ ⚺ ♅ **12:37 pm** 9:37 am
☽ ✶ ☉ **3:50 pm** 12:50 pm
☽ □ ♆ **5:54 pm** 2:54 pm
☽ ⚻ ♇ **10:03 pm** 7:03 pm
☽ □ ♄ 11:31 pm

22 WEDNESDAY
☽ □ ♄ **2:31 am**
☽ □ ♂ **5:12 am** 2:12 am
☽ □ ☿ **7:30 am** 4:30 am
☽ ☌ ♃ **6:52 pm** 3:52 pm
☉ ⚺ ♆ **11:27 pm** 8:27 pm

23 THURSDAY
☽ ✶ ♀ **2:52 pm** 11:52 am
☽ ✶ ♅ **3:28 pm** 12:28 pm
☽ △ ♆ **8:57 pm** 5:57 pm
♀ ☌ ♅ **9:58 pm** 6:58 pm
☽ □ ☉ **10:32 pm** 7:32 pm
☽ ☍ ♇ 10:13 pm

24 FRIDAY
☽ ☍ ♇ **1:13 am**
☽ △ ♄ **6:20 am** 3:20 am
☽ △ ♂ **11:49 am** 8:49 am
☽ △ ☿ **6:21 pm** 3:21 pm
☽ ⚺ ♃ **11:37 pm** 8:37 pm

25 SATURDAY
☉ □ ♇ **12:33 pm** 9:33 am
☽ □ ♅ **9:04 pm** 6:04 pm
☽ □ ♀ 10:40 pm
☽ ⚻ ♆ 11:46 pm

26 SUNDAY
☽ □ ♀ **1:40 am**
☽ ⚻ ♆ **2:46 am**
☽ ⚻ ♇ **7:08 am** 4:08 am
☽ △ ☉ **8:37 am** 5:37 am
☽ ⚻ ♄ **12:59 pm** 9:59 am
♀ ✶ ♆ **1:43 pm** 10:43 am
☿ □ ♃ **2:33 pm** 11:33 am
☽ ⚻ ♂ **9:43 pm** 6:43 pm

27 MONDAY
☽ ✶ ♃ **7:12 am** 4:12 am
☽ ⚻ ☿ **9:39 am** 6:39 am

28 TUESDAY
☽ △ ♅ **5:17 am** 2:17 am
☽ ☍ ♆ **11:07 am** 8:07 am
♀ △ ♇ **12:40 pm** 9:40 am
☽ △ ♇ **3:32 pm** 12:32 pm
☽ △ ♀ **3:50 pm** 12:50 pm
☽ ⚻ ☉ **9:49 pm** 6:49 pm
☽ ☍ ♄ **10:07 pm** 7:07 pm
☉ ⚺ ♄ 11:06 pm

29 WEDNESDAY
☉ ⚺ ♄ **2:06 am**
☽ ☍ ♂ **10:24 am** 7:24 am
☽ □ ♃ **5:06 pm** 2:06 pm

30 THURSDAY
☽ ☍ ☿ **4:52 am** 1:52 am
☽ ⚻ ♅ **3:33 pm** 12:33 pm
☽ ⚻ ♆ **9:26 pm** 6:26 pm
☽ □ ♇ 10:51 pm

Eastern time in bold type
Pacific time in medium type

APRIL 2026

DATE	SID.TIME	SUN	MOON	NODE	MERCURY	VENUS	MARS	JUPITER	SATURN	URANUS	NEPTUNE	PLUTO	CERES	PALLAS	JUNO	VESTA	CHIRON
1 W	12 37 29	11♈16 33	28♍29	8♈46R	13♈42	1♈38	23♈07	15♋47	5♈33	28♉46	2♈12	5≈13	6♐09	21♈51	0≈43	10♓25	25♈42
2 Th	12 41 25	12 15 45	11♎12	8 43	14 34	2 52	23 54	15 51	5 40	28 48	2 14	5 14	6 53	22 11	0 59	10 54	25 46
3 F	12 45 22	13 14 55	23 43	8 38	15 30	4 06	24 41	15 55	5 48	28 51	2 17	5 15	7 16	22 30	1 15	11 23	25 49
4 Sa	12 49 19	14 14 02	6♏03	8 32	16 28	5 20	25 28	15 59	5 55	28 54	2 19	5 16	7 40	22 50	1 31	11 52	25 53
5 Su	12 53 15	15 13 08	18 13	8 25	17 29	6 34	26 15	16 04	6 03	28 56	2 21	5 17	8 04	23 10	1 47	12 21	25 57
6 M	12 57 12	16 12 12	0♐14	8 19	18 33	7 47	27 01	16 09	6 10	28 59	2 23	5 18	8 28	23 29	2 02	12 50	26 00
7 T	13 1 8	17 11 14	12 09	8 13	19 39	9 01	27 48	16 13	6 17	29 02	2 26	5 18	8 51	23 49	2 18	13 18	26 04
8 W	13 5 5	18 10 14	24 02	8 08	20 48	10 15	28 35	16 18	6 25	29 05	2 28	5 19	9 15	24 09	2 33	13 47	26 07
9 Th	13 9 1	19 09 13	5♑55	8 05	21 59	11 28	29 22	16 24	6 32	29 08	2 30	5 20	9 39	24 28	2 48	14 16	26 11
10 F	13 12 58	20 08 09	17 53	8 04D	23 12	12 42	0♉09	16 29	6 40	29 10	2 32	5 21	10 03	24 48	3 03	14 44	26 14
11 Sa	13 16 54	21 07 04	0≈02	8 05	24 27	13 55	0 55	16 34	6 47	29 13	2 34	5 21	10 27	25 07	3 18	15 13	26 18
12 Su	13 20 51	22 05 58	12 26	8 06	25 44	15 09	1 42	16 40	6 54	29 16	2 37	5 22	10 51	25 27	3 32	15 41	26 22
13 M	13 24 48	23 04 49	25 10	8 07R	27 04	16 22	2 29	16 46	7 02	29 19	2 39	5 23	11 15	25 46	3 47	16 09	26 25
14 T	13 28 44	24 03 39	8♓18	8 08	28 25	17 36	3 15	16 52	7 09	29 22	2 41	5 23	11 39	26 06	4 01	16 38	26 29
15 W	13 32 41	25 02 27	21 51	8 07	29 48	18 49	4 02	16 58	7 16	29 25	2 43	5 24	12 03	26 25	4 15	17 06	26 32
16 Th	13 36 37	26 01 13	5♈51	8 04	1♉13	20 02	4 48	17 04	7 23	29 28	2 45	5 25	12 27	26 45	4 29	17 34	26 36
17 F	13 40 34	26 59 57	20 15	7 59	2 40	21 16	5 35	17 11	7 31	29 31	2 47	5 25	12 51	27 04	4 42	18 02	26 40
18 Sa	13 44 30	27 58 39	4♉57	7 52	4 09	22 29	6 21	17 17	7 38	29 34	2 49	5 26	13 16	27 23	4 56	18 30	26 43
19 Su	13 48 27	28 57 20	19 51	7 44	5 39	23 42	7 08	17 24	7 45	29 38	2 52	5 26	13 40	27 43	5 09	18 58	26 47
20 M	13 52 23	29 55 58	4♊48	7 36	7 11	24 55	7 54	17 31	7 52	29 41	2 54	5 27	14 04	28 02	5 22	19 26	26 51
21 T	13 56 20	0♉54 34	19 37	7 30	8 45	26 09	8 41	17 38	7 59	29 44	2 56	5 27	14 28	28 21	5 35	19 53	26 54
22 W	14 0 17	1 53 09	4♋14	7 25	10 21	27 22	9 27	17 45	8 06	29 47	2 58	5 28	14 52	28 40	5 48	20 21	26 58
23 Th	14 4 13	2 51 41	18 32	7 22	11 58	28 35	10 13	17 52	8 13	29 50	3 00	5 28	15 17	28 59	6 01	20 49	27 01
24 F	14 8 10	3 50 11	2♌29	7 21D	13 37	29 48	11 00	17 59	8 21	29 53	3 02	5 28	15 41	29 18	6 13	21 16	27 05
25 Sa	14 12 6	4 48 38	16 06	7 21	15 18	1♉01	11 46	18 07	8 28	29 57	3 04	5 29	16 05	29 37	6 25	21 44	27 09
26 Su	14 16 3	5 47 03	29 25	7 22R	17 00	2 14	12 32	18 15	8 34	0♊00	3 06	5 29	16 30	29 56	6 37	22 11	27 12
27 M	14 19 59	6 45 27	12♍26	7 22	18 44	3 26	13 18	18 22	8 41	0 03	3 08	5 29	16 54	0♉15	6 49	22 38	27 16
28 T	14 23 56	7 43 48	25 14	7 20	20 18	4 39	14 04	18 30	8 48	0 06	3 10	5 30	17 19	0 34	7 00	23 05	27 19
29 W	14 27 52	8 42 07	7♎50	7 16	22 18	5 52	14 50	18 38	8 55	0 10	3 12	5 30	17 43	0 52	7 12	23 32	27 23
30 Th	14 31 49	9 40 24	20 15	7 10	24 07	7 05	15 36	18 47	9 02	0 13	3 14	5 30	18 07	1 11	7 23	23 59	27 26

EPHEMERIS CALCULATED FOR 12 MIDNIGHT GREENWICH MEAN TIME. ALL OTHER DATA AND FACING ASPECTARIAN PAGE IN EASTERN TIME (BOLD) AND PACIFIC TIME (REGULAR).

MAY 2026

☽ Last Aspect day	ET / hr:mn / PT	asp	☽ Ingress sign day	ET / hr:mn / PT
2	**4:47 am** 1:47 am	△♃	♐ 2	11:33 pm
2	**4:47 am** 1:47 am	△♃	♐ 3	**2:33 am**
4	**5:33 pm** 2:33 pm	△♂	♑ 5	**3:06 pm** 12:06 pm
7	**10:18 am** 7:18 am	□♂	♒ 8	**3:27 am** 12:27 am
9	10:09 pm	✶♂	♓ 10	**1:39 pm** 10:39 am
10	**1:09 am**	✶♂	♓ 10	**1:39 pm** 10:39 am
12	**6:04 am** 3:04 am	□♀	♈ 12	**8:04 pm** 5:04 pm
14	**5:33 pm** 2:33 pm	☌♂	♉ 14	**10:31 pm** 7:31 pm
16	**9:02 pm** 6:02 pm	☌☿	♊ 16	**10:23 pm** 7:23 pm
17	**3:36 pm** 12:36 pm	✶♄	♋ 18	**9:46 pm** 6:46 pm
20	**9:27 am** 6:27 am	☌♃	♌ 20	**10:48 pm** 7:48 pm
21	**6:05 pm** 3:05 pm	△♄	♍ 22	11:57 pm
21	**6:05 pm** 3:05 pm	△♄	♍ 23	**2:57 am**
24	**8:54 pm** 5:54 pm	✶♃	♎ 25	**10:34 am** 7:34 am
27	**7:32 am** 4:32 am	□♃	♏ 27	**8:53 pm** 5:53 pm
29	**8:05 pm** 5:05 pm	△♃	♐ 30	**8:45 am** 5:45 am
31	**9:21 am** 6:21 am	△♄	♑ 6/1	**9:19 pm** 6:19 pm

☽ Phases & Eclipses phase	day	ET / hr:mn / PT
Full Moon	1	**1:23 pm** 10:23 am
4th Quarter	9	**5:10 pm** 2:10 pm
New Moon	16	**4:01 pm** 1:01 pm
2nd Quarter	23	**7:11 am** 4:11 am
Full Moon	31	**4:45 am** 1:45 am

Planet Ingress	day	ET / hr:mn / PT
☿ ♉	2	**10:57 pm** 7:57 pm
⚶ ♈	13	**12:17 am** 9:17 am
☿ ♊	17	**6:26 am** 3:26 am
♂ ♉	18	**6:25 pm** 3:25 pm
♀ ♋	18	**9:05 pm** 6:05 pm
☉ ♊	20	**8:37 pm** 5:37 pm
⚵ ♊	28	**7:52 pm** 4:52 pm

Planetary Motion	day	ET / hr:mn / PT
♇ ℞	6	**11:34 am** 8:34 am

1 FRIDAY
☽□♇ **1:51 am**
☽⚻♀ **8:36 am** 5:36 am
☽⚻♄ **9:09 am** 6:09 am
☽☍☉ **1:23 pm** 10:23 am
♀✶♄ **2:45 pm** 11:45 am
☽⚻♂ 10:12 pm

2 SATURDAY
☽⚻♂ **1:12 am**
☽△♃ **4:47 am** 1:47 am

3 SUNDAY
☽⚻☿ **3:15 am** 12:15 am
☽☍♅ **3:22 am** 12:22 am
☿⚺♅ **3:58 am** 12:58 am
☽△♆ **9:16 am** 6:16 am
☽✶♇ **1:37 pm** 10:37 am
☽△♄ **9:38 pm** 6:38 pm

4 MONDAY
☽☍♀ **3:16 am** 12:16 am
☽⚻☉ **6:43 am** 3:43 am
☿⚺♆ **4:28 pm** 1:28 pm
☽△♂ **5:33 pm** 2:33 pm
☽⚻♃ **5:48 pm** 2:48 pm
♂□♃ **10:08 pm** 7:08 pm

5 TUESDAY
☽⚻♅ **4:12 pm** 1:12 pm
☿□♇ **6:08 pm** 3:08 pm
☽□♆ **10:01 pm** 7:01 pm
☽⚺♇ 11:15 pm

6 WEDNESDAY
☽⚺♇ **2:15 am**
☽△☿ **3:55 am** 12:55 am
☽□♄ **10:52 am** 7:52 am
☽⚻♀ **10:47 pm** 7:47 pm
☽△☉ 9:44 pm

7 THURSDAY
☽△☉ **12:44 am**
☽☍♃ **7:11 am** 4:11 am
☽□♂ **10:18 am** 7:18 am
☿⚺♄ **10:13 pm** 7:13 pm

8 FRIDAY
☽△♅ **4:50 am** 1:50 am
☽✶♆ **10:23 am** 7:23 am
☽☌♇ **2:22 pm** 11:22 am
☽✶♄ **11:17 pm** 8:17 pm

9 SATURDAY
☽□☿ **4:08 am** 1:08 am
☽△♀ **4:40 pm** 1:40 pm
☽□☉ **5:10 pm** 2:10 pm
☽⚻♃ **7:05 pm** 4:05 pm
☽✶♂ 10:09 pm

10 SUNDAY
☽✶♂ **1:09 am**
☽□♅ **3:13 pm** 12:13 pm
☉⚺♀ **5:29 pm** 2:29 pm
☽⚺♆ **8:20 pm** 5:20 pm
♀⚺♃ **9:09 pm** 6:09 pm
☉✶♃ **10:14 pm** 7:14 pm
☽⚺♇ **11:57 pm** 8:57 pm

11 MONDAY
☽⚺♄ **8:48 am** 5:48 am
☽✶☿ **11:43 pm** 8:43 pm

12 TUESDAY
☽△♃ **3:29 am** 12:29 am
☽✶☉ **5:23 am** 2:23 am
☽□♀ **6:04 am** 3:04 am
☽⚺♂ **11:44 am** 8:44 am
☽✶♅ **9:44 pm** 6:44 pm
☿✶♃ 9:44 pm
☽☌♆ 11:21 pm

13 WEDNESDAY
☿✶♃ **12:44 am**
☽☌♆ **2:21 am**
☽✶♇ **5:35 am** 2:35 am
☽☌♄ **2:10 pm** 11:10 am

14 THURSDAY
☽□♃ **7:41 am** 4:41 am
☉☌☿ **10:24 am** 7:24 am
☽⚺☉ **12:31 pm** 9:31 am
☽⚺☿ **12:43 pm** 9:43 am
☽✶♀ **2:07 pm** 11:07 am
☽☌♂ **5:33 pm** 2:33 pm
☽⚺♅ 9:17 pm

15 FRIDAY
☽⚺♅ **12:17 am**
☽⚺♆ **4:29 am** 1:29 am
☽□♇ **7:25 am** 4:25 am
☿⚺♀ **7:39 am** 4:39 am
☽⚺♄ **3:51 pm** 12:51 pm

16 SATURDAY
☽✶♃ **8:39 am** 5:39 am
☿⚺♂ **11:29 am** 8:29 am
☽☌☉ **4:01 pm** 1:01 pm
☽⚺♀ **6:24 pm** 3:24 pm
☽⚺♂ **8:05 pm** 5:05 pm
☽☌☿ **9:02 pm** 6:02 pm
☽☌♅ 9:16 pm

17 SUNDAY
☽☌♅ **12:16 am**
☽✶♆ **4:15 am** 1:15 am
☽△♇ **7:01 am** 4:01 am
☽✶♄ **3:36 pm** 12:36 pm
☿☌♅ **8:10 pm** 5:10 pm

18 MONDAY
☽⚺♃ **8:29 am** 5:29 am
☽⚺☉ **6:34 pm** 3:34 pm
☽☌♀ **9:50 pm** 6:50 pm
☽✶♂ **9:57 pm** 6:57 pm
☽⚺♅ **11:52 pm** 8:52 pm
☿✶♆ 9:05 pm
♀✶♂ 10:37 pm

19 TUESDAY
☿✶♆ **12:05 am**
♀✶♂ **1:37 am**
☽□♆ **3:49 am** 12:49 am
☽⚺☿ **4:27 am** 1:27 am
☽⚻♇ **6:32 am** 3:32 am
☽□♄ **3:40 pm** 12:40 pm
☿△♇ **6:53 pm** 3:53 pm
♀⚺♅ 9:44 pm

20 WEDNESDAY
♀⚺♅ **12:44 am**
☽☌♃ **9:27 am** 6:27 am
♂⚺♅ **3:29 pm** 12:29 pm
☽✶☉ **10:57 pm** 7:57 pm
☽✶♅ 10:13 pm
☽□♂ 10:43 pm

21 THURSDAY
☽✶♅ **1:13 am**
☽□♂ **1:43 am**
☽⚺♀ **3:21 am** 12:21 am
☽△♆ **5:16 am** 2:16 am
☽☍♇ **8:02 am** 5:02 am
☽✶☿ **2:43 pm** 11:43 am
☽△♄ **6:05 pm** 3:05 pm
♀□♆ 11:32 pm

22 FRIDAY
⚳□♆ **2:32 am**
☉☌⚷ **10:26 am** 7:26 am
☽⚺♃ **1:21 pm** 10:21 am
☿✶⚵ **2:03 pm** 11:03 am

23 SATURDAY
☽□⚳ **5:46 am** 2:46 am
☽□☉ **7:11 am** 4:11 am
☽△♂ **9:12 am** 6:12 am
☽⚻♆ **9:58 am** 6:58 am
♀⚻⚳ **10:36 am** 7:36 am
☽⚻⚳ **12:48 pm** 9:48 am
☽✶⚳ **1:01 pm** 10:01 am
♂⚺♆ **10:59 pm** 7:59 pm
☽⚻♄ **11:58 pm** 8:58 pm

24 SUNDAY
☽□☿ **6:06 am** 3:06 am
☽✶♃ **8:54 pm** 5:54 pm
☉✶♆ **10:22 pm** 7:22 pm

25 MONDAY
☽△♅ **1:49 pm** 10:49 am
☽☍♆ **6:05 pm** 3:05 pm
☽△☉ **7:41 pm** 4:41 pm
☽⚻♂ **8:45 pm** 5:45 pm
☽△♇ **8:57 pm** 5:57 pm
♂□♇ 9:02 pm

26 TUESDAY
♂□♇ **12:02 am**
☽□♀ **3:08 am** 12:08 am
☽☍♄ **9:11 am** 6:11 am
☉△♇ **11:53 am** 8:53 am
☽△☿ 11:10 pm

27 WEDNESDAY
☽△☿ **2:10 am**
☽□♃ **7:32 am** 4:32 am
☽⚻♅ 9:31 pm

28 THURSDAY
☽⚻♅ **12:31 am**
☽⚻♆ **4:46 am** 1:46 am
☉⚺♂ **5:33 am** 2:33 am
☽□♇ **7:34 am** 4:34 am
☽☍♂ **11:16 am** 8:16 am
☽⚻☉ **11:22 am** 8:22 am
☿⚺♃ **3:58 pm** 12:58 pm
☽△♀ **8:26 pm** 5:26 pm
☽⚻♄ **8:40 pm** 5:40 pm
♀□♄ **11:03 pm** 8:03 pm

29 FRIDAY
☽△♃ **8:05 pm** 5:05 pm
☽⚻☿ 9:39 pm

30 SATURDAY
☽⚻☿ **12:39 am**
☽☍♅ **12:45 pm** 9:45 am
☽△♆ **4:53 pm** 1:53 pm
☽✶♇ **7:34 pm** 4:34 pm

31 SUNDAY
☽⚻♂ **3:22 am** 12:22 am
☽☍☉ **4:45 am** 1:45 am
☽△♄ **9:21 am** 6:21 am
☽⚻♀ **3:19 pm** 12:19 pm

Eastern time in bold type
Pacific time in medium type

MAY 2026

DATE	SID. TIME	SUN	MOON	NODE	MERCURY	VENUS	MARS	JUPITER	SATURN	URANUS	NEPTUNE	PLUTO	CERES	PALLAS	JUNO	VESTA	CHIRON
1 F	14 35 45	10♉38 39	21♌32	7♈01 R	25♉58	8♊17	16♈22	18♊55	9♈09	0♊16	3♈16	5≈30	18♑56	1♈48	7≈33	24♈26	27♈30
2 Sa	14 39 42	11 36 53	14 41	6 50	27 51	9 30	17 08	19 03	9 16	0 20	3 17	5 30	19 21	2 07	7 44	24 53	27 33
3 Su	14 43 39	12 35 05	26 44	6 38	29 46	10 42	17 54	19 12	9 22	0 23	3 19	5 30	19 45	2 25	7 54	25 20	27 37
4 M	14 47 35	13 33 15	8♍41	6 25	1♊42	11 55	18 40	19 20	9 29	0 27	3 21	5 30	20 10	2 44	8 05	25 47	27 40
5 T	14 51 32	14 31 24	20 34	6 14	3 40	13 07	19 26	19 29	9 36	0 30	3 23	5 31	20 34	3 02	8 14	26 13	27 44
6 W	14 55 28	15 29 31	2♎25	6 05	5 40	14 20	20 12	19 38	9 42	0 33	3 25	5 31 R	20 59	3 20	8 24	26 40	27 47
7 Th	14 59 25	16 27 36	14 18	5 58	7 41	15 32	20 58	19 47	9 49	0 37	3 27	5 31	21 23	3 39	8 33	27 06	27 51
8 F	15 3 21	17 25 41	26 15	5 54	9 44	16 45	21 43	19 56	9 55	0 40	3 28	5 31	21 48	3 57	8 43	27 32	27 54
9 Sa	15 7 18	18 23 43	8♏22	5 51 D	11 49	17 57	22 29	20 05	10 02	0 44	3 30	5 31	22 12	4 15	8 52	27 59	27 58
10 Su	15 11 15	19 21 45	20 43	5 51	13 55	19 09	23 14	20 15	10 08	0 47	3 32	5 30	22 37	4 33	9 00	28 25	28 01
11 M	15 15 11	20 19 45	3♐23	5 51 R	16 02	20 21	24 00	20 24	10 14	0 50	3 34	5 30	23 02	4 51	9 09	28 51	28 05
12 T	15 19 8	21 17 44	16 27	5 51	18 10	21 33	24 46	20 34	10 21	0 54	3 35	5 30	23 26	5 09	9 17	29 17	28 08
13 W	15 23 4	22 15 41	29 58	5 49	20 20	22 45	25 31	20 43	10 27	0 57	3 37	5 30	23 51	5 27	9 24	29 43	28 11
14 Th	15 27 1	23 13 37	13♑58	5 45	22 30	23 57	26 17	20 53	10 33	1 01	3 39	5 30	24 15	5 44	9 32	0♉08	28 15
15 F	15 30 57	24 11 32	28 27	5 38	24 41	25 09	27 02	21 03	10 39	1 04	3 40	5 30	24 40	6 02	9 39	0 34	28 18
16 Sa	15 34 54	25 09 25	13♒20	5 29	26 52	26 21	27 47	21 13	10 45	1 08	3 42	5 29	25 05	6 20	9 46	0 59	28 21
17 Su	15 38 50	26 07 18	28 29	5 18	29 03	27 33	28 33	21 23	10 51	1 11	3 43	5 29	25 29	6 37	9 53	1 25	28 25
18 M	15 42 47	27 05 08	13♓44	5 07	1♊14	28 45	29 18	21 33	10 57	1 15	3 45	5 29	25 54	6 55	9 59	1 50	28 28
19 T	15 46 44	28 02 58	28 54	4 58	3 24	29 57	0♊03	21 43	11 03	1 18	3 46	5 28	26 18	7 12	10 05	2 15	28 31
20 W	15 50 40	29 00 46	13♈48	4 50	5 34	1♋08	0 48	21 54	11 09	1 22	3 48	5 28	26 43	7 29	10 11	2 40	28 35
21 Th	15 54 37	29 58 32	28 20	4 45	7 43	2 20	1 33	22 04	11 15	1 25	3 49	5 27	27 08	7 46	10 17	3 05	28 38
22 F	15 58 33	0♊56 16	12♉27	4 43	9 50	3 32	2 18	22 15	11 21	1 29	3 51	5 27	27 32	8 03	10 22	3 30	28 41
23 Sa	16 2 30	1 53 59	26 07	4 42	11 56	4 43	3 03	22 25	11 26	1 32	3 52	5 27	27 57	8 20	10 27	3 55	28 44
24 Su	16 6 26	2 51 40	9♊23	4 42	14 00	5 55	3 48	22 36	11 32	1 36	3 54	5 26	28 22	8 37	10 31	4 19	28 47
25 M	16 10 23	3 49 20	22 18	4 41	16 02	7 06	4 33	22 47	11 38	1 39	3 55	5 25	28 46	8 54	10 35	4 44	28 50
26 T	16 14 19	4 46 58	4♋56	4 39	18 02	8 17	5 18	22 57	11 43	1 43	3 56	5 25	29 11	9 11	10 39	5 08	28 53
27 W	16 18 16	5 44 34	17 20	4 34	20 00	9 29	6 03	23 08	11 48	1 46	3 58	5 24	29 36	9 28	10 43	5 33	28 56
28 Th	16 22 13	6 42 09	29 33	4 27	21 55	10 40	6 47	23 19	11 54	1 50	3 59	5 24	0≈00	9 44	10 46	5 57	29 00
29 F	16 26 9	7 39 43	11♌39	4 16	23 47	11 51	7 32	23 30	11 59	1 53	4 00	5 23	0 25	10 01	10 49	6 21	29 03
30 Sa	16 30 6	8 37 16	23 39	4 04	25 37	13 02	8 17	23 42	12 04	1 57	4 01	5 23	0 49	10 17	10 52	6 45	29 05
31 Su	16 34 2	9 34 48	5♍35	3 50	27 25	14 13	9 01	23 53	12 10	2 00	4 02	5 23			10 54	7 08	29 08

EPHEMERIS CALCULATED FOR 12 MIDNIGHT GREENWICH MEAN TIME. ALL OTHER DATA AND FACING ASPECTARIAN PAGE IN **EASTERN TIME (BOLD)** AND PACIFIC TIME (REGULAR).

JUNE 2026

☽ Last Aspect day	ET / hr:mn / PT	asp	☽ Ingress sign	day	ET / hr:mn / PT
5/31	**9:21 am** 6:21 am	△ ♄	♑	1	**9:19 pm** 6:19 pm
3	**11:04 pm** 8:04 pm	☍ ♃	♒	4	**9:46 am** 6:46 am
5	**3:51 pm** 12:51 pm	△ ☉	♓	6	**8:43 pm** 5:43 pm
8	**8:38 pm** 5:38 pm	△ ♃	♈	9	**4:33 am** 1:33 am
11	**4:22 am** 1:22 am	□ ♀	♉	11	**8:28 am** 5:28 am
13	**3:30 am** 12:30 am	⚹ ♃	♊	13	**9:06 am** 6:06 am
14	**10:54 pm** 7:54 pm	☌ ☉	♋	15	**8:14 am** 5:14 am
17	**3:41 am** 12:41 am	☌ ♃	♌	17	**8:05 am** 5:05 am
19	**7:30 am** 4:30 am	⚹ ☉	♍	19	**10:37 am** 7:37 am
21	**1:33 pm** 10:33 am	⚹ ♃	♎	21	**4:55 pm** 1:55 pm

☽ Last Aspect day	ET / hr:mn / PT	asp	☽ Ingress sign	day	ET / hr:mn / PT
23	9:11 pm	□ ♃	♏	23	11:43 pm
24	**12:11 am**	□ ♃	♏	24	**2:43 am**
26	**1:10 pm** 10:10 am	△ ♃	♐	26	**2:41 pm** 11:41 am
27	10:05 pm	△ ♀	♑	29	**3:19 am** 12:19 am
28	**1:05 am**	△ ♀	♑	29	**3:19 am** 12:19 am

☽ Phases & Eclipses phase	day	ET / hr:mn / PT
4th Quarter	8	**3:00 am** 3:00 am
New Moon	14	**10:54 pm** 7:54 pm
2nd Quarter	21	**5:55 pm** 2:55 pm
Full Moon	29	**7:57 pm** 4:57 pm

Planet Ingress		day	ET / hr:mn / PT
☿	♋	1	**7:56 am** 4:56 am
♀	♌	13	**6:47 am** 3:47 am
⚷	♉	19	**5:20 pm** 2:20 pm
☉	♋	21	**4:24 am** 1:24 am
♂	♊	28	**3:29 pm** 12:29 pm
♃	♌	29	10:52 pm
♃	♌	30	**1:52 am**

Planetary Motion		day	ET / hr:mn / PT
⚵	℞	5	**5:55 pm** 2:55 pm
☿	℞	29	**1:36 pm** 10:36 am

1 MONDAY
☽ ⚻ ♃ **9:32 am** 6:32 am
☽ ☍ ☿ **11:32 pm** 8:32 pm
☽ ⚻ ♅ 10:38 pm

2 TUESDAY
☽ ⚻ ♅ **1:38 am**
☽ □ ♆ **5:35 am** 2:35 am
☽ ⚺ ♇ **8:08 am** 5:08 am
☿ ⚺ ♅ **3:11 pm** 12:11 pm
☉ ⚹ ♄ **6:49 pm** 3:49 pm
☽ △ ♂ **8:03 pm** 5:03 pm
☽ □ ♄ **10:25 pm** 7:25 pm
☽ ⚻ ☉ **10:43 pm** 7:43 pm

3 WEDNESDAY
☽ ☍ ♀ **10:37 am** 7:37 am
☿ □ ♆ **8:18 pm** 5:18 pm
☽ ☍ ♃ **11:04 pm** 8:04 pm

4 THURSDAY
☽ △ ♅ **2:19 pm** 11:19 am
♂ ⚺ ♄ **2:44 pm** 11:44 am
☿ ⚻ ♇ **2:51 pm** 11:51 am
☽ ⚹ ♆ **6:00 pm** 3:00 pm
☽ ☌ ♇ **8:22 pm** 5:22 pm
☽ ⚻ ☿ **9:10 pm** 6:10 pm

5 FRIDAY
☽ ⚹ ♄ **10:51 am** 7:51 am
☽ □ ♂ **12:00 pm** 9:00 am
☽ △ ☉ **3:51 pm** 12:51 pm

6 SATURDAY
☽ ⚻ ♀ **4:40 am** 1:40 am
☽ ⚻ ♃ **11:21 am** 8:21 am
☽ □ ♅ 10:21 pm

7 SUNDAY
☽ □ ♅ **1:21 am**
☽ ⚺ ♆ **4:42 am** 1:42 am
☽ ⚺ ♇ **6:49 am** 3:49 am
☽ △ ☿ **3:15 pm** 12:15 pm
☽ ⚺ ♄ **9:01 pm** 6:01 pm
☽ ⚹ ♂ 10:16 pm

8 MONDAY
☽ ⚹ ♂ **1:16 am**
☽ □ ☉ **6:00 am** 3:00 am
☽ △ ♀ **7:05 pm** 4:05 pm
☽ △ ♃ **8:38 pm** 5:38 pm

9 TUESDAY
☽ ⚹ ♅ **9:08 am** 6:08 am
☽ ☌ ♆ **12:05 pm** 9:05 am
☽ ⚹ ♇ **1:56 pm** 10:56 am
♀ ☌ ♃ **3:59 pm** 12:59 pm
☿ □ ♄ 10:39 pm

10 WEDNESDAY
☿ □ ♄ **1:39 am**
☽ ☌ ♄ **3:29 am** 12:29 am
☽ □ ☿ **3:40 am** 12:40 am
☽ ⚺ ♂ **10:09 am** 7:09 am
☽ ⚹ ☉ **3:28 pm** 12:28 pm
☽ □ ♃ 10:52 pm

11 THURSDAY
☽ □ ♃ **1:52 am**
☽ □ ♀ **4:22 am** 1:22 am
☽ ⚺ ♅ **12:55 pm** 9:55 am
☽ ⚺ ♆ **3:30 pm** 12:30 pm
☽ □ ♇ **5:08 pm** 2:08 pm

12 FRIDAY
☽ ⚺ ♄ **6:04 am** 3:04 am
☽ ⚹ ☿ **10:26 am** 7:26 am
☽ ☌ ♂ **2:37 pm** 11:37 am
☽ ⚺ ☉ **8:26 pm** 5:26 pm

13 SATURDAY
☽ ⚹ ♃ **3:30 am** 12:30 am
☽ ⚹ ♀ **9:18 am** 6:18 am
☽ ☌ ♅ **1:31 pm** 10:31 am
☽ ⚹ ♆ **3:51 pm** 12:51 pm
☽ △ ♇ **5:18 pm** 2:18 pm

14 SUNDAY
☽ ⚹ ♄ **6:00 am** 3:00 am
☽ ⚺ ☿ **1:38 pm** 10:38 am
☽ ⚺ ♂ **4:27 pm** 1:27 pm
☽ ☌ ☉ **10:54 pm** 7:54 pm

15 MONDAY
☽ ⚺ ♃ **3:20 am** 12:20 am
☽ ⚺ ♀ **12:19 pm** 9:19 am
☽ ⚺ ♅ **12:48 pm** 9:48 am
☽ □ ♆ **2:59 pm** 11:59 am
☽ ⚻ ♇ **4:21 pm** 1:21 pm
♀ ⚹ ♅ **6:53 pm** 3:53 pm

16 TUESDAY
☽ □ ♄ **5:23 am** 2:23 am
☽ ☌ ☿ **4:12 pm** 1:12 pm
☽ ⚹ ♂ **6:15 pm** 3:15 pm
♀ △ ♆ **11:41 pm** 8:41 pm
☽ ⚺ ☉ 10:42 pm

17 WEDNESDAY
☽ ⚺ ☉ **1:42 am**
☽ ☌ ♃ **3:41 am** 12:41 am
☽ ⚹ ♅ **1:00 pm** 10:00 am
☽ △ ♆ **3:09 pm** 12:09 pm
☽ ☌ ♀ **4:28 pm** 1:28 pm
☽ ☍ ♇ **4:29 pm** 1:29 pm
♀ ☍ ♇ **4:38 pm** 1:38 pm

18 THURSDAY
☽ △ ♄ **6:27 am** 3:27 am
☉ ⚺ ♃ **4:07 pm** 1:07 pm
☽ ⚺ ☿ **8:48 pm** 5:48 pm
☽ □ ♂ **10:33 pm** 7:33 pm

19 FRIDAY
☽ ⚺ ♃ **6:40 am** 3:40 am
☽ ⚹ ☉ **7:30 am** 4:30 am
☽ □ ♅ **4:05 pm** 1:05 pm
☽ ⚻ ♆ **6:13 pm** 3:13 pm
☽ ⚻ ♇ **7:33 pm** 4:33 pm
☽ ⚺ ♀ 9:22 pm

20 SATURDAY
☽ ⚺ ♀ **12:22 am**
☽ ⚻ ♄ **10:51 am** 7:51 am

21 SUNDAY
☽ ⚹ ☿ **5:03 am** 2:03 am
☽ △ ♂ **7:06 am** 4:06 am
☽ ⚹ ♃ **1:33 pm** 10:33 am
☽ □ ☉ **5:55 pm** 2:55 pm
☽ △ ♅ **11:01 pm** 8:01 pm
☽ ☍ ♆ 10:07 pm
☽ △ ♇ 11:25 pm

22 MONDAY
☽ ☍ ♆ **1:07 am**
☽ △ ♇ **2:25 am**
☽ ⚹ ♀ **1:15 pm** 10:15 am
☽ ☍ ♄ **7:07 pm** 4:07 pm

23 TUESDAY
☽ □ ☿ **4:47 pm** 1:47 pm
☽ ⚻ ♂ **7:56 pm** 4:56 pm
☽ □ ♃ 9:11 pm

24 WEDNESDAY
☽ □ ♃ **12:11 am**
☽ △ ☉ **8:43 am** 5:43 am
☽ ⚻ ♅ **9:24 am** 6:24 am
☽ ⚻ ♆ **11:22 am** 8:22 am
☽ □ ♇ **12:37 pm** 9:37 am
☉ ⚺ ♅ **5:49 pm** 2:49 pm

25 THURSDAY
☽ □ ♀ **6:13 am** 3:13 am
☽ ⚻ ♄ **6:23 am** 3:23 am
♀ △ ♄ **8:02 am** 5:02 am
☉ □ ♆ **6:38 pm** 3:38 pm

26 FRIDAY
☽ △ ☿ **6:18 am** 3:18 am
☉ ⚻ ♇ **9:19 am** 6:19 am
☽ ☍ ♂ **11:34 am** 8:34 am
☽ △ ♃ **1:10 pm** 10:10 am
☽ ☍ ♅ **9:46 pm** 6:46 pm
☽ △ ♆ **11:32 pm** 8:32 pm
☽ ⚹ ♇ 9:41 pm
☽ ⚻ ☉ 11:03 pm

27 SATURDAY
☽ ⚹ ♇ **12:41 am**
☽ ⚻ ☉ **2:03 am**
☽ △ ♄ **7:04 pm** 4:04 pm
♂ ⚹ ♃ 9:50 pm
☽ △ ♀ 10:05 pm

28 SUNDAY
♂ ⚹ ♃ **12:50 am**
☽ △ ♀ **1:05 am**
☽ ⚻ ☿ **7:42 pm** 4:42 pm
☽ ⚻ ♃ 11:54 pm

29 MONDAY
☽ ⚻ ♃ **2:54 am**
☽ ⚻ ♂ **4:04 am** 1:04 am
☽ ⚻ ♅ **10:39 am** 7:39 am
☽ □ ♆ **12:11 pm** 9:11 am
☽ ⚺ ♇ **1:12 pm** 10:12 am
☽ ☍ ☉ **7:57 pm** 4:57 pm

30 TUESDAY
☽ □ ♄ **7:51 am** 4:51 am
☽ ⚻ ♀ **7:57 pm** 4:57 pm

Eastern time in bold type
Pacific time in medium type

JUNE 2026

DATE	SID.TIME	SUN	MOON	NODE	MERCURY	VENUS	MARS	JUPITER	SATURN	URANUS	NEPTUNE	PLUTO	CERES	PALLAS	JUNO	VESTA	CHIRON
1 M	16 37 59	10♊32 18	17♐29	3♈36R	29♊09	15♊24	9♋46	24♋04	12♈15	2♊04	4♈04	5♒22R	1♉14	10♈33	10♋56	7♈32	29♈11
2 T	16 41 55	11 29 48	29 21	3 24	0♋51	16 35	10 30	24 15	12 20	2 07	4 05	5 21	1 39	10 49	10 57	7 55	29 14
3 W	16 45 52	12 27 16	11♑13	3 13	2 30	17 45	11 14	24 27	12 25	2 11	4 06	5 20	2 03	11 05	10 58	8 19	29 17
4 Th	16 49 48	13 24 44	23 08	3 05	4 06	18 56	11 59	24 38	12 30	2 14	4 07	5 20	2 28	11 21	10 59	8 42	29 20
5 F	16 53 45	14 22 11	5♒08	2 59	5 39	20 07	12 43	24 50	12 34	2 18	4 08	5 19	2 52	11 37	11 00R	9 05	29 23
6 Sa	16 57 42	15 19 37	17 17	2 56	7 09	21 17	13 27	25 02	12 39	2 21	4 09	5 18	3 17	11 53	11 00	9 28	29 25
7 Su	17 1 38	16 17 02	29 38	2 56D	8 36	22 28	14 11	25 13	12 44	2 25	4 10	5 17	3 42	12 08	11 00	9 51	29 28
8 M	17 5 35	17 14 27	12♓16	2 56R	10 01	23 38	14 56	25 25	12 48	2 28	4 11	5 17	4 06	12 24	10 59	10 13	29 31
9 T	17 9 31	18 11 51	25 16	2 56	11 22	24 48	15 40	25 37	12 53	2 31	4 12	5 16	4 31	12 39	10 58	10 36	29 34
10 W	17 13 28	19 09 14	8♈41	2 54	12 40	25 58	16 24	25 49	12 57	2 35	4 13	5 15	4 55	12 54	10 57	10 58	29 36
11 Th	17 17 24	20 06 37	22 35	2 51	13 56	27 09	17 08	26 01	13 02	2 38	4 14	5 14	5 20	13 09	10 55	11 20	29 39
12 F	17 21 21	21 04 00	6♉58	2 45	15 08	28 19	17 51	26 13	13 06	2 42	4 15	5 13	5 44	13 24	10 53	11 42	29 41
13 Sa	17 25 17	22 01 22	21 46	2 37	16 17	29 29	18 35	26 25	13 10	2 45	4 15	5 12	6 09	13 39	10 51	12 04	29 44
14 Su	17 29 14	22 58 44	6♊54	2 27	17 22	0♋38	19 19	26 37	13 14	2 48	4 16	5 11	6 33	13 54	10 48	12 26	29 46
15 M	17 33 11	23 56 05	22 12	2 18	18 24	1 48	20 03	26 49	13 18	2 52	4 17	5 10	6 58	14 09	10 45	12 48	29 49
16 T	17 37 7	24 53 25	7♋28	2 09	19 23	2 58	20 46	27 01	13 22	2 55	4 18	5 09	7 22	14 23	10 41	13 09	29 51
17 W	17 41 4	25 50 45	22 32	2 02	20 19	4 08	21 30	27 13	13 26	2 58	4 18	5 08	7 47	14 37	10 37	13 30	29 53
18 Th	17 45 0	26 48 04	7♌15	1 57	21 10	5 17	22 13	27 26	13 30	3 02	4 19	5 07	8 11	14 51	10 33	13 51	29 56
19 F	17 48 57	27 45 22	21 32	1 55D	21 59	6 27	22 57	27 38	13 34	3 05	4 20	5 06	8 36	15 05	10 28	14 12	29 58
20 Sa	17 52 53	28 42 40	5♍21	1 55	22 43	7 36	23 40	27 51	13 37	3 08	4 20	5 05	9 00	15 19	10 23	14 33	0♉00
21 Su	17 56 50	29 39 56	18 42	1 55R	23 23	8 45	24 24	28 03	13 41	3 11	4 21	5 04	9 24	15 33	10 18	14 53	0 02
22 M	18 0 47	0♋37 12	1♎39	1 55	24 00	9 54	25 07	28 15	13 44	3 15	4 21	5 03	9 49	15 47	10 12	15 14	0 05
23 T	18 4 43	1 34 27	14 15	1 55	24 32	11 03	25 50	28 28	13 48	3 18	4 22	5 02	10 13	16 00	10 06	15 34	0 07
24 W	18 8 40	2 31 42	26 35	1 52	25 00	12 12	26 33	28 41	13 51	3 21	4 22	5 01	10 37	16 13	10 00	15 54	0 09
25 Th	18 12 36	3 28 56	8♏43	1 47	25 24	13 21	27 16	28 53	13 54	3 24	4 23	5 00	11 02	16 26	9 53	16 13	0 11
26 F	18 16 33	4 26 09	20 43	1 39	25 43	14 30	27 59	29 06	13 57	3 27	4 23	4 59	11 26	16 39	9 45	16 33	0 13
27 Sa	18 20 29	5 23 22	2♐38	1 30	25 58	15 38	28 42	29 19	14 00	3 30	4 23	4 57	11 50	16 52	9 38	16 52	0 15
28 Su	18 24 26	6 20 34	14 31	1 20	26 08	16 47	29 25	29 31	14 03	3 33	4 24	4 56	12 14	17 05	9 30	17 12	0 17
29 M	18 28 22	7 17 47	26 23	1 10	26 14R	17 55	0♌08	29 44	14 06	3 36	4 24	4 55	12 39	17 17	9 22	17 31	0 18
30 T	18 32 19	8 14 59	8♑17	1 01	26 15	19 03	0 51	29 57	14 09	3 39	4 24	4 54	13 03	17 29	9 13	17 49	0 20

EPHEMERIS CALCULATED FOR 12 MIDNIGHT GREENWICH MEAN TIME. ALL OTHER DATA AND FACING ASPECTARIAN PAGE IN **EASTERN TIME (BOLD)** AND PACIFIC TIME (REGULAR).

JULY 2026

☽ Last Aspect day	ET / hr:mn / PT	asp	☽ Ingress sign day	ET / hr:mn / PT
1	**7:51 am** 4:51 am	☍ ☿	♒ 1	**3:33 pm** 12:33 pm
3	**1:27 pm** 10:27 am	☍ ♀	♓ 3	11:30 pm
3	**1:27 pm** 10:27 am	☍ ♀	♓ 4	**2:30 am**
5	10:21 pm	△ ☿	♈ 6	**11:07 am** 8:07 am
6	**1:21 am**	△ ☿	♈ 6	**11:07 am** 8:07 am
8	**2:42 pm** 11:42 am	△ ♀	♉ 8	**4:31 pm** 1:31 pm
10	**6:13 am** 3:13 am	⚹ ☿	♊ 10	**6:42 pm** 3:42 pm
11	**6:11 pm** 3:11 pm	⚹ ♄	♋ 12	**6:46 pm** 3:46 pm
14	**5:44 am** 2:44 am	☌ ☉	♌ 14	**6:35 pm** 3:35 pm
15	**6:27 pm** 3:27 pm	△ ♄	♍ 16	**8:07 pm** 5:07 pm

☽ Last Aspect day	ET / hr:mn / PT	asp	☽ Ingress sign day	ET / hr:mn / PT
18	**6:13 pm** 3:13 pm	⚹ ☉	♎ 18	9:57 pm
18	**6:13 pm** 3:13 pm	⚹ ☉	♎ 19	**12:57 am**
21	**7:06 am** 4:06 am	□ ☉	♏ 21	**9:35 am** 6:35 am
22	**5:48 pm** 2:48 pm	△ ☿	♐ 23	**9:07 pm** 6:07 pm
25	**10:58 am** 7:58 am	☍ ♂	♑ 26	**9:44 am** 6:44 am
27	11:11 pm	△ ♀	♒ 28	**9:46 pm** 6:46 pm
28	**2:11 am**	△ ♀	♒ 28	**9:46 pm** 6:46 pm
30	**5:27 pm** 2:27 pm	△ ♂	♓ 31	**8:14 am** 5:14 am

☽ Phases & Eclipses phase	day	ET / hr:mn / PT
4th Quarter	7	**3:29 pm** 12:29 pm
New Moon	14	**5:44 am** 2:44 am
2nd Quarter	21	**7:06 am** 4:06 am
Full Moon	29	**10:36 am** 7:36 am

Planet Ingress	day	ET / hr:mn / PT
♀ ♍	9	**1:22 pm** 10:22 am
☉ ♌	22	**3:13 pm** 12:13 pm

Planetary Motion	day	ET / hr:mn / PT
♆ ℞	7	**6:55 am** 3:55 am
☿ D	23	**6:58 pm** 3:58 pm
♄ ℞	26	**3:56 pm** 12:56 pm

1 WEDNESDAY
☽ ☍ ☿ **7:51 am** 4:51 am
☽ ☍ ♃ **4:14 pm** 1:14 pm
☽ △ ♂ **8:04 pm** 5:04 pm
☽ △ ♅ **11:02 pm** 8:02 pm
☽ ⚹ ♆ 9:19 pm
☽ ☌ ♇ 10:12 pm

2 THURSDAY
☽ ⚹ ♆ **12:19 am**
☽ ☌ ♇ **1:12 am**
☽ ⚻ ☉ **1:02 pm** 10:02 am
☽ ⚹ ♄ **7:49 pm** 4:49 pm

3 FRIDAY
☽ ☍ ♀ **1:27 pm** 10:27 am
☽ ⚻ ☿ **5:58 pm** 2:58 pm
♂ ☌ ♅ 11:08 pm

4 SATURDAY
♂ ☌ ♅ **2:08 am**
☽ ⚻ ♃ **4:12 am** 1:12 am
☽ □ ♅ **9:59 am** 6:59 am
☽ □ ♂ **10:26 am** 7:26 am
☽ ⚺ ♆ **11:01 am** 8:01 am
☽ ⚺ ♇ **11:45 am** 8:45 am
♂ ⚹ ♆ **8:44 pm** 5:44 pm

5 SUNDAY
☽ △ ☉ **4:01 am** 1:01 am
☿ ⚺ ♀ **4:06 am** 1:06 am
☽ ⚺ ♄ **5:58 am** 2:58 am

♂ △ ♇ **9:07 am** 6:07 am
☽ △ ☿ 10:21 pm

6 MONDAY
☽ △ ☿ **1:21 am**
☽ ⚻ ♀ **4:08 am** 1:08 am
☉ □ ♄ **6:47 am** 3:47 am
☽ △ ♃ **1:41 pm** 10:41 am
☽ ⚹ ♅ **6:26 pm** 3:26 pm
☽ ☌ ♆ **7:12 pm** 4:12 pm
☽ ⚹ ♇ **7:48 pm** 4:48 pm
☽ ⚹ ♂ **9:49 pm** 6:49 pm

7 TUESDAY
☽ ☌ ♄ **1:15 pm** 10:15 am
☽ □ ☉ **3:29 pm** 12:29 pm

8 WEDNESDAY
☽ □ ☿ **5:25 am** 2:25 am
☽ △ ♀ **2:42 pm** 11:42 am
☽ □ ♃ **7:45 pm** 4:45 pm
☽ ⚺ ♅ **11:33 pm** 8:33 pm
☽ ⚺ ♆ 9:05 pm
☽ □ ♇ 9:34 pm

9 THURSDAY
☽ ⚺ ♆ **12:05 am**
☽ □ ♇ **12:34 am**
☽ ⚺ ♂ **5:18 am** 2:18 am
☽ ⚺ ♄ **5:08 pm** 2:08 pm
☽ ⚹ ☉ **10:47 pm** 7:47 pm

10 FRIDAY
☽ ⚹ ☿ **6:13 am** 3:13 am
☽ □ ♀ **9:05 pm** 6:05 pm
☽ ⚹ ♃ **10:31 pm** 7:31 pm
☽ ☌ ♅ 10:30 pm
☽ ⚹ ♆ 10:52 pm
☽ △ ♇ 11:15 pm

11 SATURDAY
☽ ☌ ♅ **1:30 am**
☽ ⚹ ♆ **1:52 am**
☽ △ ♇ **2:15 am**
☽ ☌ ♂ **9:16 am** 6:16 am
☽ ⚹ ♄ **6:11 pm** 3:11 pm
♀ ⚺ ♃ **8:26 pm** 5:26 pm
☽ ⚺ ☉ 11:49 pm

12 SUNDAY
☽ ⚺ ☉ **2:49 am**
☽ ⚺ ☿ **4:43 am** 1:43 am
☉ ☌ ☿ **9:26 pm** 6:26 pm
☽ ⚺ ♃ **11:12 pm** 8:12 pm
☽ ⚹ ♀ 9:54 pm
☽ ⚺ ♅ 10:34 pm
☽ □ ♆ 10:46 pm
☽ ⚻ ♇ 11:05 pm

13 MONDAY
☽ ⚹ ♀ **12:54 am**
☽ ⚺ ♅ **1:34 am**
☽ □ ♆ **1:46 am**
☽ ⚻ ♇ **2:05 am**
♀ □ ♅ **10:27 am** 7:27 am

☽ ⚺ ♂ **11:23 am** 8:23 am
♀ ⚻ ♆ **12:45 pm** 9:45 am
♀ ⚻ ♇ **4:52 pm** 1:52 pm
☽ □ ♄ **5:58 pm** 2:58 pm
☽ ☌ ☿ 11:27 pm

14 TUESDAY
☽ ☌ ☿ **2:27 am**
☽ ☌ ☉ **5:44 am** 2:44 am
☽ ☌ ♃ **11:49 pm** 8:49 pm
☽ ⚹ ♅ 10:39 pm
☽ △ ♆ 10:42 pm
☽ ☍ ♇ 10:58 pm

15 WEDNESDAY
☽ ⚹ ♅ **1:39 am**
☽ △ ♆ **1:42 am**
☽ ☍ ♇ **1:58 am**
☽ ⚺ ♀ **4:41 am** 1:41 am
☽ ⚹ ♂ **1:59 pm** 10:59 am
♅ ⚹ ♆ **4:32 pm** 1:32 pm
☽ △ ♄ **6:27 pm** 3:27 pm
☽ ⚺ ☿ 10:15 pm

16 THURSDAY
☽ ⚺ ☿ **1:15 am**
☽ ⚺ ☉ **10:06 am** 7:06 am
☽ ⚺ ♃ 11:26 pm

17 FRIDAY
☽ ⚺ ♃ **2:26 am**
☽ ⚻ ♆ **3:37 am** 12:37 am
☽ □ ♅ **3:44 am** 12:44 am
☽ ⚻ ♇ **3:50 am** 12:50 am

☽ ☌ ♀ **11:06 am** 8:06 am
☽ □ ♂ **7:22 pm** 4:22 pm
☽ ⚻ ♄ **9:30 pm** 6:30 pm
♅ △ ♇ 9:45 pm
☽ ⚹ ☿ 11:50 pm

18 SATURDAY
♅ △ ♇ **12:45 am**
☽ ⚹ ☿ **2:50 am**
☽ ± ☉ **6:13 pm** 3:13 pm

19 SUNDAY
☽ ⚹ ♃ **8:39 am** 5:39 am
☽ ☍ ♆ **8:59 am** 5:59 am
☽ △ ♇ **9:08 am** 6:08 am
☽ △ ♅ **9:18 am** 6:18 am
♂ ⚹ ♄ **2:11 pm** 11:11 am
☽ ⚺ ♀ **10:02 pm** 7:02 pm

20 MONDAY
♃ △ ♆ **3:23 am** 12:23 am
☽ ☍ ♄ **4:16 am** 1:16 am
☽ △ ♂ **5:04 am** 2:04 am
☽ □ ☿ **8:19 am** 5:19 am
☽ ☍ ♇ **10:45 am** 7:45 am

21 TUESDAY
☽ □ ☉ **7:06 am** 4:06 am
♃ ⚹ ♅ **7:11 am** 4:11 am
☽ ⚻ ♆ **6:05 pm** 3:05 pm
☽ □ ♇ **6:11 pm** 3:11 pm
☽ ⚻ ♅ **6:39 pm** 3:39 pm
☽ □ ♃ **6:49 pm** 3:49 pm
☿ ⚺ ♂ 11:47 pm

22 WEDNESDAY
☿ ⚺ ♂ **2:47 am**
☽ ⚹ ♀ **1:37 pm** 10:37 am
☽ ⚻ ♄ **2:34 pm** 11:34 am
☽ △ ☿ **5:48 pm** 2:48 pm
☽ ⚻ ♂ **6:53 pm** 3:53 pm
♀ ⚻ ♄ 9:18 pm

23 THURSDAY
♀ ⚻ ♄ **12:18 am**
☽ △ ☉ **11:43 pm** 8:43 pm

24 FRIDAY
☽ △ ♆ **5:52 am** 2:52 am
☽ ⚹ ♇ **5:53 am** 2:53 am
☽ ☍ ♅ **6:41 am** 3:41 am
☽ △ ♃ **7:48 am** 4:48 am
☿ ⚹ ♀ **12:13 pm** 9:13 am
♆ ⚹ ♇ 10:49 pm
☽ △ ♄ 11:54 pm

25 SATURDAY
♆ ⚹ ♇ **1:49 am**
☽ △ ♄ **2:54 am**
☽ ⚻ ☿ **6:17 am** 3:17 am
☽ □ ♀ **7:54 am** 4:54 am
☽ ☍ ♂ **10:58 am** 7:58 am

26 SUNDAY
☽ ⚻ ☉ **5:38 pm** 2:38 pm
☽ ⚺ ♇ **6:24 pm** 3:24 pm
☽ □ ♆ **6:27 pm** 3:27 pm
☽ ⚻ ♅ **7:29 pm** 4:29 pm
☽ ⚻ ♃ **9:34 pm** 6:34 pm
☉ ☍ ♇ 11:55 pm

27 MONDAY
☉ ☍ ♇ **2:55 am**
☉ △ ♆ **3:36 am** 12:36 am
☽ □ ♄ **3:24 pm** 12:24 pm
☉ ⚹ ♅ **5:36 pm** 2:36 pm
☽ ☍ ☿ **8:08 pm** 5:08 pm
☽ △ ♀ 11:11 pm

28 TUESDAY
☽ △ ♀ **2:11 am**
☽ ⚻ ♂ **3:00 am** 12:00 am

29 WEDNESDAY
♀ □ ♂ **3:10 am** 12:10 am
☽ ☌ ♇ **6:08 am** 3:08 am
☽ ⚹ ♆ **6:14 am** 3:14 am
☽ △ ♅ **7:29 am** 4:29 am
☉ ☌ ♃ **8:18 am** 5:18 am
☽ ☍ ♃ **10:27 am** 7:27 am
☽ ☍ ☉ **10:36 am** 7:36 am
☽ ⚹ ♄ 11:44 pm

30 THURSDAY
☽ ⚹ ♄ **2:44 am**
☽ ⚻ ☿ **10:01 am** 7:01 am
☽ △ ♂ **5:27 pm** 2:27 pm
☽ ⚻ ♀ **6:41 pm** 3:41 pm

31 FRIDAY
☽ ⚺ ♇ **4:13 pm** 1:13 pm
☽ ⚺ ♆ **4:22 pm** 1:22 pm
☽ □ ♅ **5:48 pm** 2:48 pm
☽ ⚻ ♃ **9:32 pm** 6:32 pm
☽ ⚻ ☉ 10:23 pm

Eastern time in bold type
Pacific time in medium type

JULY 2026

DATE	SID.TIME	SUN	MOON	NODE	MERCURY	VENUS	MARS	JUPITER	SATURN	URANUS	NEPTUNE	PLUTO	CERES	PALLAS	JUNO	VESTA	CHIRON
1 W	18 36 16	9♋12 10	20♉13	0♋53R	26♊12R	20♊12	1♌34	0♋10	14♈11	3♊42	4♈24	4≈53R	13♊27	17♈41	9≈04R	18♈08	0♉22
2 Th	18 40 12	10 09 22	2♊14	0 47	26 04	21 20	2 16	0 23	14 14	3 45	4 25	4 51	13 51	17 53	8 55	18 26	0 24
3 F	18 44 9	11 06 34	14 22	0 43	25 51	22 27	2 59	0 35	14 16	3 48	4 25	4 50	14 15	18 05	8 45	18 44	0 25
4 Sa	18 48 5	12 03 45	26 39	0 42D	25 34	23 35	3 41	0 48	14 19	3 51	4 25	4 49	14 39	18 17	8 35	19 02	0 27
5 Su	18 52 2	13 00 57	9♋07	0 42	25 13	24 43	4 24	1 01	14 21	3 54	4 25	4 48	15 03	18 28	8 25	19 20	0 29
6 M	18 55 58	13 58 09	21 50	0 43	24 49	25 50	5 06	1 14	14 23	3 57	4 25	4 46	15 27	18 39	8 14	19 38	0 30
7 T	18 59 55	14 55 21	4♌52	0 44R	24 20	26 57	5 48	1 27	14 25	4 00	4 25R	4 45	15 51	18 50	8 03	19 55	0 32
8 W	19 3 51	15 52 34	18 15	0 45	23 49	28 05	6 31	1 40	14 27	4 03	4 25	4 44	16 15	19 01	7 52	20 12	0 33
9 Th	19 7 48	16 49 47	2♍02	0 44	23 15	29 12	7 13	1 53	14 29	4 06	4 25	4 42	16 39	19 11	7 41	20 29	0 34
10 F	19 11 45	17 47 00	16 13	0 41	22 39	0♋18	7 55	2 07	14 31	4 08	4 25	4 41	17 03	19 22	7 29	20 45	0 36
11 Sa	19 15 41	18 44 14	0♎48	0 36	22 02	1 25	8 37	2 20	14 32	4 11	4 25	4 40	17 27	19 32	7 17	21 01	0 37
12 Su	19 19 38	19 41 29	15 42	0 31	21 23	2 32	9 19	2 33	14 34	4 14	4 25	4 38	17 51	19 42	7 05	21 18	0 38
13 M	19 23 34	20 38 44	0♏46	0 25	20 44	3 38	10 01	2 46	14 35	4 16	4 24	4 37	18 15	19 51	6 52	21 33	0 39
14 T	19 27 31	21 35 59	15 53	0 20	20 06	4 44	10 43	2 59	14 37	4 19	4 24	4 36	18 38	20 01	6 40	21 49	0 40
15 W	19 31 27	22 33 15	0♐53	0 16	19 29	5 51	11 25	3 12	14 38	4 22	4 24	4 34	19 02	20 10	6 27	22 04	0 42
16 Th	19 35 24	23 30 30	15 36	0 13	18 53	6 56	12 06	3 25	14 39	4 24	4 24	4 33	19 26	20 19	6 14	22 19	0 43
17 F	19 39 20	24 27 46	0♑00	0 12D	18 20	8 02	12 48	3 39	14 40	4 27	4 23	4 32	19 49	20 28	6 00	22 34	0 44
18 Sa	19 43 17	25 25 02	13♑50	0 13	17 50	9 08	13 30	3 52	14 41	4 29	4 23	4 30	20 13	20 36	5 47	22 48	0 44
19 Su	19 47 14	26 22 18	27 17	0 14	17 23	10 13	14 11	4 05	14 42	4 32	4 23	4 29	20 36	20 44	5 33	23 03	0 45
20 M	19 51 10	27 19 35	10≈19	0 16	17 01	11 18	14 52	4 18	14 43	4 34	4 23	4 27	21 00	20 52	5 19	23 16	0 46
21 T	19 55 7	28 16 51	23 20	0 17R	16 45	12 23	15 34	4 32	14 43	4 37	4 22	4 26	21 23	21 00	5 05	23 30	0 47
22 W	19 59 3	29 14 08	5♓20	0 17	16 30	13 28	16 15	4 45	14 44	4 39	4 22	4 25	21 47	21 08	4 51	23 43	0 48
23 Th	20 3 0	0♌11 25	17 24	0 15	16 22D	14 33	16 56	4 58	14 44	4 41	4 21	4 23	22 10	21 15	4 37	23 56	0 48
24 F	20 6 56	1 08 42	29 27	0 13	16 19	15 37	17 38	5 11	14 45	4 44	4 21	4 22	22 33	21 22	4 23	24 09	0 49
25 Sa	20 10 53	2 06 00	11♈20	0 09	16 22	16 41	18 19	5 25	14 45	4 46	4 20	4 20	22 57	21 29	4 08	24 21	0 49
26 Su	20 14 49	3 03 19	23 12	0 05	16 31	17 45	19 00	5 38	14 45R	4 48	4 20	4 19	23 20	21 35	3 54	24 34	0 50
27 M	20 18 46	4 00 37	4♉49	0 00	16 45	18 49	19 41	5 51	14 45	4 50	4 19	4 18	23 43	21 41	3 40	24 45	0 50
28 T	20 22 43	4 57 57	17 03	29≈56	17 07	19 52	20 21	6 05	14 45	4 52	4 18	4 16	24 06	21 47	3 25	24 57	0 51
29 W	20 26 39	5 55 17	29 06	29 53	17 34	20 56	21 02	6 18	14 45	4 55	4 18	4 15	24 29	21 53	3 11	25 08	0 51
30 Th	20 30 36	6 52 37	11♊18	29 51	18 07	21 58	21 43	6 31	14 44	4 57	4 17	4 13	24 52	21 58	2 56	25 19	0 51
31 F	20 34 32	7 49 58	23 39	29 50D	18 46	23 01	22 24	6 44	14 44	4 59	4 16	4 12	25 15	22 03	2 42	25 29	0 52

EPHEMERIS CALCULATED FOR 12 MIDNIGHT GREENWICH MEAN TIME. ALL OTHER DATA AND FACING ASPECTARIAN PAGE IN **EASTERN TIME (BOLD)** AND PACIFIC TIME (REGULAR).

AUGUST 2026

☽ Last Aspect day	ET / hr:mn / PT		asp	☽ Ingress sign day	ET / hr:mn / PT	
2	**8:33 am**	5:33 am	☍ ♀	♈ 2	**4:37 pm**	1:37 pm
4	**2:52 pm**	11:52 am	⚹ ♂	♉ 4	**10:35 pm**	7:35 pm
6	**7:25 pm**	4:25 pm	⚹ ☿	♊ 6		11:08 pm
6	**7:25 pm**	4:25 pm	⚹ ☿	♊ 7	**2:08 am**	
8		10:27 pm	☌ ♂	♋ 9	**3:46 am**	12:46 am
9	**1:27 am**		☌ ♂	♋ 9	**3:46 am**	12:46 am
10	**3:30 am**	12:30 am	□ ♄	♌ 11	**4:38 am**	1:38 am
12	**1:37 pm**	10:37 am	☌ ☉	♍ 13	**6:18 am**	3:18 am
13	**3:24 pm**	12:24 pm	□ ♅	♎ 15	**10:20 am**	7:20 am
17	**7:31 am**	4:31 am	⚹ ☉	♏ 17	**5:46 pm**	2:46 pm
19	**10:46 pm**	7:46 pm	□ ☉	♐ 20	**4:30 am**	1:30 am
22	**4:31 pm**	1:31 pm	△ ☉	♑ 22	**4:59 pm**	1:59 pm
23		11:30 pm	□ ♀	♒ 25	**5:02 am**	2:02 am
24	**2:30 am**		□ ♀	♒ 25	**5:02 am**	2:02 am
26	**5:59 pm**	2:59 pm	△ ♀	♓ 27	**3:04 pm**	12:04 pm
28	**12:14 pm**	9:14 am	△ ♂	♈ 29	**10:38 pm**	7:38 pm
31	**3:47 pm**	12:47 pm	☍ ♀	♉ 9/1	**4:01 am**	1:01 am

☽ Phases & Eclipses phase	day	ET / hr:mn / PT	
4th Quarter	5	**10:21 pm**	7:21 pm
New Moon	12	**1:37 pm**	10:37 am
●	12	20° ♌ 02'	
2nd Quarter	19	**10:46 pm**	7:46 pm
Full Moon	27		9:18 pm
Full Moon	28	**12:18 am**	
●	28	4° ♓ 54'	

Planet Ingress	day	ET / hr:mn / PT	
☿ ♌	9	**12:28 pm**	9:28 pm
♂ ♋	11	**4:30 am**	1:30 am
⚵ ♑	11	**10:45 am**	7:45 am
⚳ ♋	12	**10:58 am**	7:48 am
☉ ♍	22	**10:19 pm**	7:19 pm
☿ ♍	25	**7:04 am**	4:04 am

Planetary Motion	day	ET / hr:mn / PT	
⚷ ℞	3	**4:10 pm**	1:10 pm
♀ ℞	14	**5:39 am**	2:39 am
⚶ ℞	25	**1:58 pm**	10:58 am

1 SATURDAY
☽ ⚻ ☉ **1:23 am**
☽ ⚺ ♄ **12:11 pm** 9:11 am
☽ △ ☿ **10:59 pm** 7:59 pm

2 SUNDAY
☽ □ ♂ **5:33 am** 2:33 am
☽ ☍ ♀ **8:33 am** 5:33 am
☽ ⚹ ♇ 9:11 pm
☽ ☌ ♆ 9:22 pm
☽ ⚹ ♅ 10:56 pm

3 MONDAY
☽ ⚹ ♇ **12:11 am**
☽ ☌ ♆ **12:22 am**
☽ ⚹ ♅ **1:56 am**
☽ △ ♃ **6:20 am** 3:20 am
☽ △ ☉ **1:25 pm** 10:25 am
☽ ☌ ♄ **7:22 pm** 4:22 pm

4 TUESDAY
☽ □ ☿ **10:17 am** 7:17 am
☽ ⚹ ♂ **2:52 pm** 11:52 am
☽ ⚻ ♀ **7:20 pm** 4:20 pm

5 WEDNESDAY
☽ □ ♇ **5:43 am** 2:43 am
☽ ⚺ ♆ **5:57 am** 2:57 am
☽ ⚺ ♅ **7:36 am** 4:36 am
☽ □ ♃ **12:34 pm** 9:34 am
☽ □ ☉ **10:21 pm** 7:21 pm
☽ ⚺ ♄ 9:04 pm

6 THURSDAY
☽ ⚺ ♄ **12:04 am**
☽ ⚹ ☿ **7:25 pm** 4:25 pm
☽ ⚺ ♂ **9:18 pm** 6:18 pm
☉ △ ♄ **10:44 pm** 7:44 pm
☽ △ ♀ 11:57 pm

7 FRIDAY
☽ △ ♀ **2:57 am**
☽ △ ♇ **8:53 am** 5:53 am
☽ ⚹ ♆ **9:07 am** 6:07 am
☽ ☌ ♅ **10:52 am** 7:52 am
☽ ⚹ ♃ **4:18 pm** 1:18 pm
☽ ⚹ ♄ 11:30 pm

8 SATURDAY
☽ ⚹ ♄ **2:30 am**
☽ ⚹ ☉ **4:30 am** 1:30 am
☿ ⚺ ♂ **5:32 am** 2:32 am
☽ ☌ ♂ 10:27 pm
☽ ⚺ ☿ 11:44 pm

9 SUNDAY
☽ ☌ ♂ **1:27 am**
☽ ⚺ ☿ **2:44 am**
☽ □ ♀ **8:11 am** 5:11 am
☽ ⚻ ♇ **10:15 am** 7:15 am
☽ □ ♆ **10:30 am** 7:30 am
☽ ⚺ ♅ **12:21 pm** 9:21 am
☽ ⚺ ♃ **6:20 pm** 3:20 pm

10 MONDAY
☽ □ ♄ **3:30 am** 12:30 am
☽ ⚺ ☉ **8:58 am** 5:58 am
♀ △ ♇ **2:09 pm** 11:09 am
♀ ☍ ♆ **6:02 pm** 3:02 pm

11 TUESDAY
☽ ⚺ ♂ **4:39 am** 1:39 am
☽ ☌ ☿ **9:41 am** 6:41 am
☽ ☍ ♇ **11:04 am** 8:04 am
☽ △ ♆ **11:20 am** 8:20 am
☽ ⚹ ♀ **12:36 pm** 9:36 am
☽ ⚹ ♅ **1:20 pm** 10:20 am
☽ ☌ ♃ **8:01 pm** 5:01 pm
☿ ☍ ♇ **9:20 pm** 6:20 pm
☿ △ ♆ **11:39 pm** 8:39 pm
♀ △ ♅ **11:46 pm** 8:46 pm

12 WEDNESDAY
☽ △ ♄ **4:28 am** 1:28 am
☽ ☌ ☉ **1:37 pm** 10:37 am
☿ ⚹ ♅ **4:48 pm** 1:48 pm

13 THURSDAY
☽ ⚹ ♂ **8:44 am** 5:44 am
☿ ⚹ ♀ **12:23 pm** 9:23 am
☽ ⚻ ♇ **12:53 pm** 9:53 am
☽ ⚻ ♆ **1:11 pm** 10:11 am
☽ □ ♅ **3:24 pm** 12:24 pm
☽ ⚺ ♀ **6:16 pm** 3:16 pm
☽ ⚺ ☿ **6:41 pm** 3:41 pm
☽ ⚺ ♃ **11:04 pm** 8:04 pm

14 FRIDAY
☽ ⚻ ♄ **7:00 am** 4:00 am
☽ ⚺ ☉ **8:33 pm** 5:33 pm

15 SATURDAY
☿ ☌ ♃ **7:23 am** 4:23 am
☽ □ ♂ **3:37 pm** 12:37 pm
☽ △ ♇ **5:13 pm** 2:13 pm
☽ ☍ ♆ **5:33 pm** 2:33 pm
☽ △ ♅ **8:04 pm** 5:04 pm

16 SUNDAY
☽ ☌ ♀ **3:11 am** 12:11 am
☽ ⚹ ♃ **5:03 am** 2:03 am
☽ ⚹ ☿ **8:20 am** 5:20 am
☽ ☍ ♄ **12:27 pm** 9:27 am
♂ ⚻ ♇ **11:15 pm** 8:15 pm

17 MONDAY
♂ □ ♆ **5:52 am** 2:52 am
☽ ⚹ ☉ **7:31 am** 4:31 am
☿ △ ♄ **11:27 am** 8:27 am
♀ ⚹ ♃ **12:16 pm** 9:16 am
☽ □ ♇ 10:01 pm
☽ ⚻ ♆ 10:23 pm
☽ △ ♂ 11:29 pm

18 TUESDAY
☽ □ ♇ **1:01 am**
☽ ⚻ ♆ **1:23 am**
☽ △ ♂ **2:29 am**
☽ ⚻ ♅ **4:15 am** 1:15 am
☽ □ ♃ **2:43 pm** 11:43 am
☽ ⚺ ♀ **4:24 pm** 1:24 pm
☽ ⚻ ♄ **9:25 pm** 6:25 pm

19 WEDNESDAY
☽ □ ☿ **4:06 am** 1:06 am
♂ ⚺ ♅ **1:00 pm** 10:00 am
☽ □ ☉ **10:46 pm** 7:46 pm

20 THURSDAY
☽ ⚹ ♇ **11:59 am** 8:59 am
☽ △ ♆ **12:22 pm** 9:22 am
☽ ☍ ♅ **3:33 pm** 12:33 pm
☽ ⚻ ♂ **5:02 pm** 2:02 pm

21 FRIDAY
☽ △ ♃ **3:26 am** 12:26 am
⚳ ☍ ♄ **8:43 am** 5:43 am
☽ △ ♄ **9:02 am** 6:02 am
☽ ⚹ ♀ **9:04 am** 6:04 am

22 SATURDAY
☽ △ ☿ **4:22 am** 1:22 am
☽ △ ☉ **4:31 pm** 1:31 pm
☽ ⚺ ♇ 9:25 pm
☽ □ ♆ 9:48 pm

23 SUNDAY
☽ ⚺ ♇ **12:25 am**
☽ □ ♆ **12:48 am**
☽ ⚻ ♅ **4:11 am** 1:11 am
☽ ☍ ♂ **9:05 am** 6:05 am
☽ ⚻ ♃ **5:07 pm** 2:07 pm
☽ □ ♄ **9:21 pm** 6:21 pm
☽ □ ♀ 11:30 pm

24 MONDAY
☽ □ ♀ **2:30 am**

25 TUESDAY
☽ ⚻ ☿ **4:38 am** 1:38 am
☽ ⚻ ☉ **9:44 am** 6:44 am
☽ ☌ ♇ **12:11 pm** 9:11 am
☽ ⚹ ♆ **12:32 pm** 9:32 am
☽ △ ♅ **4:01 pm** 1:01 pm
☽ ⚻ ♂ 9:00 pm

26 WEDNESDAY
☽ ⚻ ♂ **12:00 am**
☽ ☍ ♃ **5:32 am** 2:32 am
☽ ⚹ ♄ **8:21 am** 5:21 am
☉ ⚻ ♇ **4:10 pm** 1:10 pm
☽ △ ♀ **5:59 pm** 2:59 pm
☉ ⚻ ♆ **8:31 pm** 5:31 pm
☿ ⚻ ♇ 11:42 pm

27 THURSDAY
☿ ⚻ ♇ **2:42 am**
☿ ⚻ ♆ **4:50 am** 1:50 am
☉ ☌ ☿ **1:04 pm** 10:04 am
☽ ⚺ ♇ **9:50 pm** 6:50 pm
☽ ⚺ ♆ **10:10 pm** 7:10 pm
☽ ☍ ☉ 9:18 pm
☽ ☍ ☿ 10:20 pm
☽ □ ♅ 10:39 pm

28 FRIDAY
☽ ☍ ☉ **12:18 am**
☽ ☍ ☿ **1:20 am**
☽ □ ♅ **1:39 am**
☿ □ ♅ **3:25 am** 12:25 am
☽ △ ♂ **12:14 pm** 9:14 am
☽ ⚻ ♃ **3:29 pm** 12:29 pm
☽ ⚺ ♄ **5:01 pm** 2:01 pm
☉ □ ♅ **6:19 pm** 3:19 pm

29 SATURDAY
☽ ⚻ ♀ **6:21 am** 3:21 am

30 SUNDAY
☽ ⚹ ♇ **5:02 am** 2:02 am
☽ ☌ ♆ **5:20 am** 2:20 am
☽ ⚹ ♅ **8:49 am** 5:49 am
☽ ⚻ ☉ **11:48 am** 8:48 am
☽ ⚻ ☿ **5:46 pm** 2:46 pm
☽ □ ♂ **9:39 pm** 6:39 pm
☽ △ ♃ **10:55 pm** 7:55 pm
☽ ☌ ♄ **11:18 pm** 8:18 pm

31 MONDAY
☽ ☍ ♀ **3:47 pm** 12:47 pm
♃ △ ♄ **6:17 pm** 3:17 pm

Eastern time in bold type
Pacific time in medium type

AUGUST 2026

DATE	SID.TIME	SUN	MOON	NODE	MERCURY	VENUS	MARS	JUPITER	SATURN	URANUS	NEPTUNE	PLUTO	CERES	PALLAS	JUNO	VESTA	CHIRON
1 Sa	20 38 29	8♌47 21	6♓10	29≈50	19♋31	24♍04	23♊04	6♋58	14♈44R	5♊01	4♈16R	4≈11R	25♋38	22♈07	2≈27R	25♈39	0♉52
2 Su	20 42 25	9 44 44	18 53	29 50	20 22	25 06	23 45	7 11	14 43	5 03	4 15	4 09	26 01	22 12	2 13	25 49	0 52
3 M	20 46 22	10 42 08	1♈51	29 52	21 19	26 08	24 25	7 24	14 42	5 04	4 14	4 08	26 24	22 16	1 59	25 59	0 52R
4 T	20 50 18	11 39 33	15 03	29 53	22 22	27 09	25 05	7 38	14 42	5 06	4 13	4 06	26 47	22 20	1 44	26 08	0 52
5 W	20 54 15	12 37 00	28 32	29 54	23 30	28 10	25 46	7 51	14 41	5 08	4 12	4 05	27 09	22 23	1 30	26 17	0 52
6 Th	20 58 12	13 34 27	12♉18	29 54R	24 44	29 11	26 26	8 04	14 40	5 10	4 11	4 04	27 32	22 26	1 16	26 25	0 52
7 F	21 2 8	14 31 56	26 22	29 54	26 03	0♎12	27 06	8 17	14 39	5 12	4 10	4 02	27 54	22 29	1 02	26 33	0 52
8 Sa	21 6 5	15 29 27	10♊42	29 53	27 27	1 12	27 46	8 31	14 37	5 13	4 10	4 01	28 17	22 31	0 48	26 41	0 52
9 Su	21 10 1	16 26 59	25 15	29 52	28 56	2 12	28 26	8 44	14 36	5 15	4 09	3 59	28 39	22 34	0 35	26 48	0 51
10 M	21 13 58	17 24 32	9♋58	29 50	0♌30	3 12	29 06	8 57	14 35	5 16	4 08	3 58	29 02	22 35	0 21	26 55	0 51
11 T	21 17 54	18 22 06	24 42	29 49	2 08	4 12	29 46	9 10	14 33	5 18	4 07	3 57	29 24	22 37	0 08	27 01	0 51
12 W	21 21 51	19 19 42	9♌23	29 48D	3 50	5 10	0♋26	9 23	14 32	5 19	4 06	3 55	29 46	22 38	29♑55R	27 07	0 50
13 Th	21 25 48	20 17 19	23 52	29 48	5 35	6 09	1 05	9 37	14 30	5 21	4 04	3 54	0♌06	22 39R	29 42	27 13	0 50
14 F	21 29 44	21 14 57	8♍04	29 48	7 24	7 07	1 45	9 50	14 28	5 22	4 03	3 53	0 30	22 39	29 29	27 18	0 49
15 Sa	21 33 41	22 12 35	21 55	29 48	9 15	8 05	2 24	10 03	14 26	5 24	4 02	3 51	0 52	22 39	29 17	27 23	0 49
16 Su	21 37 37	23 10 15	5♎23	29 49	11 09	9 03	3 04	10 16	14 24	5 25	4 01	3 50	1 14	22 38	29 05	27 27	0 48
17 M	21 41 34	24 07 56	18 27	29 49	13 05	10 00	3 43	10 29	14 22	5 26	4 00	3 49	1 36	22 38	28 53	27 32	0 47
18 T	21 45 30	25 05 39	1♏10	29 49	15 03	10 56	4 23	10 42	14 20	5 27	3 59	3 47	1 58	22 36	28 41	27 35	0 47
19 W	21 49 27	26 03 22	13 35	29 50	17 02	11 52	5 02	10 55	14 18	5 29	3 58	3 46	2 20	22 35	28 30	27 38	0 46
20 Th	21 53 23	27 01 06	25 44	29 50R	19 02	12 48	5 41	11 08	14 16	5 30	3 56	3 45	2 41	22 33	28 19	27 41	0 45
21 F	21 57 20	27 58 52	7♐44	29 50	21 02	13 43	6 20	11 21	14 13	5 31	3 55	3 44	3 03	22 31	28 08	27 43	0 44
22 Sa	22 1 16	28 56 38	19 37	29 50D	23 03	14 37	6 59	11 34	14 11	5 32	3 54	3 42	3 24	22 28	27 58	27 45	0 43
23 Su	22 5 13	29 54 26	1♑30	29 50	25 04	15 31	7 38	11 47	14 08	5 33	3 52	3 41	3 45	22 25	27 48	27 47	0 42
24 M	22 9 10	0♍52 15	13 25	29 50	27 05	16 25	8 16	12 00	14 06	5 34	3 51	3 40	4 07	22 21	27 38	27 48	0 41
25 T	22 13 6	1 50 05	25 26	29 51	29 05	17 18	8 55	12 13	14 03	5 35	3 50	3 39	4 28	22 18	27 29	27 48R	0 40
26 W	22 17 3	2 47 56	7♒37	29 51R	1♍04	18 10	9 34	12 26	14 00	5 36	3 48	3 38	4 49	22 13	27 20	27 48	0 39
27 Th	22 20 59	3 45 49	20 00	29 51	3 03	19 02	10 12	12 38	13 57	5 37	3 47	3 36	5 10	22 09	27 11	27 48	0 38
28 F	22 24 56	4 43 43	2♓37	29 50	5 01	19 53	10 51	12 51	13 54	5 38	3 46	3 35	5 31	22 04	27 03	27 47	0 37
29 Sa	22 28 52	5 41 39	15 28	29 50	6 58	20 43	11 29	13 04	13 51	5 38	3 44	3 34	5 51	21 58	26 55	27 46	0 35
30 Su	22 32 49	6 39 36	28 33	29 50	8 54	21 33	12 07	13 17	13 47	5 39	3 43	3 33	6 12	21 52	26 48	27 44	0 34
31 M	22 36 45	7 37 35	11♈53	29 49	10 48	22 22	12 46	13 29	13 44	5 39	3 41	3 32	6 33	21 46	26 40	27 42	0 33

EPHEMERIS CALCULATED FOR 12 MIDNIGHT GREENWICH MEAN TIME. ALL OTHER DATA AND FACING ASPECTARIAN PAGE IN **EASTERN TIME (BOLD)** AND PACIFIC TIME (REGULAR).

SEPTEMBER 2026

☽ Last Aspect day	ET / hr:mn / PT	asp	☽ Ingress sign	day	ET / hr:mn / PT
8/31	**3:47 pm** 12:47 pm	☍♀	♉	1	**4:01 am** 1:01 am
2	**6:47 am** 3:47 am	△☿	♊	3	**7:47 am** 4:47 am
5	**4:40 am** 1:40 am	△♀	♋	5	**10:30 am** 7:30 am
7	**9:40 am** 6:40 am	□♀	♌	7	**12:49 pm** 9:49 am
9	**2:58 pm** 11:58 am	⚹♀	♍	9	**3:35 pm** 12:35 pm
10	10:52 pm	⚹♂	♎	11	**7:52 pm** 4:52 pm
11	**1:52 am**	⚹♂	♎	11	**7:52 pm** 4:52 pm
13	**10:27 am** 7:27 am	□♂	♏	13	11:44 pm
13	**10:27 am** 7:27 am	□♂	♏	14	**2:44 am**
15	**11:30 pm** 8:30 pm	⚹☉	♐	16	**12:41 pm** 9:41 am
18	**4:44 pm** 1:44 pm	□☉	♑	18	9:55 pm
18	**4:44 pm** 1:44 pm	□☉	♑	19	**12:55 am**
21	**10:31 am** 7:31 am	△☉	♒	21	**1:14 pm** 10:14 am
23	**4:18 am** 1:18 am	△☿	♓	23	**11:24 pm** 8:24 pm
26	**4:32 am** 1:32 am	△♂	♈	26	**6:23 am** 3:23 am
28	**5:50 am** 2:50 am	☍☿	♉	28	**10:40 am** 7:40 am
29	**7:36 pm** 4:36 pm	□♃	♊	30	**1:26 pm** 10:26 am

☽ Phases & Eclipses phase	day	ET / hr:mn / PT
4th Quarter	4	**3:51 am** 12:51 am
New Moon	10	**11:27 pm** 8:27 pm
2nd Quarter	18	**4:44 pm** 1:44 pm
Full Moon	26	**12:49 pm** 9:49 am

Planet Ingress	day	ET / hr:mn / PT
♀ ♏	10	**4:07 am** 1:07 am
☿ ♎	10	**12:21 pm** 9:21 am
⚷ ♈	17	**9:51 pm** 6:51 pm
☉ ♎	22	**8:05 pm** 5:05 pm
♂ ♌	27	**10:49 pm** 7:49 pm
☿ ♏	30	**7:44 am** 4:44 am

Planetary Motion		day	ET / hr:mn / PT
♅	℞	10	**2:27 pm** 11:27 am
⚵	D	16	**9:09 pm** 6:09 pm

1 TUESDAY		
♂ □ ♄	**5:59 am**	2:59 am
☿ ⚻ ♄	**8:09 am**	5:09 am
☿ ⚹ ♂	**9:21 am**	6:21 am
☽ □ ♇	**10:08 am**	7:08 am
☿ ⚺ ♃	**10:22 am**	7:22 am
☽ ⚺ ♆	**10:24 am**	7:24 am
♂ ⚺ ♃	**1:20 pm**	10:20 am
☽ ⚺ ♅	**1:54 pm**	10:54 am
☽ △ ☉	**8:43 pm**	5:43 pm
2 WEDNESDAY		
☽ ⚺ ♄	**3:40 am**	12:40 am
☽ □ ♃	**4:19 am**	1:19 am
☽ ⚹ ♂	**4:48 am**	1:48 am
☽ △ ☿	**6:47 am**	3:47 am
☽ ⚻ ♀	**10:58 pm**	7:58 pm
3 THURSDAY		
☽ △ ♇	**1:41 pm**	10:41 am
☽ ⚹ ♆	**1:55 pm**	10:55 am
☽ ☌ ♅	**5:27 pm**	2:27 pm
4 FRIDAY		
☽ □ ☉	**3:51 am**	12:51 am
☽ ⚹ ♄	**6:40 am**	3:40 am
☽ ⚹ ♃	**8:17 am**	5:17 am
☽ ⚺ ♂	**10:22 am**	7:22 am
☽ □ ☿	**5:29 pm**	2:29 pm
5 SATURDAY		
☽ △ ♀	**4:40 am**	1:40 am
☽ ⚻ ♇	**4:16 pm**	1:16 pm
☽ □ ♆	**4:28 pm**	1:28 pm
☉ ⚻ ♄	**6:48 pm**	3:48 pm
☽ ⚺ ♅	**8:03 pm**	5:03 pm
6 SUNDAY		
☽ □ ♄	**8:54 am**	5:54 am
☽ ⚹ ☉	**10:00 am**	7:00 am
☽ ⚺ ♃	**11:27 am**	8:27 am
☽ ☌ ♂	**3:06 pm**	12:06 pm
7 MONDAY		
☽ ⚹ ☿	**3:01 am**	12:01 am
☽ □ ♀	**9:40 am**	6:40 am
☉ ⚺ ♃	**12:59 pm**	9:59 am
☽ ☍ ♇	**6:31 pm**	3:31 pm
☽ △ ♆	**6:41 pm**	3:41 pm
☽ ⚹ ♅	**10:24 pm**	7:24 pm
8 TUESDAY		
☽ △ ♄	**11:04 am**	8:04 am
☽ ☌ ♃	**2:37 pm**	11:37 am
☽ ⚺ ☉	**4:06 pm**	1:06 pm
☽ ⚺ ♂	**7:52 pm**	4:52 pm
9 WEDNESDAY		
☽ ⚺ ☿	**12:43 pm**	9:43 am
☽ ⚹ ♀	**2:58 pm**	11:58 am
☽ ⚻ ♇	**9:21 pm**	6:21 pm
☽ ⚻ ♆	**9:28 pm**	6:28 pm
☽ □ ♅		10:22 pm
10 THURSDAY		
☽ □ ♅	**1:22 am**	
☽ ⚻ ♄	**2:07 pm**	11:07 am
☿ ⚺ ♀	**5:30 pm**	2:30 pm
☽ ⚺ ♃	**6:46 pm**	3:46 pm
☽ ☌ ☉	**11:27 pm**	8:27 pm
☽ ⚹ ♂		10:52 pm
11 FRIDAY		
☽ ⚹ ♂	**1:52 am**	
☽ ⚺ ♀	**9:51 pm**	6:51 pm
☽ ☌ ☿		9:21 pm
☽ △ ♇		10:48 pm
☽ ☍ ♆		10:54 pm
12 SATURDAY		
☽ ☌ ☿	**12:21 am**	
☽ △ ♇	**1:48 am**	
☽ ☍ ♆	**1:54 am**	
☽ △ ♅	**6:03 am**	3:03 am
☿ △ ♇	**11:59 am**	8:59 am
☿ ☍ ♆	**12:38 pm**	9:38 am
☽ ☍ ♄	**7:08 pm**	4:08 pm
☽ ⚹ ♃		10:08 pm
13 SUNDAY		
☽ ⚹ ♃	**1:08 am**	
☽ ⚺ ☉	**9:33 am**	6:33 am
☽ □ ♂	**10:27 am**	7:27 am
☿ △ ♅	**10:40 pm**	7:40 pm
14 MONDAY		
☽ ☌ ♀	**7:33 am**	4:33 am
☽ □ ♇	**8:57 am**	5:57 am
☽ ⚻ ♆	**8:59 am**	5:59 am
☽ ⚻ ♅	**1:29 pm**	10:29 am
☽ ⚺ ☿	**3:41 pm**	12:41 pm
☉ ⚹ ♂	**3:53 pm**	12:53 pm
15 TUESDAY		
☽ ⚻ ♄	**3:01 am**	12:01 am
☽ □ ♃	**10:36 am**	7:36 am
♀ □ ♇	**2:35 pm**	11:35 am
♀ ⚻ ♆	**2:46 pm**	11:46 am
♆ ⚹ ♇	**9:47 pm**	6:47 pm
☽ △ ♂	**10:31 pm**	7:31 pm
☽ ⚹ ☉	**11:30 pm**	8:30 pm
16 WEDNESDAY		
☽ △ ♆	**7:08 pm**	4:08 pm
☽ ⚹ ♇	**7:09 pm**	4:09 pm
☽ ⚺ ♀	**8:30 pm**	5:30 pm
☽ ☍ ♅	**11:58 pm**	8:58 pm
17 THURSDAY		
☽ ⚹ ☿	**11:14 am**	8:14 am
☽ △ ♄	**1:47 pm**	10:47 am
☽ △ ♃	**11:01 pm**	8:01 pm
18 FRIDAY		
☿ ☍ ♄	**6:01 am**	3:01 am
☽ ⚻ ♂	**1:35 pm**	10:35 am
☽ □ ☉	**4:44 pm**	1:44 pm
19 SATURDAY		
☽ □ ♆	**7:21 am**	4:21 am
☽ ⚺ ♇	**7:27 am**	4:27 am
☽ ⚹ ♀	**11:27 am**	8:27 am
☽ ⚻ ♅	**12:22 pm**	9:22 am
☽ □ ♄		10:59 pm
20 SUNDAY		
☽ □ ♄	**1:59 am**	
☽ □ ☿	**8:48 am**	5:48 am
♀ ⚻ ♅	**11:49 am**	8:49 am
☽ ⚻ ♃	**12:37 pm**	9:37 am
21 MONDAY		
☽ ☍ ♂	**5:17 am**	2:17 am
☽ △ ☉	**10:31 am**	7:31 am
☿ ⚹ ♃	**6:51 pm**	3:51 pm
☽ ⚹ ♆	**7:24 pm**	4:24 pm
☽ ☌ ♇	**7:35 pm**	4:35 pm
☽ △ ♅		9:24 pm
☽ □ ♀		10:40 pm
22 TUESDAY		
☽ △ ♅	**12:24 am**	
☽ □ ♀	**1:40 am**	
☽ ⚹ ♄	**1:17 pm**	10:17 am
☽ ☍ ♃		9:47 pm
23 WEDNESDAY		
☽ ☍ ♃	**12:47 am**	
☽ △ ☿	**4:18 am**	1:18 am
☽ ⚻ ♂	**6:43 pm**	3:43 pm
☽ ⚻ ☉		10:40 pm
24 THURSDAY		
☽ ⚻ ☉	**1:40 am**	
☽ ⚺ ♆	**5:07 am**	2:07 am
☽ ⚺ ♇	**5:22 am**	2:22 am
☽ □ ♅	**9:56 am**	6:56 am
☽ △ ♀	**12:46 pm**	9:46 am
☽ ⚺ ♄	**9:50 pm**	6:50 pm
25 FRIDAY		
☽ ⚻ ♃	**9:51 am**	6:51 am
☽ ⚻ ☿	**7:13 pm**	4:13 pm
☉ ☍ ♆	**9:36 pm**	6:36 pm
☉ △ ♇		10:35 pm
26 SATURDAY		
☉ △ ♇	**1:35 am**	
☽ △ ♂	**4:32 am**	1:32 am
☽ ☌ ♆	**11:41 am**	8:41 am
☽ ⚹ ♇	**12:00 pm**	9:00 am
☽ ☍ ☉	**12:49 pm**	9:49 am
☽ ⚹ ♅	**4:18 pm**	1:18 pm
☽ ⚻ ♀	**8:07 pm**	5:07 pm
27 SUNDAY		
☽ ☌ ♄	**3:20 am**	12:20 am
☽ △ ♃	**3:46 pm**	12:46 pm
28 MONDAY		
☽ ☍ ☿	**5:50 am**	2:50 am
☽ □ ♂	**11:11 am**	8:11 am
☉ △ ♅	**12:22 pm**	9:22 am
☽ ⚺ ♆	**3:39 pm**	12:39 pm
☽ □ ♇	**4:02 pm**	1:02 pm
☽ ⚺ ♅	**8:09 pm**	5:09 pm
☽ ⚻ ☉	**8:44 pm**	5:44 pm
☽ ☍ ♀		9:35 pm
29 TUESDAY		
☽ ☍ ♀	**12:35 am**	
☽ ⚺ ♄	**6:34 am**	3:34 am
☽ □ ♃	**7:36 pm**	4:36 pm
30 WEDNESDAY		
☽ ⚻ ☿	**2:01 pm**	11:01 am
☽ ⚹ ♂	**4:07 pm**	1:07 pm
☽ ⚹ ♆	**6:15 pm**	3:15 pm
☽ △ ♇	**6:41 pm**	3:41 pm
☽ ☌ ♅	**10:43 pm**	7:43 pm

Eastern time in bold type
Pacific time in medium type

SEPTEMBER 2026

DATE	SID. TIME	SUN	MOON	NODE	MERCURY	VENUS	MARS	JUPITER	SATURN	URANUS	NEPTUNE	PLUTO	CERES	PALLAS	JUNO	VESTA	CHIRON
1 T	22 40 42	8♍35 36	25♈26	29♒48R	12♍42	23♎10	13♋24	13♌43	13♈41R	5♊39	3♈40R	3♒31R	6♋53	21♍39R	26♉34R	27♈40R	0♈31R
2 W	22 44 39	9 33 39	9♉11	29 47	14 35	23 58	14 02	13 55	13 37	5 40	3 38	3 30	7 13	21 32	26 27	27 36	0 30
3 Th	22 48 35	10 31 43	23 06	29 46	16 26	24 45	14 40	14 07	13 34	5 40	3 37	3 29	7 34	21 25	26 21	27 33	0 28
4 F	22 52 32	11 29 50	7♊11	29 46D	18 16	25 30	15 17	14 20	13 30	5 41	3 36	3 28	7 54	21 17	26 16	27 29	0 27
5 Sa	22 56 28	12 27 58	21 23	29 46	20 05	26 15	15 55	14 32	13 27	5 41	3 34	3 27	8 14	21 09	26 10	27 24	0 25
6 Su	23 0 25	13 26 09	5♋39	29 46	21 52	27 00	16 33	14 44	13 23	5 41	3 32	3 25	8 34	21 00	26 06	27 20	0 23
7 M	23 4 21	14 24 22	19 58	29 48	23 39	27 43	17 10	14 57	13 19	5 41	3 31	3 25	8 53	20 51	26 01	27 14	0 22
8 T	23 8 18	15 22 36	4♌16	29 49	25 24	28 25	17 48	15 09	13 15	5 42	3 29	3 24	9 13	20 41	25 57	27 08	0 21
9 W	23 12 14	16 20 53	18 30	29 49	27 08	29 06	18 25	15 21	13 12	5 42	3 28	3 23	9 33	20 31	25 54	27 02	0 18
10 Th	23 16 11	17 19 11	2♍35	29 50	28 51	29 47	19 03	15 34	13 08	5 42R	3 26	3 22	9 52	20 21	25 51	26 55	0 16
11 F	23 20 8	18 17 31	16 27	29 49	0♎32	0♏26	19 40	15 46	13 04	5 42	3 25	3 21	10 11	20 10	25 48	26 48	0 14
12 Sa	23 24 4	19 15 53	0♎05	29 47	2 13	1 04	20 17	15 58	13 00	5 42	3 23	3 20	10 30	19 59	25 45	26 40	0 12
13 Su	23 28 1	20 14 17	13 24	29 45	3 52	1 41	20 54	16 10	12 55	5 42	3 21	3 19	10 49	19 47	25 44	26 32	0 11
14 M	23 31 57	21 12 42	26 25	29 42	5 31	2 16	21 31	16 22	12 51	5 41	3 20	3 18	11 08	19 35	25 42	26 24	0 09
15 T	23 35 54	22 11 10	9♏06	29 38	7 08	2 51	22 07	16 34	12 47	5 41	3 18	3 17	11 27	19 23	25 41	26 15	0 06
16 W	23 39 50	23 09 39	21 31	29 35	8 44	3 24	22 44	16 46	12 43	5 41	3 17	3 17	11 46	19 11	25 40	26 06	0 04
17 Th	23 43 47	24 08 09	3♐41	29 33	10 19	3 56	23 21	16 58	12 38	5 41	3 15	3 16	12 04	18 58	25 40D	25 56	0 02
18 F	23 47 43	25 06 41	15 41	29 31D	11 53	4 26	23 57	17 09	12 34	5 40	3 13	3 15	12 22	18 44	25 41	25 46	0 00
19 Sa	23 51 40	26 05 15	27 34	29 31	13 26	4 55	24 34	17 21	12 30	5 40	3 12	3 14	12 40	18 31	25 42	25 35	29♓58
20 Su	23 55 37	27 03 51	9♑26	29 31	14 58	5 22	25 10	17 33	12 25	5 40	3 10	3 14	12 58	18 17	25 42	25 24	29 56
21 M	23 59 33	28 02 28	21 21	29 33	16 29	5 46	25 46	17 44	12 21	5 39	3 08	3 13	13 16	18 02	25 43	25 13	29 54
22 T	0 3 30	29 01 07	3♒25	29 35	17 59	6 12	26 22	17 56	12 16	5 39	3 07	3 12	13 34	17 48	25 45	25 01	29 51
23 W	0 7 26	29 59 47	15 41	29 37R	19 28	6 35	26 58	18 07	12 12	5 38	3 05	3 12	13 51	17 33	25 47	24 49	29 49
24 Th	0 11 23	0♎58 30	28 12	29 36	20 56	6 55	27 34	18 18	12 07	5 37	3 03	3 11	14 09	17 18	25 50	24 37	29 47
25 F	0 15 19	1 57 14	11♓02	29 36	22 23	7 13	28 09	18 30	12 03	5 37	3 02	3 10	14 26	17 02	25 53	24 25	29 44
26 Sa	0 19 16	2 56 00	24 12	29 34	23 49	7 30	28 45	18 41	11 58	5 36	3 00	3 10	14 43	16 47	25 56	24 12	29 42
27 Su	0 23 12	3 54 47	7♈41	29 30	25 13	7 45	29 20	18 52	11 53	5 35	2 58	3 09	15 00	16 31	26 00	23 59	29 39
28 M	0 27 9	4 53 37	21 28	29 25	26 37	7 58	29 56	19 03	11 49	5 34	2 57	3 09	15 16	16 15	26 04	23 45	29 37
29 T	0 31 6	5 52 29	5♉28	29 20	27 59	8 08	0♌31	19 14	11 44	5 33	2 55	3 08	15 33	15 58	26 09	23 31	29 34
30 W	0 35 2	6 51 23	19 39	29 14	29 21	8 17	1 06	19 25	11 39	5 33	2 53	3 08	15 49	15 42	26 14	23 17	29 32

EPHEMERIS CALCULATED FOR 12 MIDNIGHT GREENWICH MEAN TIME. ALL OTHER DATA AND FACING ASPECTARIAN PAGE IN **EASTERN TIME (BOLD)** AND PACIFIC TIME (REGULAR).

OCTOBER 2026

D Last Aspect

day	ET / hr:mn / PT	asp
1	10:42 pm 7:42 pm	✶ ♄
3	11:08 am 8:08 am	♂ ⚷
6	6:22 am 3:22 am	□ ♂
7	2:57 pm 11:57 am	✶ ♀
10	7:07 pm 4:07 pm	✶ ♀
13	4:46 am 1:46 am	✶ ♆
15	5:56 pm 2:56 pm	△ ♀
18	12:13 pm 9:13 am	△ ♄
21	4:42 am 1:42 am	□ ♂
22	11:31 pm 8:31 pm	□ ♀

D Ingress

sign	day	ET / hr:mn / PT
⚷	2	3:54 am 12:54 am
♐	4	6:54 am 3:54 am
♑	6	10:53 am 7:53 am
≈	9	5:43 pm 2:43 pm
♓	11	11:21 am 8:21 am
♈	13	6:59 pm 3:59 pm
♉	16	8:57 am 5:57 am

D Last Aspect

day	ET / hr:mn / PT	asp
25	6:59 pm 3:59 pm	□ ♀
27	10:51 am 7:51 am	♂ ♂
29	5:43 pm 2:43 pm	△ ♀
31	6:00 am 3:00 am	✶ ♀
31	6:00 am 3:00 am	□ ♀

D Ingress

sign	day	ET / hr:mn / PT
♊	25	7:35 pm 4:35 pm
♋	27	9:02 pm 6:02 pm
♌	29	10:06 pm 7:06 pm
♍	31	12:18 am 9:18 pm

Phases & Eclipses

phase	day	ET / hr:mn / PT	
4th Quarter	9	9:25 am 6:25 am	
New Moon	1C	11:50 am 8:50 am	
2nd Quarter	1C	12:13 pm 9:13 am	
Full Moon	25	12:12 am	
Full Moon	26	12:12 am	

Planet Ingress

	day	ET / hr:mn / PT
⊙ ♏	23	5:38 am 2:38 am
♀ ♏	23	10:39 pm 7:39 pm
♀ ≏	5	5:10 am 2:10 am

Planetary Motion

	day	ET / hr:mn / PT		day	ET / hr:mn / PT
♀ ℞	3	3:16 am 12:16 am			
♀ D	15	10:41 am 7:41 am			
♀ ℞	24	3:13 am 12:13 am			

---

1 THURSDAY
ET / hr:mn / PT
3:06 am 12:06 am
8:08 am 5:08 am
8:49 am 5:49 am
10:35 am 7:35 am
10:42 pm 7:42 pm

2 FRIDAY
ET / hr:mn / PT
5:14 am 2:14 am
11:15 am 8:15 am
4:43 am 1:43 am
6:18 pm 3:18 pm
8:38 pm 5:38 pm
8:45 pm 5:45 pm
9:09 pm 6:09 pm
9:36 pm 6:36 pm

3 SATURDAY
ET / hr:mn / PT
1:10 am
6:15 am 3:15 am
6:39 am 3:39 am
9:25 am 6:25 am
11:08 am 8:08 am
11:06 am

4 SUNDAY
ET / hr:mn / PT
2:06 am
8:29 am 5:29 am
11:53 am 8:53 am
1:21 pm 10:21 am
11:37 pm 8:37 pm

5 MONDAY
ET / hr:mn / PT
9:13 am
11:01 am
12:13 am
2:01 am
5:43 am 2:43 am
9:20 am 6:20 am
2:11 pm 11:11 am
4:38 pm 1:38 pm

6 TUESDAY
ET / hr:mn / PT
6:22 am 3:22 am
8:10 pm 5:10 pm

7 WEDNESDAY
ET / hr:mn / PT
12:36 am
3:36 am 1:18 am
4:18 am
6:42 am 3:42 am
8:26 am 5:26 am
1:08 pm 10:08 am
2:57 pm 11:57 am
6:18 pm 3:18 pm

8 THURSDAY
ET / hr:mn / PT
1:14 am
4:55 am 1:55 am
8:56 am 5:56 am

9 FRIDAY
ET / hr:mn / PT
9:44 am 6:44 am
1:52 pm 10:52 am
4:26 pm 1:26 pm
6:00 pm 3:00 pm
11:54 am 8:54 am
10:44 pm

10 SATURDAY
ET / hr:mn / PT
1:44 am
11:50 am 8:50 am
5:31 pm 2:31 pm
7:07 pm 4:07 pm

11 SUNDAY
ET / hr:mn / PT
4:11 am 1:11 am
5:08 am 2:08 am
6:20 pm 3:20 pm
9:20 pm 6:20 pm
9:27 pm
11:43 pm

12 MONDAY
ET / hr:mn / PT
12:27 am
2:43 am
7:34 am 4:34 am
2:48 pm 11:48 am
10:17 pm

13 TUESDAY
ET / hr:mn / PT
1:17 am
4:46 am 1:46 am
1:46 pm
10:55 pm

14 WEDNESDAY
ET / hr:mn / PT
1:55 am
3:02 pm 12:02 pm

15 THURSDAY
ET / hr:mn / PT
4:22 am 1:22 am
6:25 am 3:25 am
4:58 am 1:58 am
5:56 pm 2:56 pm
7:18 am 4:18 am
8:52 am 5:52 am
3:51 pm 12:51 pm
5:45 pm 2:45 pm

16 FRIDAY
ET / hr:mn / PT
4:32 am 1:32 am
4:39 am 1:39 am
3:10 pm 12:10 pm
6:51 pm 3:51 pm
7:25 pm 4:25 pm
1:54 pm 10:54 am

17 SATURDAY
ET / hr:mn / PT
5:50 am 2:50 am
7:14 am 4:14 am
11:07 am 8:07 am

18 SUNDAY
ET / hr:mn / PT
6:30 am 3:30 am
12:13 pm 9:13 am
11:26 pm

19 MONDAY
ET / hr:mn / PT
2:26 am
3:49 am 12:49 am
7:52 am 4:52 am
5:52 am 2:52 am

20 TUESDAY
ET / hr:mn / PT
2:56 am
1:42 am
6:49 am 3:49 am

21 WEDNESDAY
ET / hr:mn / PT
4:42 am 1:42 am
9:39 am 6:39 am
12:51 pm 9:51 am
1:00 pm 10:00 am
2:26 pm 11:26 am
6:07 pm 3:07 pm

22 THURSDAY
ET / hr:mn / PT
3:21 am 12:21 am
10:26 am 7:26 am
11:31 am 8:31 am

23 FRIDAY
ET / hr:mn / PT
3:40 am 12:40 am
4:42 am 1:42 am
5:30 am 2:30 am
7:54 am 4:54 am
11:44 am 8:44 am

24 SATURDAY
ET / hr:mn / PT
12:38 am
9:05 am 6:05 am

25 SUNDAY
ET / hr:mn / PT
4:13 am 1:13 am
8:37 am 5:37 am
11:15 am 8:15 am
6:59 pm 3:59 pm
11:17 pm 9:12 pm
9:45 pm

26 MONDAY
ET / hr:mn / PT
12:12 am
12:45 am
3:43 am 12:43 am
8:12 am 5:12 am
11:37 am 8:37 am
10:18 am 7:18 am

27 TUESDAY
ET / hr:mn / PT
5:11 am 2:11 am
10:51 am 7:51 am
6:31 pm 3:31 pm
9:34 pm
10:29 pm
11:06 pm

28 WEDNESDAY
ET / hr:mn / PT
12:34 am
1:29 am
2:06 am
4:52 am 1:52 am
5:07 am 2:07 am
12:32 pm 9:32 am
10:06 pm

29 THURSDAY
ET / hr:mn / PT
1:56 am
4:16 am 1:16 am
12:17 pm 9:17 am
5:43 pm 2:43 pm
10:36 pm

30 FRIDAY
ET / hr:mn / PT
1:36 am
3:14 am 12:14 am
5:55 am 2:55 am
9:55 am 6:55 am
1:20 pm 10:20 am
1:36 pm 10:36 am

31 SATURDAY
ET / hr:mn / PT
3:02 am 12:02 am
4:30 am 1:30 am
2:37 pm 11:37 am
6:00 pm 3:00 pm

Eastern time in bold type
Pacific time in medium type

OCTOBER 2026

DATE	SID. TIME	SUN	MOON	NODE	MERCURY	VENUS	MARS	JUPITER	SATURN	URANUS	NEPTUNE	PLUTO	CERES	PALLAS	JUNO	VESTA	CHIRON
1 Th	0 38 59	7♎50 20	3♊54	29♓09R	0♏41	8♎23	1♎41	19♋35	11♈35R	5♊32R	2♈52R	3♒07R	16♋05	15♍25R	26♑19	23♈03R	29♈29R
2 F	0 42 55	8 49 18	16 35	29 06	2 00	8 28	2 16	19 46	11 30	5 31	2 50	3 07	16 21	15 08	26 25	22 48	29 27
3 Sa	0 46 52	9 48 20	0♋38	29 04	3 17	8 29R	2 51	19 57	11 25	5 29	2 48	3 07	16 37	14 51	26 31	22 34	29 24
4 Su	0 50 48	10 47 23	14 34	29 04	4 33	8 29	3 26	20 07	11 20	5 28	2 47	3 06	16 52	14 34	26 38	22 19	29 22
5 M	0 54 45	11 46 29	28 21	29 05	5 48	8 26	4 00	20 18	11 16	5 27	2 45	3 06	17 08	14 16	26 44	22 04	29 19
6 T	0 58 41	12 45 37	12♌00	29 06	7 01	8 21	4 35	20 28	11 11	5 26	2 43	3 06	17 23	13 59	26 52	21 49	29 16
7 W	1 02 38	13 44 47	25 27	29 07R	8 13	8 13	5 09	20 38	11 06	5 25	2 42	3 05	17 38	13 41	26 59	21 34	29 14
8 Th	1 06 35	14 43 59	8♍44	29 06	9 23	8 03	5 43	20 49	11 02	5 23	2 40	3 05	17 52	13 24	27 07	21 19	29 11
9 F	1 10 31	15 43 14	21 46	29 03	10 31	7 51	6 17	20 59	10 57	5 22	2 39	3 05	18 07	13 06	27 15	21 03	29 08
10 Sa	1 14 28	16 42 31	4♎35	28 58	11 36	7 36	6 51	21 09	10 52	5 21	2 37	3 05	18 21	12 48	27 24	20 47	29 06
11 Su	1 18 24	17 41 50	17 10	28 51	12 40	7 19	7 25	21 18	10 48	5 19	2 35	3 05	18 35	12 31	27 33	20 32	29 03
12 M	1 22 21	18 41 10	29 30	28 42	13 41	7 00	7 58	21 28	10 43	5 18	2 34	3 04	18 49	12 13	27 42	20 16	29 00
13 T	1 26 17	19 40 33	11♏38	28 32	14 40	6 38	8 32	21 38	10 38	5 16	2 32	3 04	19 02	11 55	27 52	20 00	28 57
14 W	1 30 14	20 39 58	23 35	28 23	15 36	6 15	9 05	21 47	10 34	5 15	2 31	3 04	19 16	11 38	28 02	19 45	28 55
15 Th	1 34 10	21 39 25	5♐27	28 15	16 29	5 49	9 38	21 57	10 29	5 13	2 29	3 04	19 29	11 20	28 12	19 29	28 52
16 F	1 38 7	22 38 54	17 17	28 09	17 18	5 21	10 11	22 06	10 25	5 12	2 28	3 04D	19 41	11 03	28 23	19 14	28 49
17 Sa	1 42 4	23 38 24	29 10	28 04	18 03	4 52	10 44	22 15	10 20	5 10	2 26	3 04	19 54	10 45	28 33	18 58	28 46
18 Su	1 46 0	24 37 56	11♑12	28 02D	18 44	4 21	11 17	22 24	10 16	5 08	2 25	3 04	20 06	10 28	28 45	18 43	28 44
19 M	1 49 57	25 37 30	23 27	28 02	19 21	3 48	11 49	22 34	10 11	5 06	2 23	3 04	20 18	10 11	28 56	18 28	28 41
20 T	1 53 53	26 37 06	6♒01	28 03	19 53	3 14	12 22	22 42	10 07	5 05	2 22	3 04	20 30	9 54	29 08	18 13	28 38
21 W	1 57 50	27 36 43	18 58	28 04R	20 19	2 39	12 54	22 51	10 02	5 03	2 20	3 04	20 41	9 37	29 20	17 58	28 35
22 Th	2 1 46	28 36 22	2♓19	28 01	20 39	2 04	13 26	23 00	9 58	5 01	2 19	3 05	20 53	9 21	29 33	17 43	28 32
23 F	2 5 43	29 36 03	16 06	28 01	20 52	1 27	13 58	23 08	9 54	4 59	2 17	3 05	21 03	9 04	29 45	17 29	28 30
24 Sa	2 9 39	0♏35 45	0♈15	27 57	20 58R	0 51	14 30	23 17	9 49	4 57	2 16	3 05	21 14	8 48	29 59	17 15	28 27
25 Su	2 13 36	1 35 29	14 43	27 50	20 57	0 14	15 01	23 25	9 45	4 55	2 14	3 05	21 24	8 32	0♒12	17 01	28 24
26 M	2 17 32	2 35 16	29 22	27 41	20 47	29♍37	15 33	23 33	9 41	4 53	2 13	3 06	21 34	8 17	0 25	16 47	28 21
27 T	2 21 29	3 35 04	14♉05	27 30	20 28	29 01	16 04	23 41	9 37	4 51	2 12	3 06	21 44	8 02	0 39	16 33	28 18
28 W	2 25 26	4 34 54	28 44	27 20	20 00	28 26	16 35	23 49	9 33	4 49	2 10	3 06	21 54	7 47	0 54	16 20	28 16
29 Th	2 29 22	5 34 47	13♊13	27 11	19 23	27 51	17 06	23 57	9 29	4 47	2 09	3 06	22 03	7 32	1 08	16 07	28 13
30 F	2 33 19	6 34 41	28 11	27 03	18 37	27 18	17 36	24 05	9 25	4 45	2 08	3 07	22 12	7 17	1 23	15 54	28 10
31 Sa	2 37 15	7 34 38	13♋13	26 59	17 42	26 45	18 07	24 12	9 21	4 43	2 06	3 07	22 20	7 03	1 38	15 42	28 07

EPHEMERIS CALCULATED FOR 12 MIDNIGHT GREENWICH MEAN TIME. ALL OTHER DATA AND FACING ASPECTARIAN PAGE IN **EASTERN TIME (BOLD)** AND PACIFIC TIME (REGULAR).

NOVEMBER 2026

☽ Last Aspect day	ET / hr:mn / PT	asp	☽ Ingress sign	day	ET / hr:mn / PT
10/31	**6:00 pm** 3:00 pm	□♀	♌	10/31	9:18 pm
10/31	**6:00 pm** 3:00 pm	□♀	♌	1	**12:18 am**
2	**7:10 pm** 4:10 pm	⚹♀	♍	3	**3:28 am** 12:28 am
3	10:57 pm	⚹☿	♎	5	**9:38 am** 6:38 am
4	**1:57 am**	⚹☿	♎	5	**9:38 am** 6:38 am
7	**8:20 am** 5:20 am	⚹♃	♏	7	**5:40 pm** 2:40 pm
9	**6:25 pm** 3:25 pm	□♃	♐	10	**3:36 am** 12:36 am
12	**6:29 am** 3:29 am	△♃	♑	12	**3:27 pm** 12:27 pm
14	**1:56 pm** 10:56 am	□♀	♒	15	**4:24 am** 1:24 am
17	**9:26 am** 6:26 am	☍♂	♓	17	**4:19 pm** 1:19 pm

☽ Last Aspect day	ET / hr:mn / PT	asp	☽ Ingress sign	day	ET / hr:mn / PT
19	**8:46 pm** 5:46 pm	△☉	♈	19	9:52 pm
19	**8:46 pm** 5:46 pm	△☉	♈	20	**12:52 am**
21	11:38 pm	△♂	♉	22	**5:10 am** 2:10 am
22	**2:38 am**	△♂	♉	22	**5:10 am** 2:10 am
24	**5:09 am** 2:09 am	□♂	♊	24	**6:10 am** 3:10 am
25	9:24 pm	⚹♃	♋	26	**5:51 am** 2:51 am
26	**12:24 am**	⚹♃	♋	26	**5:51 am** 2:51 am
27	9:40 pm	□♀	♌	28	**6:21 am** 3:21 am
28	**12:40 am**	□♀	♌	28	**6:21 am** 3:21 am
30	**5:10 am** 2:10 am	⚹♀	♍	30	**9:13 am** 6:13 am

☽ Phases & Eclipses phase	day	ET / hr:mn / PT
4th Quarter	1	**3:28 pm** 12:28 pm
New Moon	8	11:02 pm
New Moon	9	**2:02 am**
2nd Quarter	17	**6:48 am** 3:48 am
Full Moon	24	**9:53 am** 6:53 am
4th Quarter	30	10:09 pm
4th Quarter	12/1	**1:09 am**

Planet Ingress	day	ET / hr:mn / PT
☉ ♐	21	11:23 pm
☉ ♐	22	**2:23 am**
♂ ♍	25	**6:37 pm** 3:37 pm

Planetary Motion		day	ET / hr:mn / PT
☿	D	13	**10:54 am** 7:54 am
♀	D	13	**7:27 pm** 4:27 pm
⚳	℞	21	9:58 pm
⚳	℞	22	**12:58 am**
⚶	D	28	**8:17 am** 5:17 am
⚴	D	30	**11:34 pm** 8:34 pm

1 SUNDAY
☽ △ ♆ **2:51 am** 12:51 am
☽ ☍ ♇ **4:39 am** 1:39 am
☽ ⚹ ♅ **7:16 am** 4:16 am
☉ ⚻ ♄ **11:01 am** 8:01 am
☽ △ ♄ **3:08 pm** 12:08 pm
☽ □ ☉ **3:28 pm** 12:28 pm
☽ □ ☿ 10:26 pm

2 MONDAY
☽ □ ☿ **1:26 am**
☽ ☌ ♂ **8:49 am** 5:49 am
☽ ☌ ♃ **5:51 pm** 2:51 pm
☽ ⚹ ♀ **7:10 pm** 4:10 pm

3 TUESDAY
☽ ⚻ ♆ **7:04 am** 4:04 am
☽ ⚻ ♇ **9:04 am** 6:04 am
☽ □ ♅ **11:36 am** 8:36 am
☽ ⚻ ♄ **7:42 pm** 4:42 pm
☽ ⚹ ☉ 9:34 pm
☽ ⚹ ☿ 10:57 pm

4 WEDNESDAY
☽ ⚹ ☉ **12:34 am**
☽ ⚹ ☿ **1:57 am**
♀ ⚹ ♃ **5:31 am** 2:31 am
☉ ☌ ☿ **9:24 am** 6:24 am
☽ ⚺ ♂ **4:23 pm** 1:23 pm
☽ ⚺ ♀ **11:28 pm** 8:28 pm
☽ ⚺ ♃ 9:08 pm

5 THURSDAY
☽ ⚺ ♃ **12:08 am**
☽ ☍ ♆ **1:18 pm** 10:18 am
☽ △ ♇ **3:28 pm** 12:28 pm
☽ △ ♅ **5:55 pm** 2:55 pm
☽ ☍ ♄ 11:12 pm

6 FRIDAY
☽ ☍ ♄ **2:12 am**
☽ ⚺ ☿ **3:58 am** 12:58 am
☽ ⚺ ☉ **12:07 pm** 9:07 am
☿ ⚻ ♄ 9:24 pm
☽ ⚹ ♂ 11:02 pm

7 SATURDAY
☿ ⚻ ♄ **12:24 am**
☽ ⚹ ♂ **2:02 am**
☽ ☌ ♀ **5:50 am** 2:50 am
☽ ⚹ ♃ **8:20 am** 5:20 am
☽ ⚻ ♆ **9:22 pm** 6:22 pm
☽ □ ♇ **11:44 pm** 8:44 pm
☽ ⚻ ♅ 11:02 pm

8 SUNDAY
☽ ⚻ ♅ **2:02 am**
☽ ☌ ☿ **8:02 am** 5:02 am
☽ ⚻ ♄ **10:32 am** 7:32 am
☽ ☌ ☉ 11:02 pm

9 MONDAY
☽ ☌ ☉ **2:02 am**
☽ □ ♂ **1:44 pm** 10:44 am
☽ ⚺ ♀ **2:20 pm** 11:20 am
☽ □ ♃ **6:25 pm** 3:25 pm
♀ ⚹ ♂ 10:48 pm

10 TUESDAY
♀ ⚹ ♂ **1:48 am**
☽ △ ♆ **7:20 am** 4:20 am
☽ ⚹ ♇ **9:56 am** 6:56 am
☽ ☍ ♅ **12:04 pm** 9:04 am
☽ ⚺ ☿ **3:02 pm** 12:02 pm
☽ △ ♄ **8:48 pm** 5:48 pm

11 WEDNESDAY
☽ ⚺ ☉ **6:29 pm** 3:29 pm
☽ ⚹ ♀ 10:11 pm

12 THURSDAY
☽ ⚹ ♀ **1:11 am**
☽ △ ♂ **3:35 am** 12:35 am
☽ △ ♃ **6:29 am** 3:29 am
☽ □ ♆ **7:13 pm** 4:13 pm
☽ ⚺ ♇ **10:02 pm** 7:02 pm
☽ ⚻ ♅ **11:58 pm** 8:58 pm
☽ ⚹ ☿ 10:41 pm

13 FRIDAY
☽ ⚹ ☿ **1:41 am**
☽ □ ♄ **8:52 am** 5:52 am

14 SATURDAY
☽ ⚹ ☉ **12:54 pm** 9:54 am
☽ □ ♀ **1:56 pm** 10:56 am
☽ ⚻ ♂ **6:54 pm** 3:54 pm
☽ ⚻ ♃ **7:51 pm** 4:51 pm
☉ ⚺ ♀ 10:17 pm

15 SUNDAY
☉ ⚺ ♀ **1:17 am**
☽ ⚹ ♆ **8:06 am** 5:06 am
☽ ☌ ♇ **11:04 am** 8:04 am
☽ △ ♅ **12:43 pm** 9:43 am
☽ □ ☿ **3:28 pm** 12:28 pm
☽ ⚹ ♄ **9:33 pm** 6:33 pm
♂ ☌ ♃ 10:24 pm

16 MONDAY
♂ ☌ ♃ **1:24 am**
☽ △ ♀ 11:44 pm

17 TUESDAY
☽ △ ♀ **2:44 am**
☽ □ ☉ **6:48 am** 3:48 am
☽ ☍ ♃ **8:28 am** 5:28 am
☽ ☍ ♂ **9:26 am** 6:26 am
☽ ⚺ ♆ **7:48 pm** 4:48 pm
☽ ⚺ ♇ **10:48 pm** 7:48 pm
☽ □ ♅ 9:06 pm

18 WEDNESDAY
☽ □ ♅ **12:06 am**
☉ □ ♃ **4:39 am** 1:39 am
☽ △ ☿ **5:46 am** 2:46 am
☽ ⚺ ♄ **8:32 am** 5:32 am

19 THURSDAY
☉ □ ♂ **12:49 pm** 9:49 am
☽ ⚻ ♀ **12:59 pm** 9:59 am
☽ ⚻ ♃ **5:54 pm** 2:54 pm
☽ ⚻ ♂ **8:24 pm** 5:24 pm
☽ △ ☉ **8:46 pm** 5:46 pm
☿ ⚻ ♄ **9:16 pm** 6:16 pm

20 FRIDAY
☽ ☌ ♆ **4:03 am** 1:03 am
☽ ⚹ ♇ **6:56 am** 3:56 am
☽ ⚹ ♅ **7:54 am** 4:54 am
☽ ☌ ♄ **3:44 pm** 12:44 pm
☽ ⚻ ☿ **5:12 pm** 2:12 pm

21 SATURDAY
☽ ☍ ♀ **7:10 pm** 4:10 pm
☽ △ ♃ **10:58 pm** 7:58 pm
☽ △ ♂ 11:38 pm

22 SUNDAY
☽ △ ♂ **2:38 am**
☽ ⚻ ☉ **5:22 am** 2:22 am
☽ ⚺ ♆ **8:03 am** 5:03 am
☽ □ ♇ **10:51 am** 7:51 am
☽ ⚺ ♅ **11:32 am** 8:32 am
☽ ⚺ ♄ **6:51 pm** 3:51 pm
☽ ☍ ☿ 9:27 pm

23 MONDAY
☽ ☍ ☿ **12:27 am**
☉ △ ♆ **7:08 pm** 4:08 pm
☽ ⚻ ♀ **9:48 pm** 6:48 pm
☽ □ ♃ 9:29 pm

24 TUESDAY
☽ □ ♃ **12:29 am**
☽ □ ♂ **5:09 am** 2:09 am
☽ ⚹ ♆ **8:53 am** 5:53 am
☽ ☍ ☉ **9:53 am** 6:53 am
☽ △ ♇ **11:39 am** 8:39 am
☽ ☌ ♅ **12:07 pm** 9:07 am
☽ ⚹ ♄ **7:10 pm** 4:10 pm

25 WEDNESDAY
☽ ⚻ ☿ **4:58 am** 1:58 am
☉ ⚹ ♇ **12:28 pm** 9:28 am
☉ ☍ ♅ **5:41 pm** 2:41 pm
☽ △ ♀ **10:51 pm** 7:51 pm
☽ ⚹ ♃ 9:24 pm

26 THURSDAY
☽ ⚹ ♃ **12:24 am**
☽ ⚹ ♂ **6:09 am** 3:09 am
☽ □ ♆ **8:33 am** 5:33 am
☽ ⚻ ♇ **11:23 am** 8:23 am
☽ ⚺ ♅ **11:40 am** 8:40 am
☽ ⚻ ☉ **1:01 pm** 10:01 am
☽ □ ♄ **6:48 pm** 3:48 pm

27 FRIDAY
☽ △ ☿ **9:31 am** 6:31 am
☽ □ ♀ 9:40 pm
☽ ⚺ ♃ 9:52 pm

28 SATURDAY
☽ □ ♀ **12:40 am**
☽ ⚺ ♃ **12:52 am**
♀ ⚹ ♃ **7:05 am** 4:05 am
☽ ⚺ ♂ **8:00 am** 5:00 am
☽ △ ♆ **9:06 am** 6:06 am
☽ ☍ ♇ **12:09 pm** 9:09 am
☽ ⚹ ♅ **12:14 pm** 9:14 am
☽ △ ☉ **5:28 pm** 2:28 pm
☽ △ ♄ **7:44 pm** 4:44 pm

29 SUNDAY
♅ △ ♇ **6:21 am** 3:21 am
☽ □ ☿ **4:44 pm** 1:44 pm
☉ △ ♄ 10:06 pm
♂ ⚻ ♆ 10:20 pm

30 MONDAY
☉ △ ♄ **1:06 am**
♂ ⚻ ♆ **1:20 am**
☽ ☌ ♃ **3:35 am** 12:35 am
☽ ⚹ ♀ **5:10 am** 2:10 am
☽ ⚻ ♆ **12:06 pm** 9:06 am
☽ ☌ ♂ **12:25 pm** 9:25 am
☽ □ ♅ **3:17 pm** 12:17 pm
☽ ⚻ ♇ **3:26 pm** 12:26 pm
☽ ⚻ ♄ **11:19 pm** 8:19 pm
☽ □ ☉ 10:09 pm

Eastern time in bold type
Pacific time in medium type

NOVEMBER 2026

DATE	SID.TIME	SUN	MOON	NODE	MERCURY	VENUS	MARS	JUPITER	SATURN	URANUS	NEPTUNE	PLUTO	CERES	PALLAS	JUNO	VESTA	CHIRON
1 Su	2 41 12	8♏34 37	27♎28	26♊56D	16♏40R	26♎15R	18♎37	24♌19	9♈17R	4♊41R	2♓05R	3♒08	22♋28	6♈50R	1♎53	15♈30R	28♈04R
2 M	2 45 8	9 34 38	11♏28	26 56	15 30	25 46	19 07	24 27	9 13	4 38	2 04	3 08	22 36	6 36	2 08	15 18	28 02
3 T	2 49 5	10 34 41	25 13	26 56R	14 16	25 19	19 37	24 34	9 10	4 36	2 03	3 09	22 44	6 23	2 24	15 07	27 59
4 W	2 53 2	11 34 47	8♐43	26 56	12 58	24 54	20 07	24 41	9 06	4 34	2 01	3 09	22 51	6 11	2 40	14 56	27 56
5 Th	2 56 58	12 34 54	22 00	26 48	11 40	24 31	20 37	24 47	9 03	4 32	2 00	3 10	22 58	5 58	2 56	14 45	27 54
6 F	3 0 55	13 35 03	5♑05	26 40	10 23	24 10	21 06	24 54	8 59	4 29	1 59	3 10	23 04	5 46	3 13	14 35	27 51
7 Sa	3 4 51	14 35 15	17 59	26 40	9 10	23 52	21 35	25 01	8 56	4 27	1 58	3 11	23 10	5 35	3 30	14 25	27 48
8 Su	3 8 48	15 35 28	0♒42	26 29	8 05	23 36	22 04	25 07	8 52	4 25	1 57	3 12	23 16	5 24	3 47	14 16	27 46
9 M	3 12 44	16 35 43	13 15	26 16	7 07	23 23	22 32	25 13	8 49	4 22	1 56	3 12	23 21	5 13	4 04	14 07	27 43
10 T	3 16 41	17 36 00	25 37	26 02	6 19	23 12	23 01	25 19	8 46	4 20	1 55	3 13	23 26	5 03	4 21	13 58	27 40
11 W	3 20 37	18 36 19	7♓48	25 48	5 43	23 03	23 29	25 25	8 43	4 18	1 54	3 13	23 31	4 54	4 39	13 50	27 38
12 Th	3 24 34	19 36 40	19 51	25 35	5 18	22 57	23 57	25 31	8 40	4 15	1 53	3 14	23 35	4 44	4 57	13 43	27 35
13 F	3 28 31	20 37 02	1♈45	25 24	5 04D	22 53	24 25	25 36	8 37	4 13	1 52	3 15	23 39	4 36	5 15	13 35	27 33
14 Sa	3 32 27	21 37 25	13 35	25 17	5 03	22 52D	24 52	25 42	8 34	4 10	1 51	3 16	23 43	4 27	5 34	13 29	27 30
15 Su	3 36 24	22 37 50	25 22	25 12	5 12	22 53	25 19	25 47	8 32	4 08	1 50	3 17	23 46	4 19	5 52	13 22	27 28
16 M	3 40 20	23 38 16	7♉13	25 09	5 31	22 57	25 46	25 52	8 29	4 05	1 49	3 18	23 49	4 12	6 11	13 16	27 25
17 T	3 44 17	24 38 44	19 11	25 09	6 00	23 02	26 13	25 57	8 26	4 03	1 48	3 19	23 51	4 05	6 30	13 11	27 23
18 W	3 48 13	25 39 13	1♊22	25 09	6 37	23 11	26 39	26 02	8 24	4 00	1 47	3 19	23 53	3 58	6 49	13 06	27 20
19 Th	3 52 10	26 39 43	13 53	25 08	7 22	23 21	27 05	26 06	8 22	3 58	1 46	3 20	23 54	3 52	7 09	13 01	27 18
20 F	3 56 6	27 40 15	26 47	25 06	8 14	23 34	27 31	26 11	8 19	3 55	1 46	3 21	23 55	3 47	7 28	12 57	27 16
21 Sa	4 0 3	28 40 47	10♋08	25 01	9 12	23 48	27 57	26 15	8 17	3 53	1 45	3 22	23 56	3 42	7 48	12 54	27 13
22 Su	4 3 59	29 41 21	23 59	24 53	10 15	24 05	28 24	26 19	8 15	3 50	1 44	3 23	23 57R	3 37	8 08	12 50	27 11
23 M	4 7 56	0♐41 56	8♌19	24 43	11 22	24 24	28 47	26 23	8 13	3 48	1 44	3 24	23 56	3 33	8 29	12 48	27 09
24 T	4 11 53	1 42 33	23 03	24 32	12 33	24 45	29 12	26 26	8 11	3 45	1 43	3 25	23 56	3 30	8 49	12 45	27 07
25 W	4 15 49	2 43 11	8♍03	24 20	13 48	25 07	29 36	26 30	8 10	3 43	1 42	3 27	23 54	3 26	9 09	12 44	27 05
26 Th	4 19 46	3 43 51	23 10	24 09	15 05	25 32	0♏00	26 33	8 08	3 40	1 42	3 28	23 53	3 24	9 30	12 42	27 02
27 F	4 23 42	4 44 32	8♎14	24 01	16 25	25 58	0 24	26 37	8 06	3 38	1 41	3 29	23 52	3 22	9 51	12 41	27 00
28 Sa	4 27 39	5 45 14	23 05	23 55	17 47	26 26	0 48	26 39	8 05	3 35	1 41	3 30	23 50	3 20	10 12	12 41D	27 00
29 Su	4 31 35	6 45 58	7♏34	23 52	19 11	26 56	1 11	26 42	8 04	3 33	1 40	3 31	23 47	3 19	10 34	12 41	26 56
30 M	4 35 32	7 46 44	21 47	23 51D	20 36	27 27	1 34	26 45	8 02	3 30	1 40	3 32	23 44	3 18	10 55	12 41	26 54

EPHEMERIS CALCULATED FOR 12 MIDNIGHT GREENWICH MEAN TIME. ALL OTHER DATA AND FACING ASPECTARIAN PAGE IN **EASTERN TIME (BOLD)** AND PACIFIC TIME (REGULAR).

DECEMBER 2026

☽ Last Aspect day	ET / hr:mn / PT	asp	☽ Ingress sign	day	ET / hr:mn / PT
2	**4:11 am** 1:11 am	⚹ ☿	♎	2	**3:04 pm** 12:04 pm
4	**5:40 pm** 2:40 pm	⚹ ♃	♏	4	**11:35 pm** 8:35 pm
7	**4:08 am** 1:08 am	□ ♃	♐	7	**10:07 am** 7:07 am
9	**4:06 pm** 1:06 pm	△ ♃	♑	9	**10:09 pm** 7:09 pm
10	**2:12 pm** 11:12 am	□ ♄	♒	12	**11:06 am** 8:06 am
14	**5:40 pm** 2:40 pm	☍ ♃	♓	14	**11:36 pm** 8:36 pm
16	9:43 pm	□ ☉	♈	17	**9:34 am** 6:34 am
17	**12:43 am**	□ ☉	♈	17	**9:34 am** 6:34 am
19	**11:40 am** 8:40 am	△ ☉	♉	19	**3:30 pm** 12:30 pm
21	**12:26 pm** 9:26 am	□ ♃	♊	21	**5:27 pm** 2:27 pm
23	**12:01 pm** 9:01 am	⚹ ♃	♋	23	**4:58 pm** 1:58 pm
24	**7:09 pm** 4:09 pm	△ ♀	♌	25	**4:12 pm** 1:12 pm
27	**11:39 am** 8:39 am	☌ ♃	♍	27	**5:13 pm** 2:13 pm
29	**5:18 am** 2:18 am	⚹ ♀	♎	29	**9:27 pm** 6:27 pm
31	**10:27 pm** 7:27 pm	⚹ ♃	♏	1/1	**5:16 am** 2:16 am

☽ Phases & Eclipses phase	day	ET / hr:mn / PT
4th Quarter	11/30	10:09 pm
4th Quarter	1	**1:09 am**
New Moon	8	**7:52 pm** 4:52 pm
2nd Quarter	16	9:43 pm
2nd Quarter	17	**12:43 am**
Full Moon	23	**8:28 pm** 5:28 pm
4th Quarter	30	**1:59 pm** 10:59 am

Planet Ingress		day	ET / hr:mn / PT
♀	♏	4	**3:13 am** 12:13 am
☿	♐	6	**3:33 am** 12:33 am
☉	♑	21	**3:50 pm** 12:50 pm
☿	♑	25	**1:22 pm** 10:22 am

Planetary Motion		day	ET / hr:mn / PT
♄	D	10	**6:31 pm** 3:31 pm
♆	D	12	**5:18 pm** 2:18 pm
♃	℞	12	**7:57 pm** 4:57 pm

1 TUESDAY
☽ □ ☉ **1:09 am**

2 WEDNESDAY
☽ ⚹ ☿ **4:11 am** 1:11 am
☽ ⊻ ♃ **9:16 am** 6:16 am
☽ ⊻ ♀ **1:16 pm** 10:16 am
☽ ☍ ♆ **6:06 pm** 3:06 pm
☽ ⊻ ♂ **8:01 pm** 5:01 pm
☽ △ ♅ **9:18 pm** 6:18 pm
☽ △ ♇ **9:43 pm** 6:43 pm

3 THURSDAY
☽ ☍ ♄ **5:52 am** 2:52 am
☽ ⚹ ☉ **12:34 pm** 9:34 am
☿ □ ♃ 11:03 pm

4 FRIDAY
☿ □ ♃ **2:03 am**
♂ □ ♅ **2:28 pm** 11:28 am
☽ ⚹ ♃ **5:40 pm** 2:40 pm
☽ ⊻ ☿ **7:45 pm** 4:45 pm
☽ ☌ ♀ 9:42 pm
☽ ⊼ ♆ 11:43 pm

5 SATURDAY
☽ ☌ ♀ **12:42 am**
☽ ⊼ ♆ **2:43 am**
☽ ⊼ ♅ **5:54 am** 2:54 am
☽ ⚹ ♂ **6:23 am** 3:23 am
☽ □ ♇ **6:37 am** 3:37 am
☽ ⊼ ♄ **2:56 pm** 11:56 am
♂ ⊼ ♇ **3:24 pm** 12:24 pm

6 SUNDAY
☽ ⊻ ☉ **3:05 am** 12:05 am
♀ ⊼ ♆ **2:05 pm** 11:05 am

7 MONDAY
☽ □ ♃ **4:08 am** 1:08 am
☿ △ ♆ **5:15 am** 2:15 am
☽ △ ♆ **1:19 pm** 10:19 am
☽ ☌ ☿ **2:28 pm** 11:28 am
☽ ⊻ ♀ **2:44 pm** 11:44 am
☽ ☍ ♅ **4:24 pm** 1:24 pm
☽ ⚹ ♇ **5:28 pm** 2:28 pm
☿ ⊻ ♀ **6:12 pm** 3:12 pm
☽ □ ♂ **6:47 pm** 3:47 pm
☽ △ ♄ 10:52 pm

8 TUESDAY
☽ △ ♄ **1:52 am**
☿ ☍ ♅ **5:29 am** 2:29 am
☿ ⚹ ♇ **2:32 pm** 11:32 am
♀ ⊼ ♅ **5:27 pm** 2:27 pm
☽ ☌ ☉ **7:52 pm** 4:52 pm

9 WEDNESDAY
☿ □ ♂ **8:41 am** 5:41 am
♀ □ ♇ **1:38 pm** 10:38 am
☽ △ ♃ **4:06 pm** 1:06 pm
☽ □ ♆ 10:25 pm

10 THURSDAY
☽ □ ♆ **1:25 am**
☽ ⊼ ♅ **4:22 am** 1:22 am
☽ ⊻ ♇ **5:46 am** 2:46 am

☽ ⚹ ♀ **6:49 am** 3:49 am
☽ △ ♂ **8:40 am** 5:40 am
☽ ⊻ ☿ **11:30 am** 8:30 am
☽ □ ♄ **2:12 pm** 11:12 am

11 FRIDAY
☿ △ ♄ **8:25 am** 5:25 am
☽ ⊻ ☉ **2:15 pm** 11:15 am

12 SATURDAY
♀ ⚹ ♂ **4:15 am** 1:15 am
☽ ⊼ ♃ **5:02 am** 2:02 am
☽ ⚹ ♆ **2:22 pm** 11:22 am
☽ △ ♅ **5:09 pm** 2:09 pm
☽ ☌ ♇ **6:53 pm** 3:53 pm
☽ ⊼ ♂ **11:14 pm** 8:14 pm
☽ □ ♀ 9:06 pm

13 SUNDAY
☽ □ ♀ **12:06 am**
☽ ⚹ ♄ **3:13 am** 12:13 am
☽ ⚹ ☿ **9:36 am** 6:36 am

14 MONDAY
☽ ⚹ ☉ **8:47 am** 5:47 am
☽ ☍ ♃ **5:40 pm** 2:40 pm
♀ ⊼ ♄ **9:58 pm** 6:58 pm
☽ ⊻ ♆ 11:48 pm

15 TUESDAY
☽ ⊻ ♆ **2:48 am**
☽ □ ♅ **5:18 am** 2:18 am
☽ ⊻ ♇ **7:19 am** 4:19 am
☽ ☍ ♂ **12:49 pm** 9:49 am

☽ ⊻ ♄ **3:18 pm** 12:18 pm
☽ △ ♀ **4:32 pm** 1:32 pm

16 WEDNESDAY
☽ □ ☿ **5:57 am** 2:57 am
☽ □ ☉ 9:43 pm

17 THURSDAY
☽ □ ☉ **12:43 am**
☽ ⊼ ♃ **3:56 am** 12:56 am
☽ ☌ ♆ **12:36 pm** 9:36 am
☽ ⚹ ♅ **2:46 pm** 11:46 am
☽ ⚹ ♇ **4:56 pm** 1:56 pm
☽ ⊼ ♂ **11:08 pm** 8:08 pm
☽ ☌ ♄ 9:20 pm

18 FRIDAY
☽ ☌ ♄ **12:20 am**
☽ ⊼ ♀ **5:23 am** 2:23 am
☉ △ ♃ **4:21 pm** 1:21 pm
☽ △ ☿ **9:14 pm** 6:14 pm

19 SATURDAY
☽ △ ♃ **10:13 am** 7:13 am
☽ △ ☉ **11:40 am** 8:40 am
☽ ⊻ ♆ **6:18 pm** 3:18 pm
☽ ⊻ ♅ **8:09 pm** 5:09 pm
☽ □ ♇ **10:23 pm** 7:23 pm

20 SUNDAY
☽ △ ♂ **4:55 am** 1:55 am
☽ ⊻ ♄ **5:11 am** 2:11 am
☽ ☍ ♀ **1:14 pm** 10:14 am
♂ ⊼ ♄ **11:13 pm** 8:13 pm

21 MONDAY
☽ ⊼ ☿ **6:33 am** 3:33 am
☽ □ ♃ **12:26 pm** 9:26 am
☽ ⊼ ☉ **5:34 pm** 2:34 pm
☽ ⚹ ♆ **8:05 pm** 5:05 pm
☽ ☌ ♅ **9:41 pm** 6:41 pm
☽ △ ♇ 9:00 pm

22 TUESDAY
☽ △ ♇ **12:00 am**
☽ ⚹ ♄ **6:21 am** 3:21 am
☽ □ ♂ **6:46 am** 3:46 am
☽ ⊼ ♀ **5:00 pm** 2:00 pm

23 WEDNESDAY
☉ □ ♆ **6:37 am** 3:37 am
☽ ☍ ☿ **11:54 am** 8:54 am
☽ ⚹ ♃ **12:01 pm** 9:01 am
☿ △ ♃ **1:03 pm** 10:03 am
☽ □ ♆ **7:33 pm** 4:33 pm
☽ ☍ ☉ **8:28 pm** 5:28 pm
☽ ⊻ ♅ **8:59 pm** 5:59 pm
☽ ⊼ ♇ **11:26 pm** 8:26 pm

24 THURSDAY
☉ ⊼ ♅ **3:58 am** 12:58 am
☽ □ ♄ **5:39 am** 2:39 am
☽ ⚹ ♂ **6:37 am** 3:37 am
☽ △ ♀ **7:09 pm** 4:09 pm

25 FRIDAY
☽ ⊻ ♃ **11:04 am** 8:04 am
☽ ⊼ ☿ **4:32 pm** 1:32 pm
☉ ⊻ ♇ **6:18 pm** 3:18 pm

☽ △ ♆ **6:51 pm** 3:51 pm
☽ ⚹ ♅ **8:11 pm** 5:11 pm
☽ ☍ ♇ **10:53 pm** 7:53 pm
☽ ⊼ ☉ **11:13 pm** 8:13 pm

26 SATURDAY
☽ △ ♄ **5:16 am** 2:16 am
☽ ⊻ ♂ **6:46 am** 3:46 am
☿ □ ♆ **2:47 pm** 11:47 am
☽ □ ♀ **10:29 pm** 7:29 pm
☿ ⊼ ♅ 11:40 pm

27 SUNDAY
☿ ⊼ ♅ **2:40 am**
☽ ☌ ♃ **11:39 am** 8:39 am
☽ ⊼ ♆ **8:03 pm** 5:03 pm
☽ □ ♅ **9:18 pm** 6:18 pm
☽ △ ☿ **11:42 pm** 8:42 pm
☽ ⊼ ♇ 9:23 pm

28 MONDAY
☽ ⊼ ♇ **12:23 am**
☽ △ ☉ **4:29 am** 1:29 am
☿ ⊻ ♇ **5:54 am** 2:54 am
☽ ⊼ ♄ **7:09 am** 4:09 am
☽ ☌ ♂ **9:13 am** 6:13 am

29 TUESDAY
☽ ⚹ ♀ **5:18 am** 2:18 am
☽ ⊻ ♃ **3:17 pm** 12:17 pm
☉ □ ♄ **6:28 pm** 3:28 pm
☽ ☍ ♆ 9:31 pm
☽ △ ♅ 10:42 pm

30 WEDNESDAY
☽ ☍ ♆ **12:31 am**
☽ △ ♅ **1:42 am**
☽ △ ♇ **5:15 am** 2:15 am
☽ □ ☿ **11:39 am** 8:39 am
☽ ☍ ♄ **12:31 pm** 9:31 am
☽ □ ☉ **1:59 pm** 10:59 am
☽ ⊻ ♂ **3:10 pm** 12:10 pm
☿ □ ♄ **6:55 pm** 3:55 pm

31 THURSDAY
☉ △ ♂ **7:03 am** 4:03 am
☽ ⊻ ♀ **4:41 pm** 1:41 pm
☿ △ ♂ **6:30 pm** 3:30 pm
☽ ⚹ ♃ **10:27 pm** 7:27 pm

Eastern time in bold type
Pacific time in medium type

DECEMBER 2026

DATE	SID.TIME	SUN	MOON	NODE	MERCURY	VENUS	MARS	JUPITER	SATURN	URANUS	NEPTUNE	PLUTO	CERES	PALLAS	JUNO	VESTA	CHIRON
1 T	4 39 29	8♐47 30	5♍35	23♒52R	22♏03	28♎00	1♏56	26♌47	8♓01R	3♊28R	1♈39R	3♒34	23♋41R	3♈18D	11♒17	12♈42	26♈52R
2 W	4 43 25	9 48 19	19 01	23 51	23 30	28 34	2 18	26 50	8 00	3 25	1 39	3 35	23 37	3 18	11 39	12 43	26 50
3 Th	4 47 22	10 49 09	2♎08	23 49	24 59	29 10	2 40	26 53	7 59	3 23	1 38	3 36	23 32	3 18	12 01	12 45	26 49
4 F	4 51 18	11 50 00	14 59	23 45	26 28	29 47	3 01	26 55	7 59	3 20	1 38	3 37	23 28	3 19	12 23	12 47	26 47
5 Sa	4 55 15	12 50 53	27 37	23 38	27 57	0♏25	3 22	26 58	7 58	3 18	1 38	3 39	23 22	3 21	12 45	12 50	26 45
6 Su	4 59 11	13 51 47	10♏03	23 28	29 28	1 05	3 43	26 59	7 57	3 15	1 37	3 40	23 17	3 23	13 08	12 53	26 43
7 M	5 3 8	14 52 42	22 20	23 16	0♐58	1 46	4 03	27 00	7 57	3 13	1 37	3 41	23 11	3 25	13 30	12 56	26 42
8 T	5 7 4	15 53 39	4♐29	23 02	2 29	2 28	4 23	27 01	7 56	3 10	1 37	3 43	23 05	3 28	13 53	13 00	26 40
9 W	5 11 1	16 54 36	16 31	22 49	4 01	3 11	4 42	27 01	7 56	3 08	1 37	3 44	22 58	3 32	14 16	13 04	26 38
10 Th	5 14 58	17 55 35	28 27	22 37	5 33	3 55	5 01	27 01	7 56D	3 06	1 37	3 46	22 51	3 35	14 39	13 09	26 37
11 F	5 18 54	18 56 34	10♑18	22 27	7 04	4 40	5 20	27 01R	7 56	3 03	1 37	3 47	22 43	3 40	15 02	13 14	26 36
12 Sa	5 22 51	19 57 34	22 06	22 20	8 36	5 27	5 38	27 01	7 56	3 01	1 37D	3 48	22 35	3 44	15 26	13 20	26 34
13 Su	5 26 47	20 58 35	3♒53	22 15	10 09	6 14	5 55	27 00	7 56	2 58	1 37	3 50	22 27	3 49	15 50	13 25	26 33
14 M	5 30 44	21 59 36	15 44	22 13D	11 41	7 02	6 13	27 00	7 57	2 56	1 37	3 51	22 18	3 55	16 13	13 32	26 31
15 T	5 34 40	23 00 38	27 41	22 13	13 14	7 51	6 29	26 59	7 57	2 54	1 37	3 53	22 09	4 01	16 37	13 38	26 30
16 W	5 38 37	24 01 41	9♓51	22 14	14 46	8 40	6 46	26 58	7 57	2 51	1 37	3 54	21 59	4 07	17 01	13 45	26 29
17 Th	5 42 33	25 02 43	22 17	22 15R	16 19	9 31	7 01	26 57	7 58	2 49	1 37	3 56	21 49	4 14	17 25	13 53	26 28
18 F	5 46 30	26 03 47	5♈05	22 14	17 52	10 22	7 17	26 55	7 59	2 47	1 37	3 58	21 39	4 21	17 50	14 00	26 27
19 Sa	5 50 27	27 04 50	18 19	22 12	19 25	11 14	7 31	26 54	7 59	2 45	1 38	3 59	21 29	4 28	18 14	14 09	26 26
20 Su	5 54 23	28 05 54	2♉02	22 07	20 59	12 07	7 46	26 52	8 00	2 42	1 38	4 01	21 18	4 36	18 39	14 17	26 25
21 M	5 58 20	29 06 58	16 16	21 58	22 32	13 00	7 59	26 50	8 01	2 40	1 38	4 02	21 07	4 45	19 03	14 26	26 24
22 T	6 2 16	0♑08 03	0♊58	21 53	24 06	13 55	8 12	26 48	8 03	2 38	1 39	4 04	20 55	4 53	19 28	14 35	26 23
23 W	6 6 13	1 09 08	16 01	21 45	25 40	14 50	8 25	26 46	8 04	2 36	1 39	4 06	20 44	5 02	19 53	14 45	26 22
24 Th	6 10 9	2 10 14	1♋18	21 37	27 14	15 45	8 37	26 43	8 05	2 34	1 39	4 07	20 32	5 12	20 18	14 54	26 21
25 F	6 14 6	3 11 20	16 36	21 31	28 48	16 41	8 49	26 41	8 07	2 32	1 40	4 09	20 19	5 22	20 44	15 05	26 20
26 Sa	6 18 3	4 12 26	1♌04	21 27	0♑22	17 38	9 00	26 39	8 08	2 30	1 40	4 11	20 07	5 32	21 09	15 15	26 20
27 Su	6 21 59	5 13 33	15 04	21 26D	1 57	18 35	9 10	26 36	8 10	2 28	1 40	4 12	19 54	5 43	21 34	15 26	26 19
28 M	6 25 56	6 14 40	28 39	21 26	3 32	19 33	9 20	26 34	8 12	2 26	1 41	4 14	19 41	5 53	22 00	15 37	26 18
29 T	6 29 52	7 15 47	11♍48	21 27	5 07	20 30	9 29	26 32	8 14	2 24	1 41	4 16	19 28	6 05	22 26	15 48	26 18
30 W	6 33 49	8 16 56	24 42	21 28R	6 42	21 30	9 37	26 30	8 16	2 22	1 42	4 18	19 15	6 16	22 51	16 00	26 17
31 Th	6 37 45	9 18 04	7♎18	21 29	8 18	22 30	9 45	26 27	8 18	2 20	1 42	4 19	19 01	6 28	23 17	16 12	26 17

EPHEMERIS CALCULATED FOR 12 MIDNIGHT GREENWICH MEAN TIME. ALL OTHER DATA AND FACING ASPECTARIAN PAGE IN EASTERN TIME (BOLD) AND PACIFIC TIME (REGULAR).

Notes

Notes

Notes

Notes

Notes